2

MONS
WRES
INTER

Art:
Original Story: Ty...
Producer: Takeo Ao...

Translation: Ko Ransom   Lettering: Takeshi Kamura

Yen Press
150 West 30th St., 19th Floor
New York, NY 10001

Visit us at yenpress.com
facebook.com/yenpress
twitter.com/yenpress
yenpress.tumblr.com
instagram.com/yenpress

MONWRES -ISHUKAKUTOU MONSTER MUSUME- Vol.2
© 2019 Ganmarei, Tyataniyou, Takeo Aoki
All rights reserved.
First published in Japan in 2019 by MICRO MAGAZINE,INC., Tokyo.
English translation rights arranged with MICRO MAGAZINE,INC., through
Tuttle-Mori Agency, Inc., Tokyo.

English translation © 2019 by Yen Press, LLC

First Yen Press Edition: November 2019

Yen Press is an imprint of Yen Press, LLC.
The Yen Press name and logo are trademarks
of Yen Press, LLC.

The publisher is not responsible for websites
(or their content) that are not owned by
the publisher.

Library of Congress Control Number: 2018958634

ISBNs: 978-1-9753-5958-4 (paperback)
978-1-9753-0634-2 (ebook)

10 9 8 7 6 5 4 3 2 1

WOR

This book is a work
of fiction. Names,
characters, places,
and incidents are
the product of the
author's imagination
or are used
fictitiously.
Any resemblance
to actual events,
locales, or persons,
living or dead,
is coincidental.

Printed in the United States of America

ILLUSTRATION FROM SHAKE-O

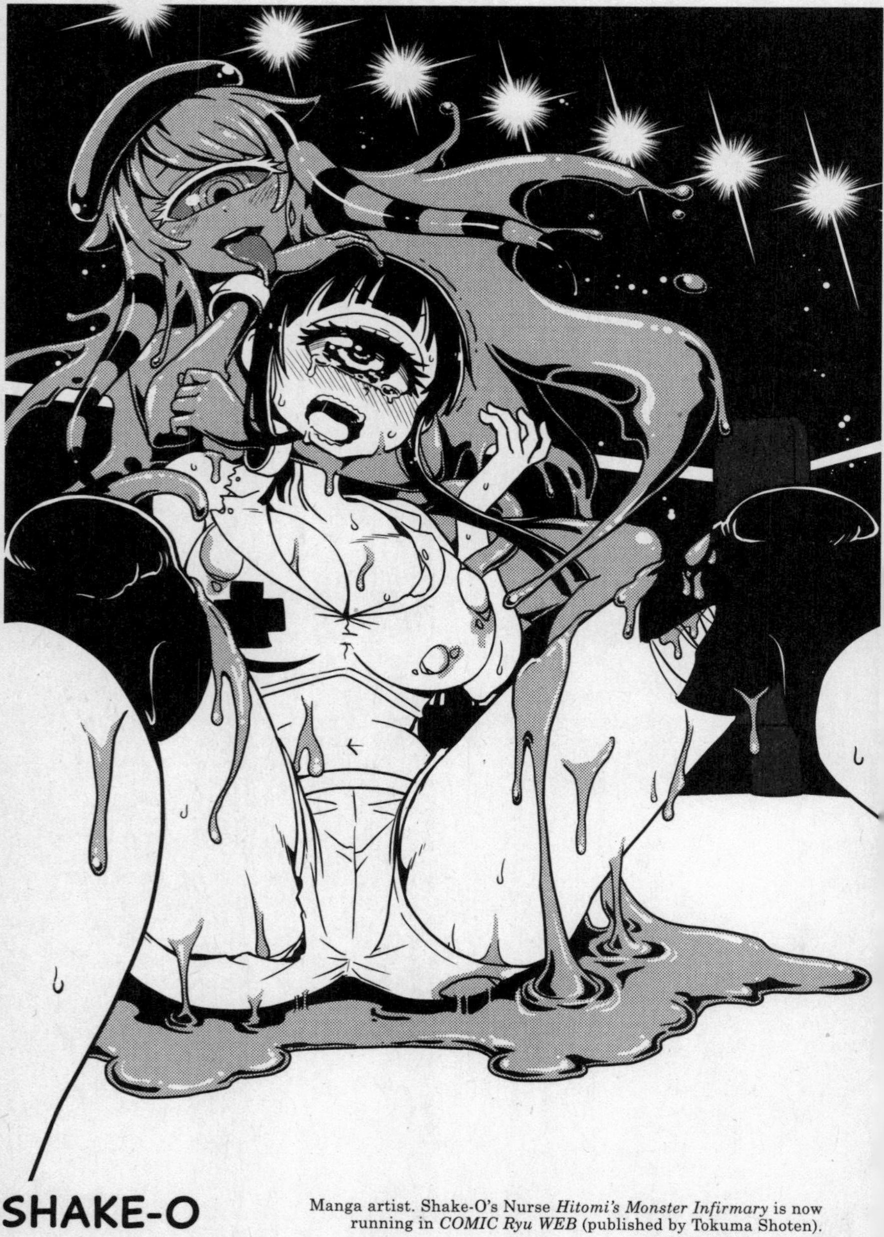

SHAKE-O

Manga artist. Shake-O's Nurse *Hitomi's Monster Infirmary* is now running in *COMIC Ryu WEB* (published by Tokuma Shoten).

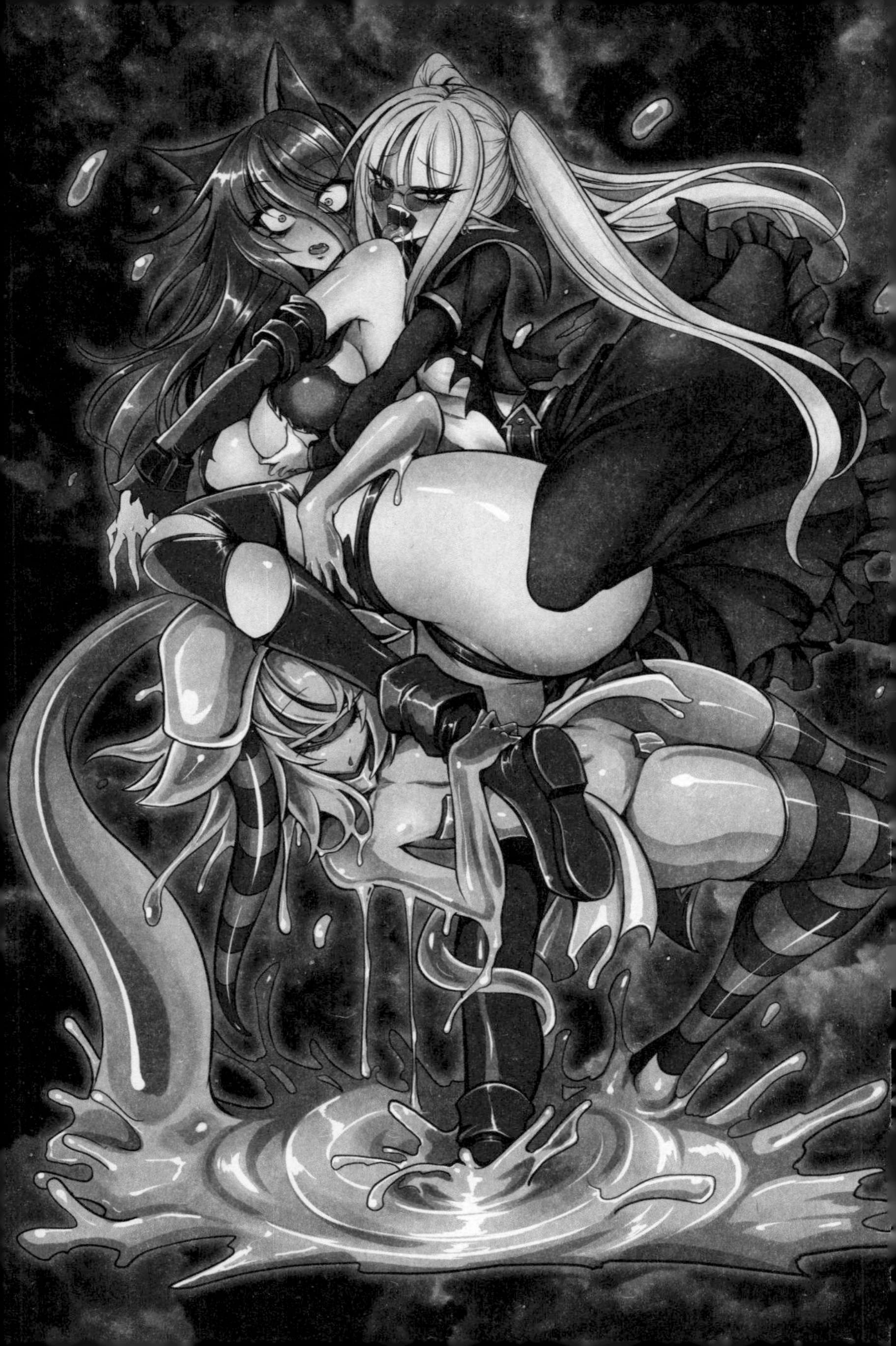

CONTENTS

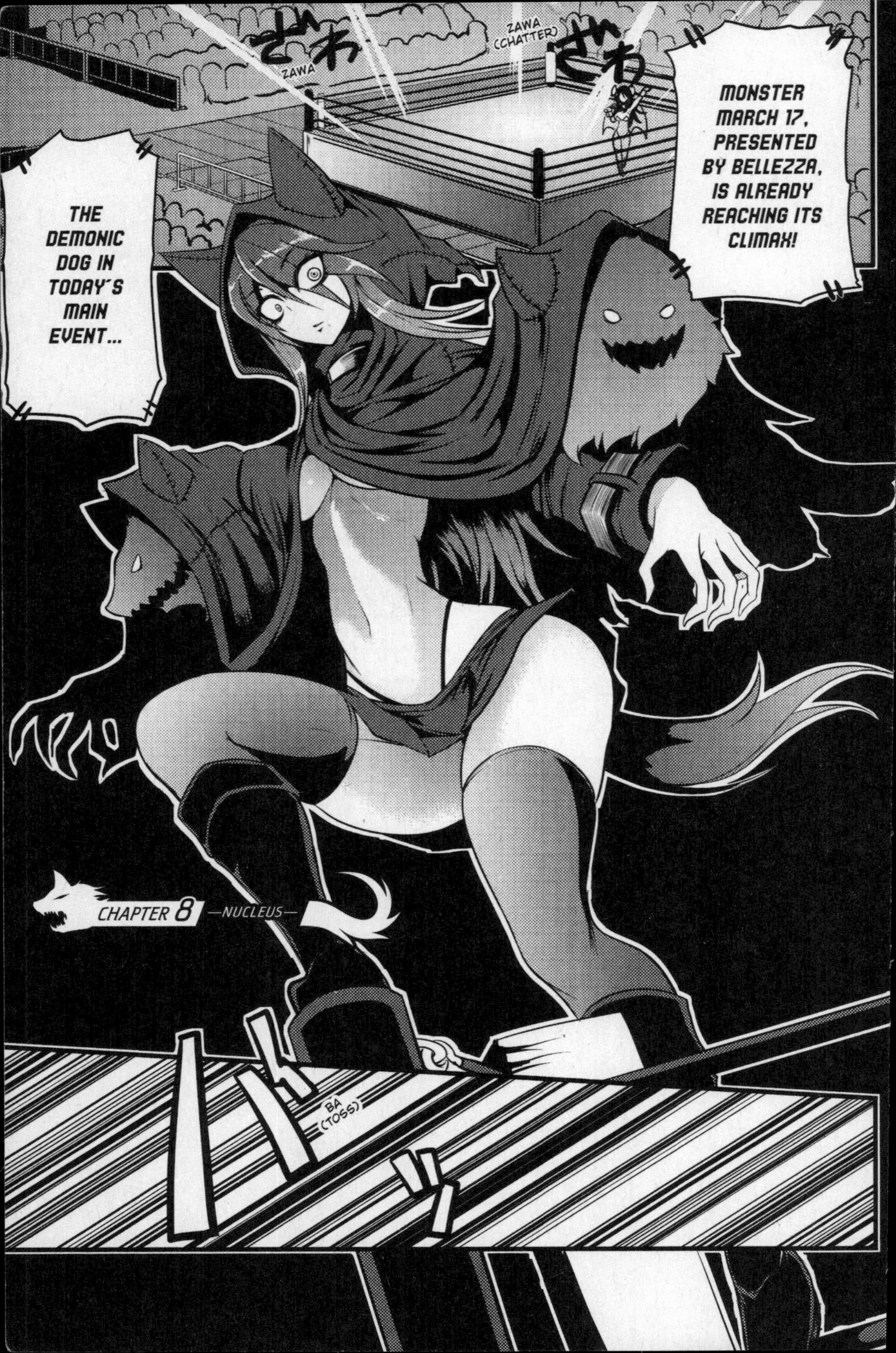
ZAWA (CHATTER)
ZAWA
MONSTER MARCH 17, PRESENTED BY BELLEZZA, IS ALREADY REACHING ITS CLIMAX!
THE DEMONIC DOG IN TODAY'S MAIN EVENT...
CHAPTER 8 —NUCLEUS—
BA (TOSS)

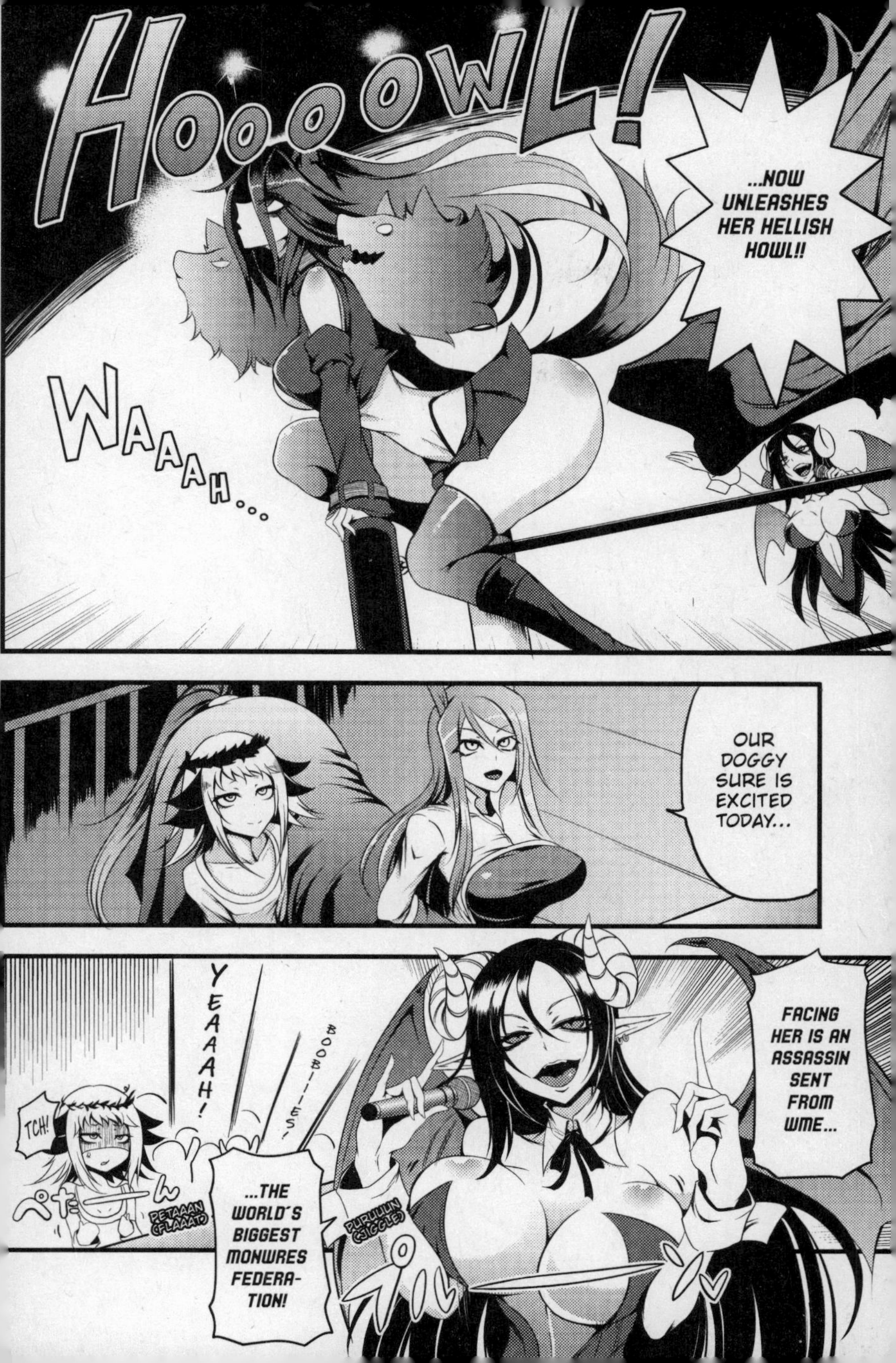
HOOOOWL!
...NOW UNLEASHES HER HELLISH HOWL!!
WAAAAH...
OUR DOGGY SURE IS EXCITED TODAY...
FACING HER IS AN ASSASSIN SENT FROM WME...
...THE WORLD'S BIGGEST MONWRES FEDERA-TION!
PURUUUN (JIGGLE)
BOOBIIIES!
YEAAAAH!
TCH!
PETAAAN (FLAAAT)

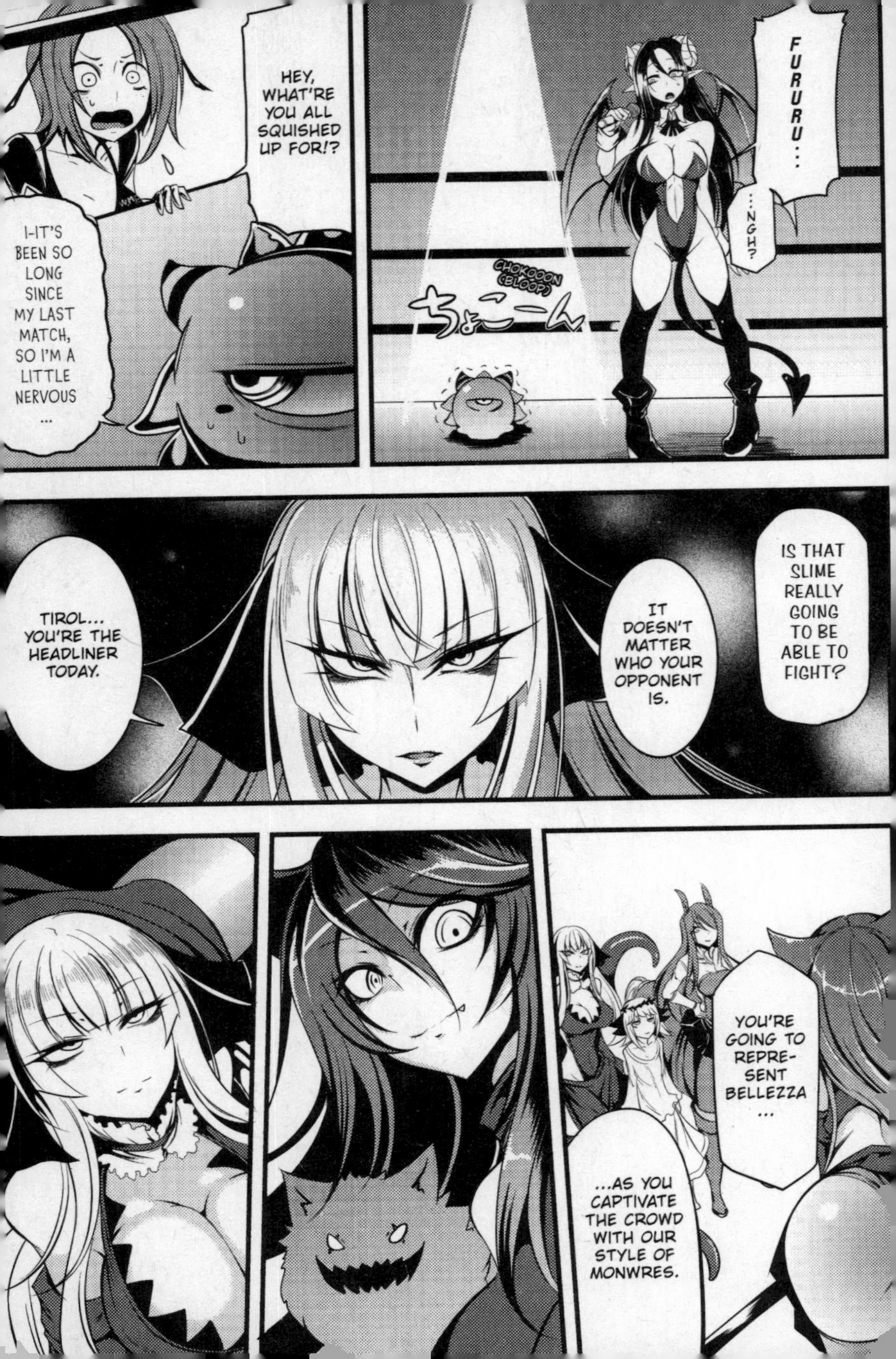
FURURU...
...NGH?
CHOKOOON (BLOOP)
ちょこーん
HEY, WHAT'RE YOU ALL SQUISHED UP FOR!?
I-IT'S BEEN SO LONG SINCE MY LAST MATCH, SO I'M A LITTLE NERVOUS...
IS THAT SLIME REALLY GOING TO BE ABLE TO FIGHT?
IT DOESN'T MATTER WHO YOUR OPPONENT IS.
TIROL... YOU'RE THE HEADLINER TODAY.
YOU'RE GOING TO REPRESENT BELLEZZA...
...AS YOU CAPTIVATE THE CROWD WITH OUR STYLE OF MONWRES.

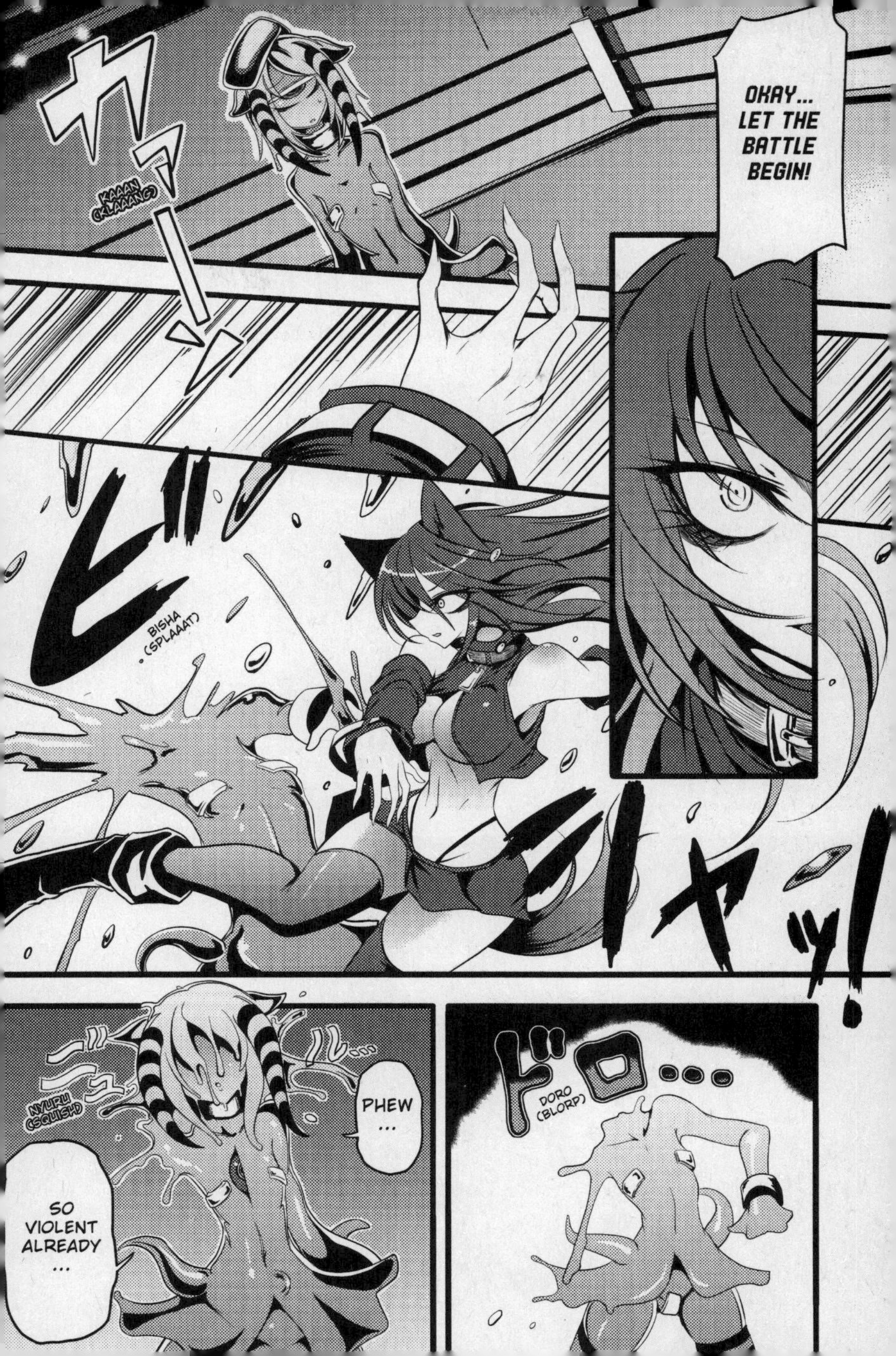
OKAY... LET THE BATTLE BEGIN!
KAAAN (KLAAANG)
BISHA (SPLAAAT)
DORO (BLORP)
NYURU (SQUISH)
PHEW ...
SO VIOLENT ALREADY ...

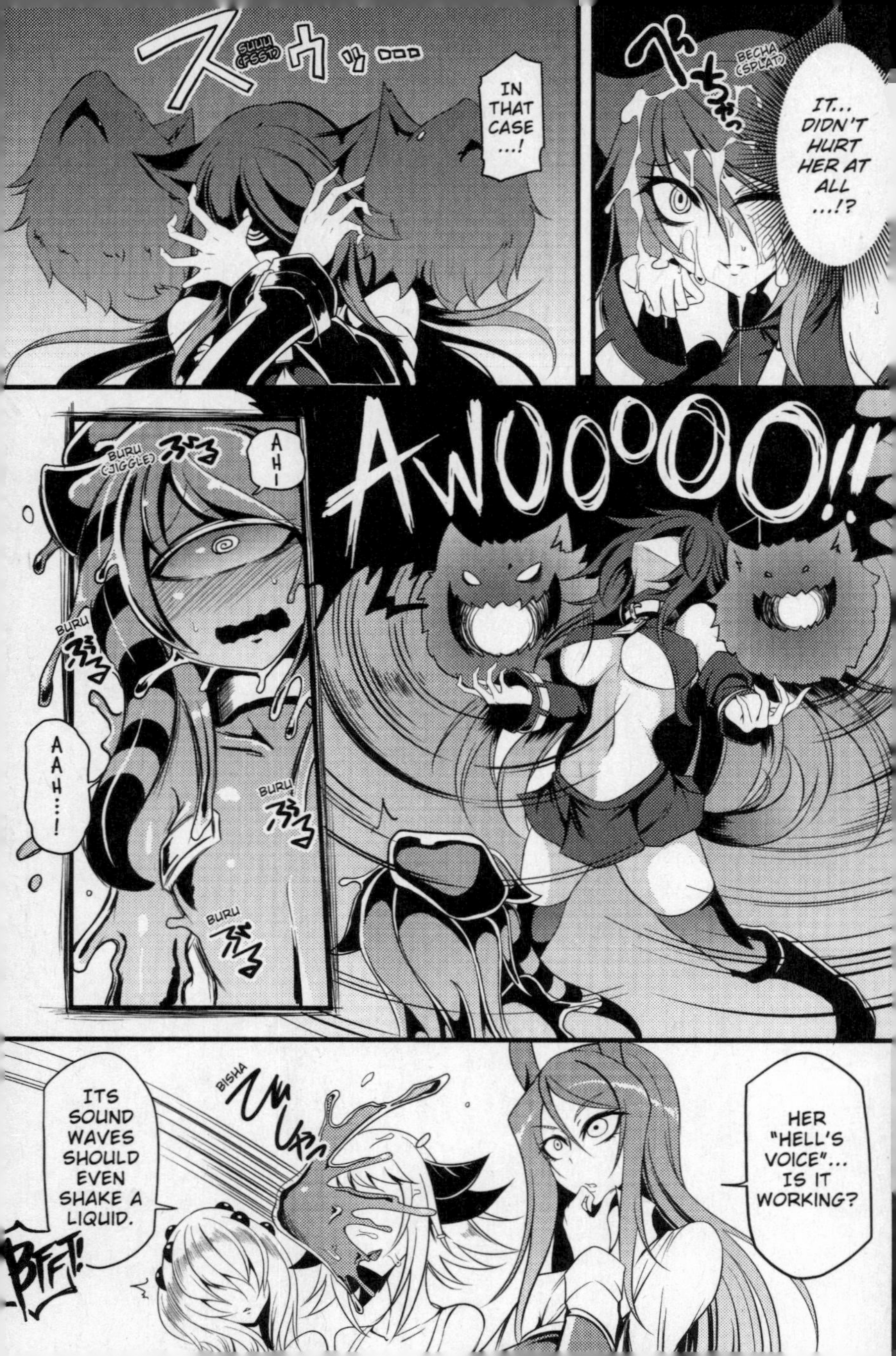
BECHA (SPLAT)
IT... DIDN'T HURT HER AT ALL ...!?
SUUU (FSSST)
IN THAT CASE ...!
AWOOOOOO!!
BURU (JIGGLE)
AHI
BURU
AAH...!
BURU
BURU
HER "HELL'S VOICE"... IS IT WORKING?
BISHA
ITS SOUND WAVES SHOULD EVEN SHAKE A LIQUID.
BFFT!

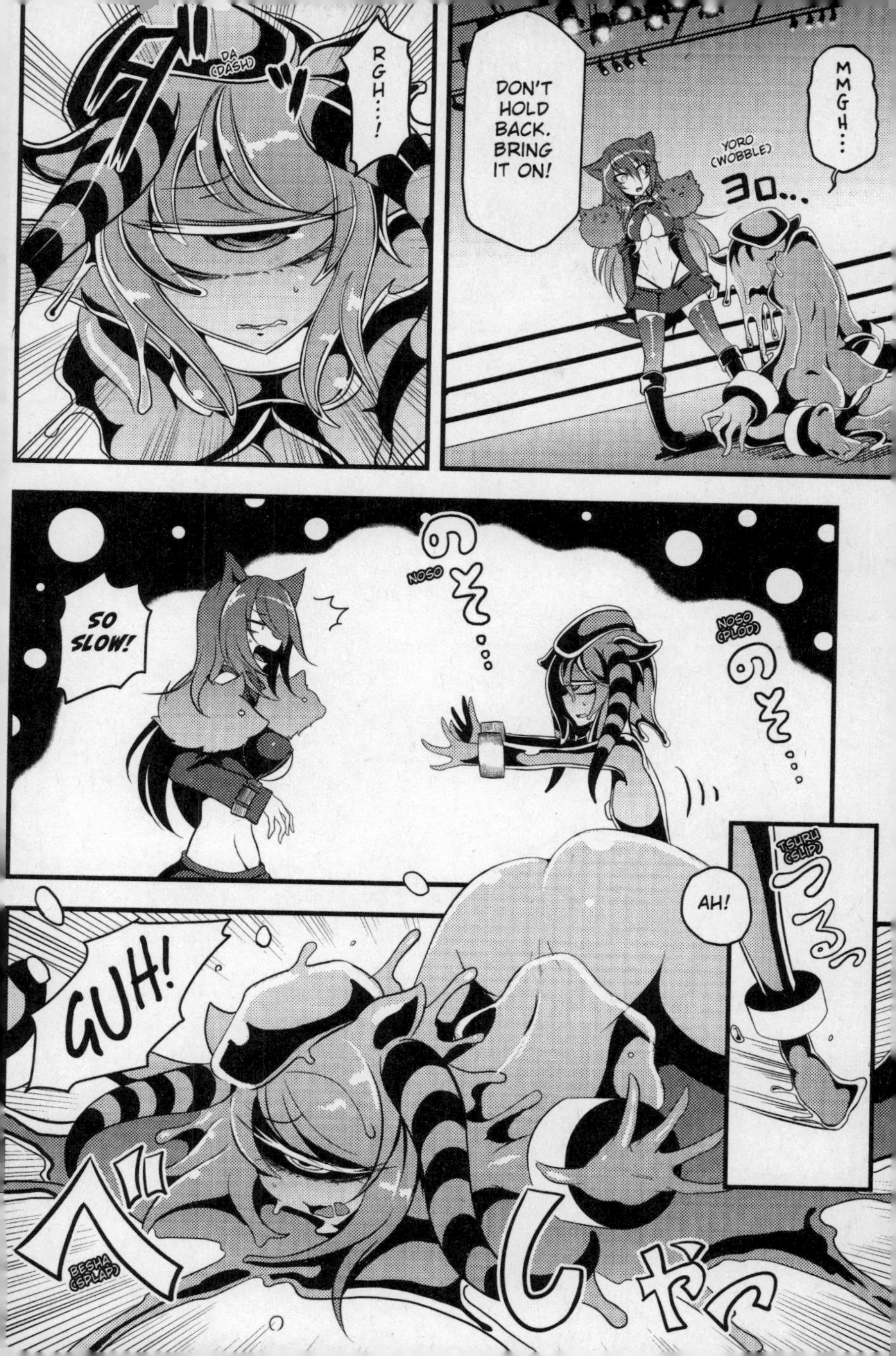
MMGH...
YORO (WOBBLE)
ヨロ...
DON'T HOLD BACK. BRING IT ON!
RGH...!
DA (DASH)
NOSO (PLOD)
のそ...
NOSO
のそ...
SO SLOW!
TSURU (SLIP)
AH!
GUH!
BESHA (SPLAP)

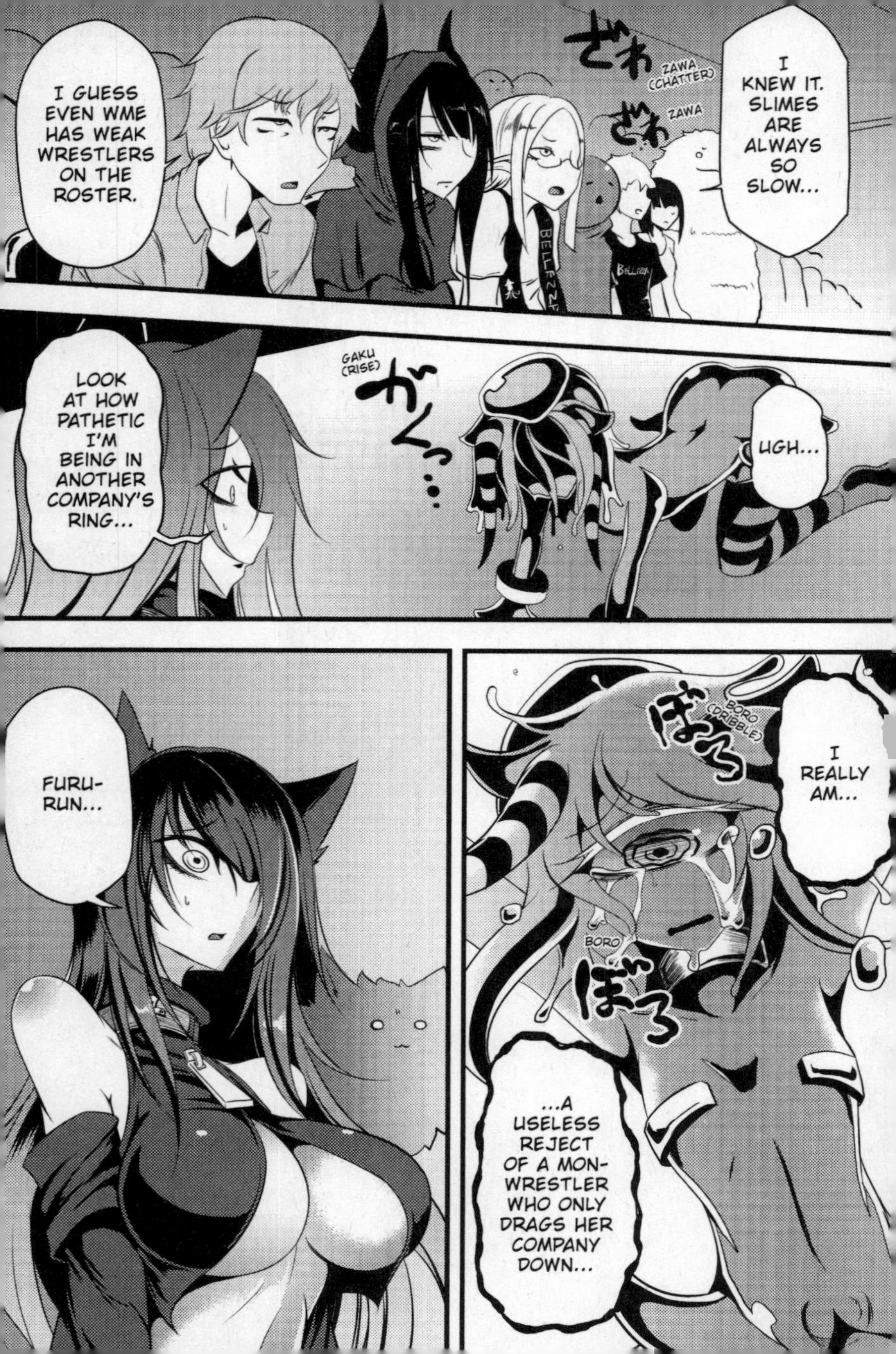

I KNEW IT. SLIMES ARE ALWAYS SO SLOW...
ざわ
ZAWA (CHATTER)
ざわ
ZAWA
I GUESS EVEN WME HAS WEAK WRESTLERS ON THE ROSTER.
UGH...
がくっ
GAKU (RISE)
LOOK AT HOW PATHETIC I'M BEING IN ANOTHER COMPANY'S RING...
ぼろ
BORO (DRIBBLE)
I REALLY AM...
BORO
ぼろ
...A USELESS REJECT OF A MON-WRESTLER WHO ONLY DRAGS HER COMPANY DOWN...
FURU-RUN...

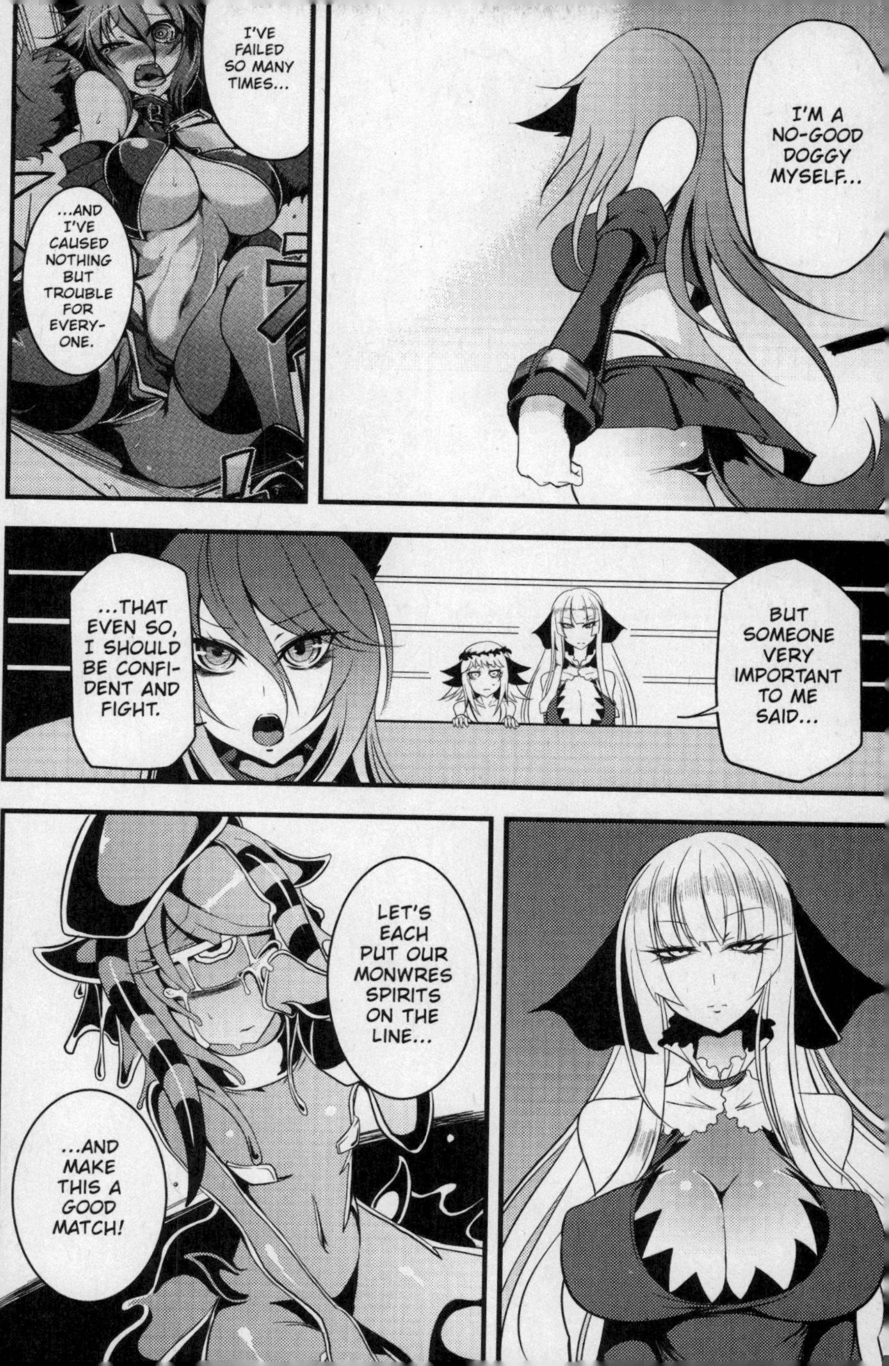
I'M A NO-GOOD DOGGY MYSELF...
I'VE FAILED SO MANY TIMES...
...AND I'VE CAUSED NOTHING BUT TROUBLE FOR EVERY-ONE.
BUT SOMEONE VERY IMPORTANT TO ME SAID...
...THAT EVEN SO, I SHOULD BE CONFI-DENT AND FIGHT.
LET'S EACH PUT OUR MONWRES SPIRITS ON THE LINE...
...AND MAKE THIS A GOOD MATCH!

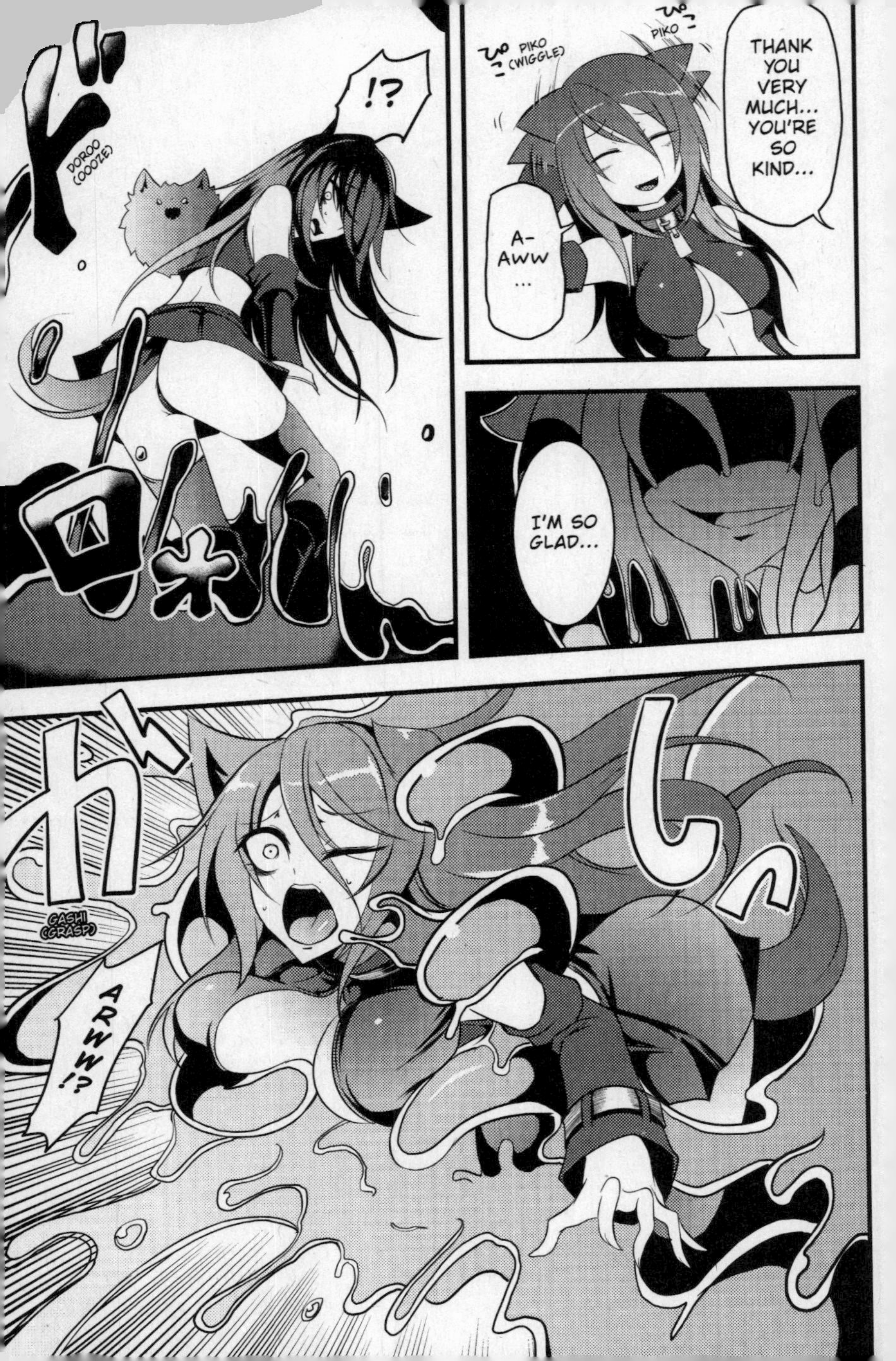
PIKO
THANK YOU VERY MUCH... YOU'RE SO KIND...
PIKO (WIGGLE)
A-AWW ...
I'M SO GLAD...
!?
DOROO (OOOZE)
GASHI (GRASP)
ARWW!?

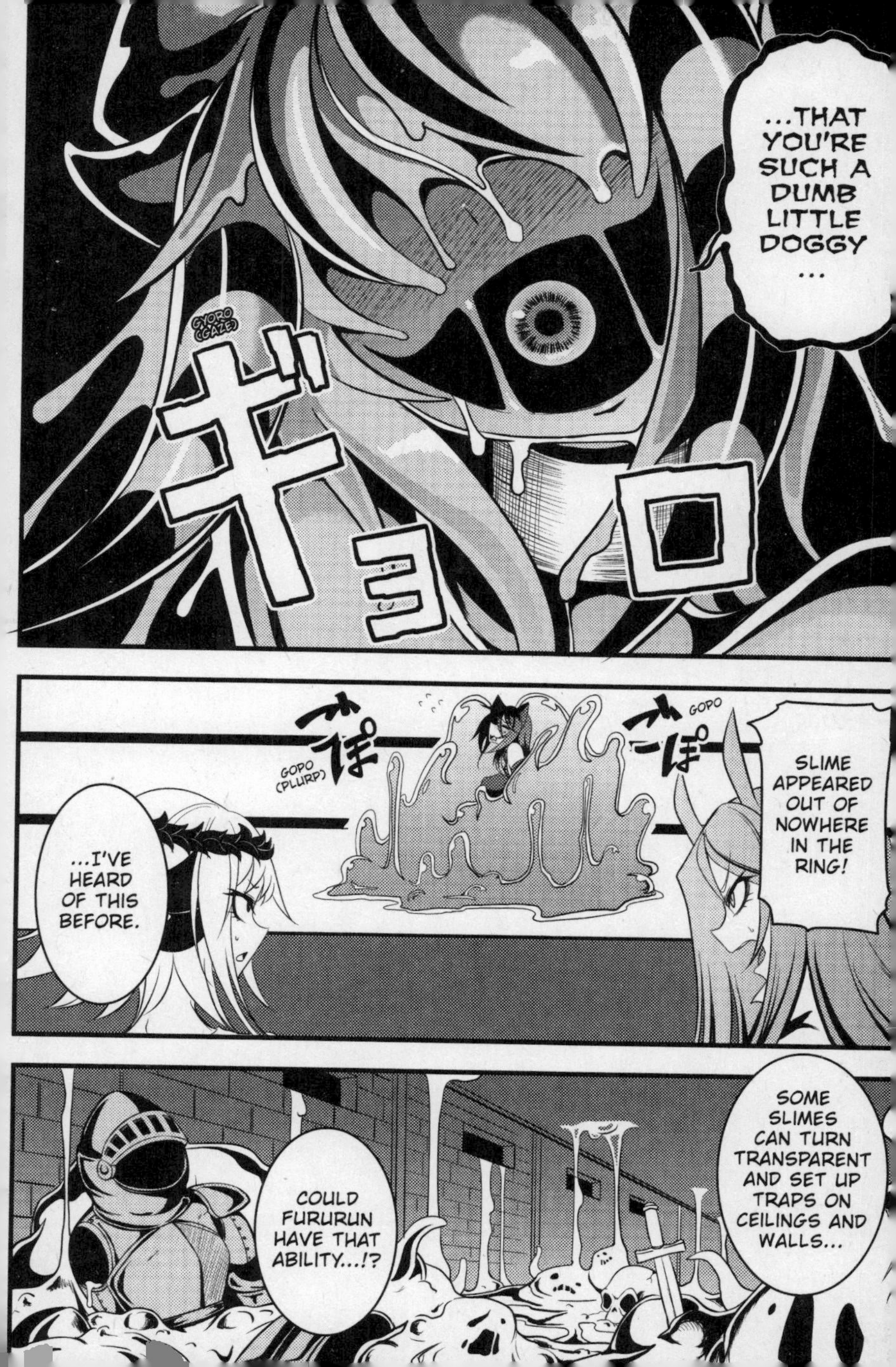
...THAT YOU'RE SUCH A DUMB LITTLE DOGGY...
GYORO (GAZE)
ギョロ
SLIME APPEARED OUT OF NOWHERE IN THE RING!
GOPO
ごぽ
GOPO (PLURP)
ごぽ
...I'VE HEARD OF THIS BEFORE.
SOME SLIMES CAN TURN TRANSPARENT AND SET UP TRAPS ON CEILINGS AND WALLS...
COULD FURURUN HAVE THAT ABILITY...!?

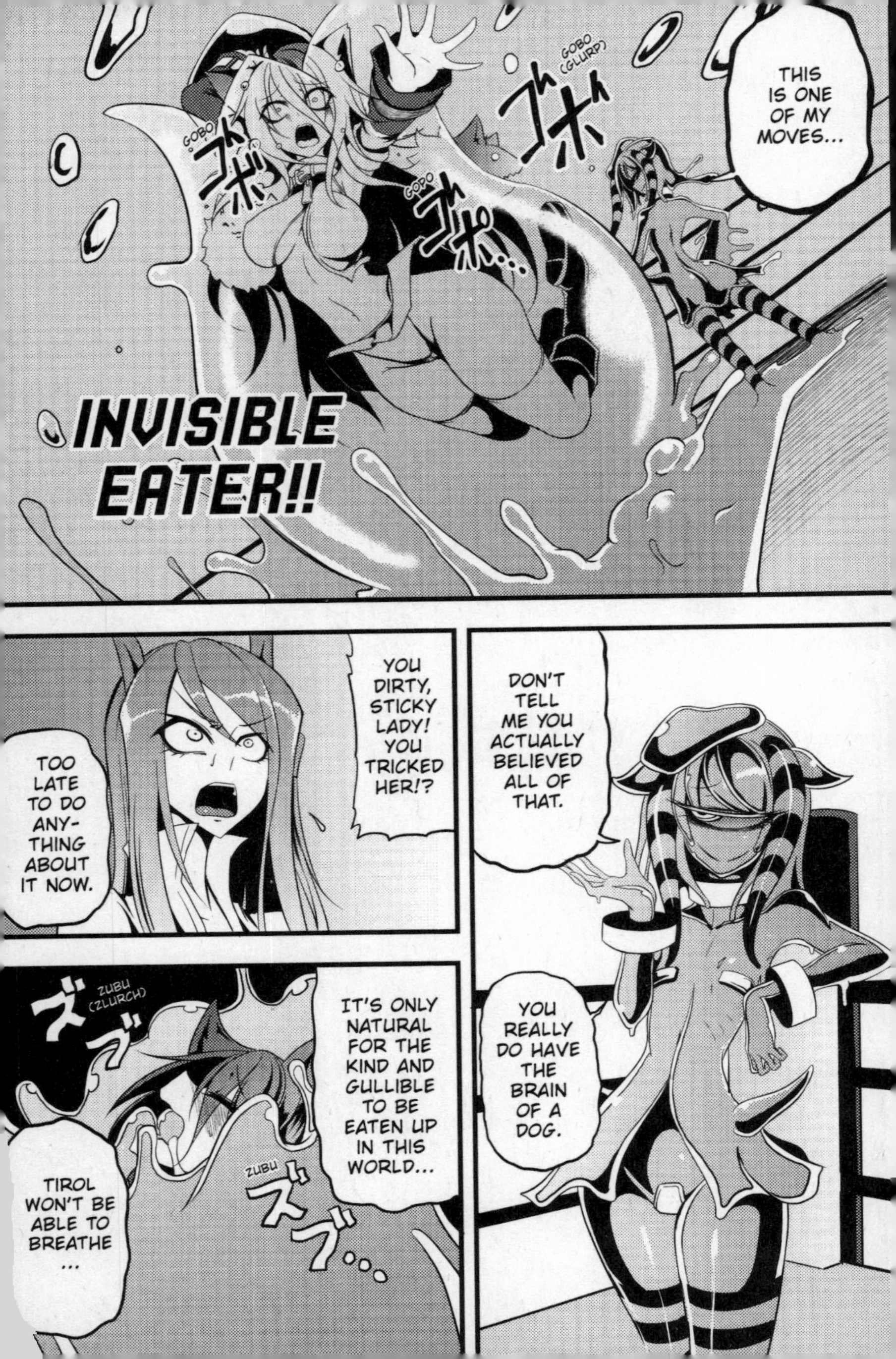
THIS IS ONE OF MY MOVES...
GOBO (GLURP)
GOBO
GOBO
INVISIBLE EATER!!
DON'T TELL ME YOU ACTUALLY BELIEVED ALL OF THAT.
YOU REALLY DO HAVE THE BRAIN OF A DOG.
YOU DIRTY, STICKY LADY! YOU TRICKED HER!?
TOO LATE TO DO ANY-THING ABOUT IT NOW.
IT'S ONLY NATURAL FOR THE KIND AND GULLIBLE TO BE EATEN UP IN THIS WORLD...
ZUBU (ZLURCH)
ZUBU
TIROL WON'T BE ABLE TO BREATHE...

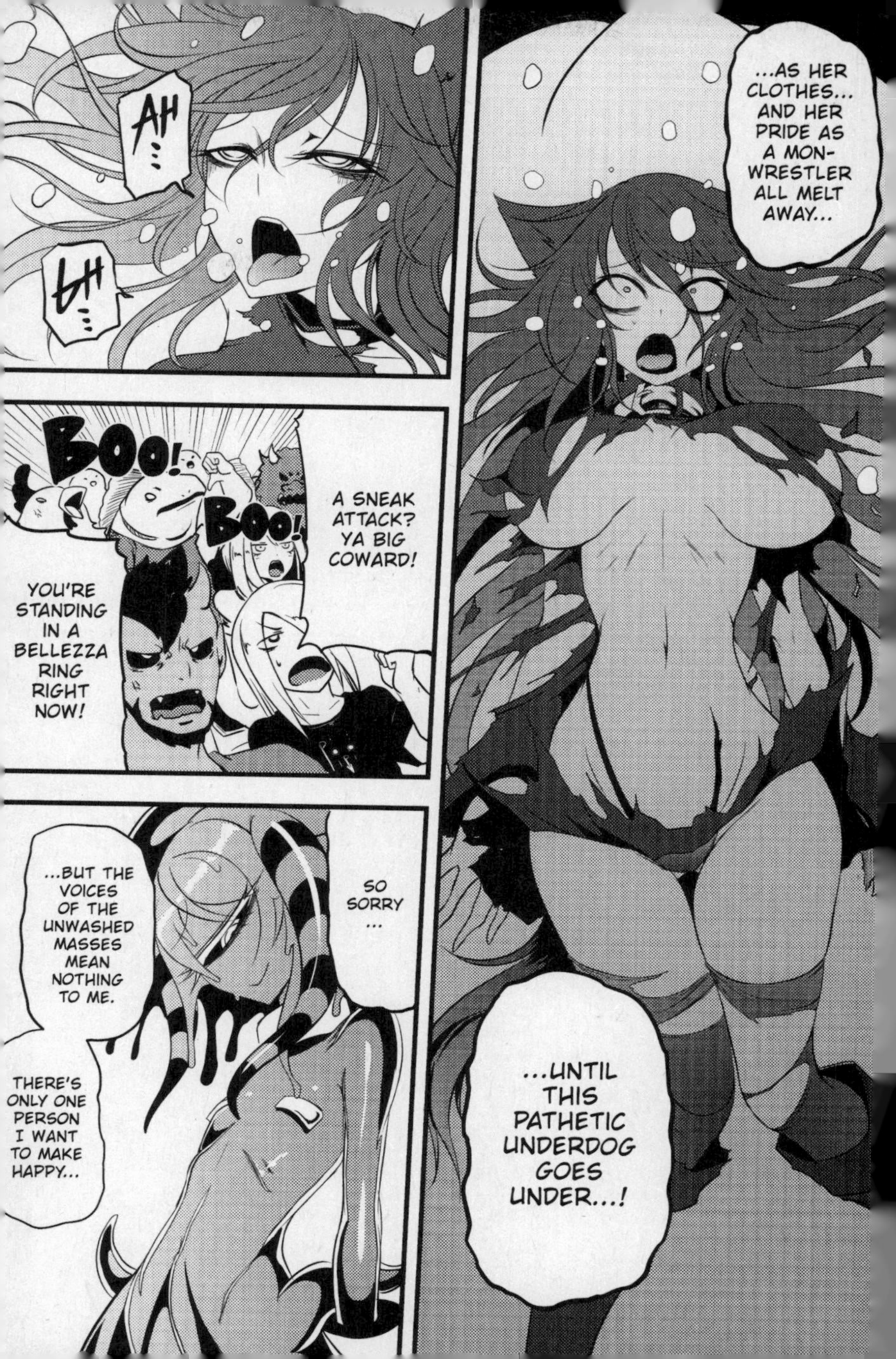
...AS HER CLOTHES... AND HER PRIDE AS A MON-WRESTLER ALL MELT AWAY...
...UNTIL THIS PATHETIC UNDERDOG GOES UNDER...!
AH...
UH...
A SNEAK ATTACK? YA BIG COWARD!
BOO! BOO!
YOU'RE STANDING IN A BELLEZZA RING RIGHT NOW!
SO SORRY...
...BUT THE VOICES OF THE UNWASHED MASSES MEAN NOTHING TO ME.
THERE'S ONLY ONE PERSON I WANT TO MAKE HAPPY...

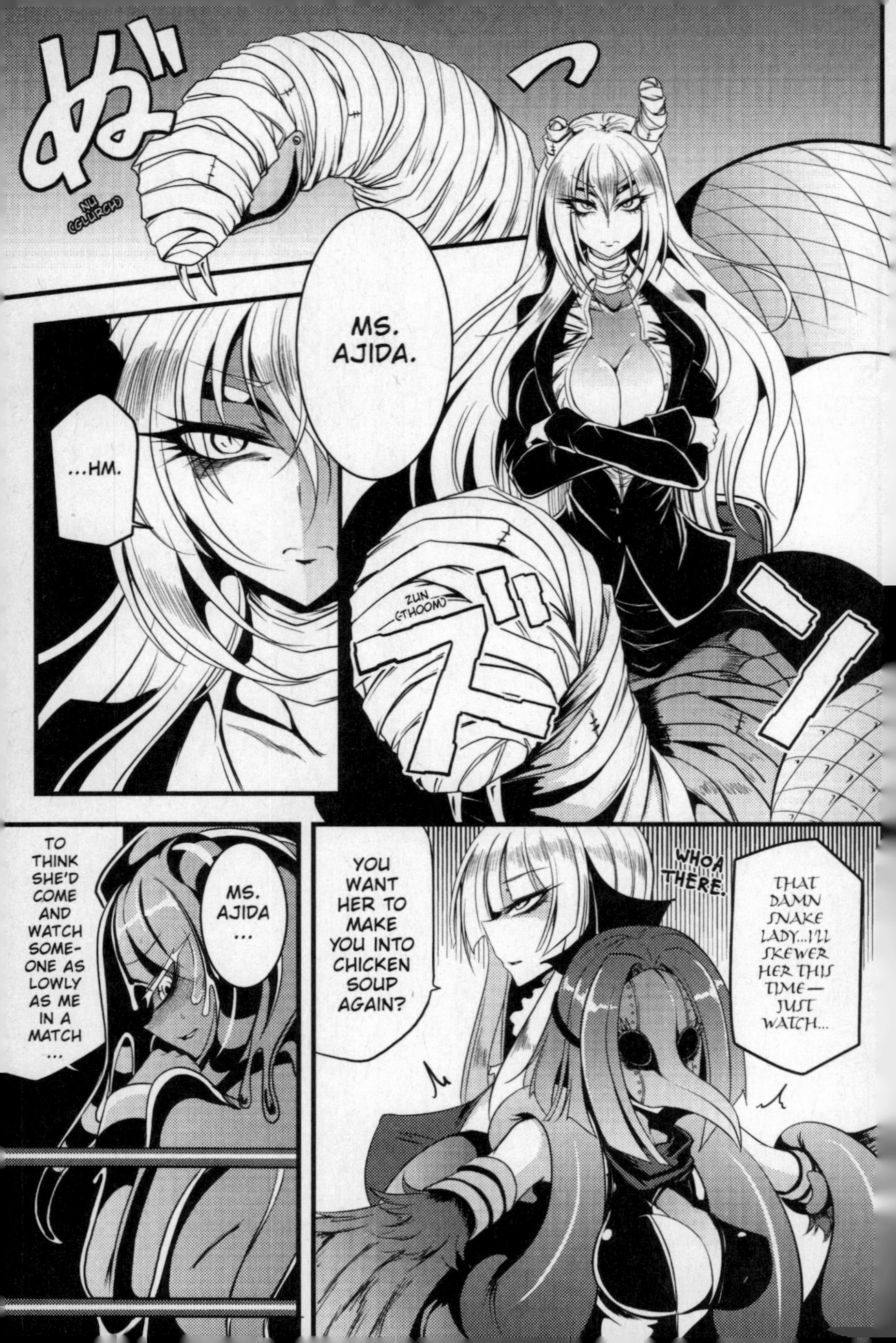

ぬ゛っ
NU (GLURCH)
MS. AJIDA.
ZUN (THOOM)
ズン
...HM.
THAT DAMN SNAKE LADY...I'LL SKEWER HER THIS TIME— JUST WATCH...
WHOA THERE.
YOU WANT HER TO MAKE YOU INTO CHICKEN SOUP AGAIN?
MS. AJIDA ...
TO THINK SHE'D COME AND WATCH SOME-ONE AS LOWLY AS ME IN A MATCH ...

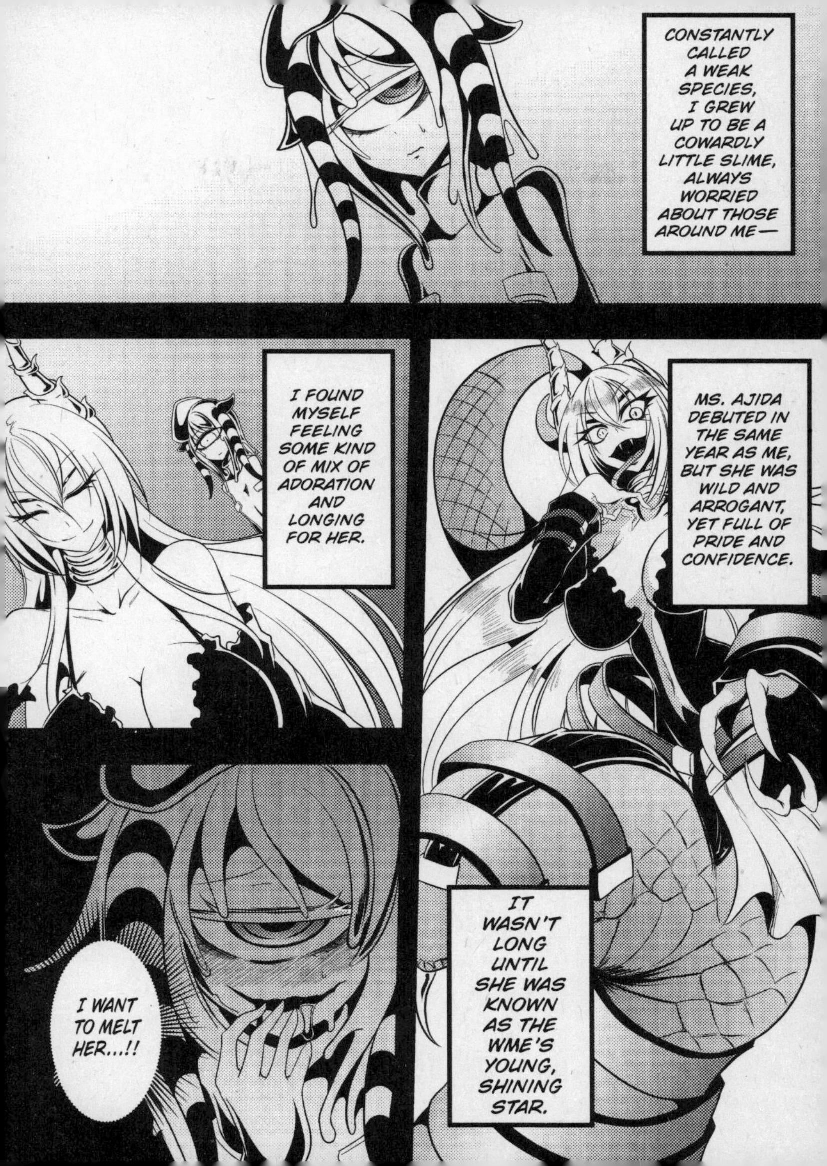
CONSTANTLY CALLED A WEAK SPECIES, I GREW UP TO BE A COWARDLY LITTLE SLIME, ALWAYS WORRIED ABOUT THOSE AROUND ME—
MS. AJIDA DEBUTED IN THE SAME YEAR AS ME, BUT SHE WAS WILD AND ARROGANT, YET FULL OF PRIDE AND CONFIDENCE.
IT WASN'T LONG UNTIL SHE WAS KNOWN AS THE WME'S YOUNG, SHINING STAR.
I FOUND MYSELF FEELING SOME KIND OF MIX OF ADORATION AND LONGING FOR HER.
I WANT TO MELT HER...!!

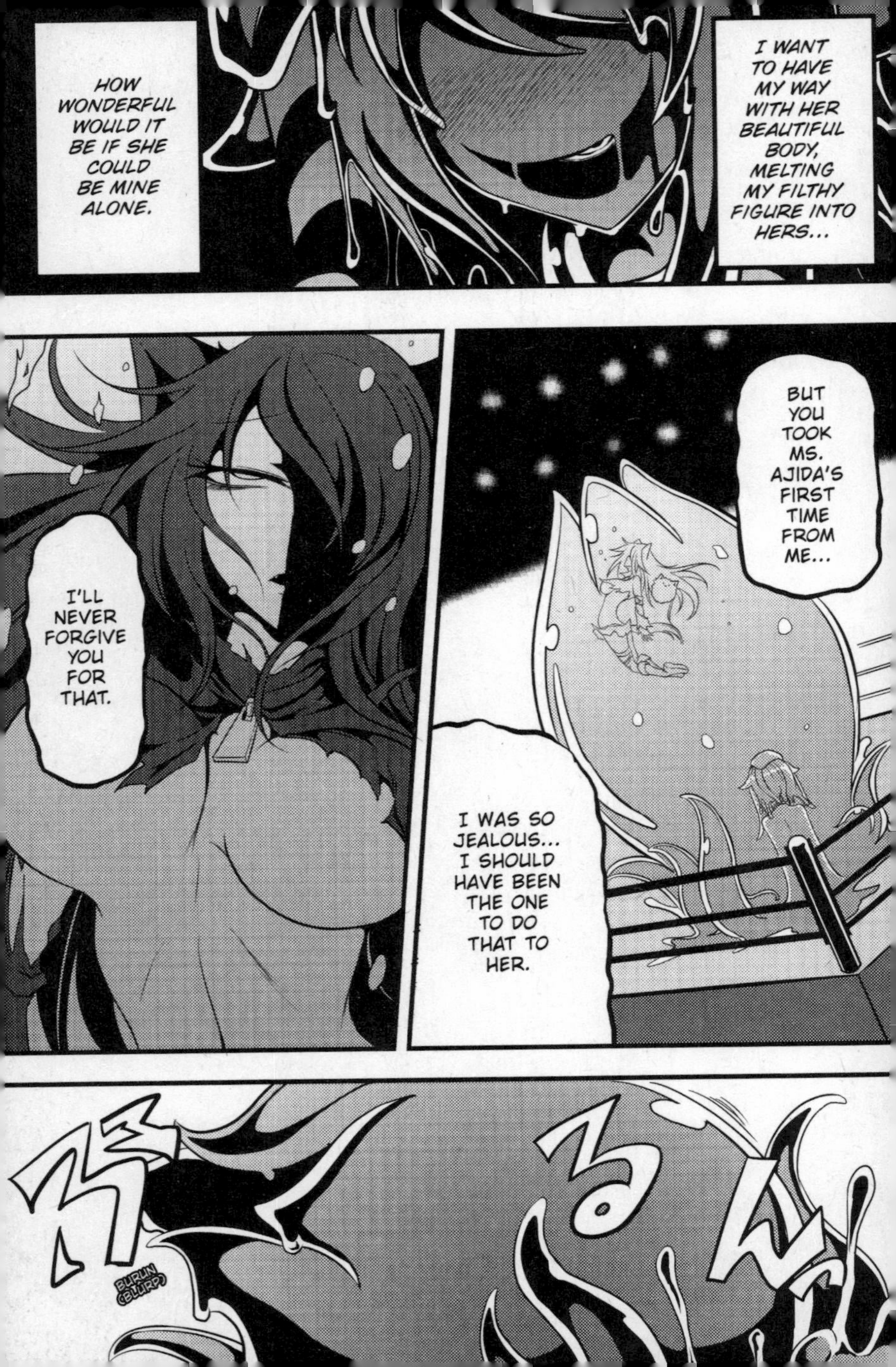
I WANT TO HAVE MY WAY WITH HER BEAUTIFUL BODY, MELTING MY FILTHY FIGURE INTO HERS...
HOW WONDERFUL WOULD IT BE IF SHE COULD BE MINE ALONE.
BUT YOU TOOK MS. AJIDA'S FIRST TIME FROM ME...
I WAS SO JEALOUS... I SHOULD HAVE BEEN THE ONE TO DO THAT TO HER.
I'LL NEVER FORGIVE YOU FOR THAT.
BURUN (BLURP)

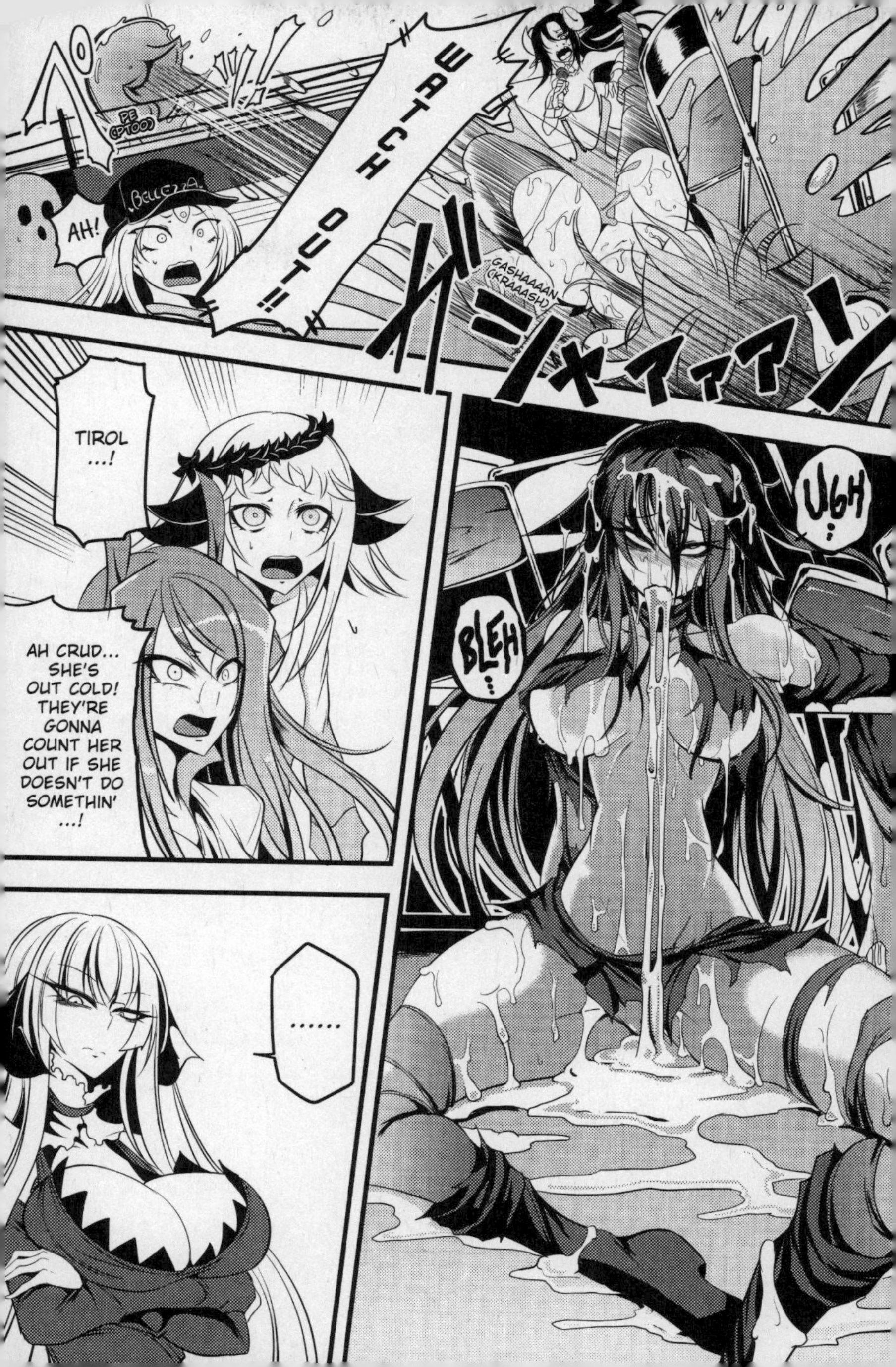
WATCH OUT!!
GASHAAAAN (KRAAASH)
PE (PTOO)
AH!
UGH...
BLEH...
TIROL ...!
AH CRUD... SHE'S OUT COLD! THEY'RE GONNA COUNT HER OUT IF SHE DOESN'T DO SOMETHIN' ...!
......

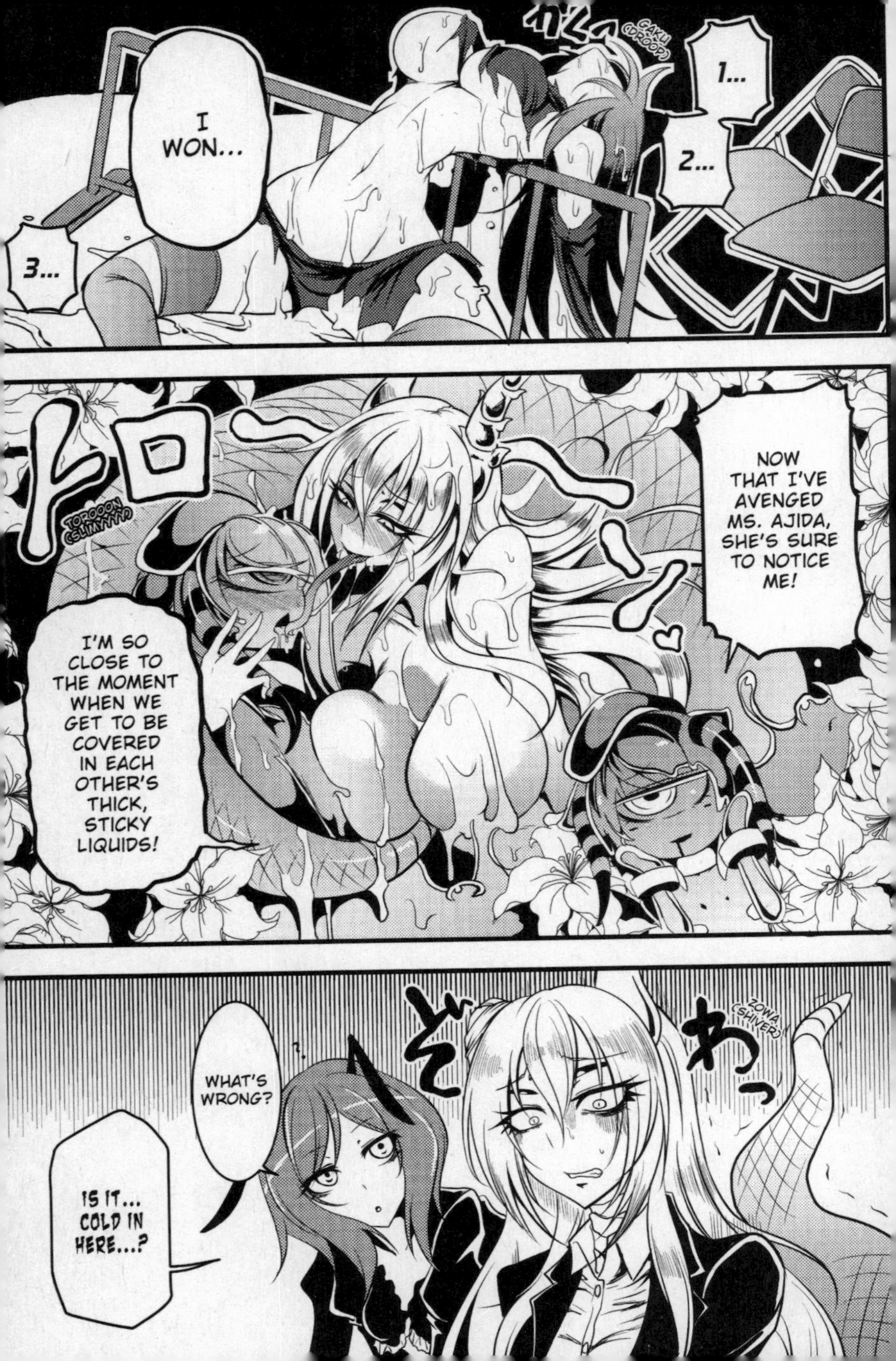GAKU (DROOP)
1...
2...
I WON...
3...
NOW THAT I'VE AVENGED MS. AJIDA, SHE'S SURE TO NOTICE ME!
TOROOON (SLIMYYYY)
I'M SO CLOSE TO THE MOMENT WHEN WE GET TO BE COVERED IN EACH OTHER'S THICK, STICKY LIQUIDS!
ZOWA (SHIVER)
WHAT'S WRONG?
IS IT... COLD IN HERE...?

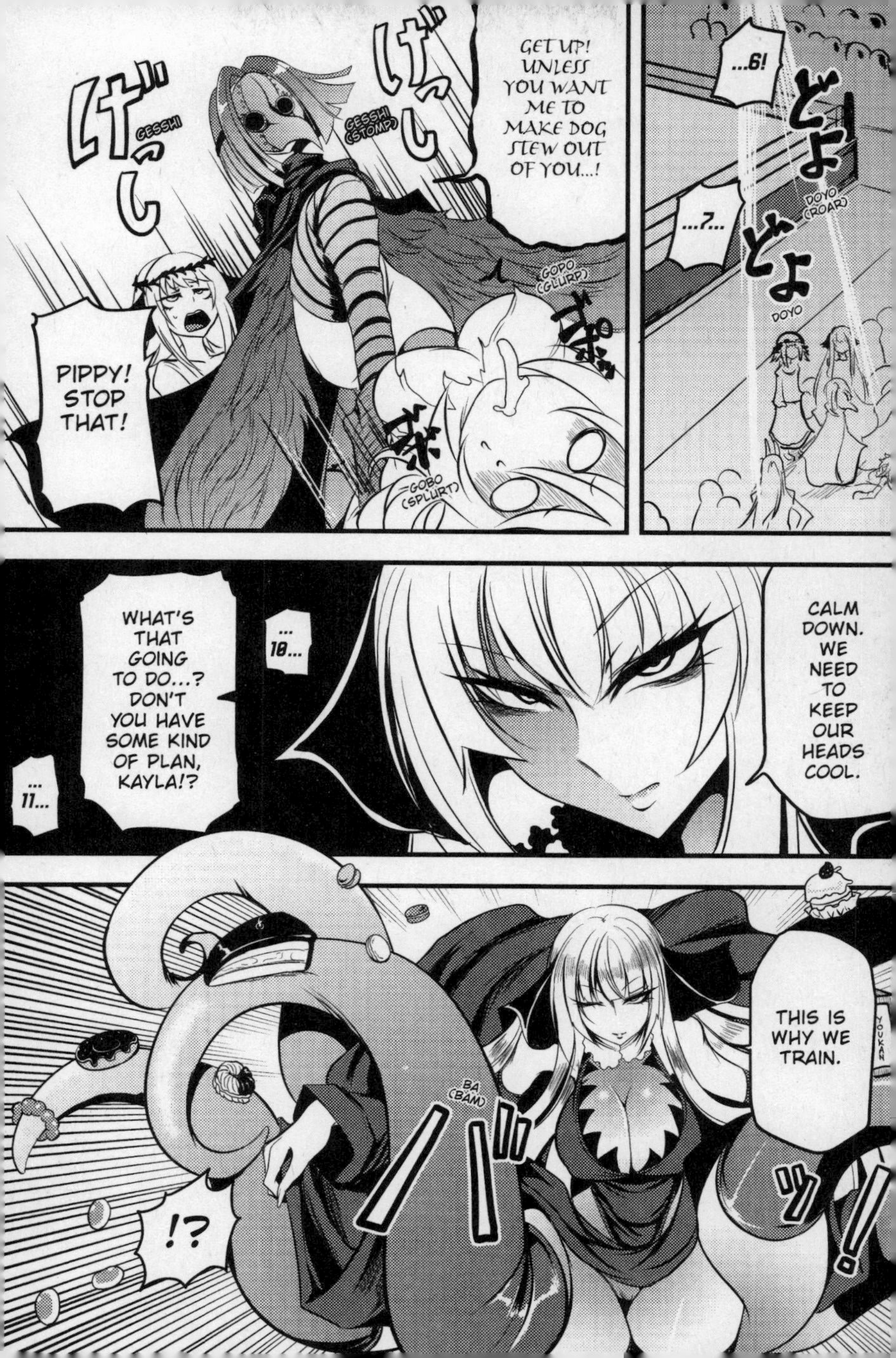

...6!
どよ
DOYO (ROAR)
...7...
どよ
DOYO
GET UP! UNLESS YOU WANT ME TO MAKE DOG STEW OUT OF YOU...!
げっし
GESSHI (STOMP)
げっし
GESSHI
GOPO (GLURP)
PIPPY! STOP THAT!
GOBO (SPLURT)
CALM DOWN. WE NEED TO KEEP OUR HEADS COOL.
WHAT'S THAT GOING TO DO...? DON'T YOU HAVE SOME KIND OF PLAN, KAYLA!?
... 10...
... 11...
THIS IS WHY WE TRAIN.
YOUKAN
BA (BAM)
!?

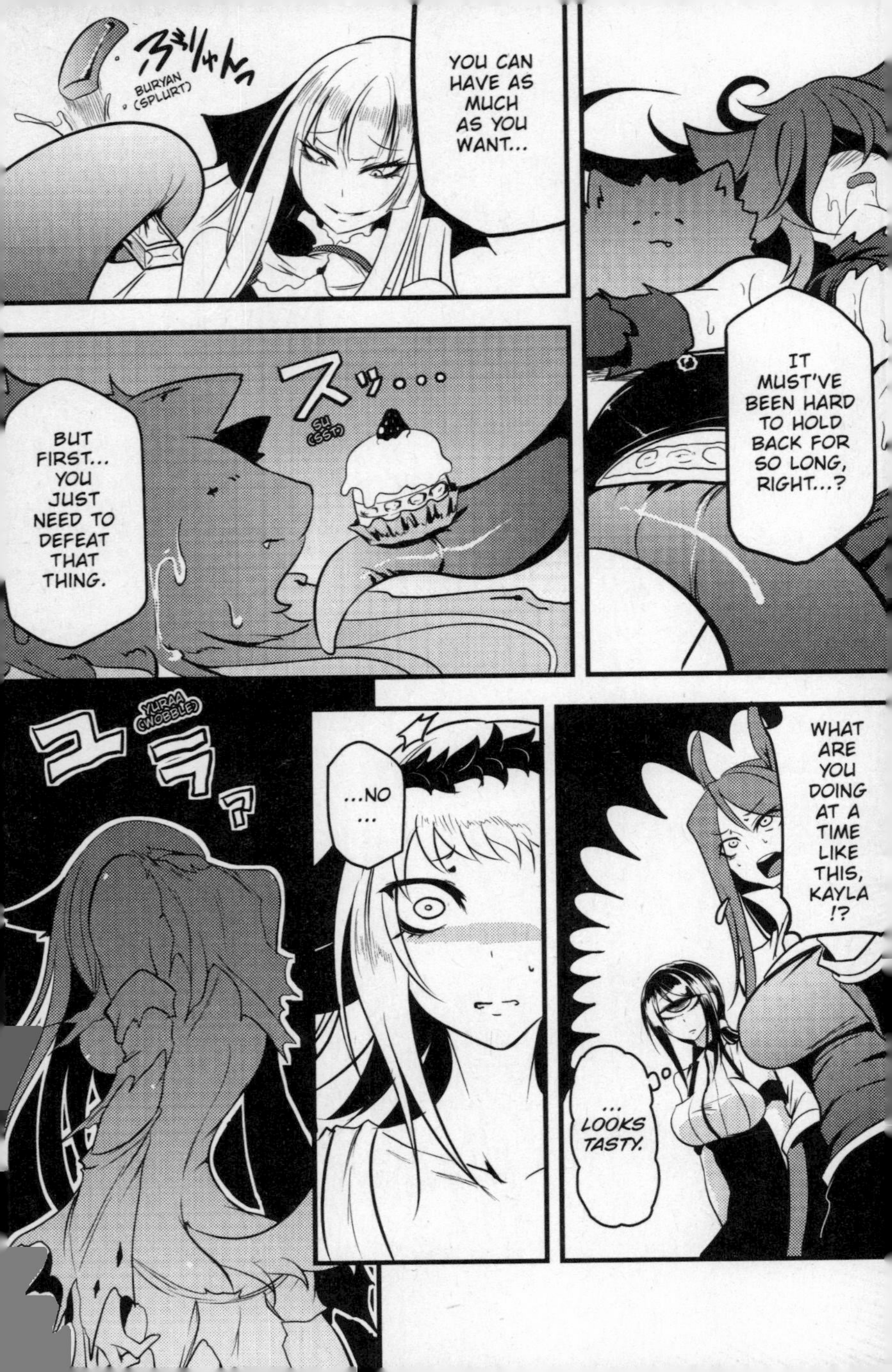
IT MUST'VE BEEN HARD TO HOLD BACK FOR SO LONG, RIGHT...?
YOU CAN HAVE AS MUCH AS YOU WANT...
BURYAN (SPLURT)
SU (SST)
BUT FIRST... YOU JUST NEED TO DEFEAT THAT THING.
WHAT ARE YOU DOING AT A TIME LIKE THIS, KAYLA!?
... LOOKS TASTY.
...NO ...
YURAA (WOBBLE)

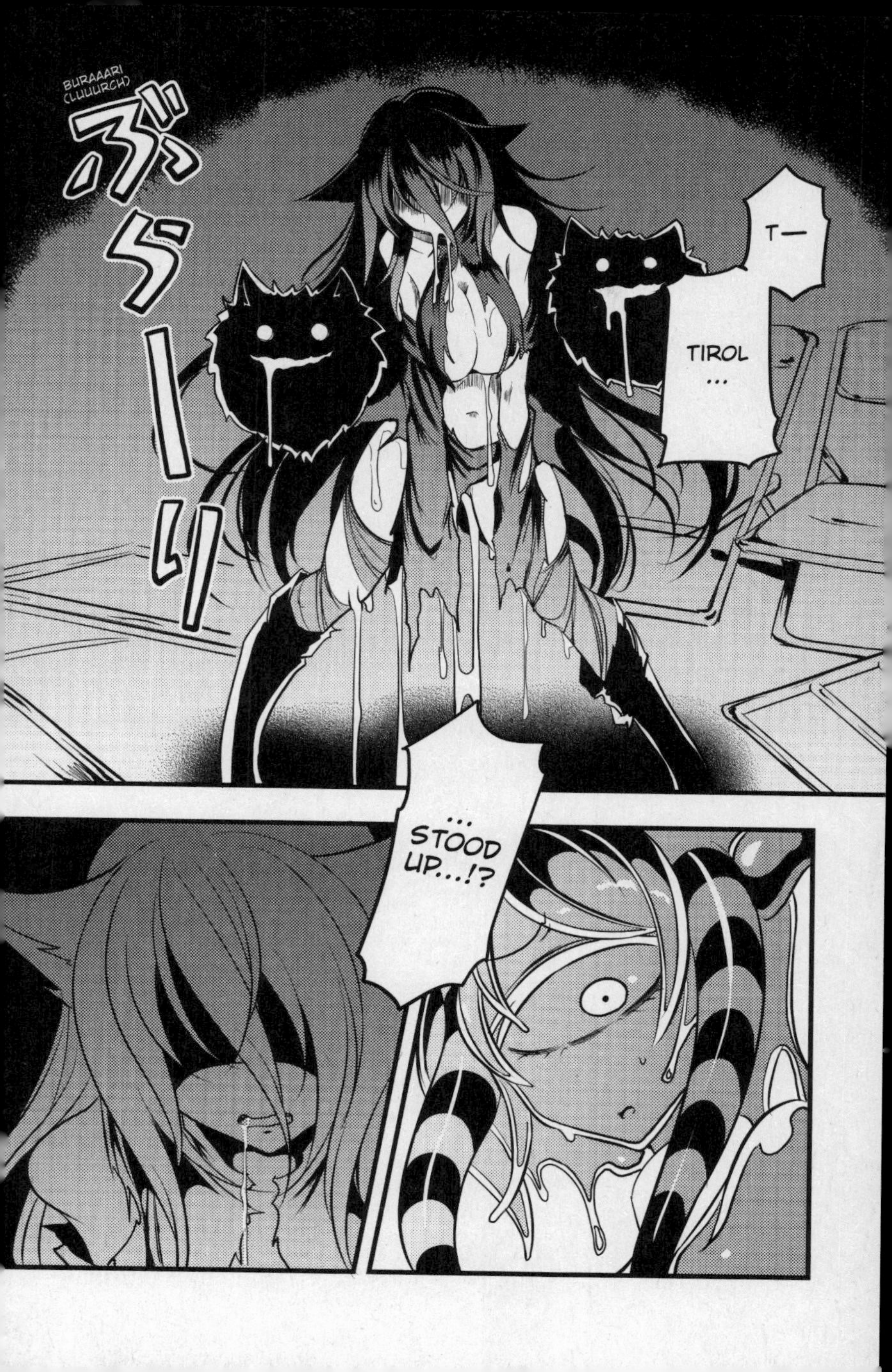
T— TIROL ...
BURAAARI (LUUURCH)
ぶらーり
... STOOD UP...!?

YURAA
(WOBBLE)

CHAPTER 9 —BETTER OF
TWO EVILS—

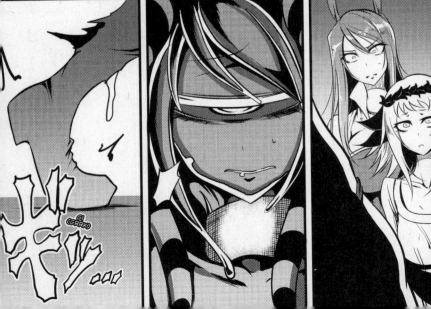

GI
(GRRK)

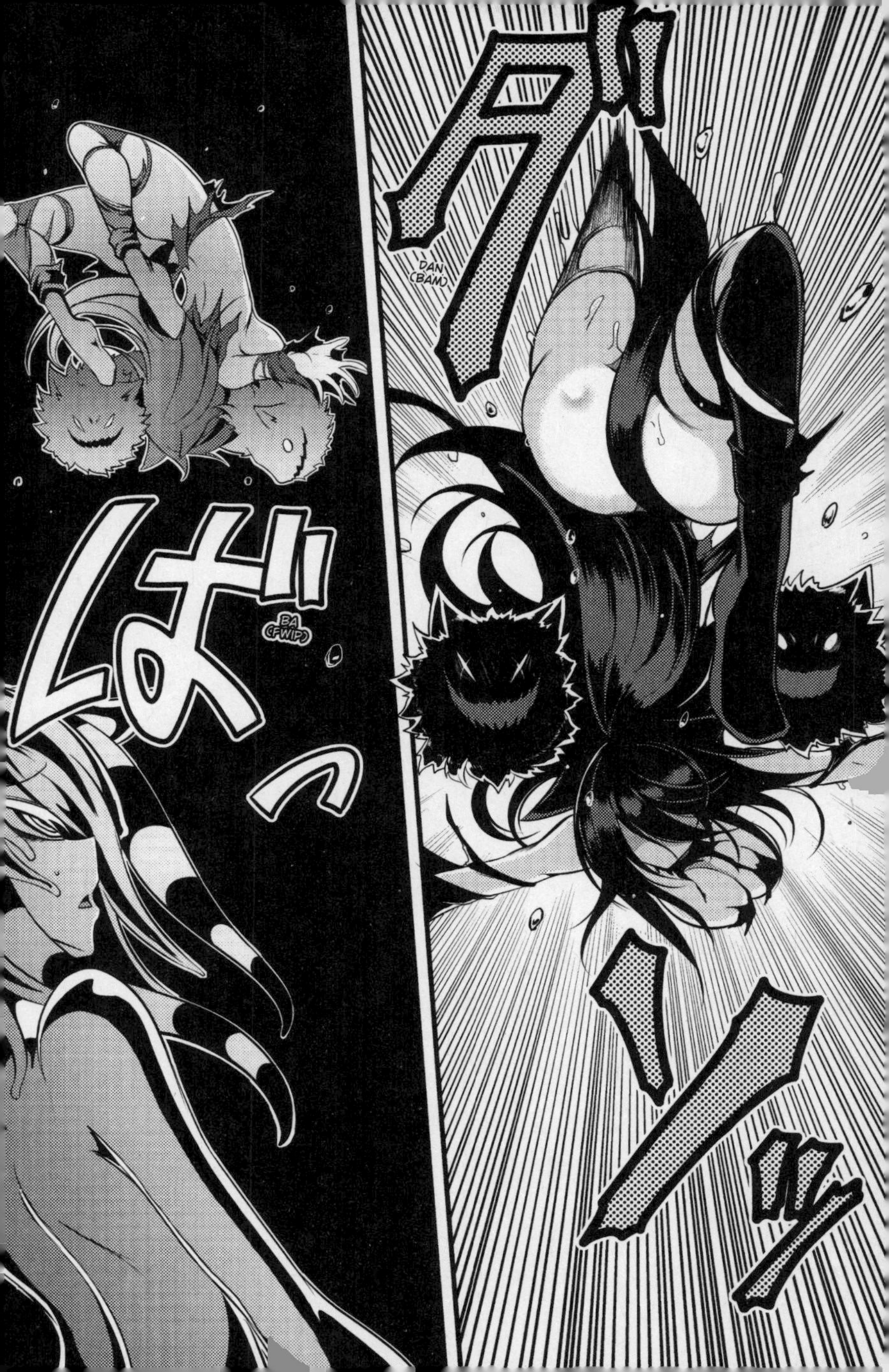
ダンッ
DAN (BAM)
ばっ
BA (FWIP)

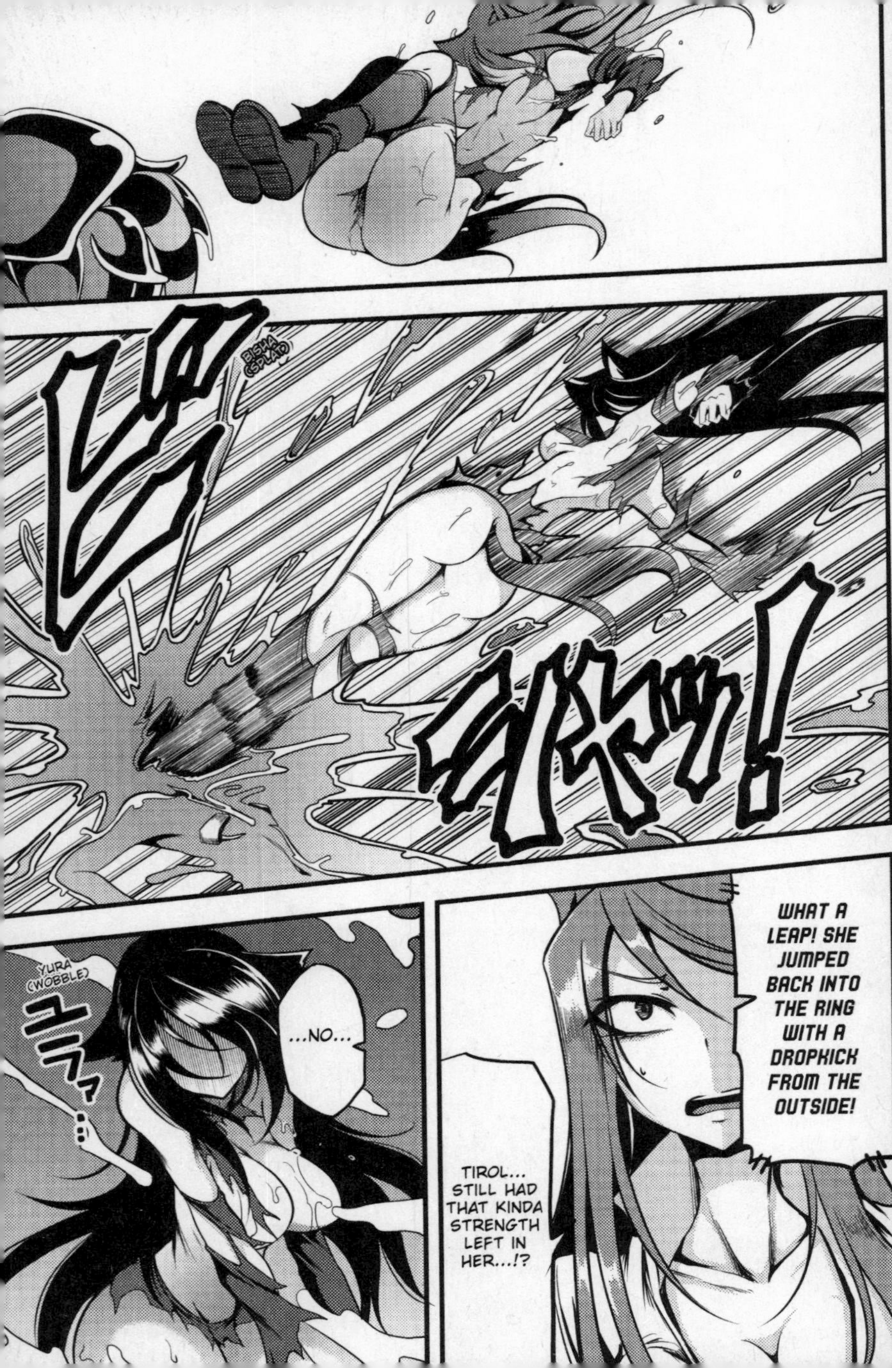
BISHA (SPLAT)
WHAT A LEAP! SHE JUMPED BACK INTO THE RING WITH A DROPKICK FROM THE OUTSIDE!
TIROL... STILL HAD THAT KINDA STRENGTH LEFT IN HER...!?
YURA (WOBBLE)
...NO...

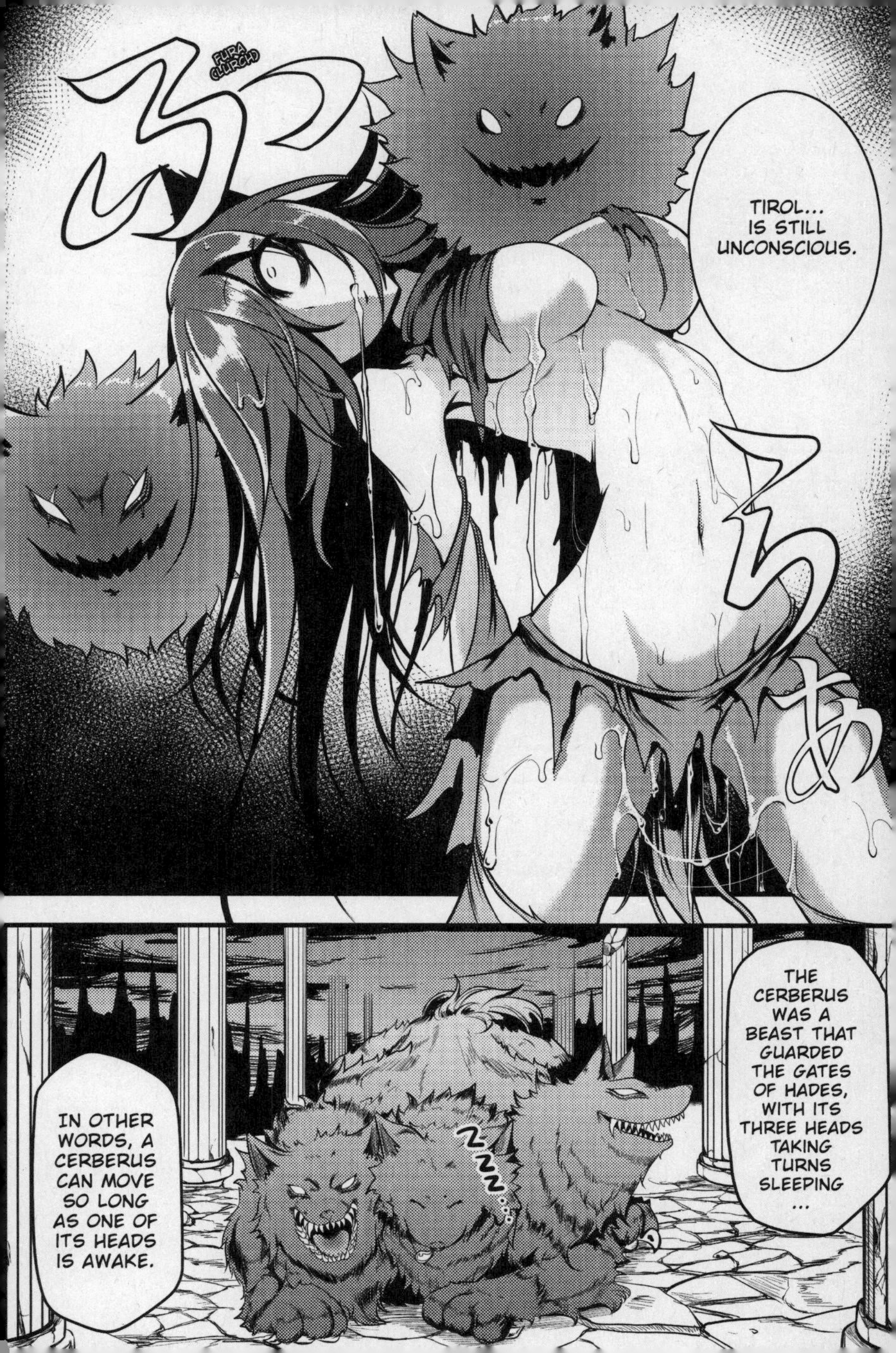
FURA (LURCH)
TIROL... IS STILL UNCONSCIOUS.
THE CERBERUS WAS A BEAST THAT GUARDED THE GATES OF HADES, WITH ITS THREE HEADS TAKING TURNS SLEEPING...
ZZZ...
IN OTHER WORDS, A CERBERUS CAN MOVE SO LONG AS ONE OF ITS HEADS IS AWAKE.

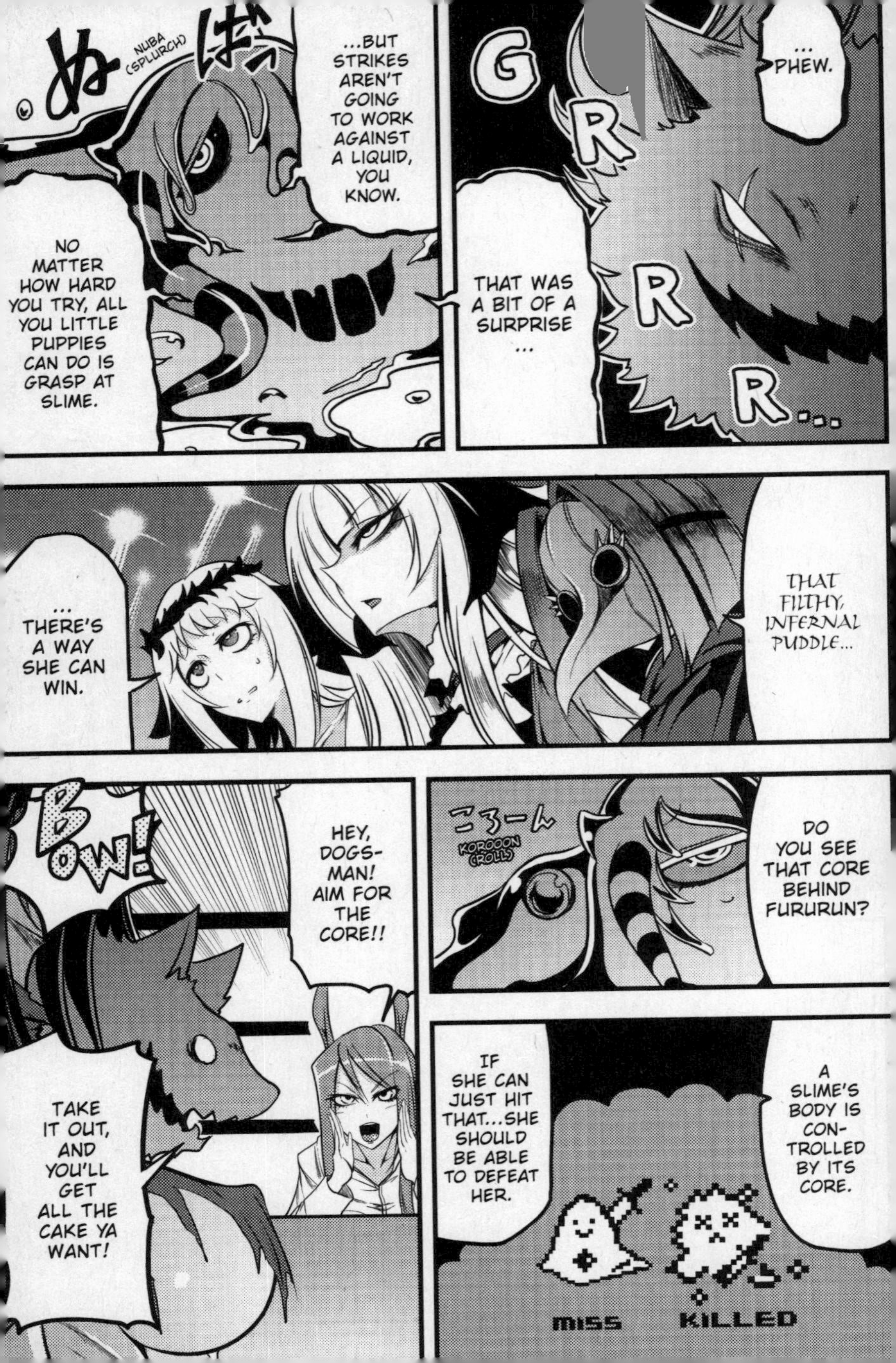
GRRR...
...PHEW.
THAT WAS A BIT OF A SURPRISE...
ぬぱっ
NUBA (SPLURCH)
...BUT STRIKES AREN'T GOING TO WORK AGAINST A LIQUID, YOU KNOW.
NO MATTER HOW HARD YOU TRY, ALL YOU LITTLE PUPPIES CAN DO IS GRASP AT SLIME.
THAT FILTHY, INFERNAL PUDDLE...
...THERE'S A WAY SHE CAN WIN.
ころーん
KOROOON (ROLL)
DO YOU SEE THAT CORE BEHIND FURURUN?
A SLIME'S BODY IS CON-TROLLED BY ITS CORE.
IF SHE CAN JUST HIT THAT...SHE SHOULD BE ABLE TO DEFEAT HER.
MISS
KILLED
BOW!
HEY, DOGS-MAN! AIM FOR THE CORE!!
TAKE IT OUT, AND YOU'LL GET ALL THE CAKE YA WANT!

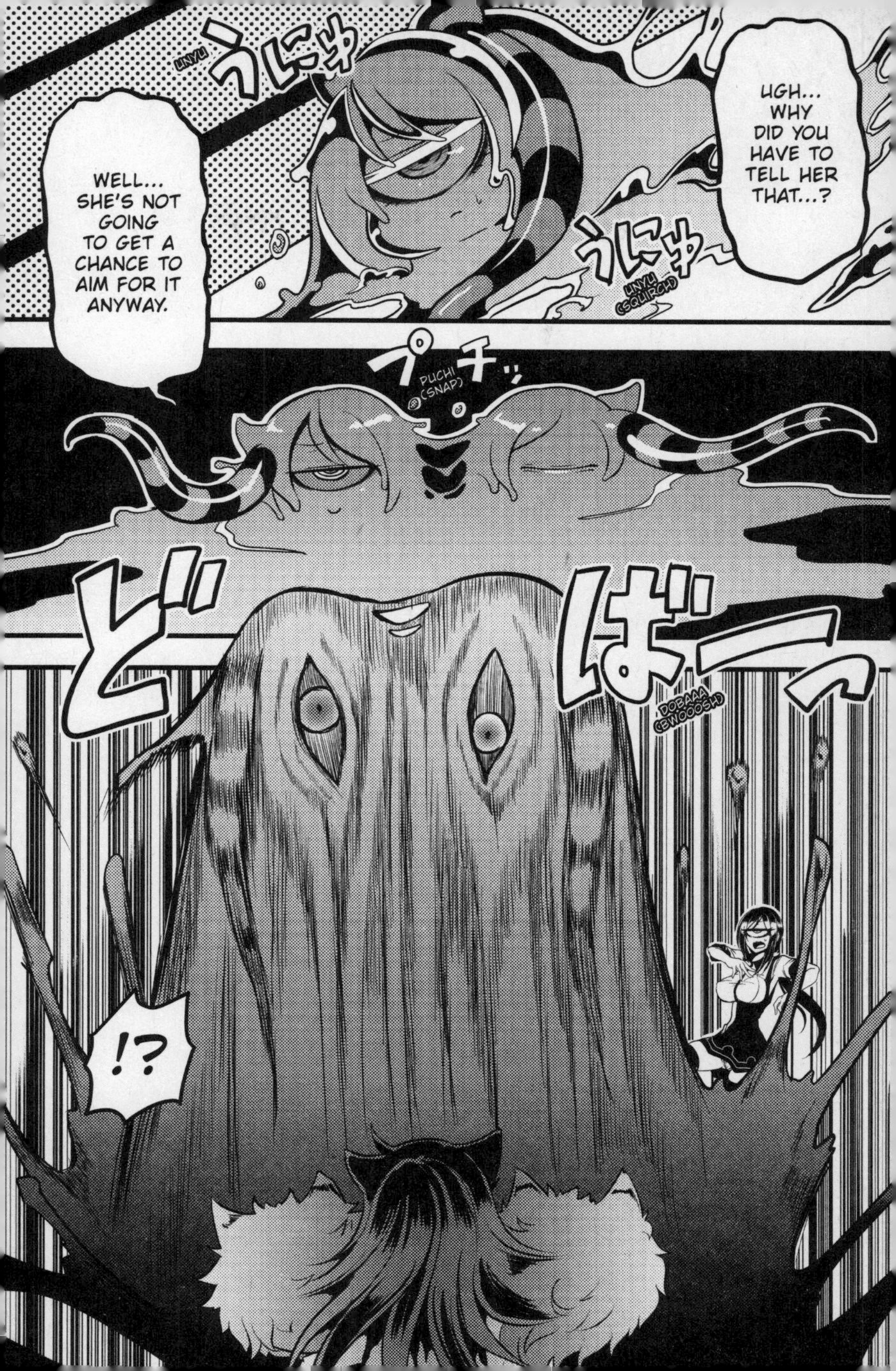
UGH... WHY DID YOU HAVE TO TELL HER THAT...?
うにゅ
UNYU
うにゅ
UNYU (SQUIRCH)
WELL... SHE'S NOT GOING TO GET A CHANCE TO AIM FOR IT ANYWAY.
プチッ
PUCHI (SNAP)
どばーっ
DOBAAA (BWOOOSH)
!?

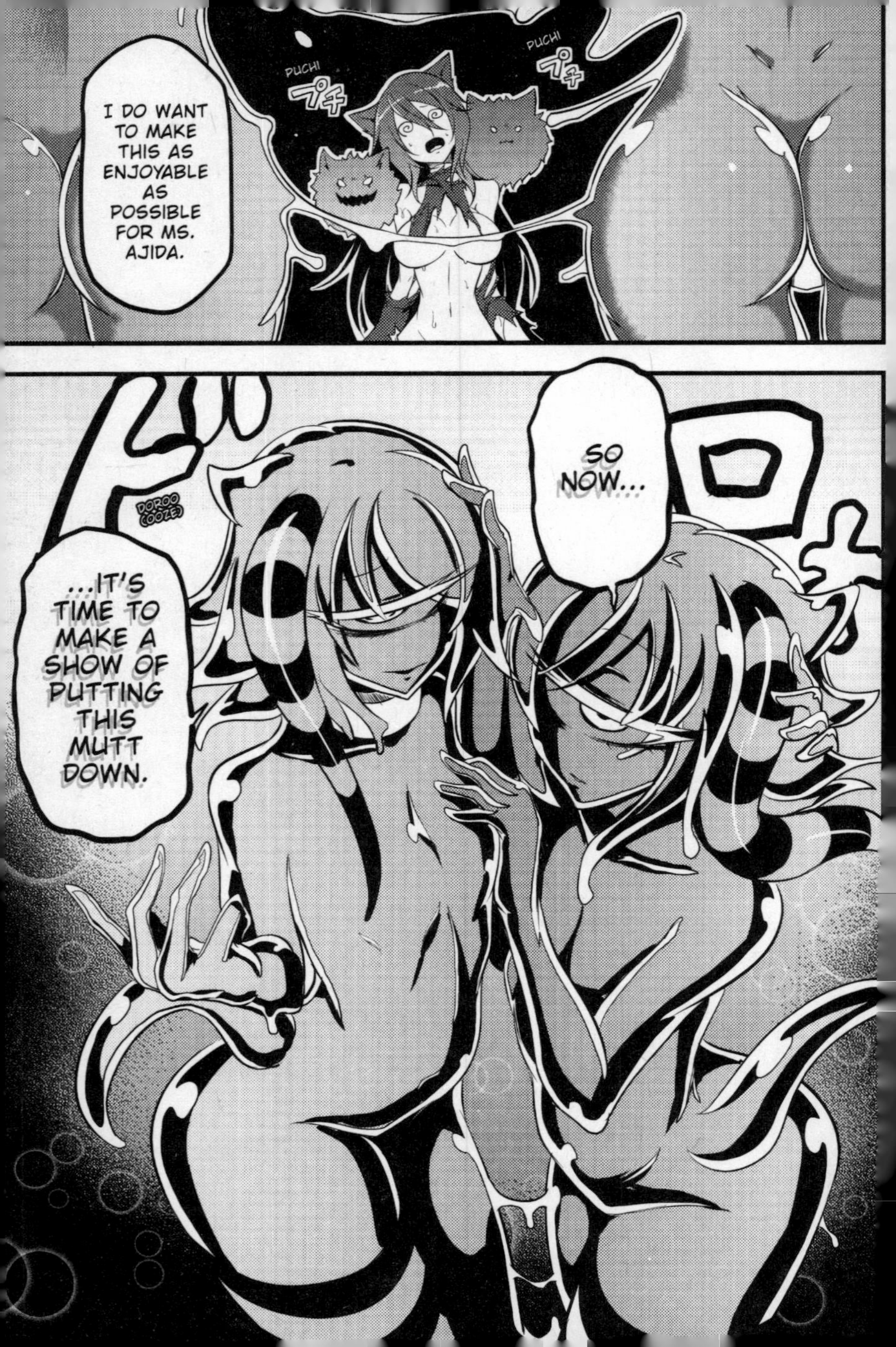
PUCHI
プチ
PUCHI
プチ
I DO WANT TO MAKE THIS AS ENJOYABLE AS POSSIBLE FOR MS. AJIDA.
SO NOW...
DOROO (OOZE)
...IT'S TIME TO MAKE A SHOW OF PUTTING THIS MUTT DOWN.

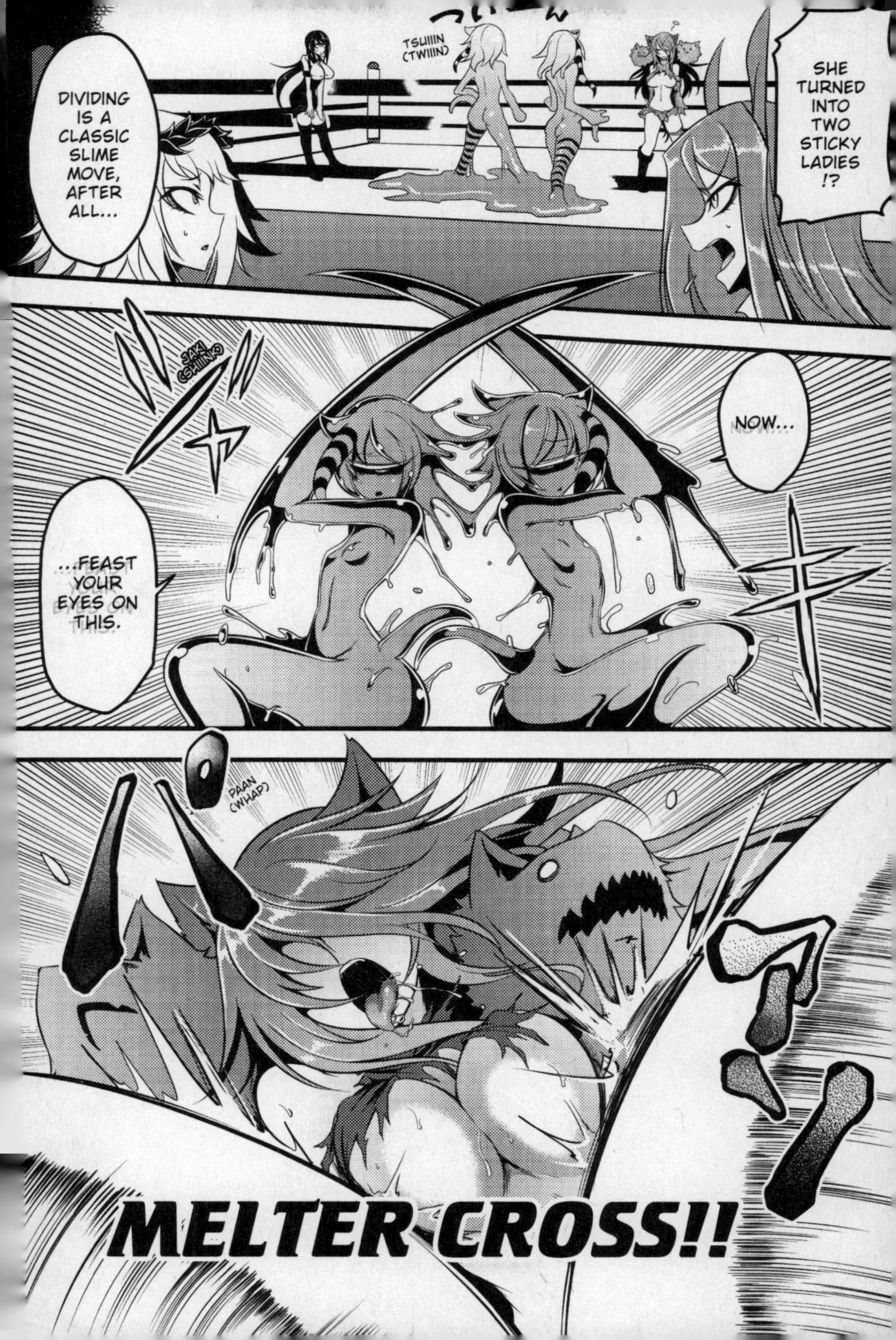
SHE TURNED INTO TWO STICKY LADIES !?
TSUIIIN (TWIIIN)
DIVIDING IS A CLASSIC SLIME MOVE, AFTER ALL...
SAKI (SHIIING)
NOW...
...FEAST YOUR EYES ON THIS.
PAAN (WHAP)
MELTER CROSS!!

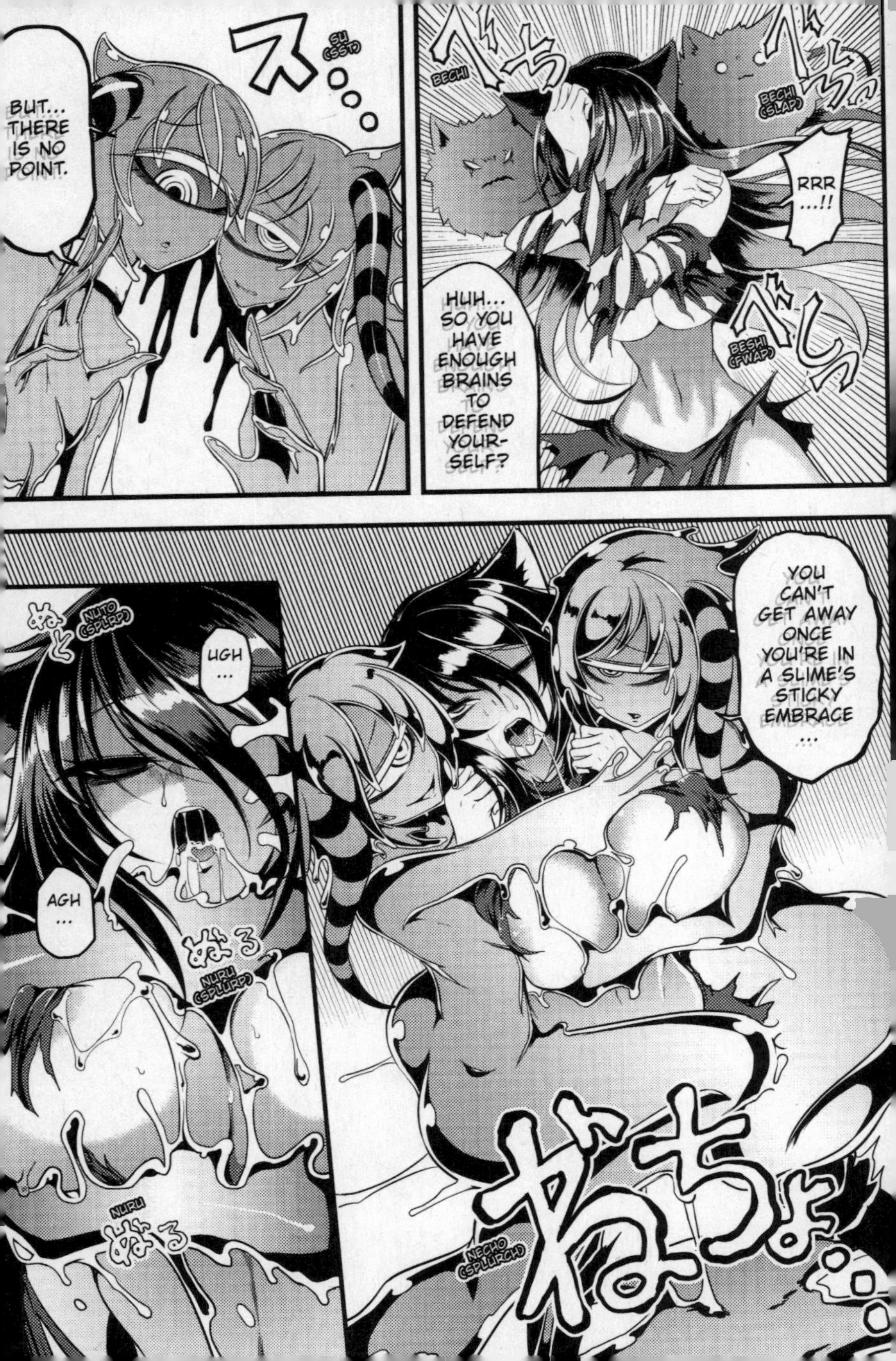

べち
BECHI (SLAP)
べち
BECHI
RRR ...!!
HUH... SO YOU HAVE ENOUGH BRAINS TO DEFEND YOURSELF?
べし
BESHI (FWAP)
ス
SU (SSST)
BUT... THERE IS NO POINT.
YOU CAN'T GET AWAY ONCE YOU'RE IN A SLIME'S STICKY EMBRACE...
ぬと
NUTO (SPLRP)
UGH ...
AGH ...
ぬる
NURU (SPLURP)
ねちょ
NECHO (SPLURCH)
ぬる
NURU

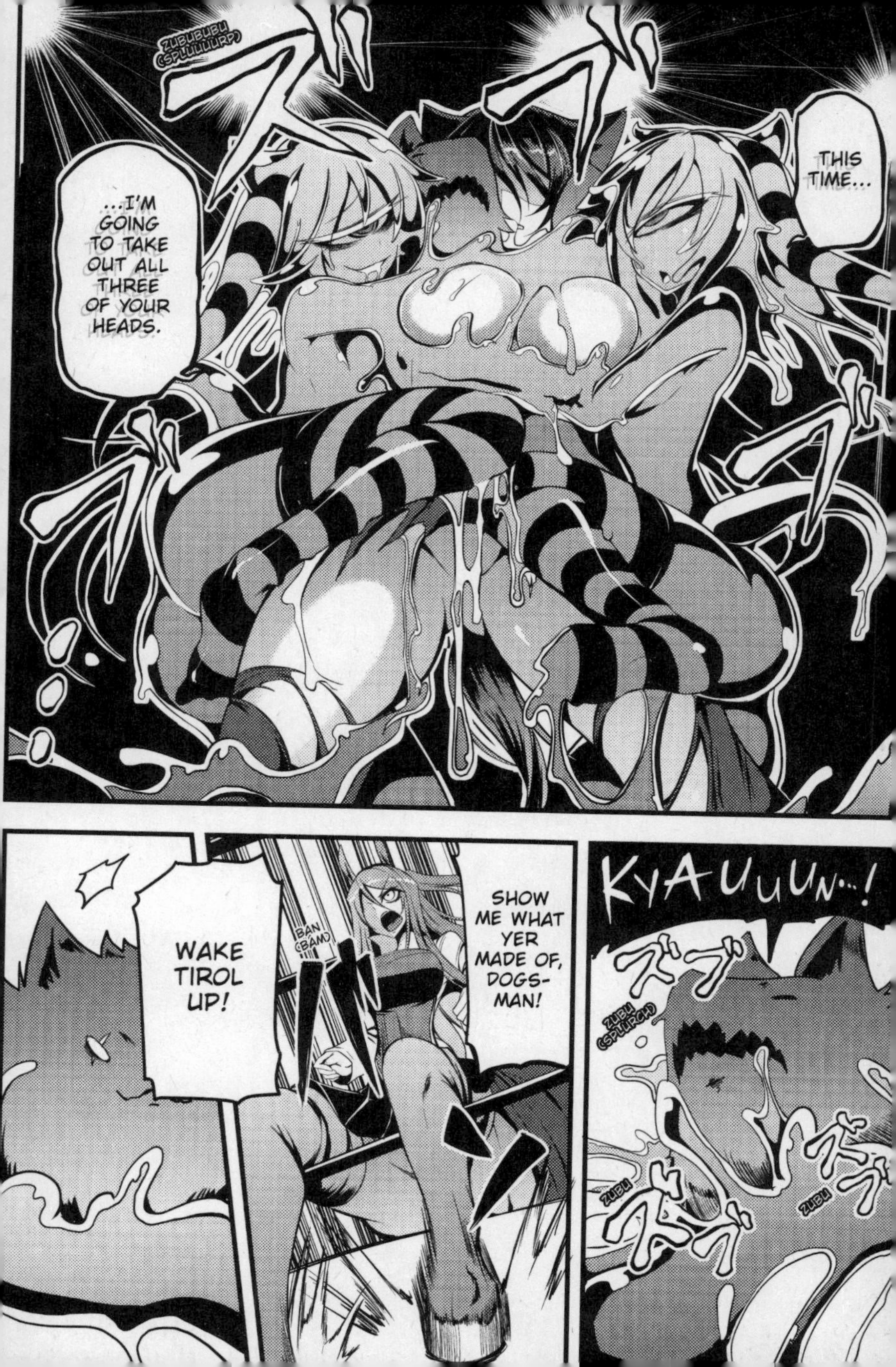
THIS TIME...
ZUBUBUBU (SPLUUUURP)
...I'M GOING TO TAKE OUT ALL THREE OF YOUR HEADS.
KYAUUUN...!
ZUBU (SPLURGH)
ZUBU
ZUBU
SHOW ME WHAT YER MADE OF, DOGS-MAN!
BAN (BAM)
WAKE TIROL UP!

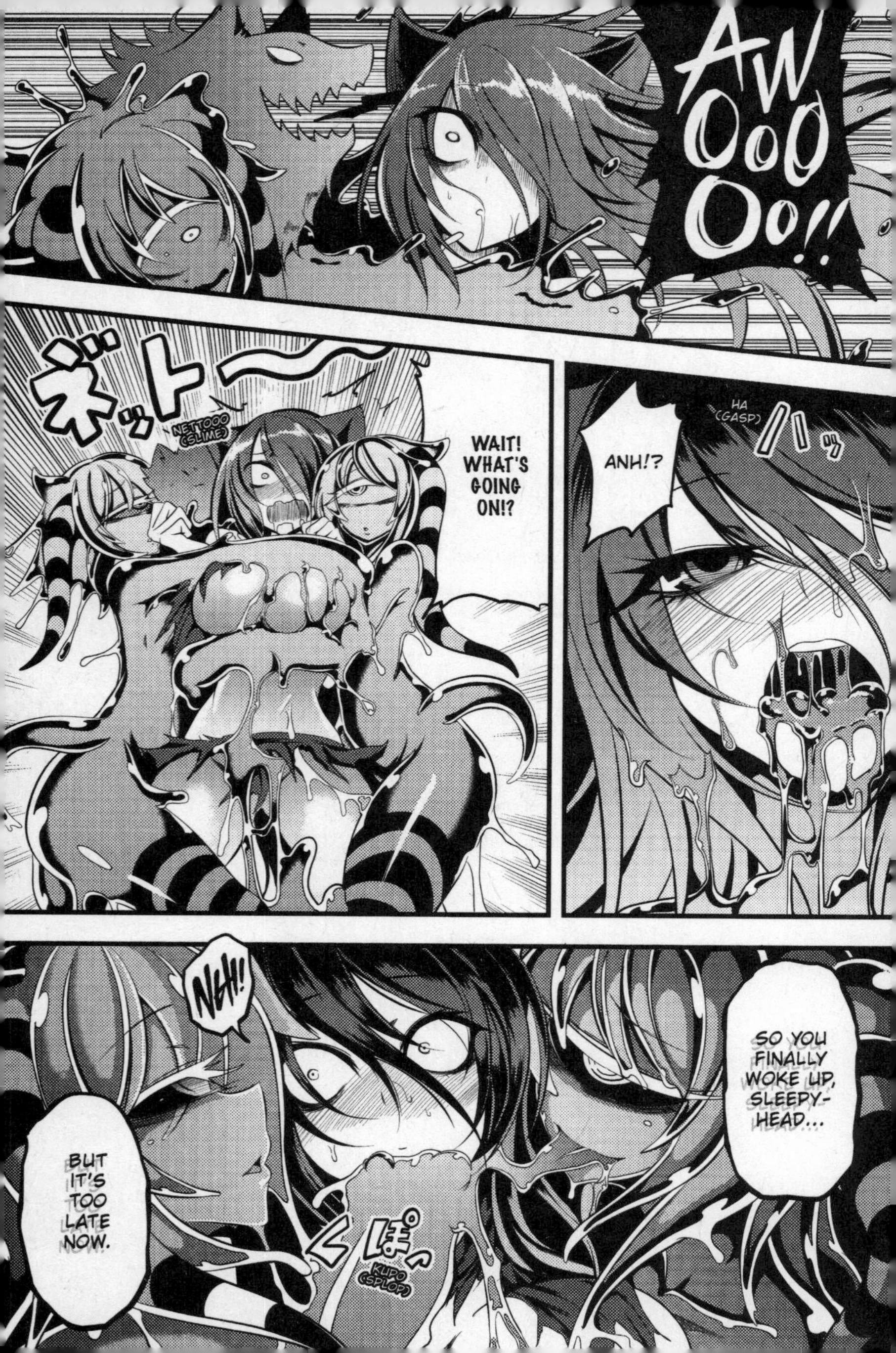
AWOOOOOO!!
HA (GASP)
ハッ
ANH!?
ネ゛ットーー
NETTOOO (SLIME)
WAIT! WHAT'S GOING ON!?
SO YOU FINALLY WOKE UP, SLEEPY-HEAD...
NGH!
BUT IT'S TOO LATE NOW.
くぽっ
KUPO (SPLOP)

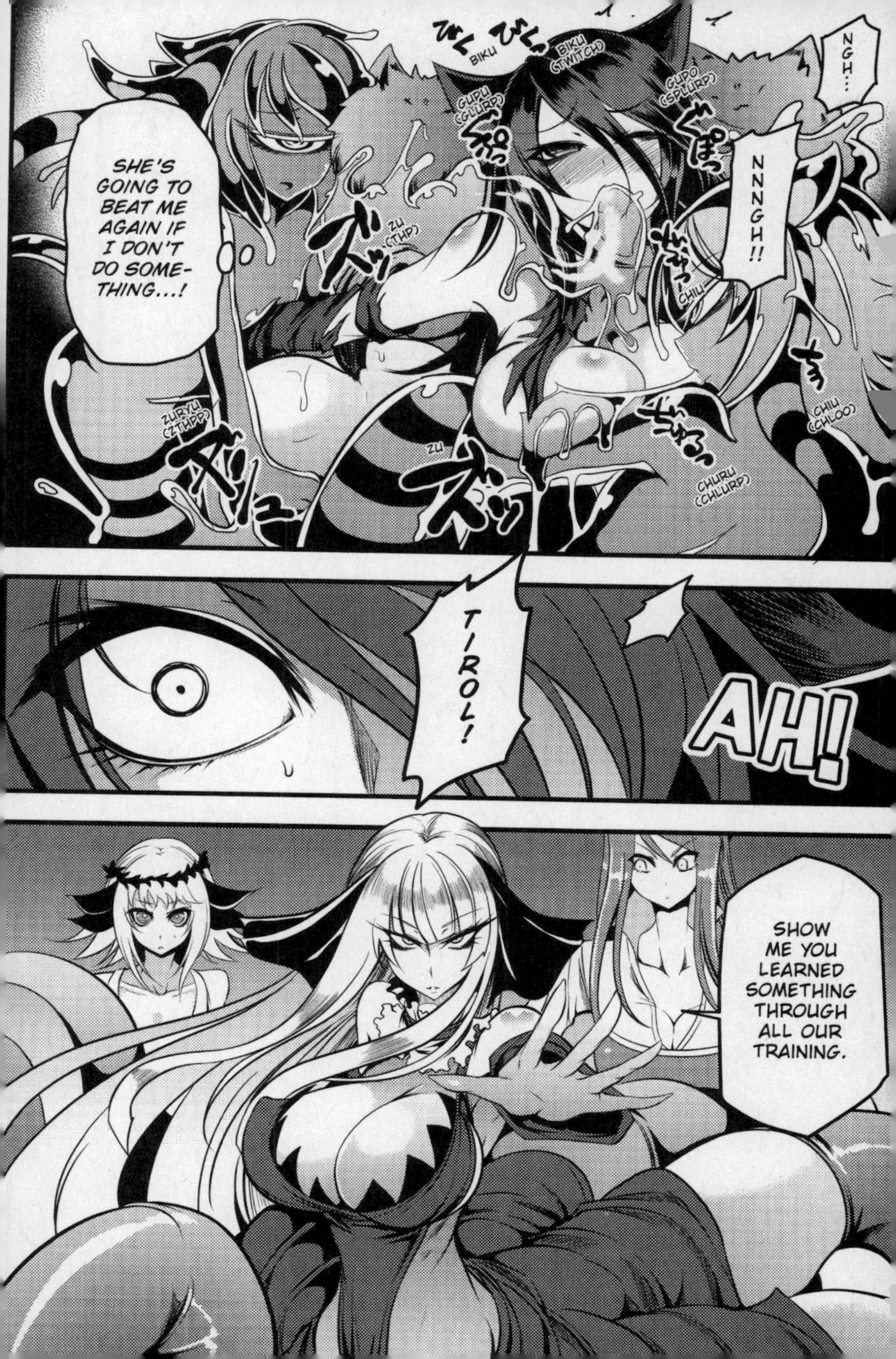
NGH...
BIKU (TWITCH)
BIKU
GUPO (SPLURP)
NNNGH!!
GUPU (GLURP)
SHE'S GOING TO BEAT ME AGAIN IF I DON'T DO SOME-THING...!
ZU (THP)
CHIU
CHIU (CHLOO)
CHURU (CHLURP)
ZU
ZURYU (ZTHPP)
AH!
TIROL!
SHOW ME YOU LEARNED SOMETHING THROUGH ALL OUR TRAINING.

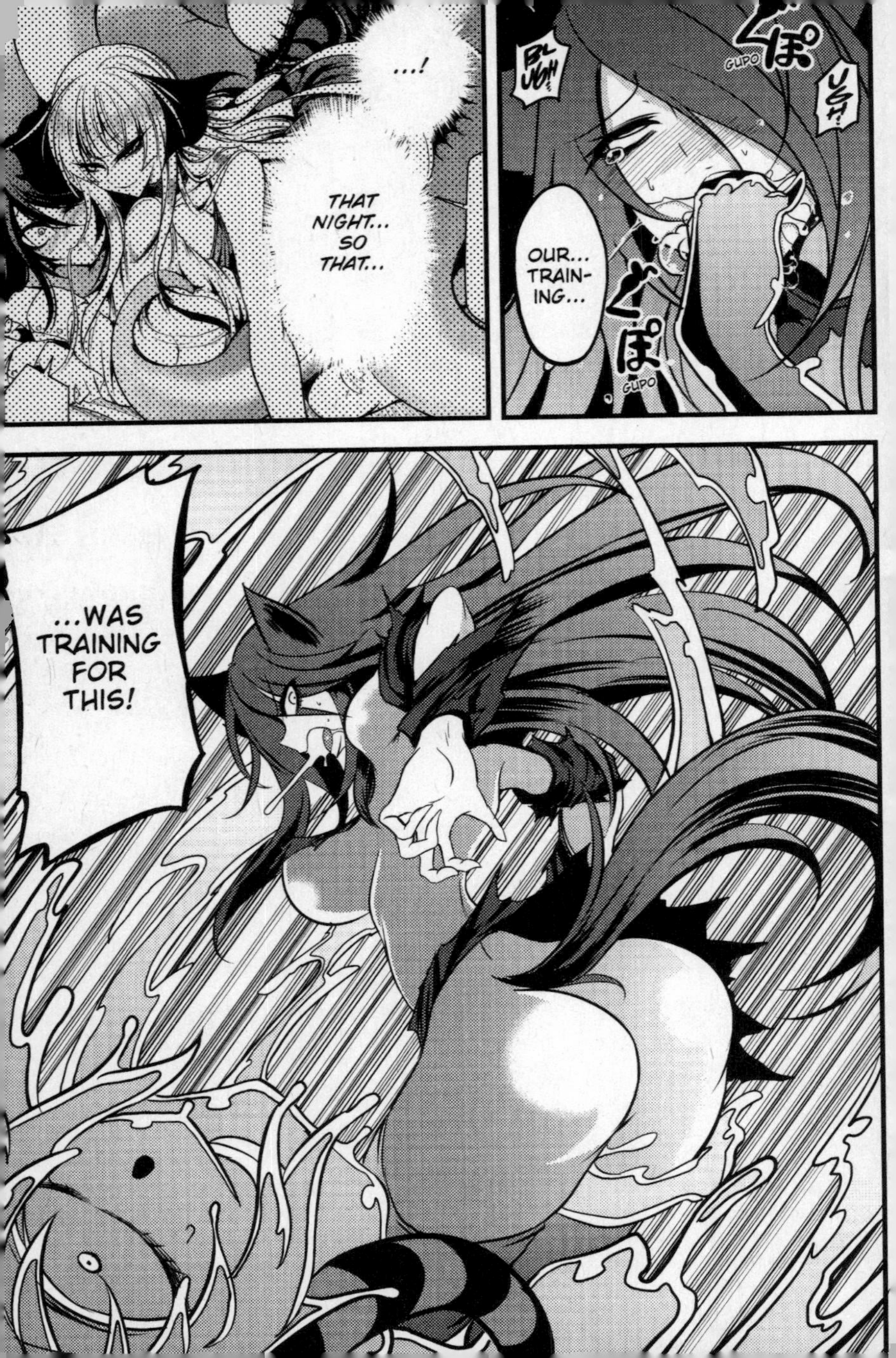
ぐぽ
GUPO
UGH!
BLUGH!
OUR... TRAIN-ING...
ぐぽ
GUPO
...!
THAT NIGHT... SO THAT...
...WAS TRAINING FOR THIS!

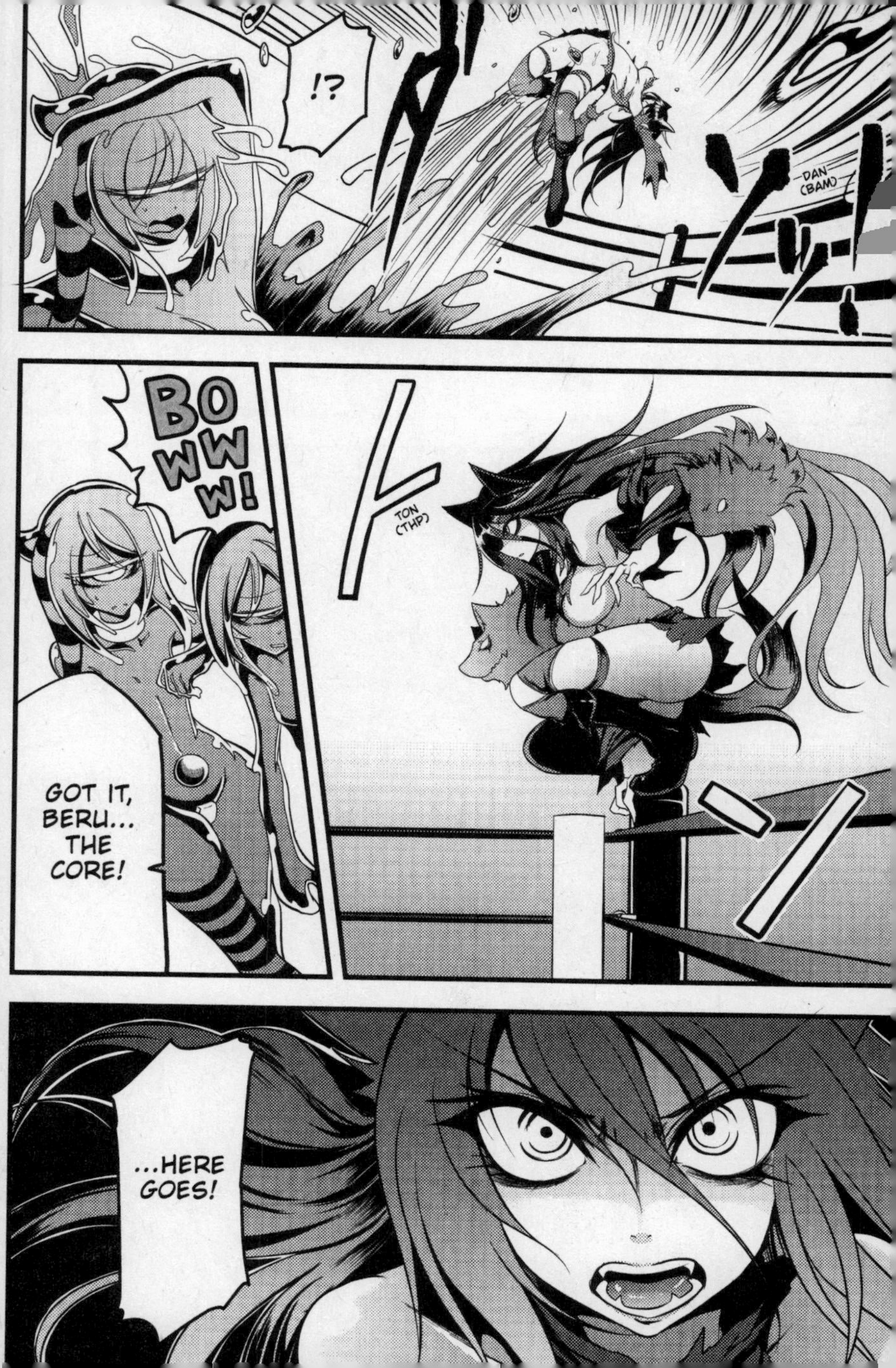

DAN (BAM)
!?
TON (THP)
BOWWWW!
GOT IT, BERU... THE CORE!
...HERE GOES!

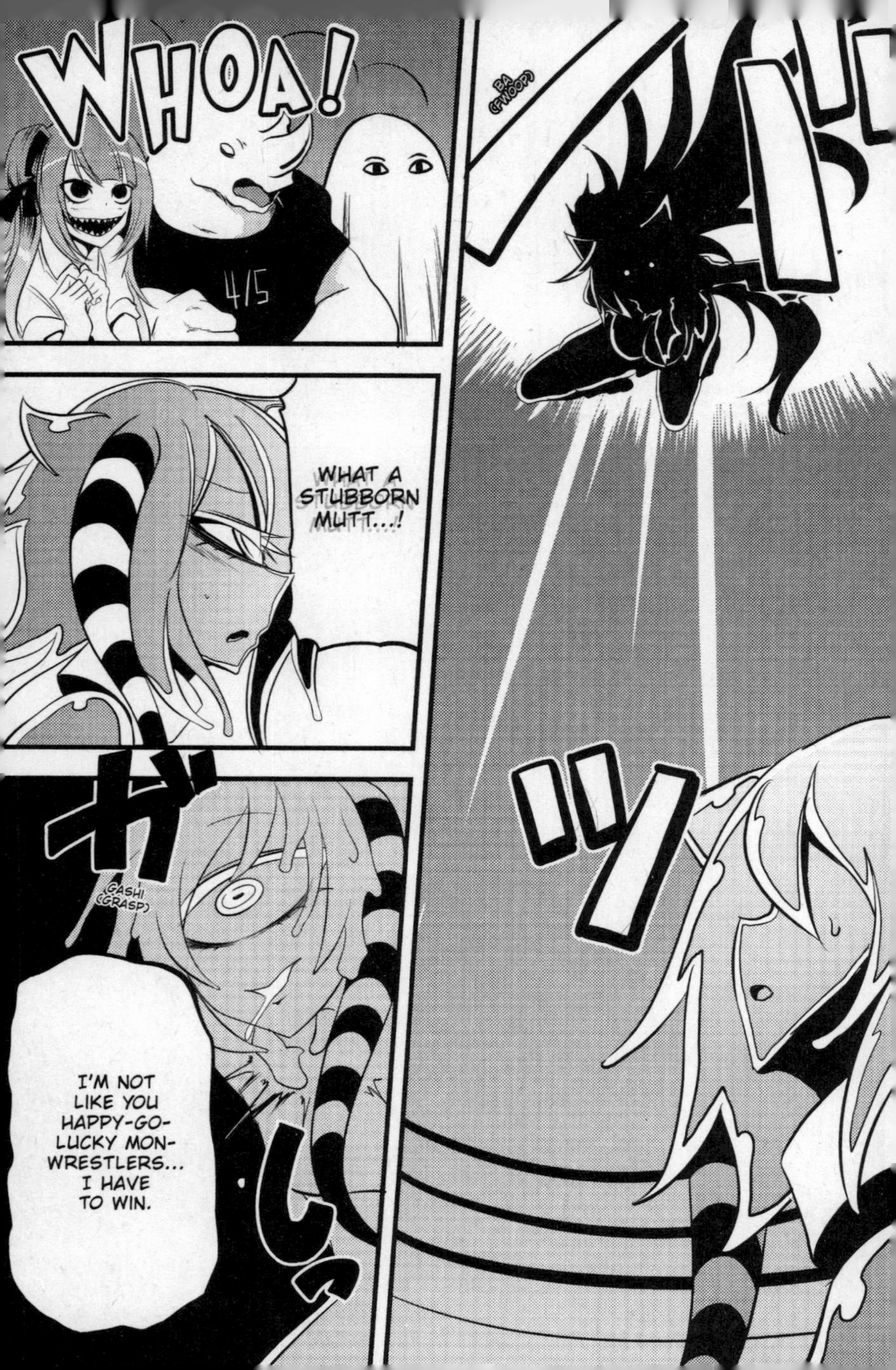
BA (FWOOP)
WHOA!
WHAT A STUBBORN MUTT...!
GASHI (GRASP)
I'M NOT LIKE YOU HAPPY-GO-LUCKY MON-WRESTLERS... I HAVE TO WIN.

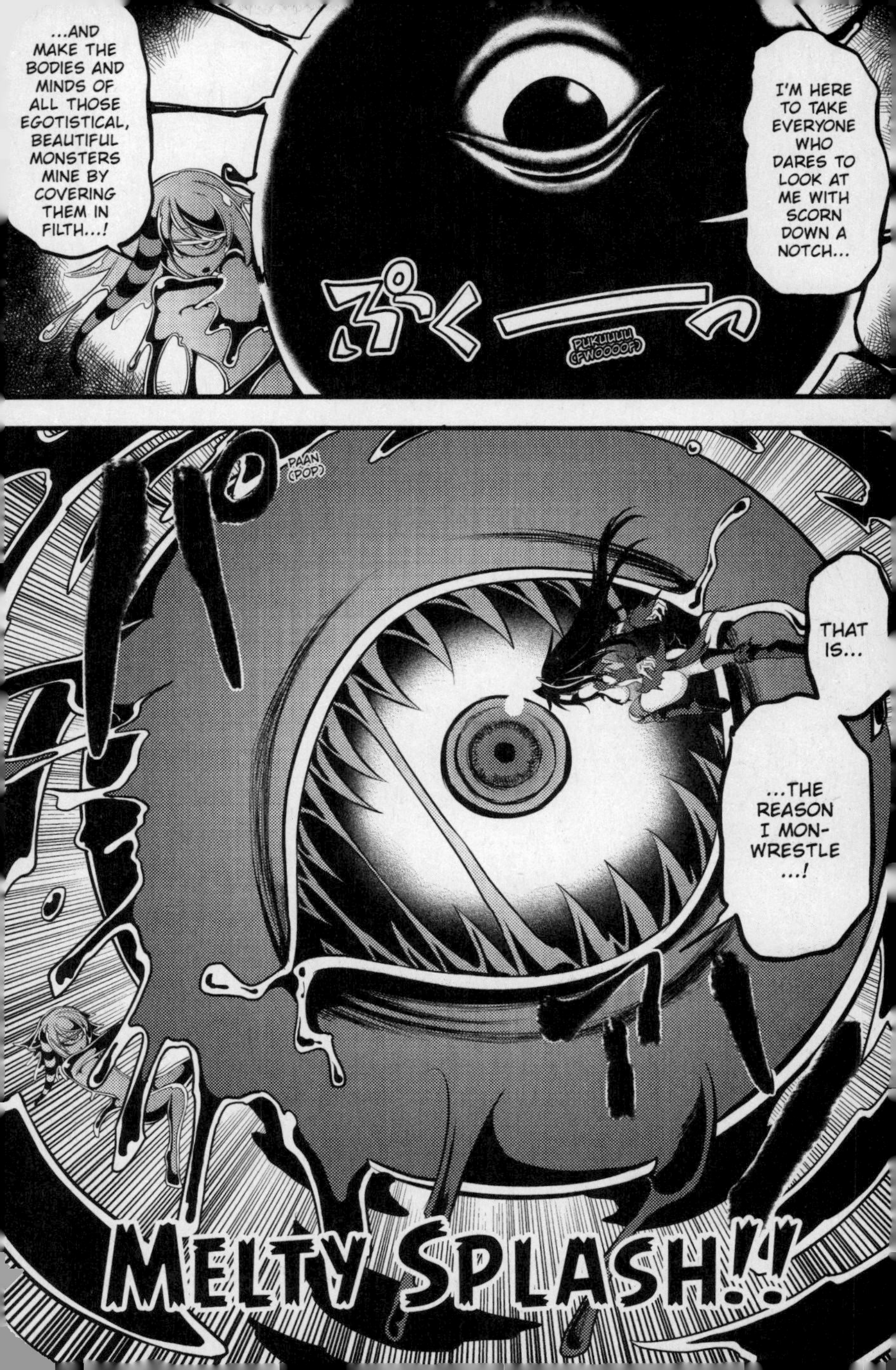
I'M HERE TO TAKE EVERYONE WHO DARES TO LOOK AT ME WITH SCORN DOWN A NOTCH...
ぷくーーっ
PUKUUUU (FWOOOOP)
...AND MAKE THE BODIES AND MINDS OF ALL THOSE EGOTISTICAL, BEAUTIFUL MONSTERS MINE BY COVERING THEM IN FILTH...!
THAT IS...
...THE REASON I MON-WRESTLE ...!
PAAN (POP)
MELTY SPLASH!!

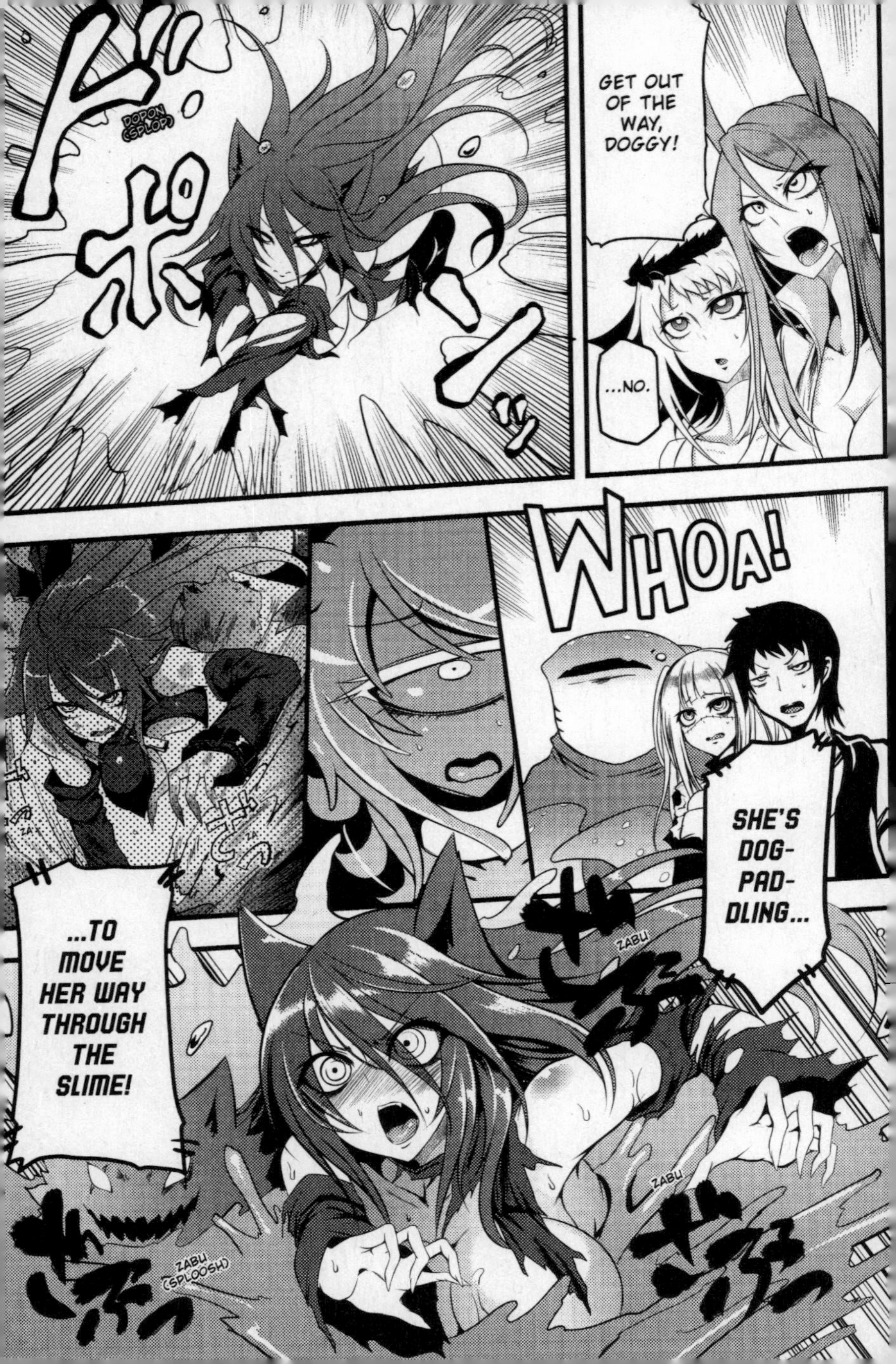

GET OUT OF THE WAY, DOGGY!
...NO.
DOPON (SPLOP)
WHOA!
SHE'S DOG-PADDLING...
ZA
ZA
...TO MOVE HER WAY THROUGH THE SLIME!
ZABU
ZABU
ZABU (SPLOOSH)

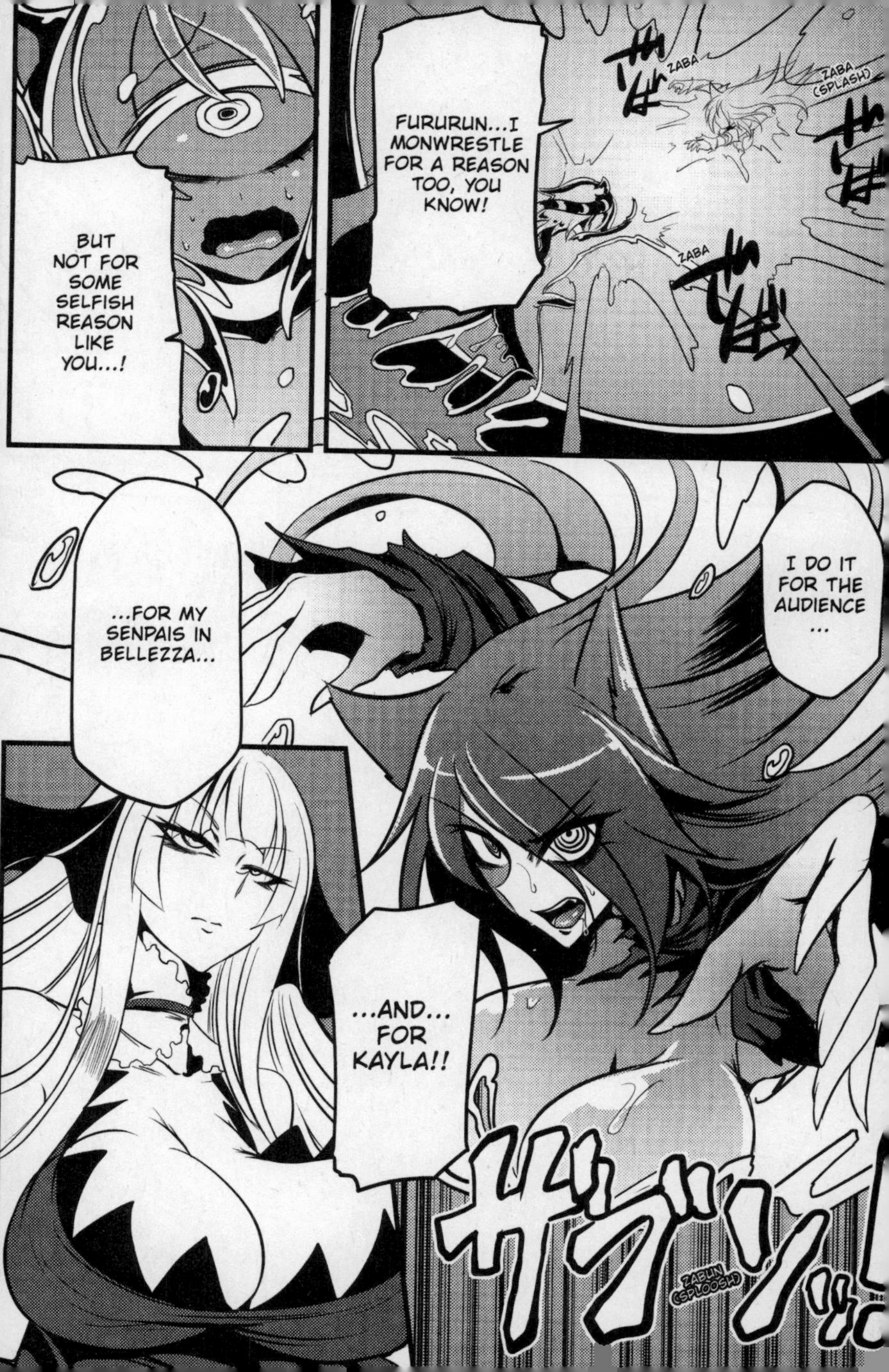
ZABA
ZABA (SPLASH)
FURURUN...I MONWRESTLE FOR A REASON TOO, YOU KNOW!
ZABA
BUT NOT FOR SOME SELFISH REASON LIKE YOU...!
I DO IT FOR THE AUDIENCE ...
...FOR MY SENPAIS IN BELLEZZA...
...AND... FOR KAYLA!!
ZABUN (SPLOOSH)

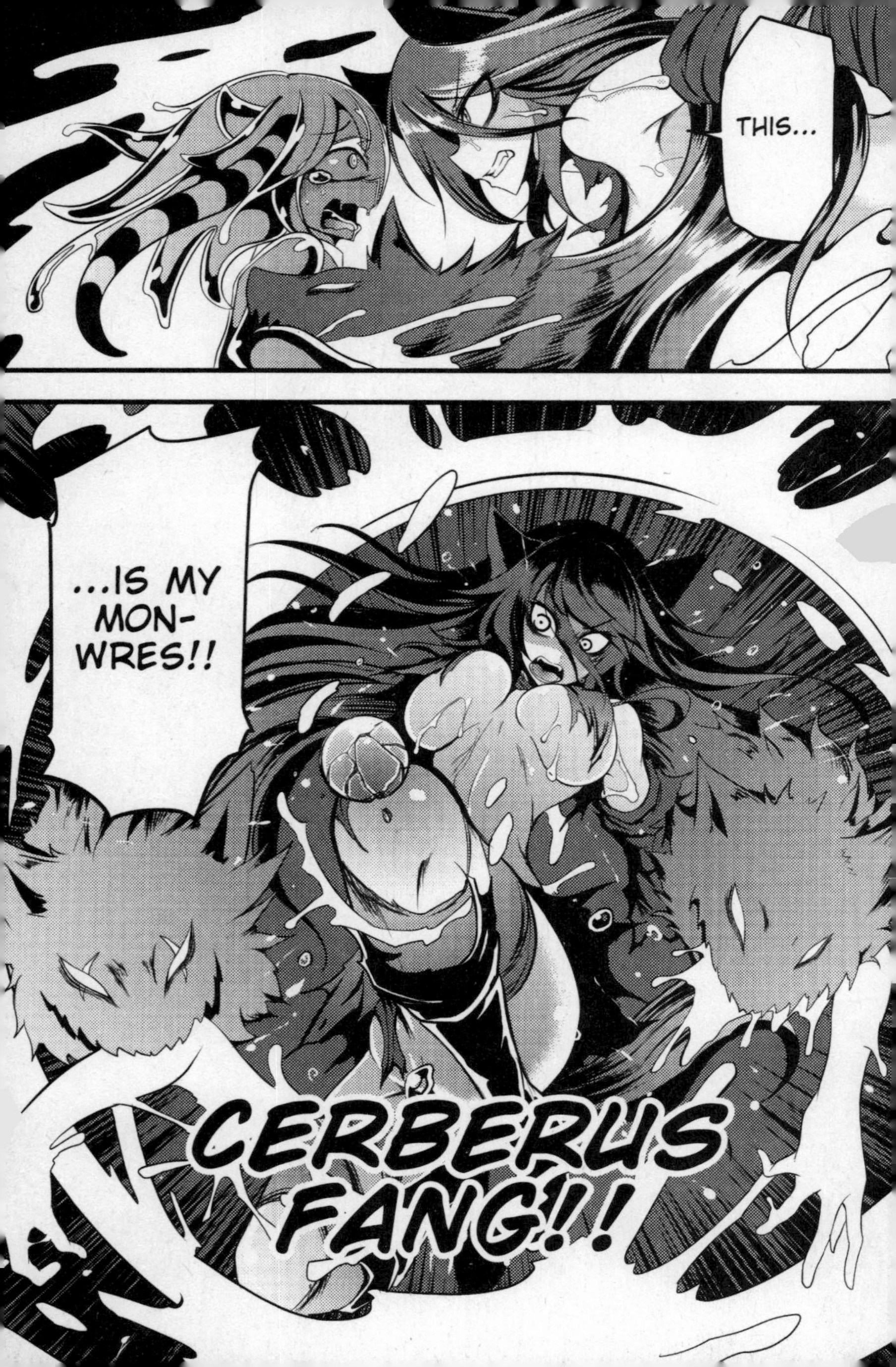
THIS...
...IS MY MON-WRES!!
CERBERUS FANG!!!

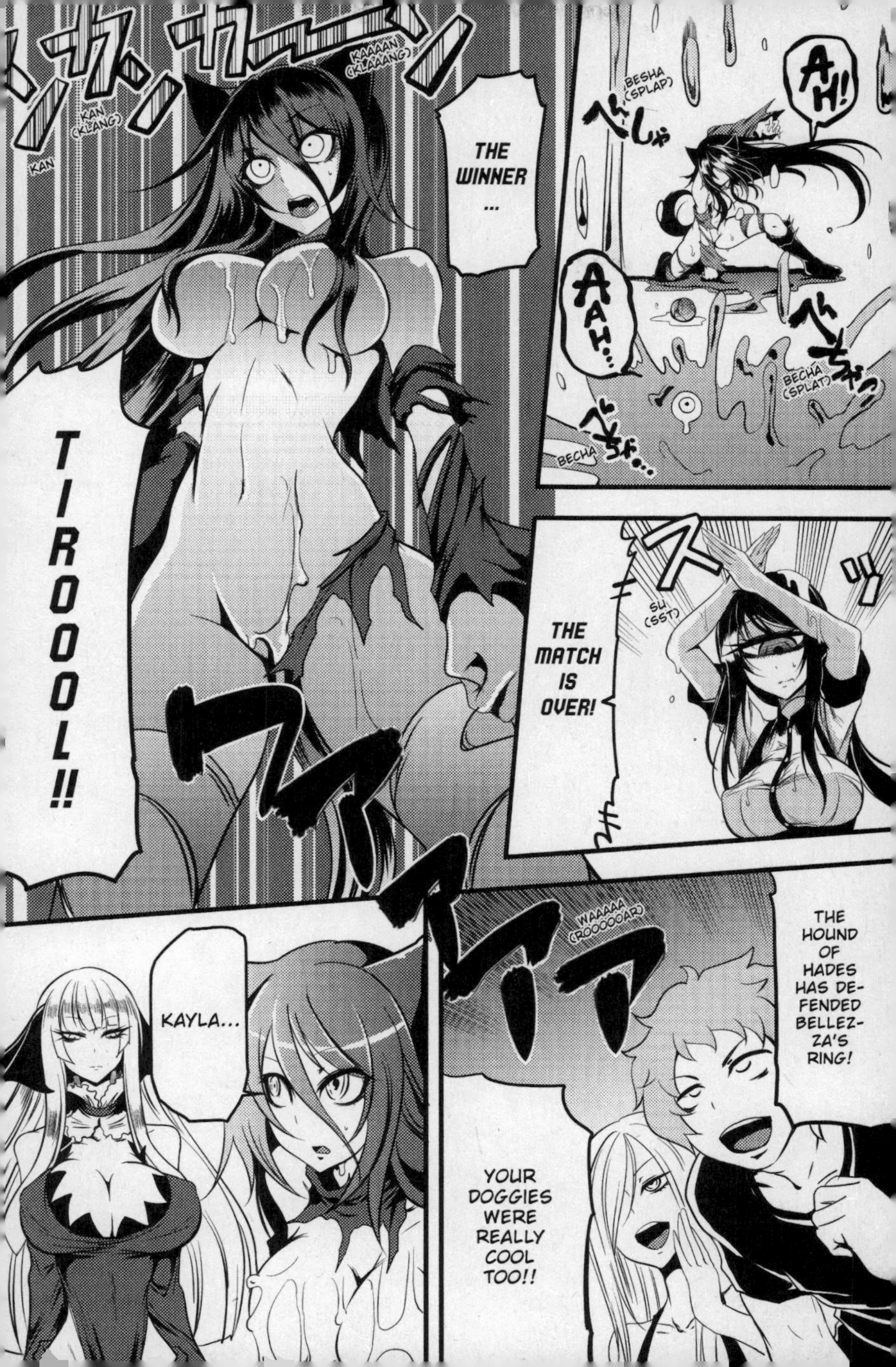

AH!
BESHA (SPLAP)
AAH...
BECHA (SPLAT)
BECHA
SU (SST)
THE MATCH IS OVER!
KAN
KAN (KLANG)
KAAAAN (KLAAANG)
THE WINNER...
TIROOOOOL!!
WAAAAA (ROOOOOAR)
THE HOUND OF HADES HAS DE-FENDED BELLEZ-ZA'S RING!
YOUR DOGGIES WERE REALLY COOL TOO!!
KAYLA...

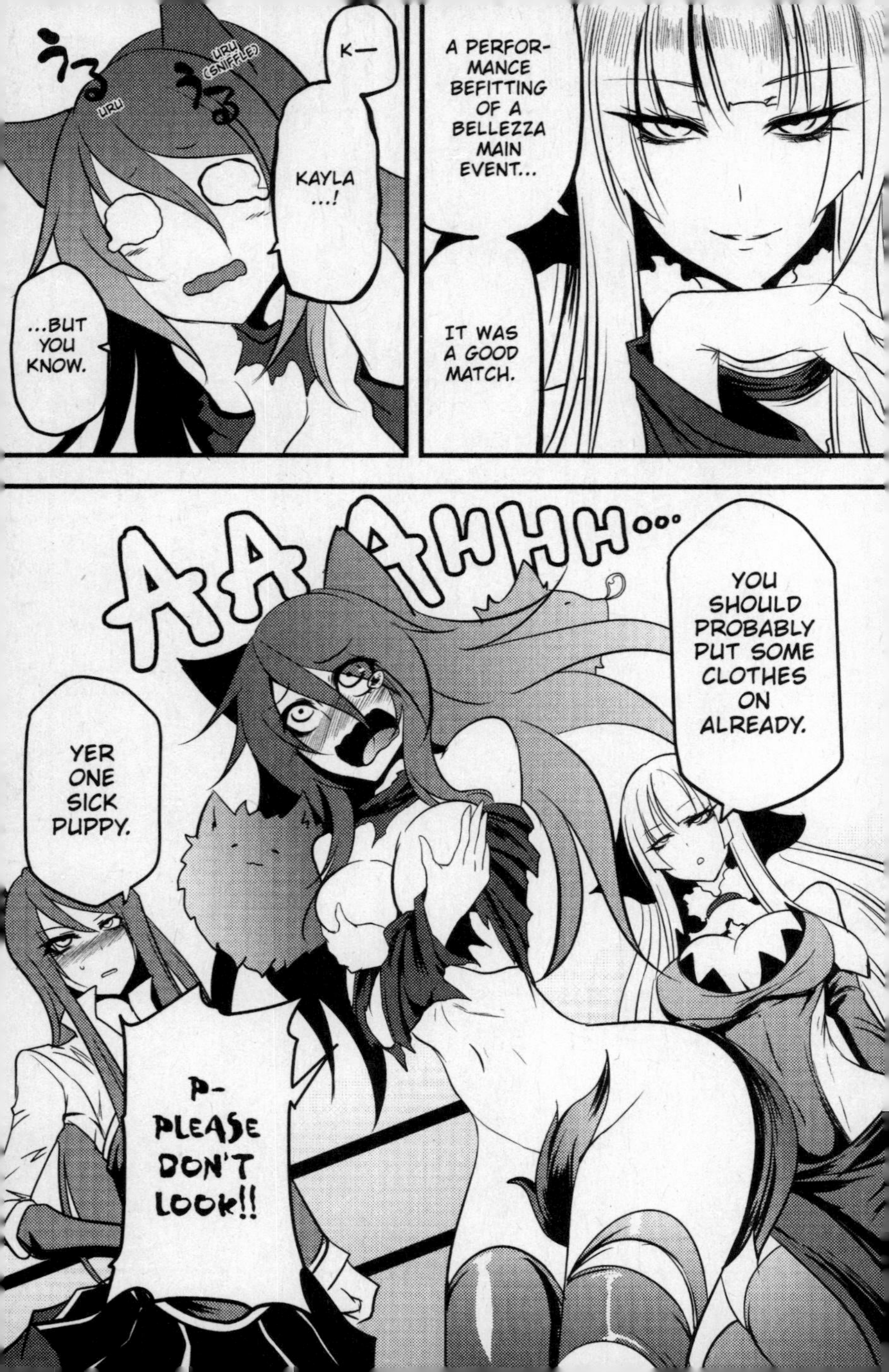
A PERFORMANCE BEFITTING OF A BELLEZZA MAIN EVENT...
IT WAS A GOOD MATCH.
K—
うる URU (SNIFFLE)
KAYLA ...!
うる URU
...BUT YOU KNOW.
YOU SHOULD PROBABLY PUT SOME CLOTHES ON ALREADY.
AAAHHH...
YER ONE SICK PUPPY.
P-PLEASE DON'T LOOK!!

Only Women Bleed

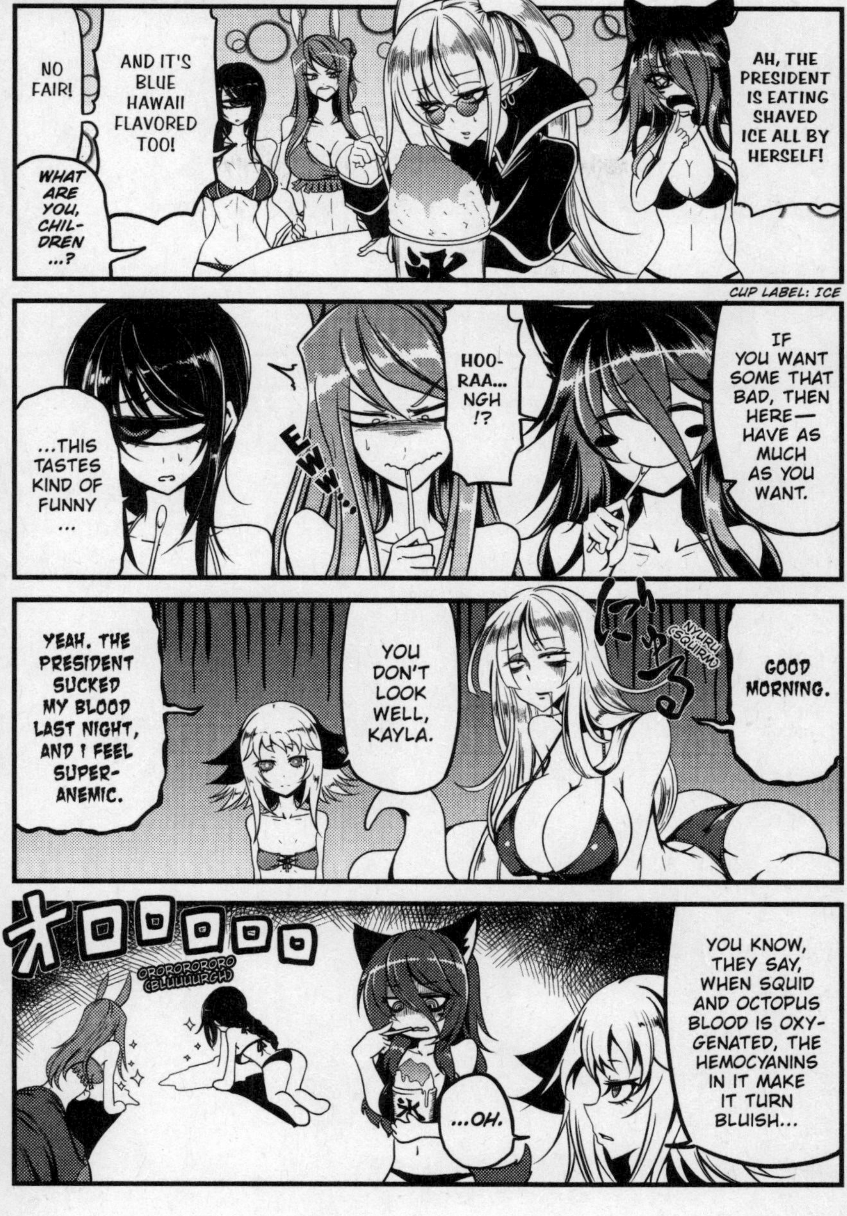
AH, THE PRESIDENT IS EATING SHAVED ICE ALL BY HERSELF!
AND IT'S BLUE HAWAII FLAVORED TOO!
NO FAIR!
WHAT ARE YOU, CHIL-DREN ...?
CUP LABEL: ICE
IF YOU WANT SOME THAT BAD, THEN HERE—HAVE AS MUCH AS YOU WANT.
HOO-RAA... NGH !?
EWW...
...THIS TASTES KIND OF FUNNY ...
GOOD MORNING.
NYURU (SQUIRM)
YOU DON'T LOOK WELL, KAYLA.
YEAH. THE PRESIDENT SUCKED MY BLOOD LAST NIGHT, AND I FEEL SUPER-ANEMIC.
YOU KNOW, THEY SAY, WHEN SQUID AND OCTOPUS BLOOD IS OXY-GENATED, THE HEMOCYANINS IN IT MAKE IT TURN BLUISH...
...OH.
オロロロロロロ
ORORORORORO (BLUUUURGH)

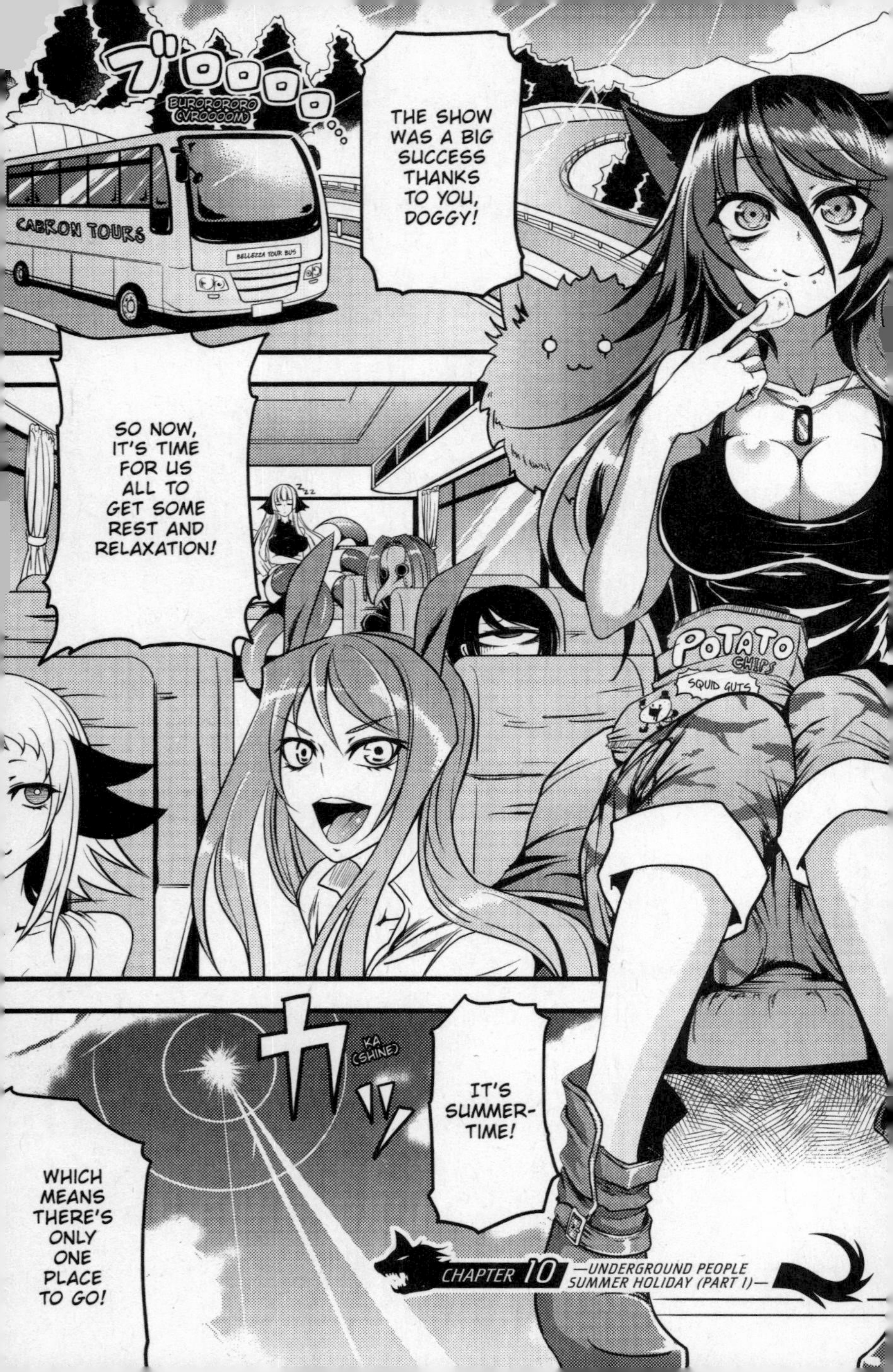
BUROROROROR (VROOOOM)
CABRON TOURS
BELLEZZA TOUR BUS
THE SHOW WAS A BIG SUCCESS THANKS TO YOU, DOGGY!
SO NOW, IT'S TIME FOR US ALL TO GET SOME REST AND RELAXATION!
POTATO CHIPS
SQUID GUTS
IT'S SUMMER-TIME!
KA (SHINE)
WHICH MEANS THERE'S ONLY ONE PLACE TO GO!
CHAPTER 10 —UNDERGROUND PEOPLE SUMMER HOLIDAY (PART 1)—

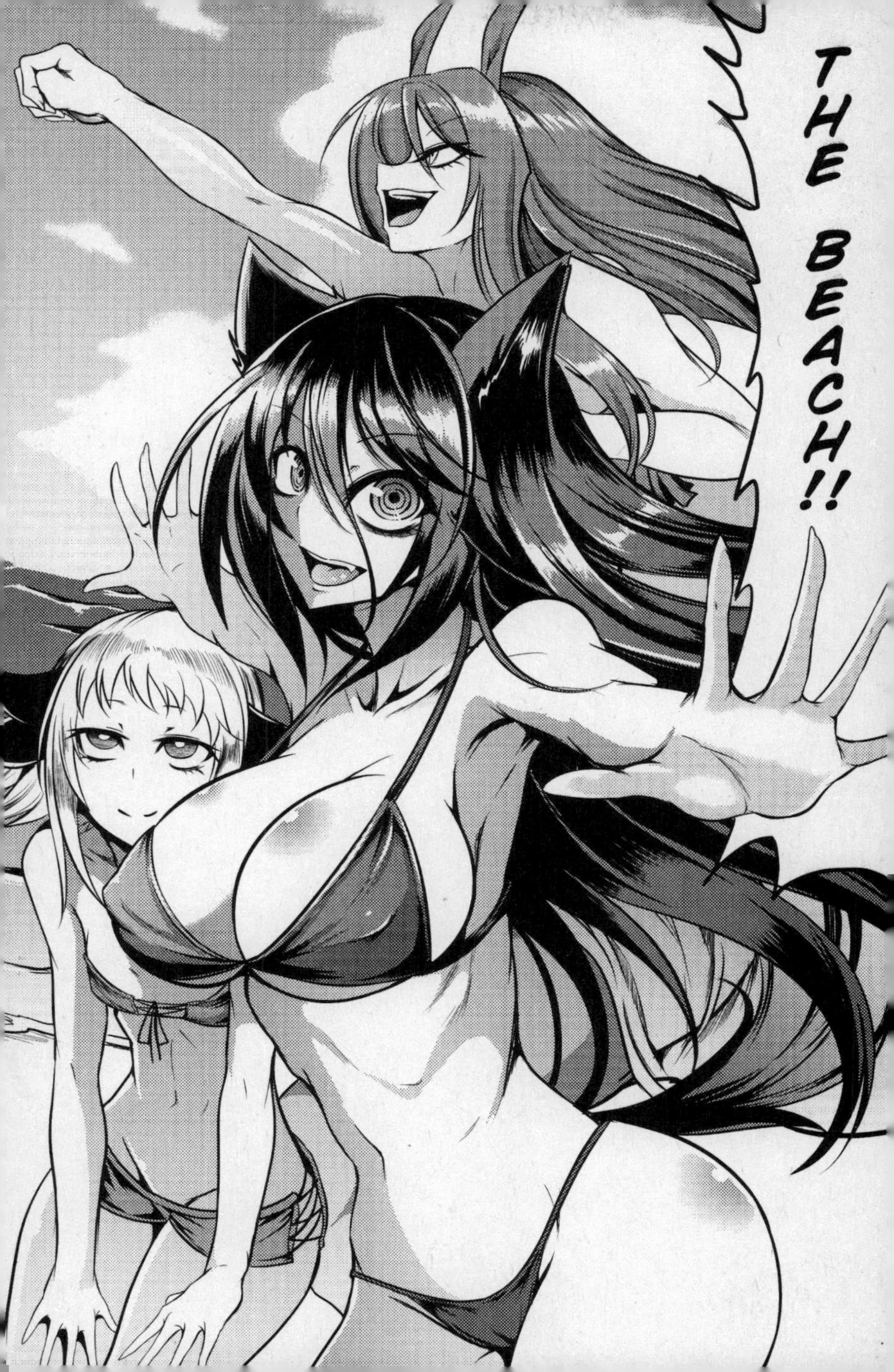
THE BEACH!!

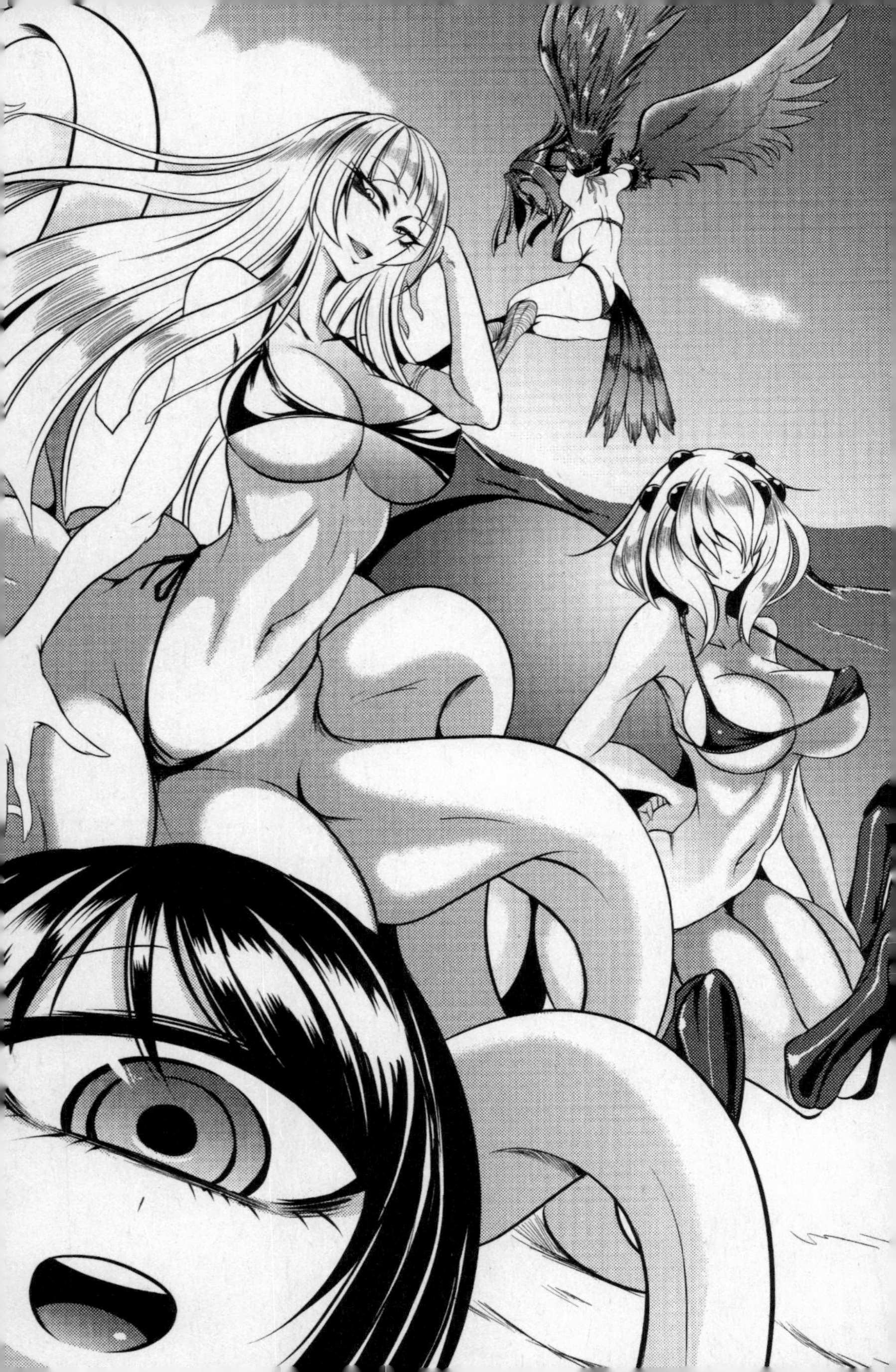

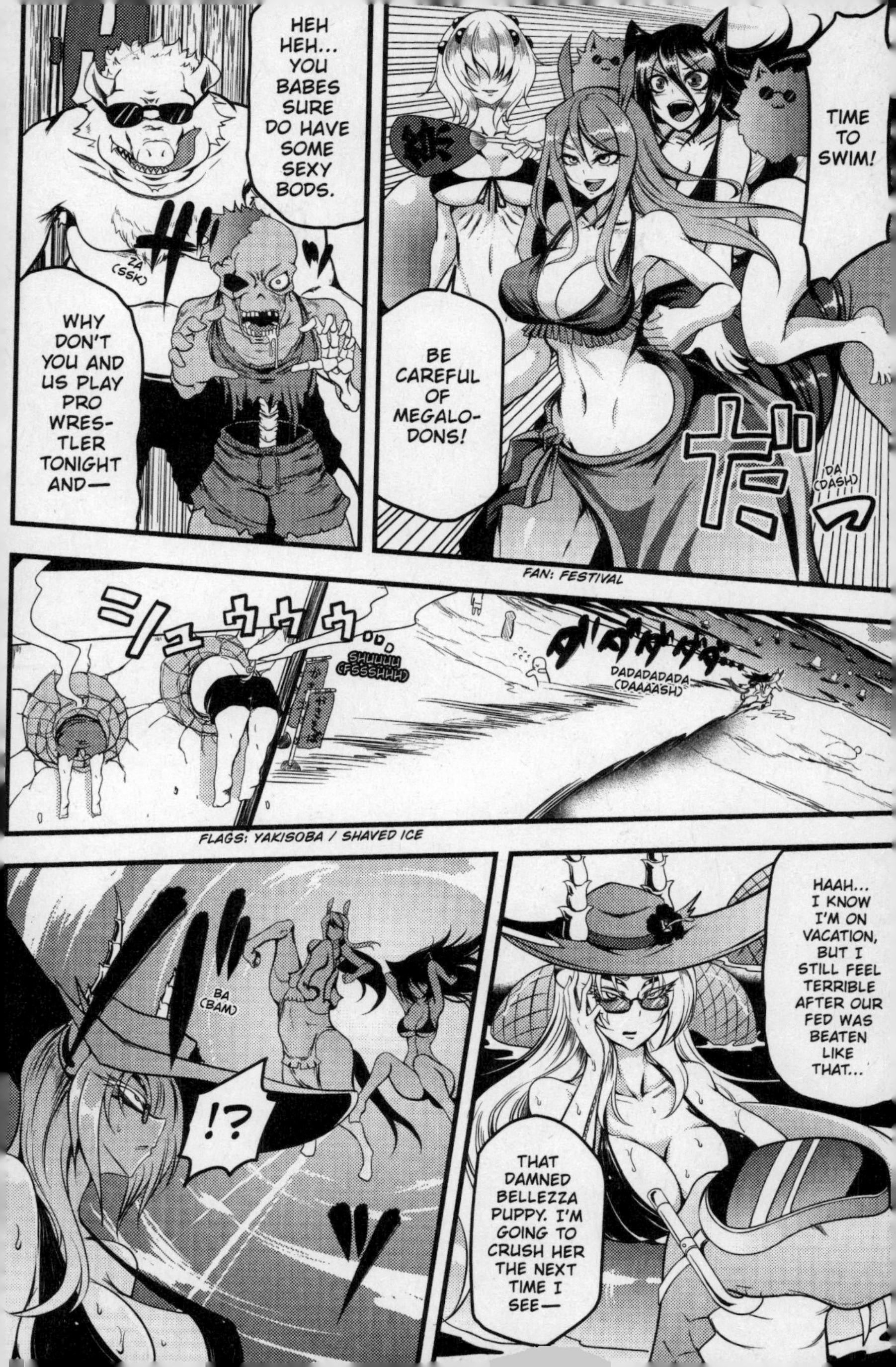
TIME TO SWIM!
BE CAREFUL OF MEGALO-DONS!
DA (DASH)
FAN: FESTIVAL
HEH HEH... YOU BABES SURE DO HAVE SOME SEXY BODS.
ZA (SSK)
WHY DON'T YOU AND US PLAY PRO WRES-TLER TONIGHT AND—
DADADADADA (DAAAASH)
SHUUUU (FSSSHHH)
FLAGS: YAKISOBA / SHAVED ICE
HAAH... I KNOW I'M ON VACATION, BUT I STILL FEEL TERRIBLE AFTER OUR FED WAS BEATEN LIKE THAT...
THAT DAMNED BELLEZZA PUPPY. I'M GOING TO CRUSH HER THE NEXT TIME I SEE—
BA (BAM)
!?

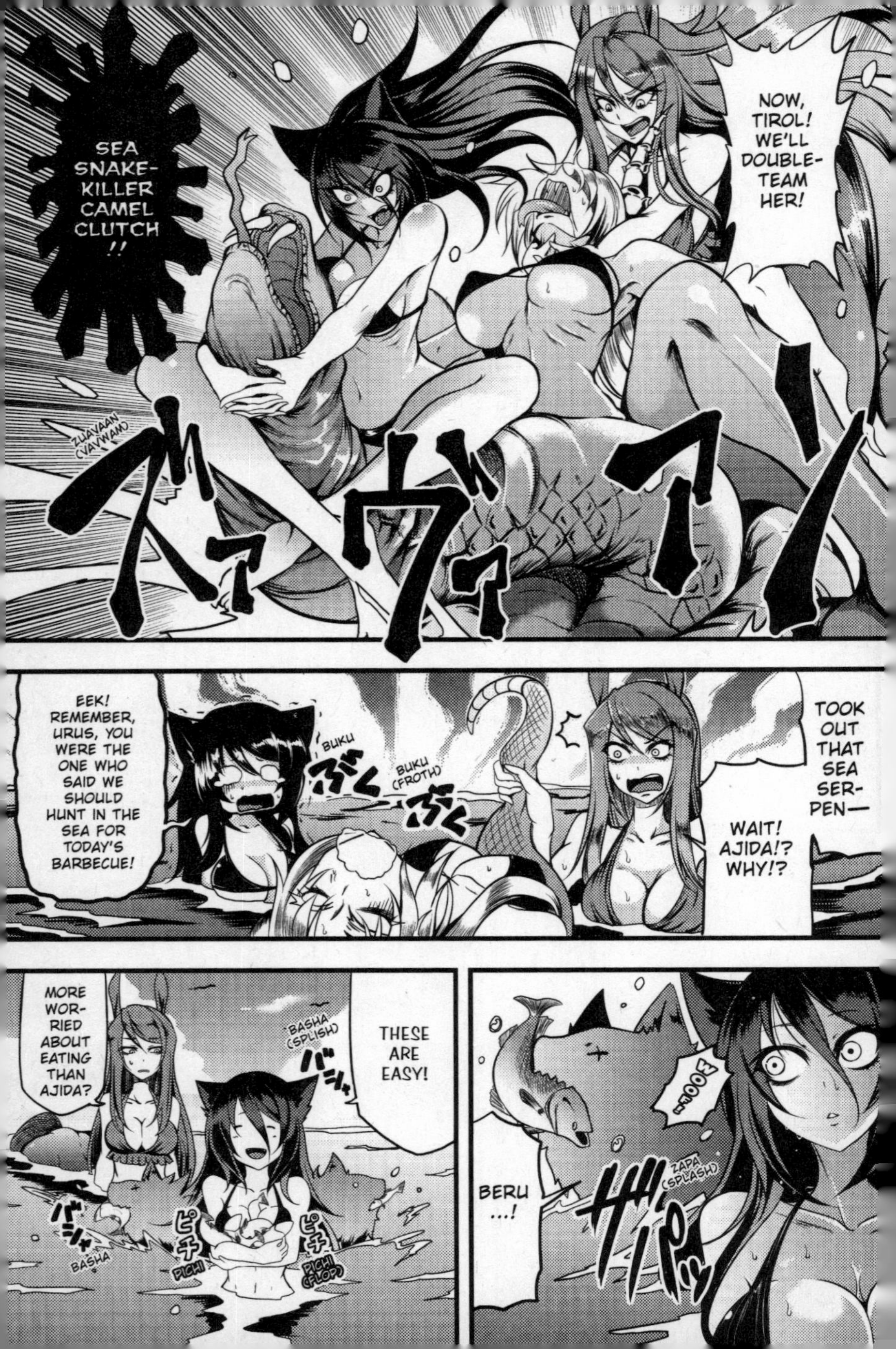
NOW, TIROL! WE'LL DOUBLE-TEAM HER!
SEA SNAKE-KILLER CAMEL CLUTCH!!
ZUAVAAN (VAVWAM)
TOOK OUT THAT SEA SER-PEN—
WAIT! AJIDA!? WHY!?
BUKU (FROTH)
ぶく
BUKU
ぶく
EEK! REMEMBER, URUS, YOU WERE THE ONE WHO SAID WE SHOULD HUNT IN THE SEA FOR TODAY'S BARBECUE!
WOOF!!
ZAPA (SPLASH)
BERU ...!
THESE ARE EASY!
BASHA (SPLISH)
バシャ
MORE WOR-RIED ABOUT EATING THAN AJIDA?
ピチ
PICHI (PLOP)
ピチ
PICHI
バシャ
BASHA

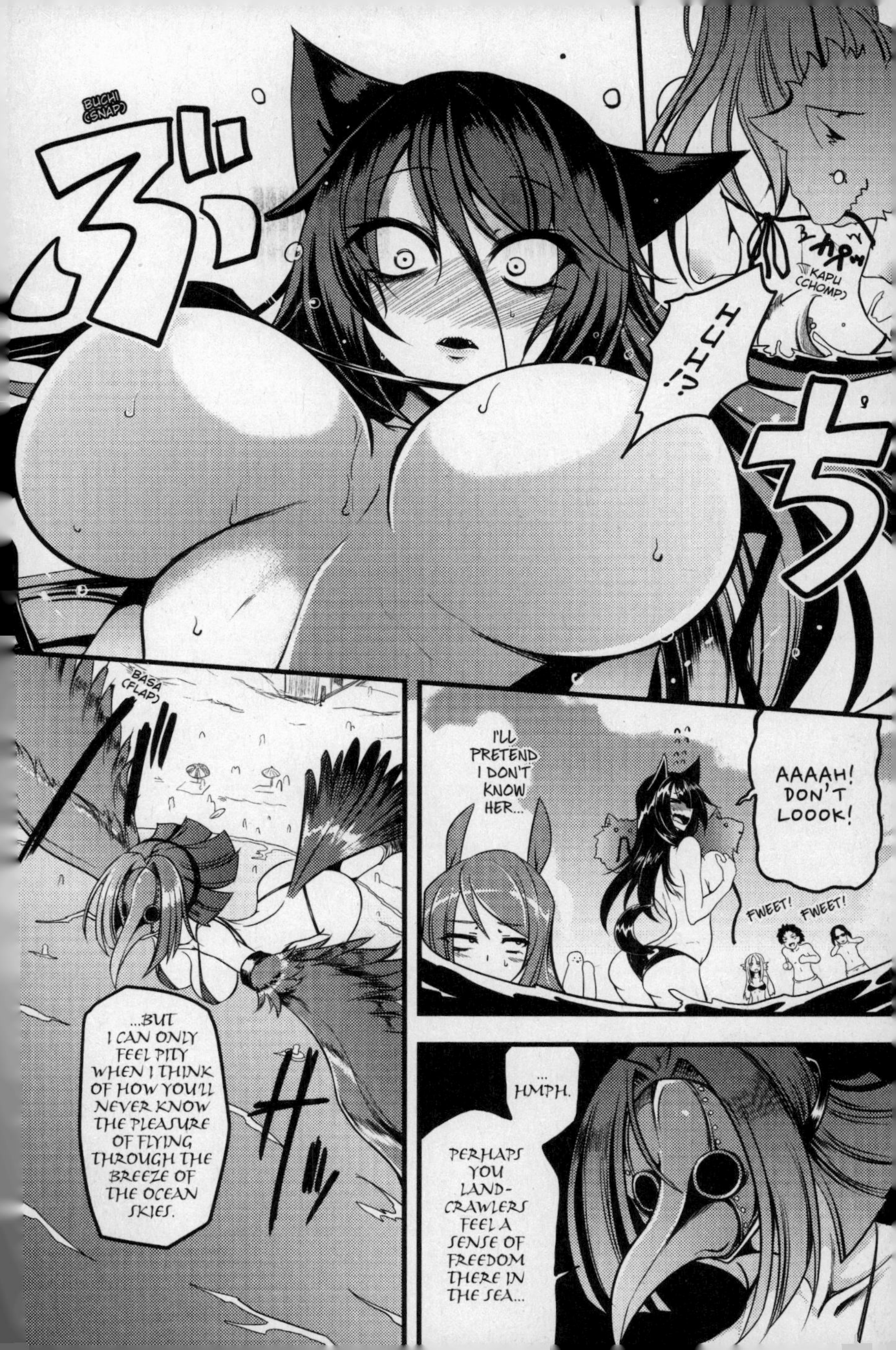

KAPU (CHOMP)
BUCHI (SNAP)
HUH?!
AAAAH! DON'T LOOOK!
I'LL PRETEND I DON'T KNOW HER...
FWEET! FWEET!
... HMPH.
PERHAPS YOU LAND-CRAWLERS FEEL A SENSE OF FREEDOM THERE IN THE SEA...
BASA (FLAP)
...BUT I CAN ONLY FEEL PITY WHEN I THINK OF HOW YOU'LL NEVER KNOW THE PLEASURE OF FLYING THROUGH THE BREEZE OF THE OCEAN SKIES.

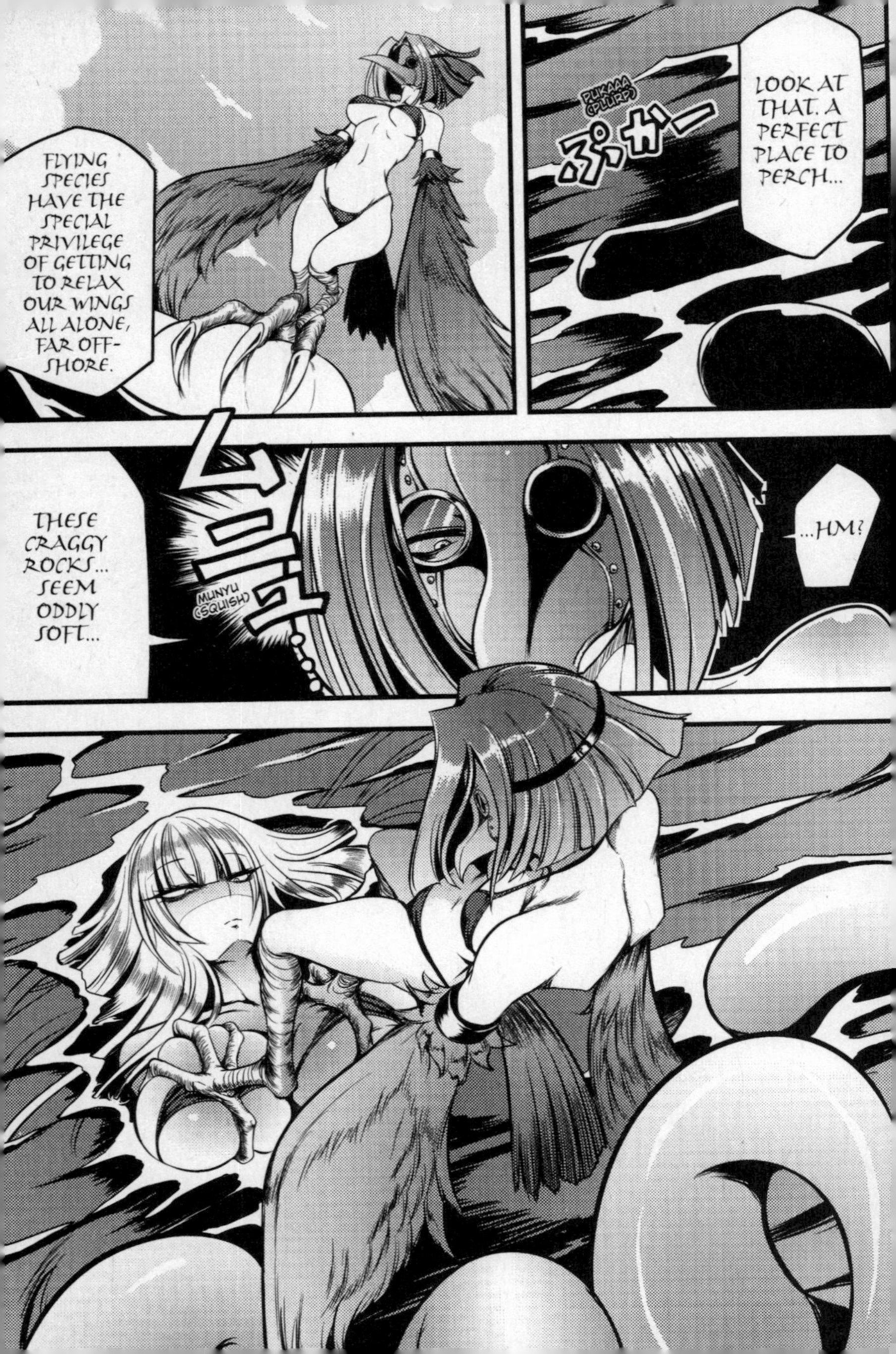
PUKAAA (PLURP)
LOOK AT THAT. A PERFECT PLACE TO PERCH...
FLYING SPECIES HAVE THE SPECIAL PRIVILEGE OF GETTING TO RELAX OUR WINGS ALL ALONE, FAR OFF-SHORE.
...HM?
MUNYU (SQUISH)
THESE CRAGGY ROCKS... SEEM ODDLY SOFT...

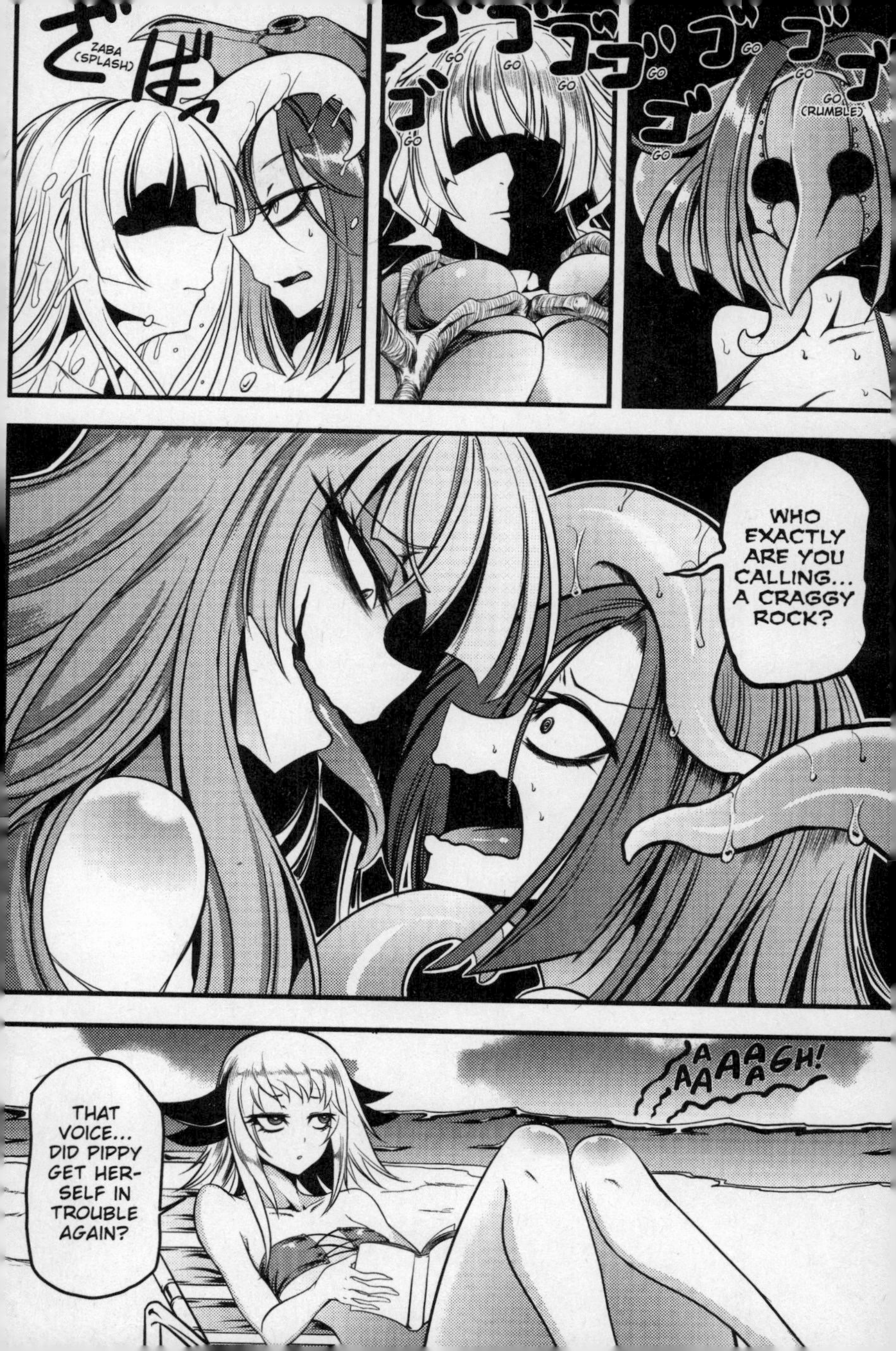
GO
GO
GO
GO
(RUMBLE)
GO
GO
GO
GO
GO
ZABA
(SPLASH)
WHO EXACTLY ARE YOU CALLING... A CRAGGY ROCK?
AAAAAGH!
THAT VOICE... DID PIPPY GET HER-SELF IN TROUBLE AGAIN?

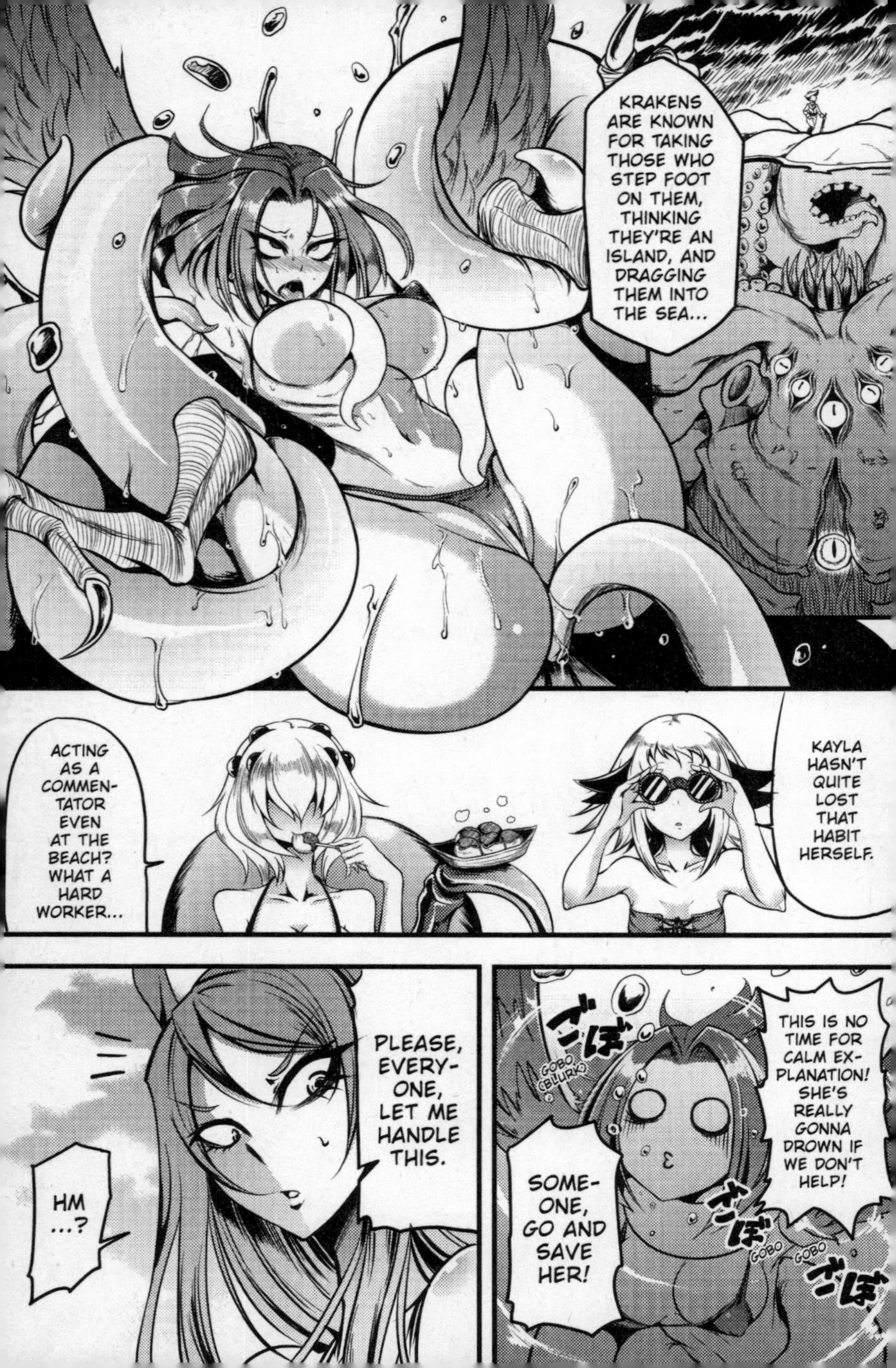
KRAKENS ARE KNOWN FOR TAKING THOSE WHO STEP FOOT ON THEM, THINKING THEY'RE AN ISLAND, AND DRAGGING THEM INTO THE SEA...
KAYLA HASN'T QUITE LOST THAT HABIT HERSELF.
ACTING AS A COMMENTATOR EVEN AT THE BEACH? WHAT A HARD WORKER...
ごぼ
GOBO (BLURK)
THIS IS NO TIME FOR CALM EXPLANATION! SHE'S REALLY GONNA DROWN IF WE DON'T HELP!
SOMEONE, GO AND SAVE HER!
ごぼ
GOBO
GOBO
ごぼ
PLEASE, EVERYONE, LET ME HANDLE THIS.
HM ...?

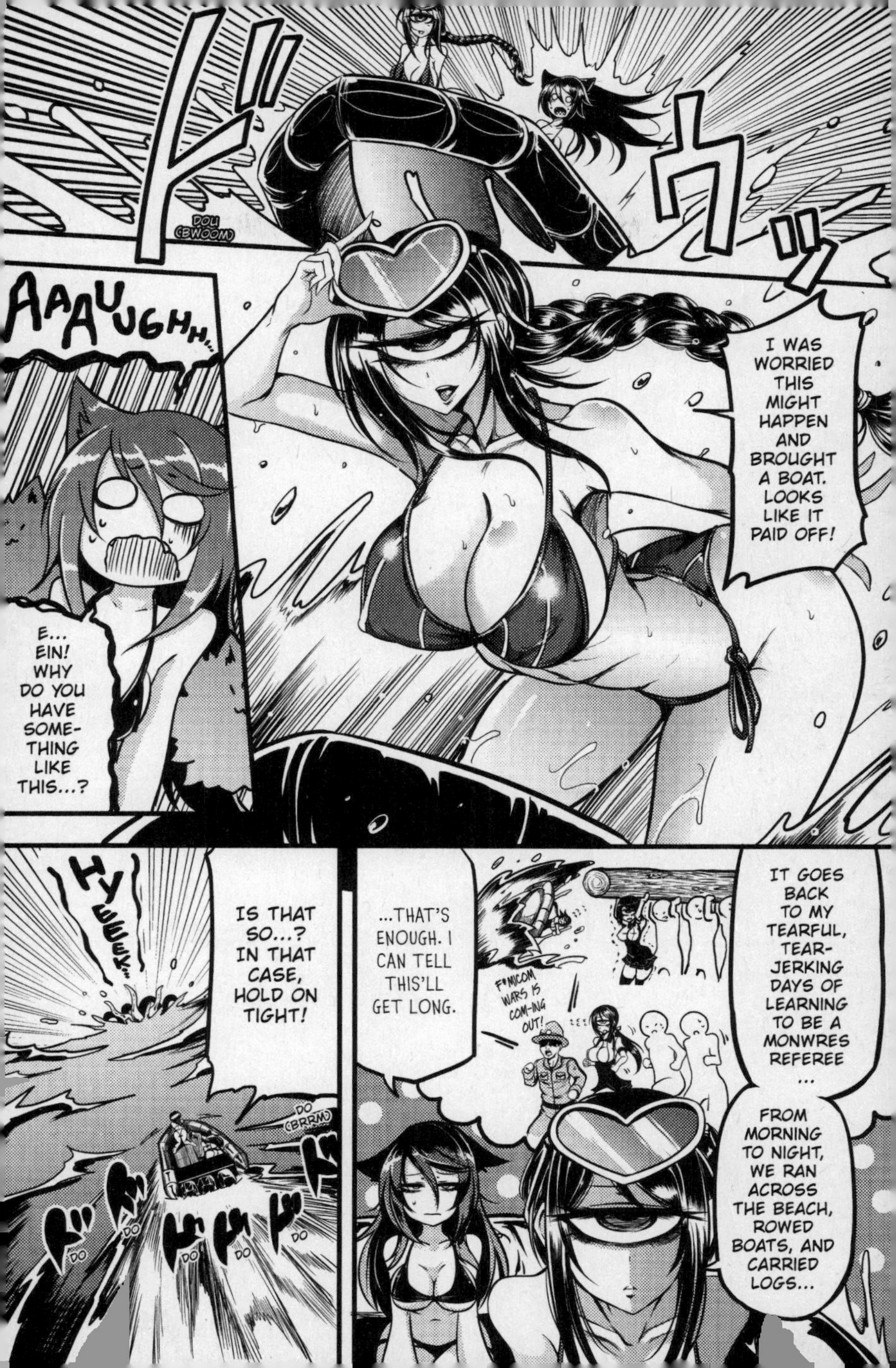
DOU (BWOOM)
I WAS WORRIED THIS MIGHT HAPPEN AND BROUGHT A BOAT. LOOKS LIKE IT PAID OFF!
AAAUUGHH...
E... EIN! WHY DO YOU HAVE SOME-THING LIKE THIS...?
IT GOES BACK TO MY TEARFUL, TEAR-JERKING DAYS OF LEARNING TO BE A MONWRES REFEREE...
FROM MORNING TO NIGHT, WE RAN ACROSS THE BEACH, ROWED BOATS, AND CARRIED LOGS...
F*MICOM WARS IS COM-ING OUT!
...THAT'S ENOUGH. I CAN TELL THIS'LL GET LONG.
IS THAT SO...? IN THAT CASE, HOLD ON TIGHT!
HYEEEEK...
DO (BRRM)
DO
DO
DO
DO
DO

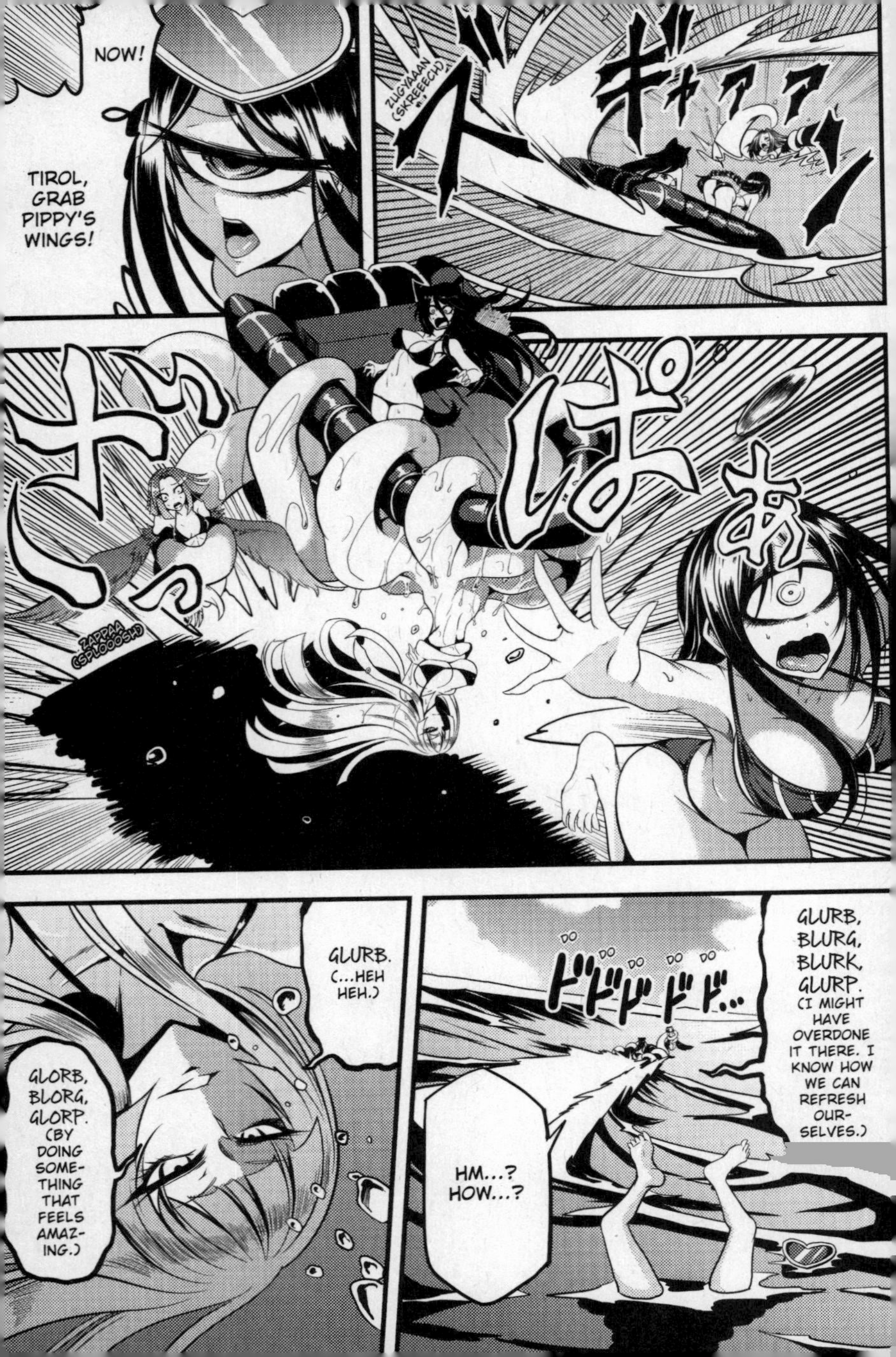
ZUGYAAAN (SKREEECH)
NOW!
TIROL, GRAB PIPPY'S WINGS!
ZAPPAA (SPLOOOSH)
GLURB, BLURG, BLURK, GLURP. (I MIGHT HAVE OVERDONE IT THERE. I KNOW HOW WE CAN REFRESH OURSELVES.)
DO DO DO DO DO
ドドドドド…
HM...? HOW...?
GLURB. (...HEH HEH.)
GLORB, BLORG, GLORP. (BY DOING SOMETHING THAT FEELS AMAZING.)

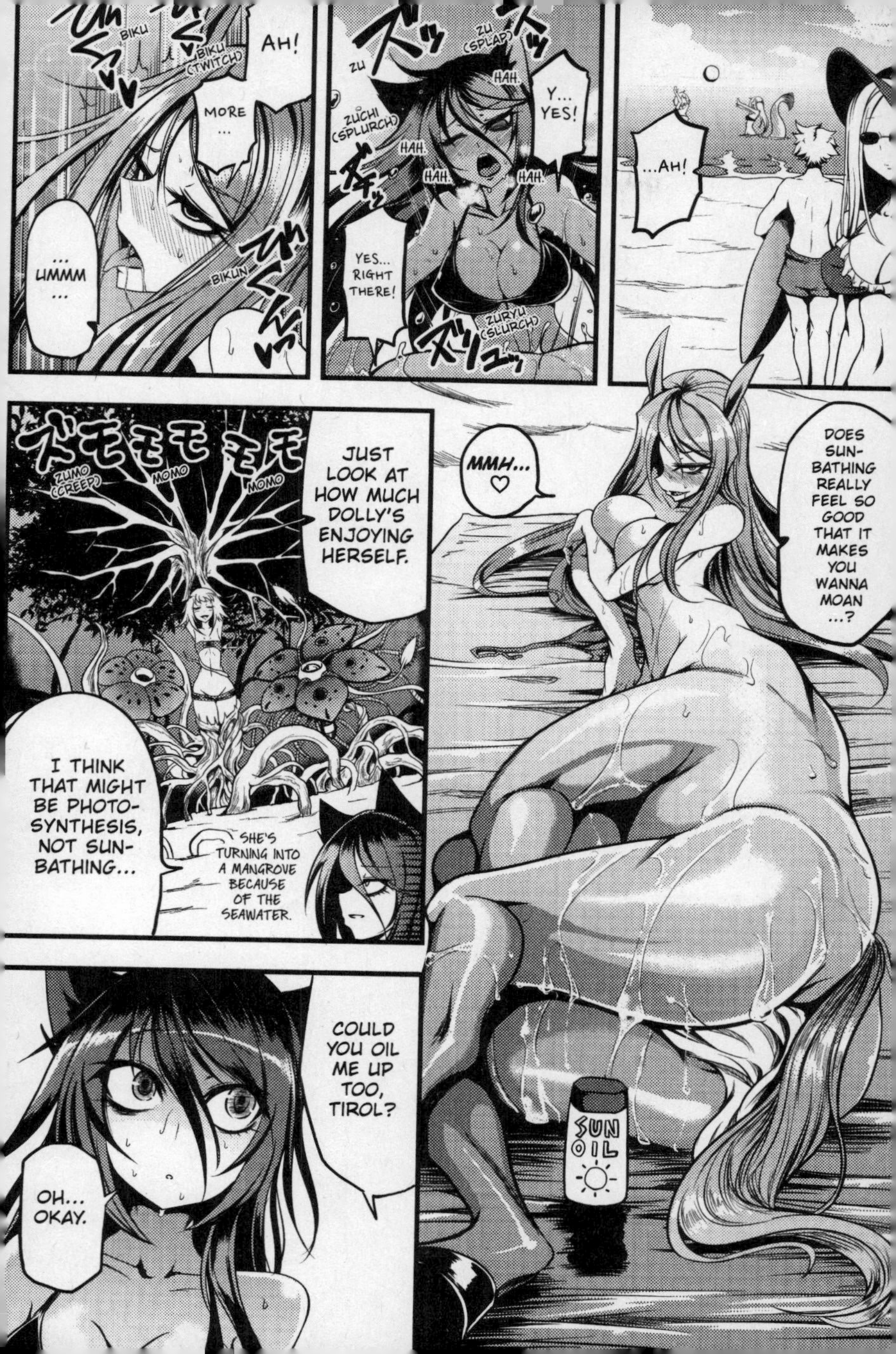
...AH!
ZU (SPLAP)
ZU
Y... YES!
HAH.
ZUCHI (SPLURCH)
HAH.
HAH.
HAH.
YES... RIGHT THERE!
ZURYU (SLURCH)
AH!
BIKU (TWITCH)
BIKU
MORE ...
BIKUN
... UMMM ...
DOES SUN-BATHING REALLY FEEL SO GOOD THAT IT MAKES YOU WANNA MOAN ...?
MMH... ♡
JUST LOOK AT HOW MUCH DOLLY'S ENJOYING HERSELF.
MOMO
MOMO
ZUMO (CREEP)
I THINK THAT MIGHT BE PHOTO-SYNTHESIS, NOT SUN-BATHING...
SHE'S TURNING INTO A MANGROVE BECAUSE OF THE SEAWATER.
SUN OIL
COULD YOU OIL ME UP TOO, TIROL?
OH... OKAY.

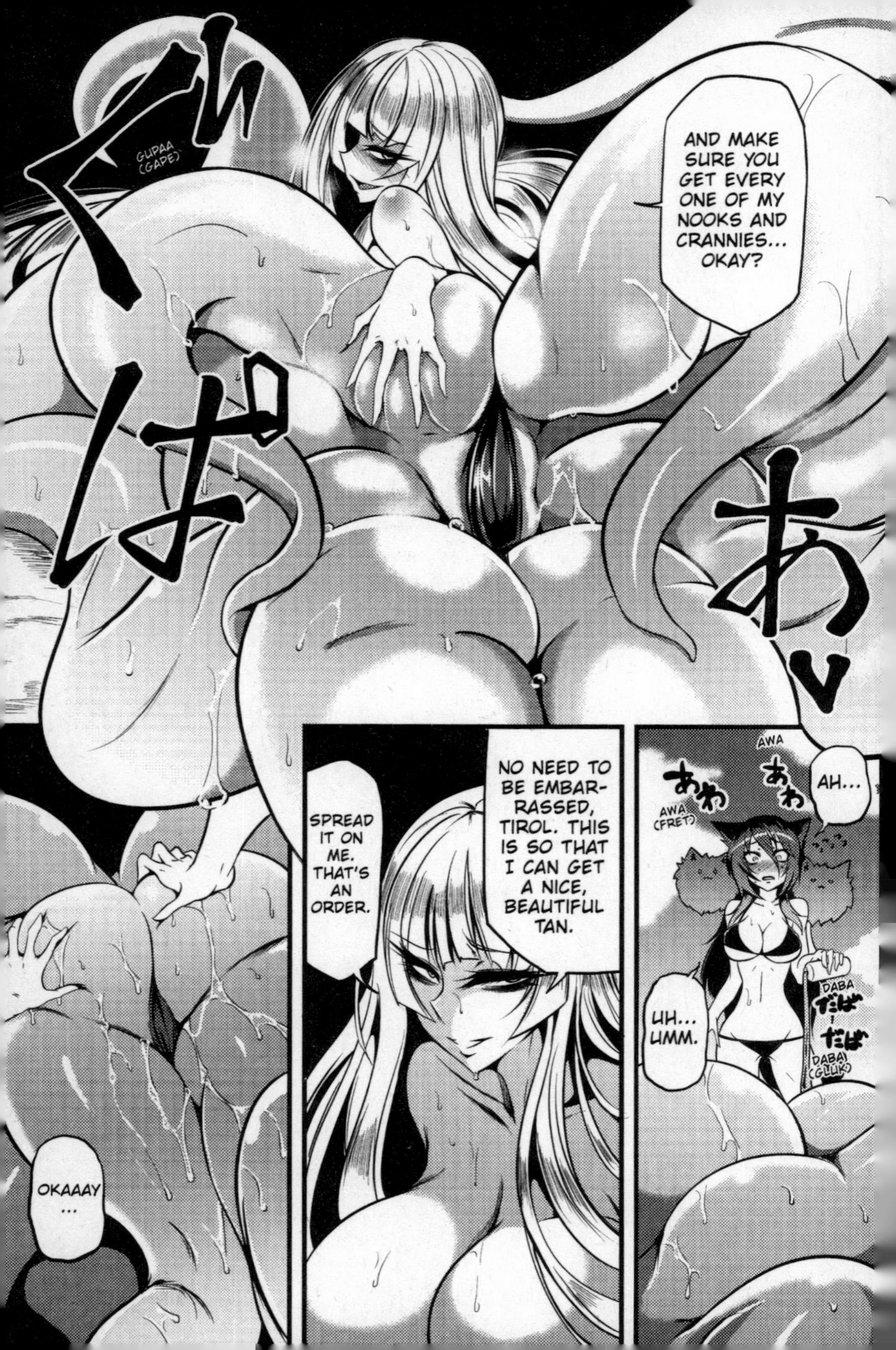

ぐぱ
GUPAA (GAPE)
AND MAKE SURE YOU GET EVERY ONE OF MY NOOKS AND CRANNIES... OKAY?
あ
AWA
あわ
AWA (FRET)
あわ
AH...
UH... UMM.
DABA
だば
だば
DABA (GLUK)
NO NEED TO BE EMBAR-RASSED, TIROL. THIS IS SO THAT I CAN GET A NICE, BEAUTIFUL TAN.
SPREAD IT ON ME. THAT'S AN ORDER.
OKAAAY...

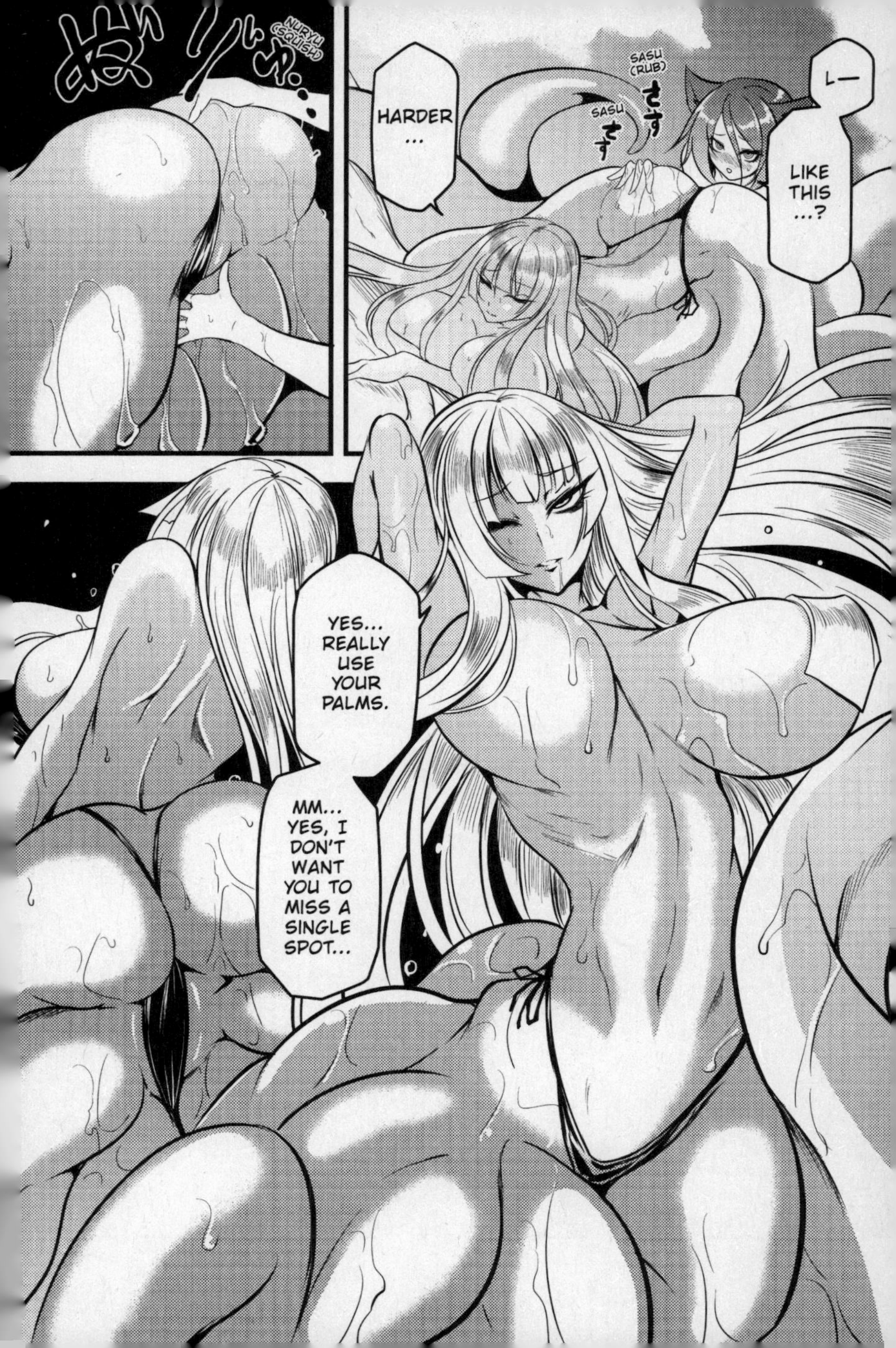
L—
LIKE THIS ...?
SASU (RUB) さす
SASU さす
HARDER ...
ぬりゅ
NURYU (SQUISH)
YES... REALLY USE YOUR PALMS.
MM... YES, I DON'T WANT YOU TO MISS A SINGLE SPOT...

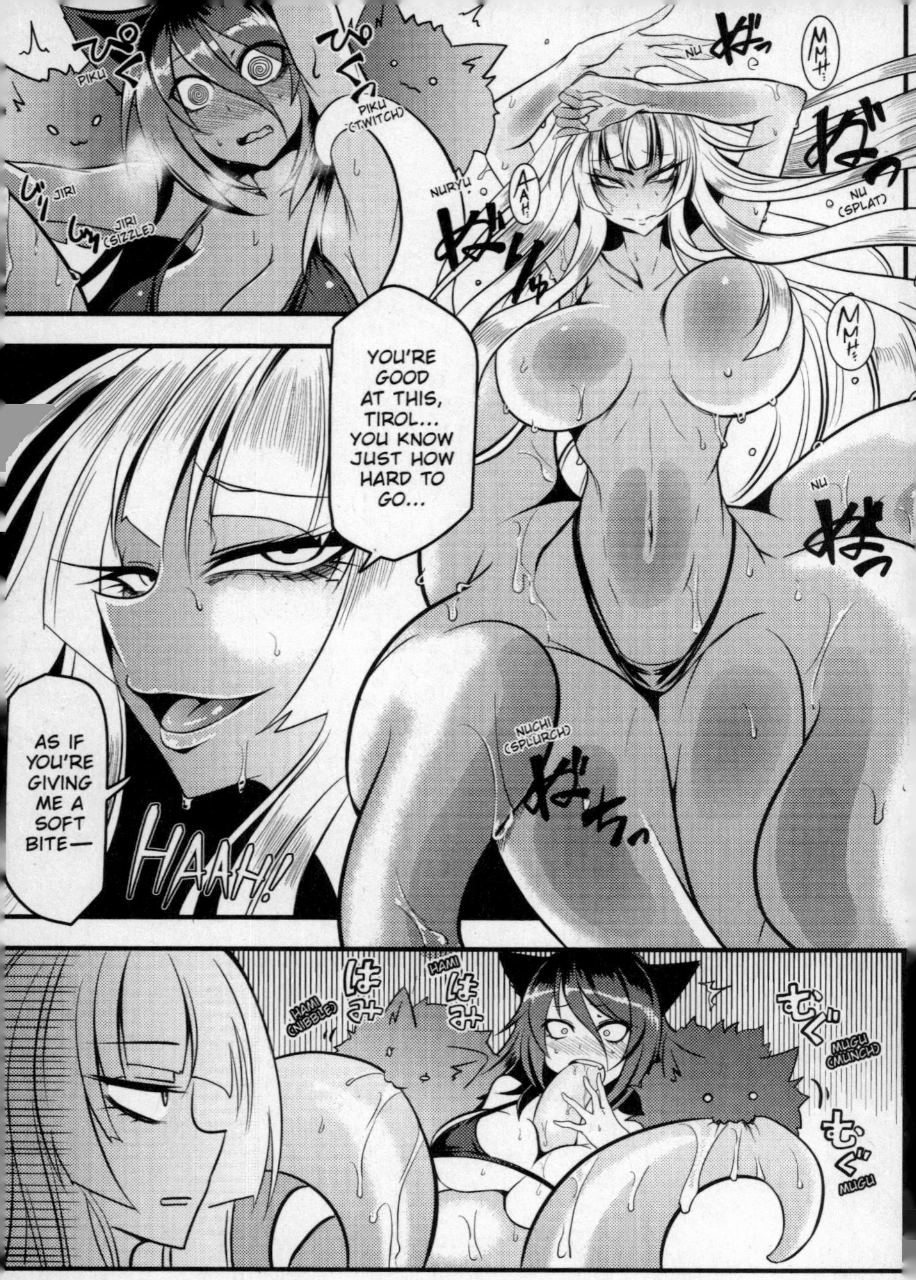

ぬっ NU
MMH...
ぬっ NU (SPLAT)
AAH...
ぬりゅ NURYU
MMH...
ぬっ NU
ぬちっ NUCHI (SPLURCH)
ぴく PIKU
ぴくっ PIKU (TWITCH)
じりじり JIRI JIRI (SIZZLE)
YOU'RE GOOD AT THIS, TIROL... YOU KNOW JUST HOW HARD TO GO...
AS IF YOU'RE GIVING ME A SOFT BITE—
HAAH!
はみ HAMI
はみ HAMI (NIBBLE)
むぐ MUGU (MUNCH)
むぐ MUGU

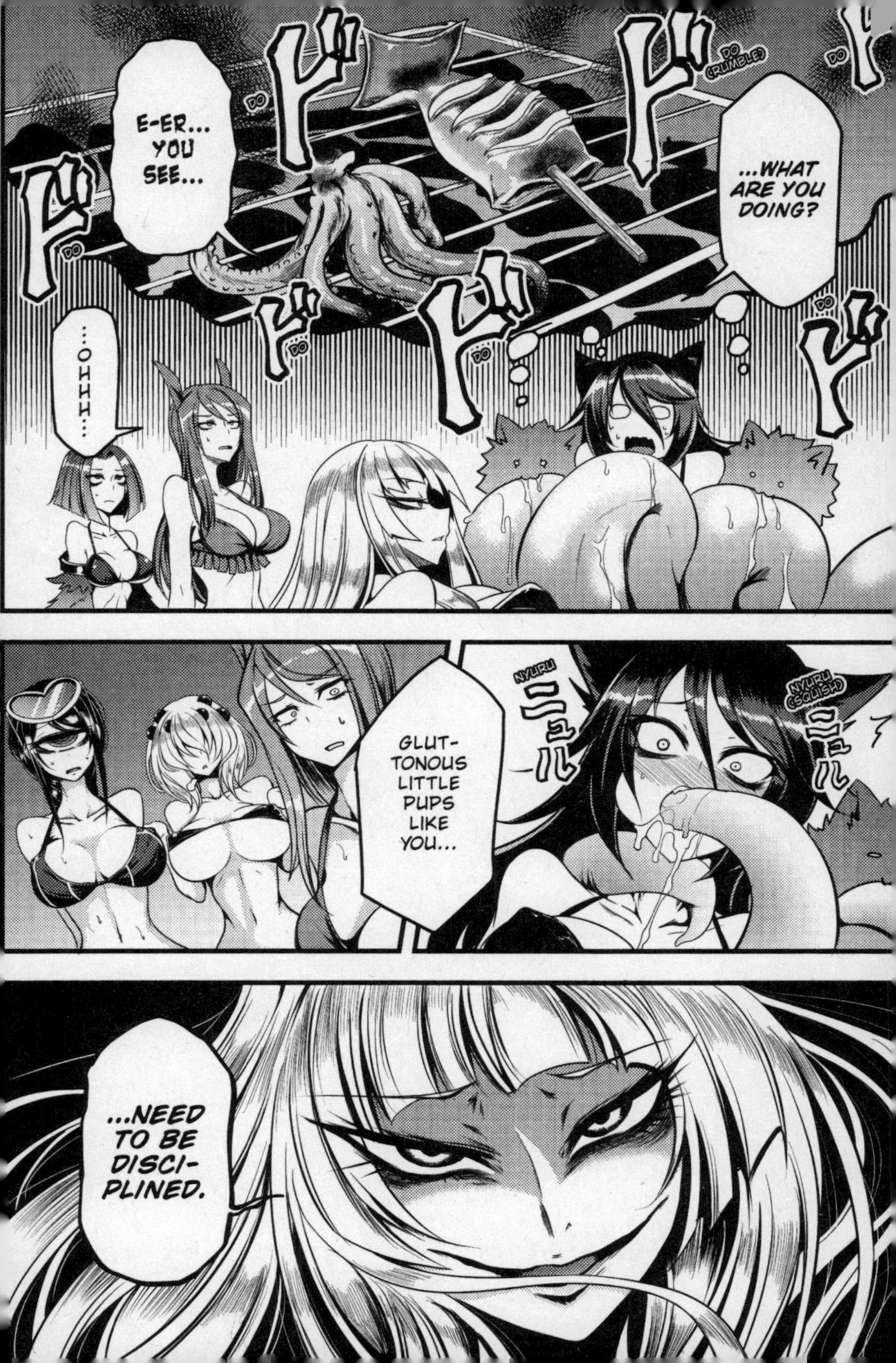
DO
DO (RUMBLE)
...WHAT ARE YOU DOING?
DO
E-ER... YOU SEE...
DO
DO
DO
DO
...OHHH...
NYURU (SQUISH)
NYURU
GLUT-TONOUS LITTLE PUPS LIKE YOU...
...NEED TO BE DISCI-PLINED.

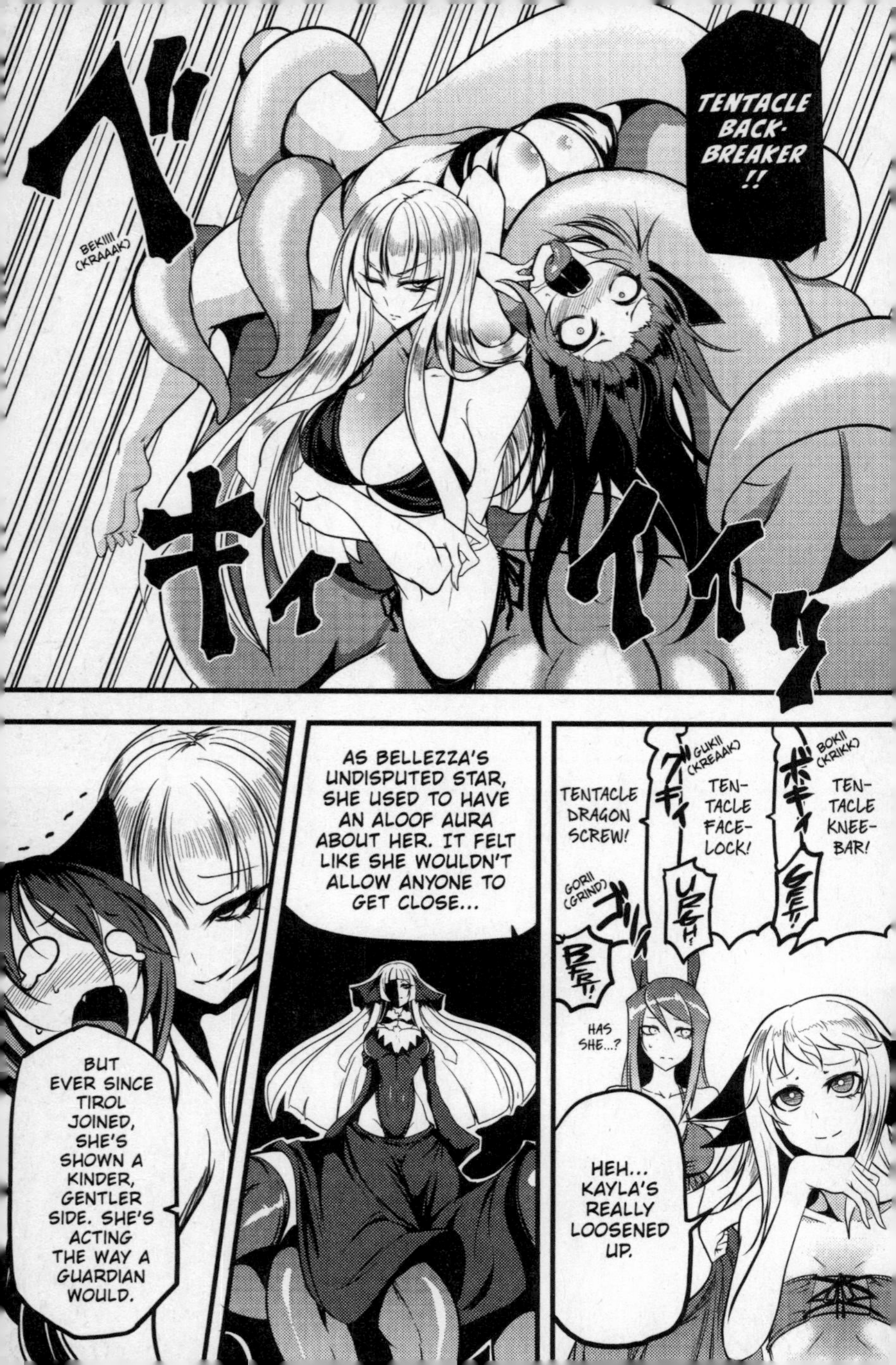
TENTACLE BACK-BREAKER!!
BEKIIII (KRAAAK)
BOKII (KRIKK)
TEN-TACLE KNEE-BAR!
GEE!!
GUKII (KREAAK)
TEN-TACLE FACE-LOCK!
URGH!
TENTACLE DRAGON SCREW!
GORII (GRIND)
BLERT!
HAS SHE...?
HEH... KAYLA'S REALLY LOOSENED UP.
AS BELLEZZA'S UNDISPUTED STAR, SHE USED TO HAVE AN ALOOF AURA ABOUT HER. IT FELT LIKE SHE WOULDN'T ALLOW ANYONE TO GET CLOSE...
BUT EVER SINCE TIROL JOINED, SHE'S SHOWN A KINDER, GENTLER SIDE. SHE'S ACTING THE WAY A GUARDIAN WOULD.

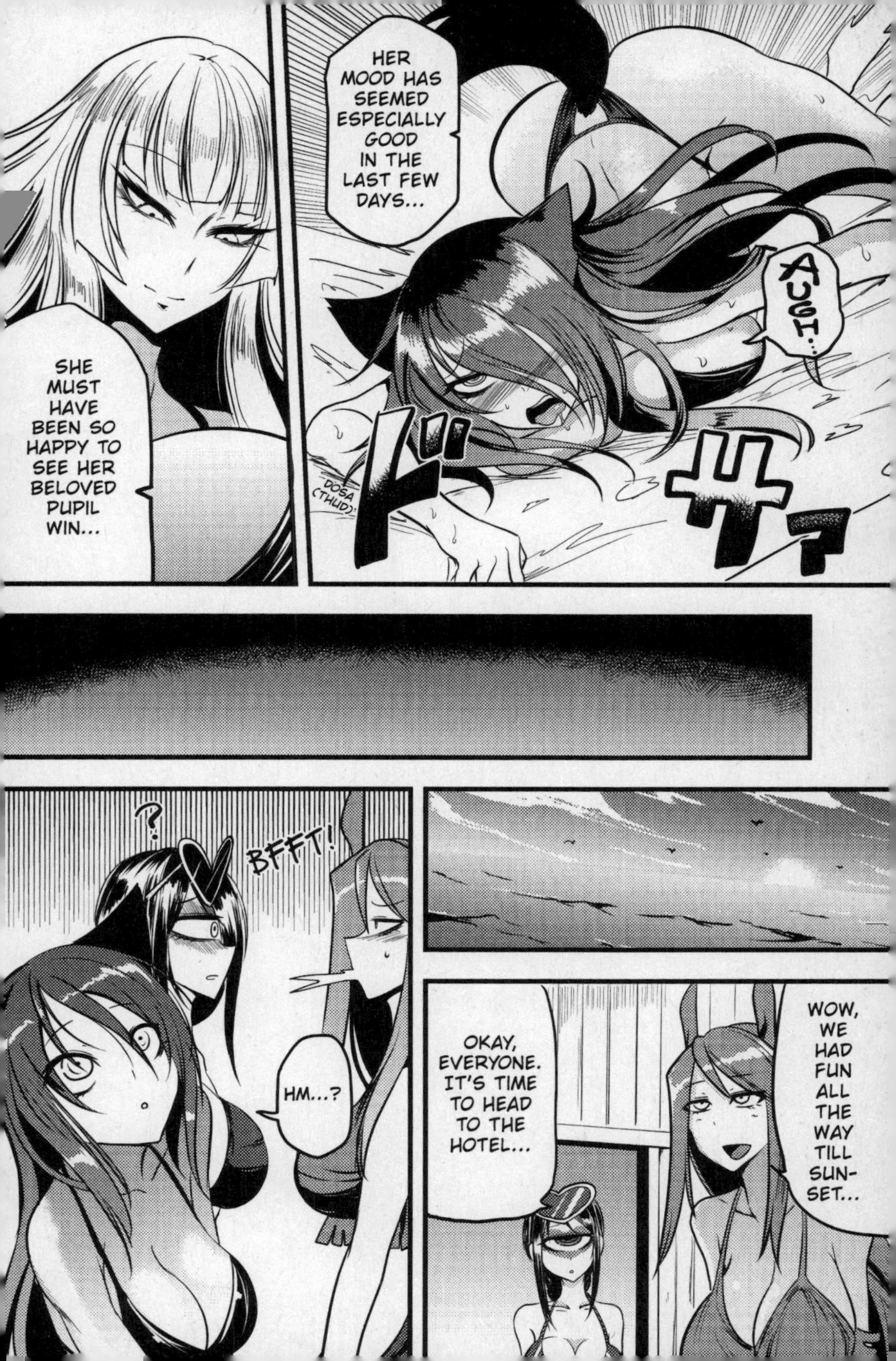
HER MOOD HAS SEEMED ESPECIALLY GOOD IN THE LAST FEW DAYS...
AUGH...
ドサァ
DOSA (THUD)
SHE MUST HAVE BEEN SO HAPPY TO SEE HER BELOVED PUPIL WIN...
WOW, WE HAD FUN ALL THE WAY TILL SUN-SET...
OKAY, EVERYONE. IT'S TIME TO HEAD TO THE HOTEL...
?
BFFT!
HM...?

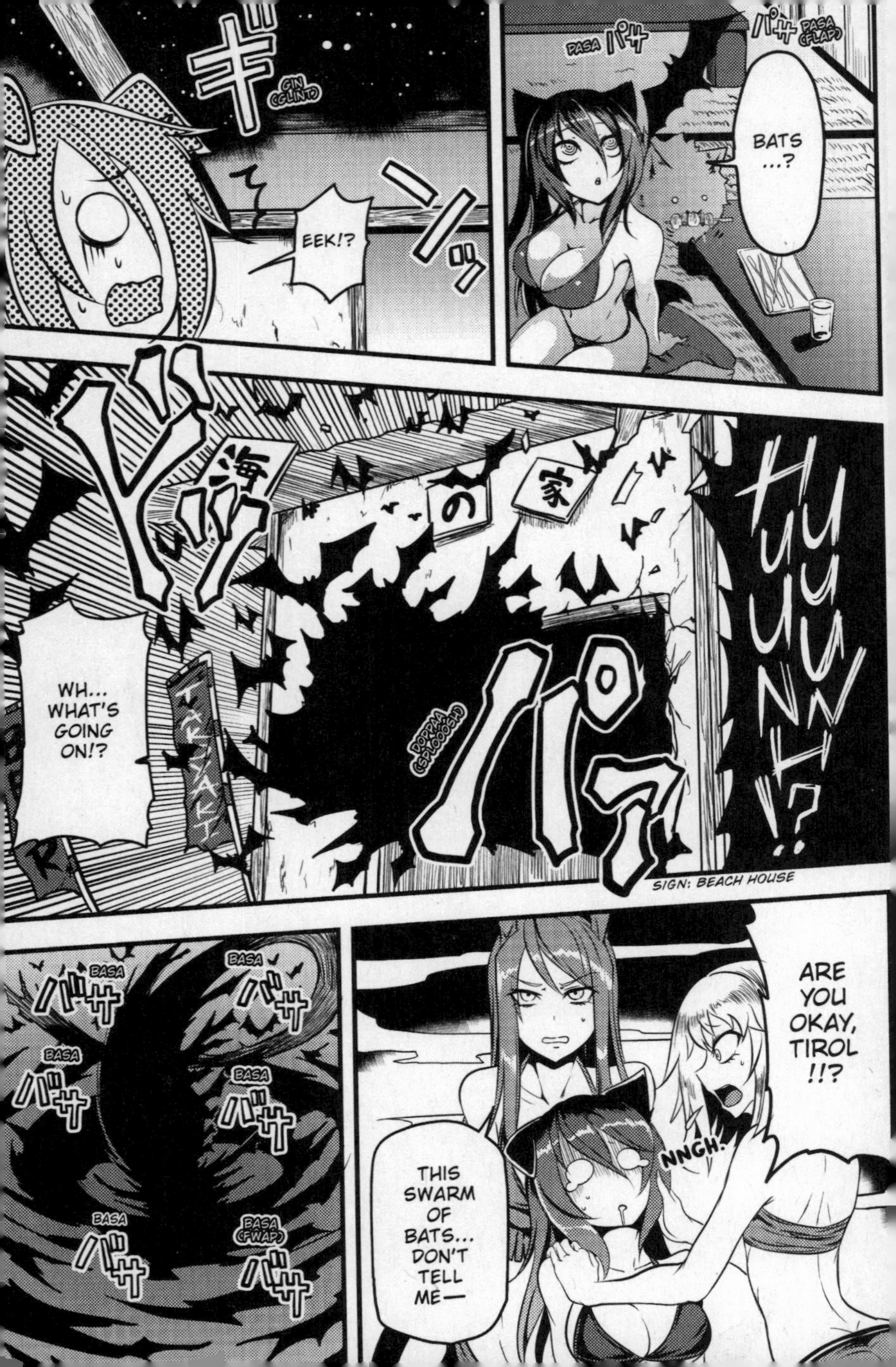
PASA (FLAP)
PASA
BATS ...?
GIN (GLINT)
EEK!?
HYUUUUUNNNH!?
DOPPA (SPLOOOSH)
WH... WHAT'S GOING ON!?
SIGN: BEACH HOUSE
ARE YOU OKAY, TIROL!!?
NNGH!
THIS SWARM OF BATS... DON'T TELL ME—
BASA
BASA
BASA
BASA
BASA
BASA (FWAP)

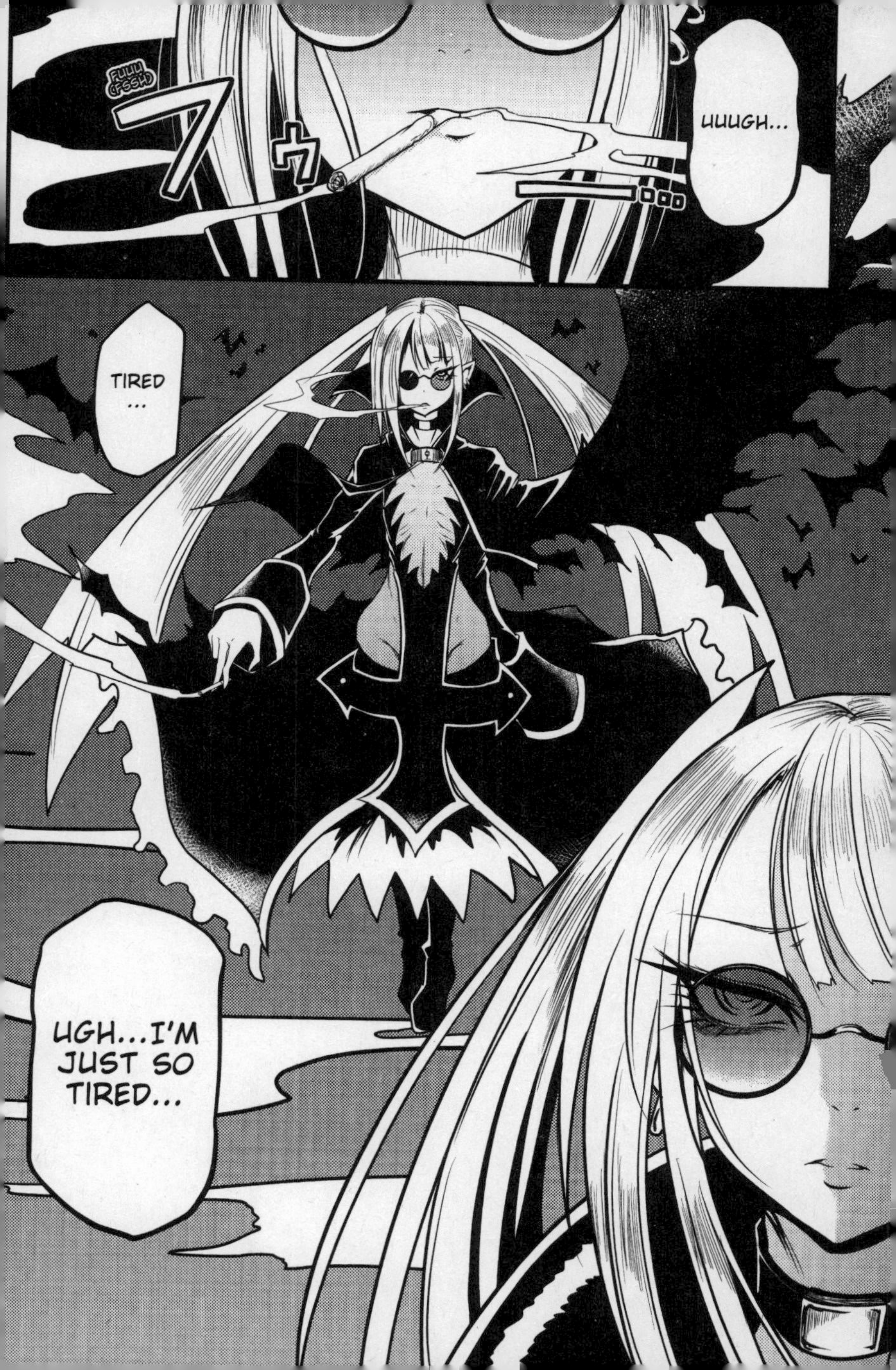
UUUGH...
FUUU (FSSH)
TIRED ...
UGH...I'M JUST SO TIRED...

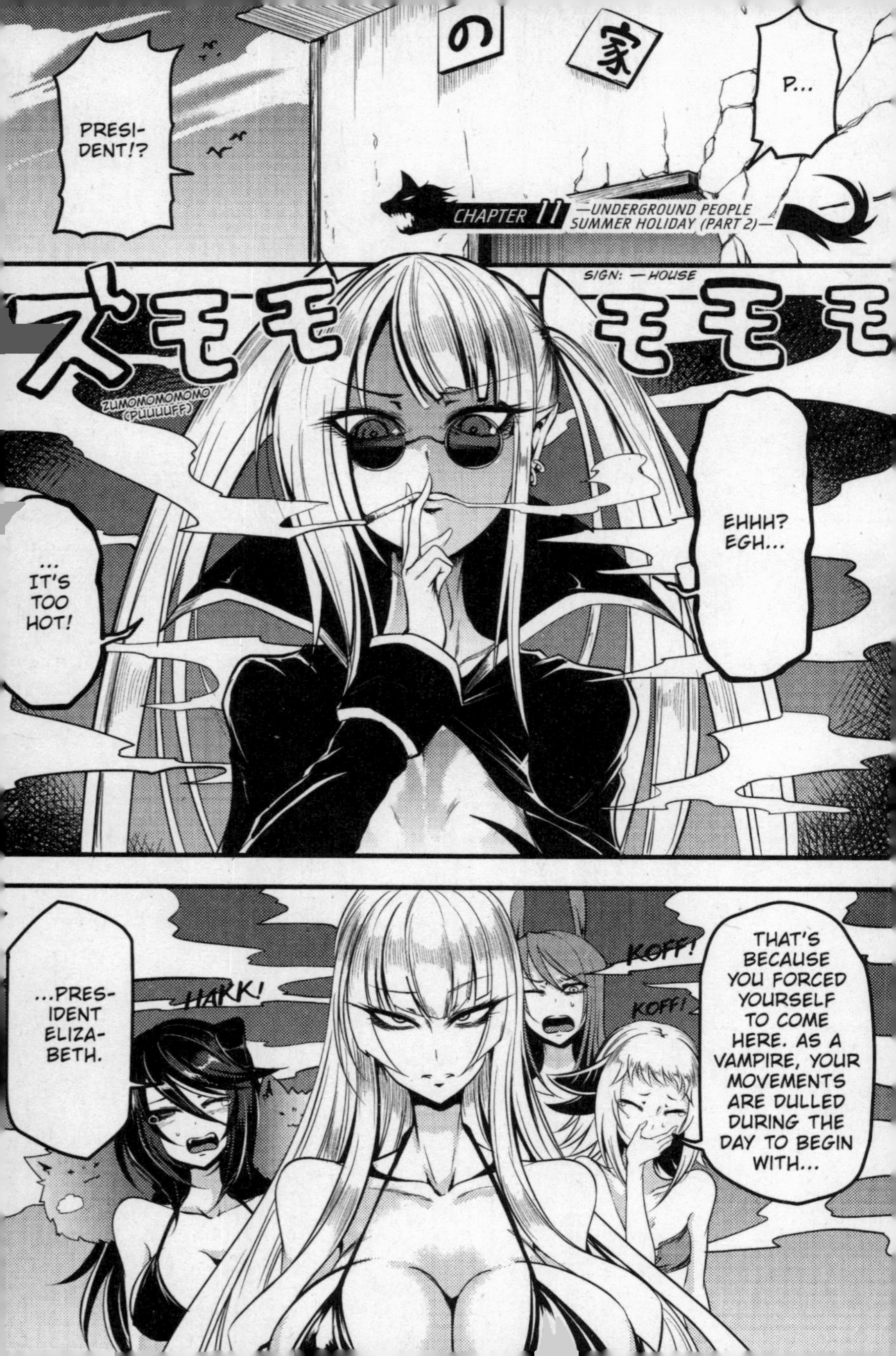
P...
の
家
CHAPTER 11 —UNDERGROUND PEOPLE SUMMER HOLIDAY (PART 2)—
PRESI-DENT!?
SIGN: —HOUSE
ズモモ モモモ
ZUMOMOMOMOMO (PUUUUFF)
EHHH? EGH...
... IT'S TOO HOT!
THAT'S BECAUSE YOU FORCED YOURSELF TO COME HERE. AS A VAMPIRE, YOUR MOVEMENTS ARE DULLED DURING THE DAY TO BEGIN WITH...
KOFF!
KOFF!
HAKK!
...PRES-IDENT ELIZA-BETH.

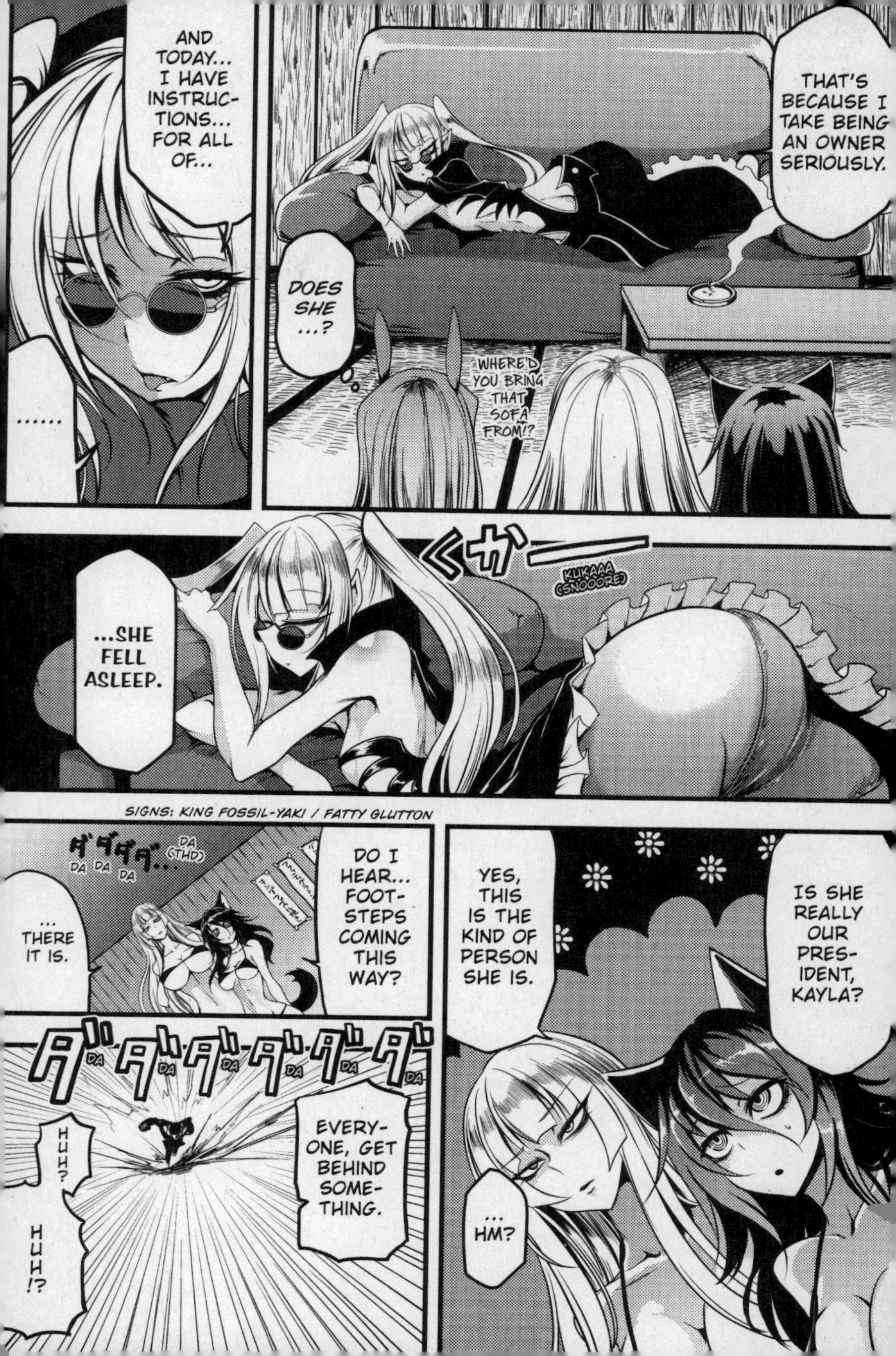
THAT'S BECAUSE I TAKE BEING AN OWNER SERIOUSLY.
DOES SHE ...?
WHERE'D YOU BRING THAT SOFA FROM!?
AND TODAY... I HAVE INSTRUCTIONS... FOR ALL OF...
......
KUKAAA (SNOOORE)
...SHE FELL ASLEEP.
IS SHE REALLY OUR PRESIDENT, KAYLA?
YES, THIS IS THE KIND OF PERSON SHE IS.
...HM?
SIGNS: KING FOSSIL-YAKI / FATTY GLUTTON
DO I HEAR... FOOTSTEPS COMING THIS WAY?
DA DA DA DA (THD)
...THERE IT IS.
DA DA DA DA DA DA
EVERYONE, GET BEHIND SOMETHING.
HUH?
HUH!?

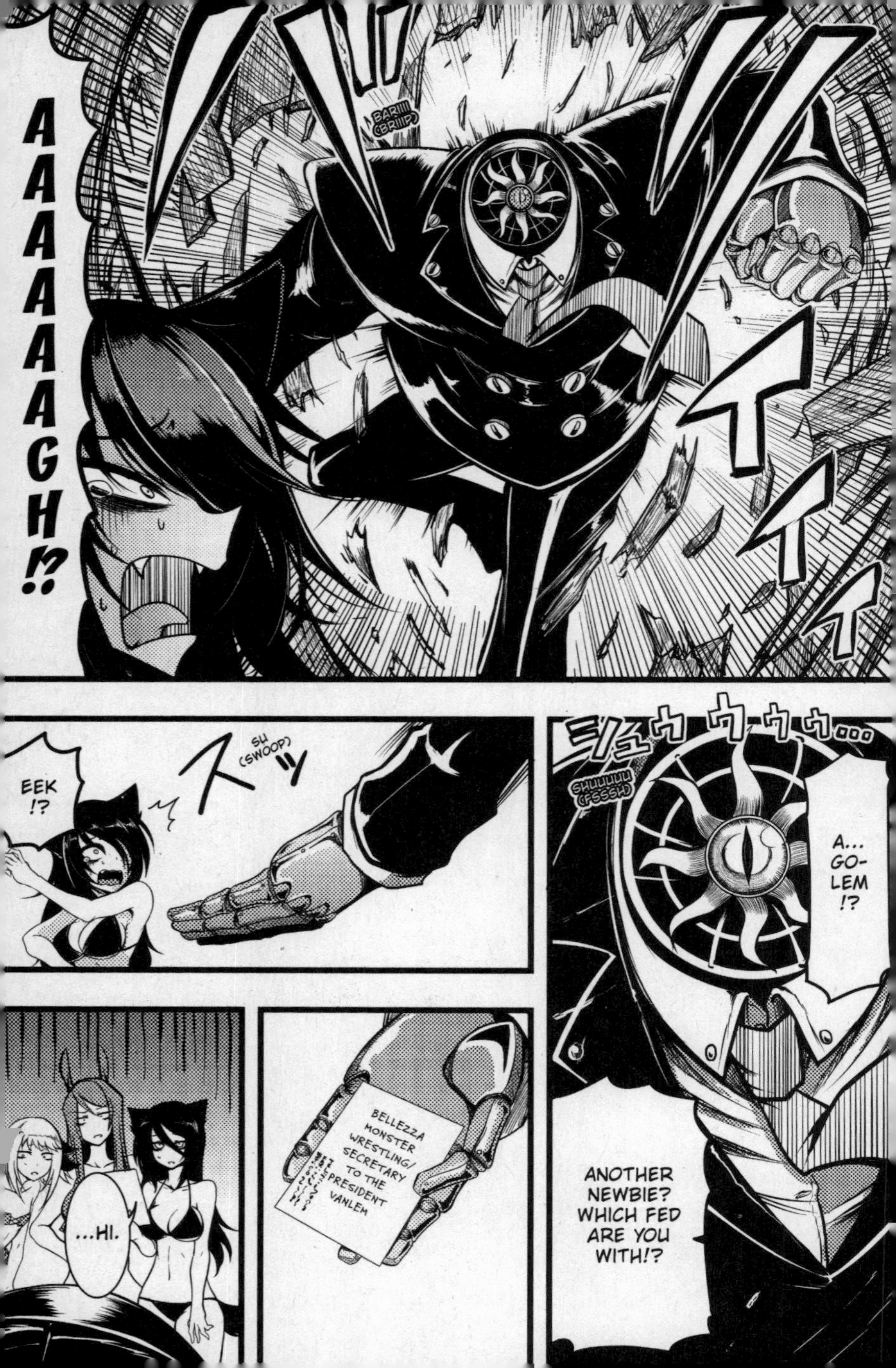
BARIIII (BRIIP)
AAAAAAGH!?
ミシュウ ウ ウ ウ...
SHUUUUU (FSSSH)
A... GO-LEM!?
ANOTHER NEWBIE? WHICH FED ARE YOU WITH!?
SU (SWOOP)
スッ
EEK!?
BELLEZZA MONSTER WRESTLING/ SECRETARY TO THE PRESIDENT VANLEM
...HI.

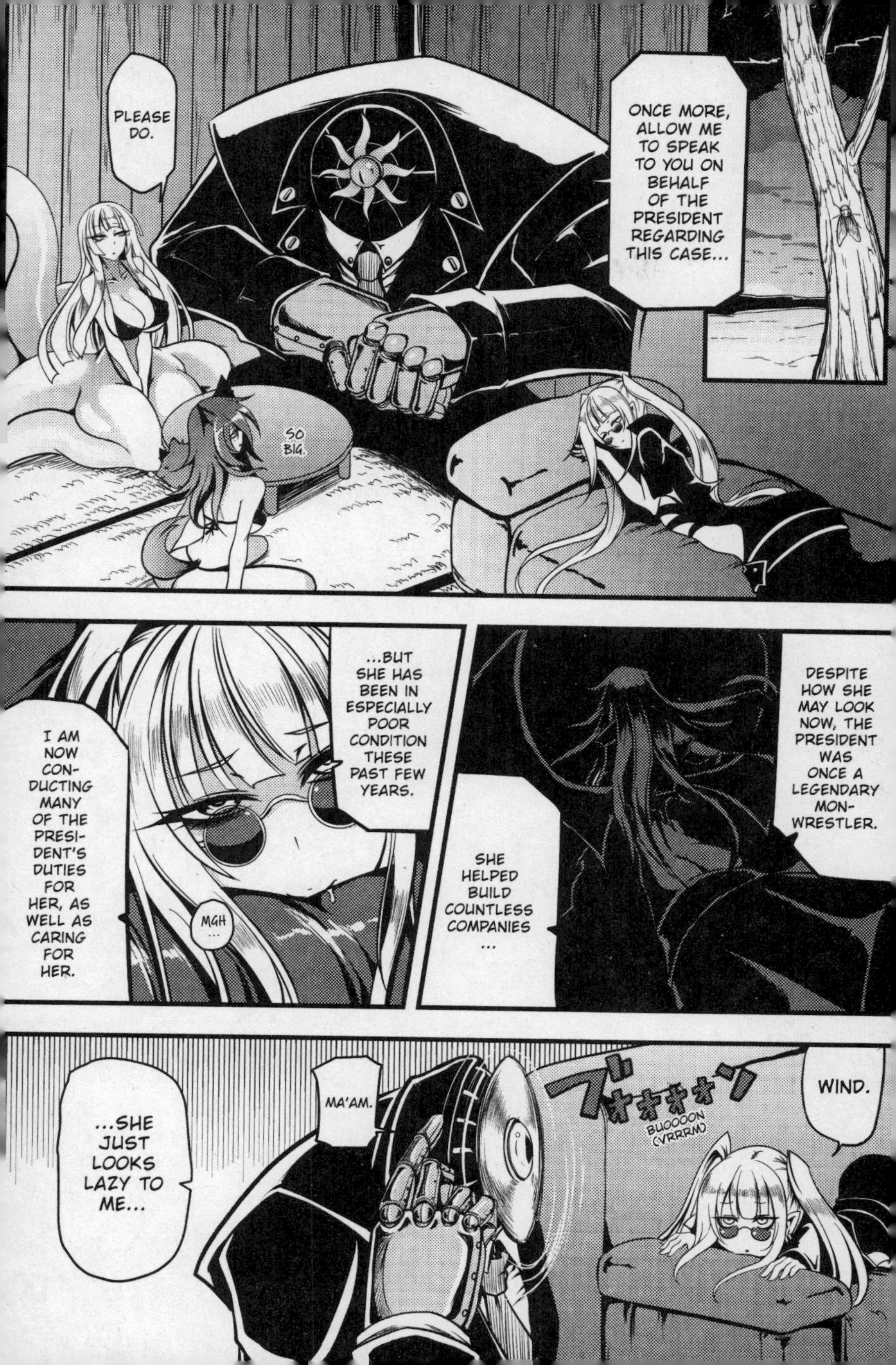
ONCE MORE, ALLOW ME TO SPEAK TO YOU ON BEHALF OF THE PRESIDENT REGARDING THIS CASE...
PLEASE DO.
SO BIG.
DESPITE HOW SHE MAY LOOK NOW, THE PRESIDENT WAS ONCE A LEGENDARY MON-WRESTLER.
SHE HELPED BUILD COUNTLESS COMPANIES...
...BUT SHE HAS BEEN IN ESPECIALLY POOR CONDITION THESE PAST FEW YEARS.
I AM NOW CONDUCTING MANY OF THE PRESIDENT'S DUTIES FOR HER, AS WELL AS CARING FOR HER.
MGH...
WIND.
BUOOOON (VRRRM)
MA'AM.
...SHE JUST LOOKS LAZY TO ME...

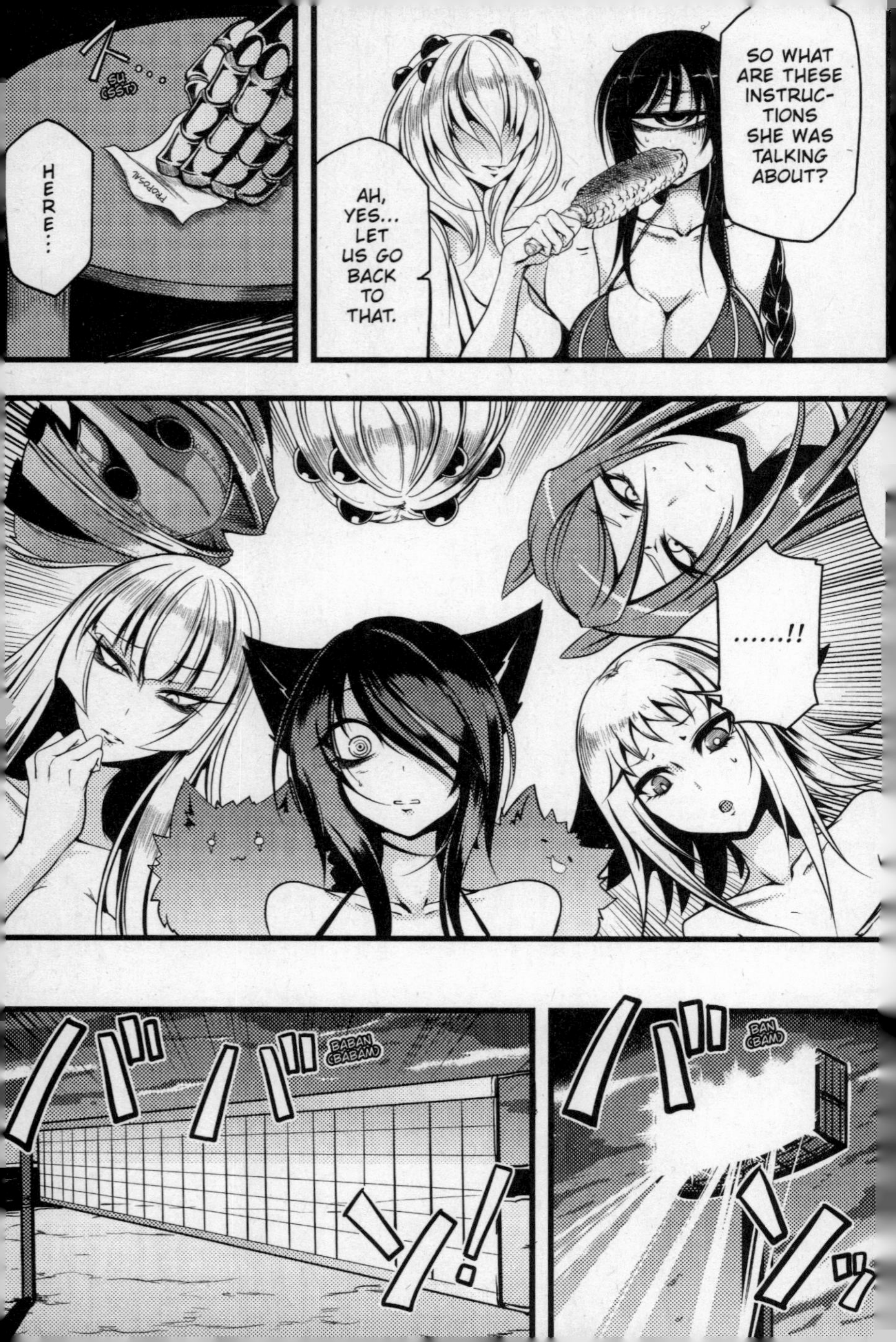
SO WHAT ARE THESE INSTRUCTIONS SHE WAS TALKING ABOUT?
AH, YES... LET US GO BACK TO THAT.
SU (SST)
PROPOSAL
HERE...
......!!
BAN (BAM)
BABAN (BABAM)

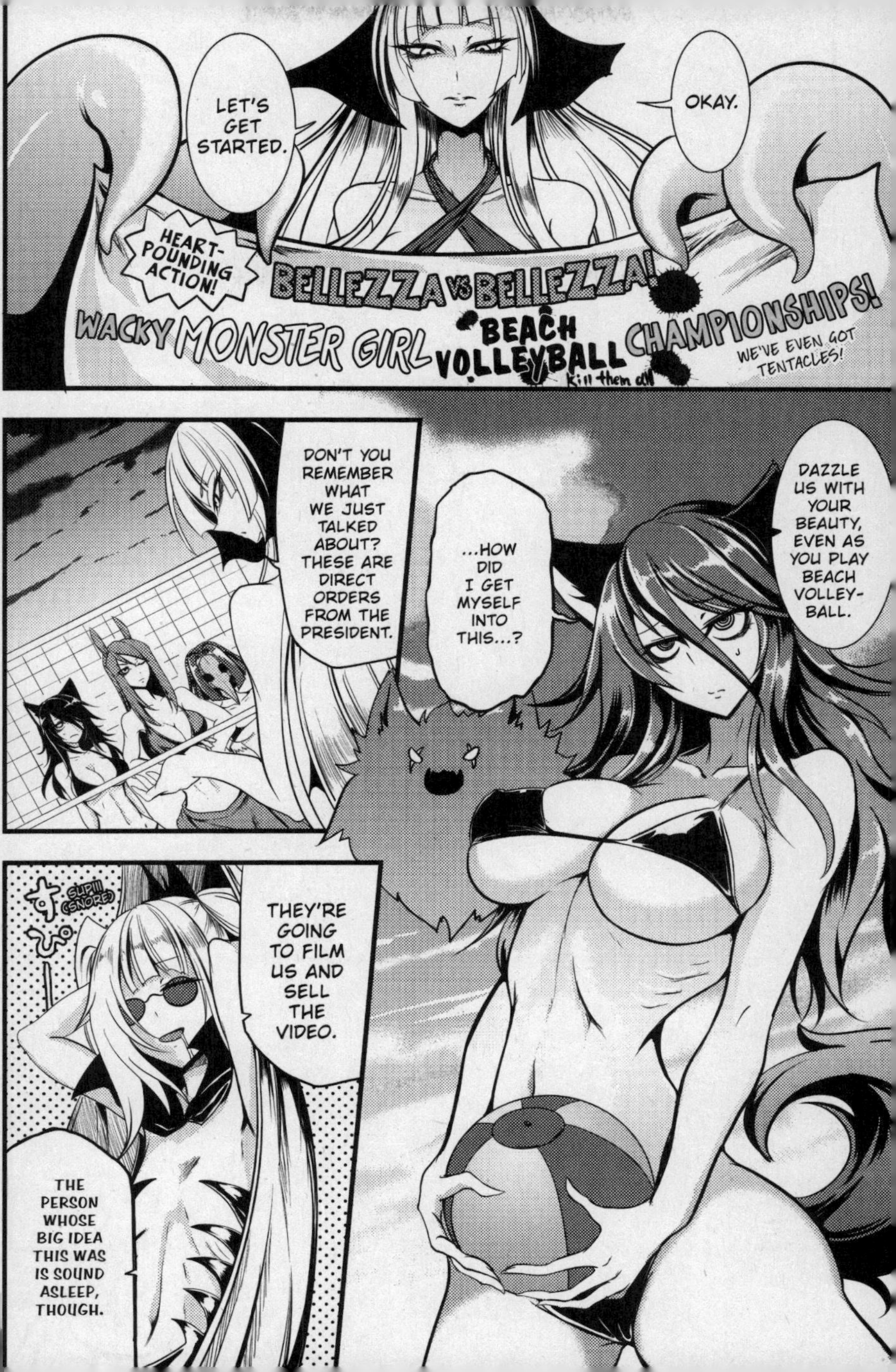
OKAY.
LET'S GET STARTED.
HEART-POUNDING ACTION!
BELLEZZA VS BELLEZZA!
WACKY MONSTER GIRL BEACH VOLLEYBALL CHAMPIONSHIPS!
kill them all
WE'VE EVEN GOT TENTACLES!
DAZZLE US WITH YOUR BEAUTY, EVEN AS YOU PLAY BEACH VOLLEY-BALL.
...HOW DID I GET MYSELF INTO THIS...?
DON'T YOU REMEMBER WHAT WE JUST TALKED ABOUT? THESE ARE DIRECT ORDERS FROM THE PRESIDENT.
THEY'RE GOING TO FILM US AND SELL THE VIDEO.
SUPIII (SNORE)
THE PERSON WHOSE BIG IDEA THIS WAS IS SOUND ASLEEP, THOUGH.

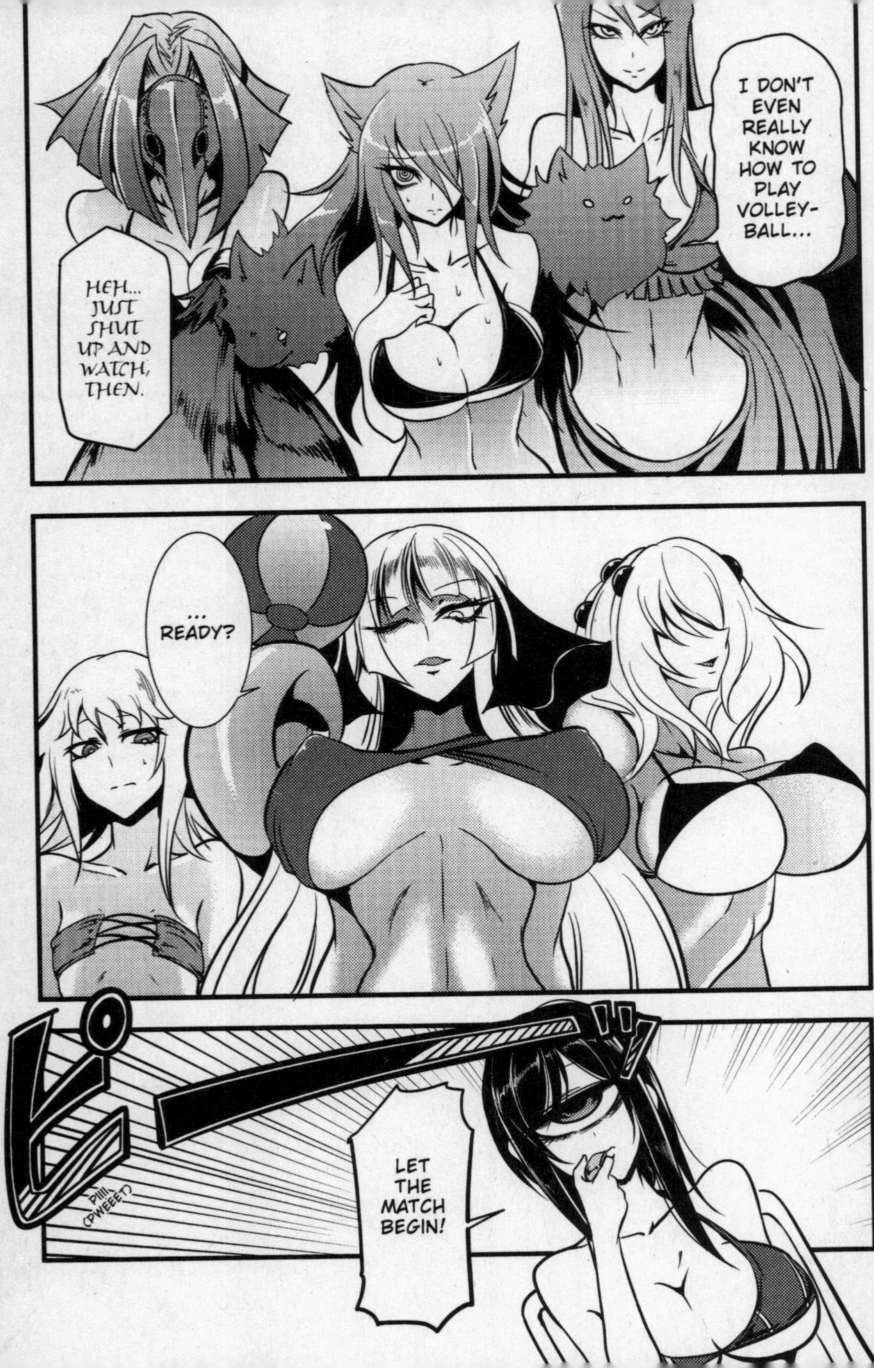
I DON'T EVEN REALLY KNOW HOW TO PLAY VOLLEY-BALL...
HEH... JUST SHUT UP AND WATCH, THEN.
... READY?
LET THE MATCH BEGIN!
PIIII (PWEEET)

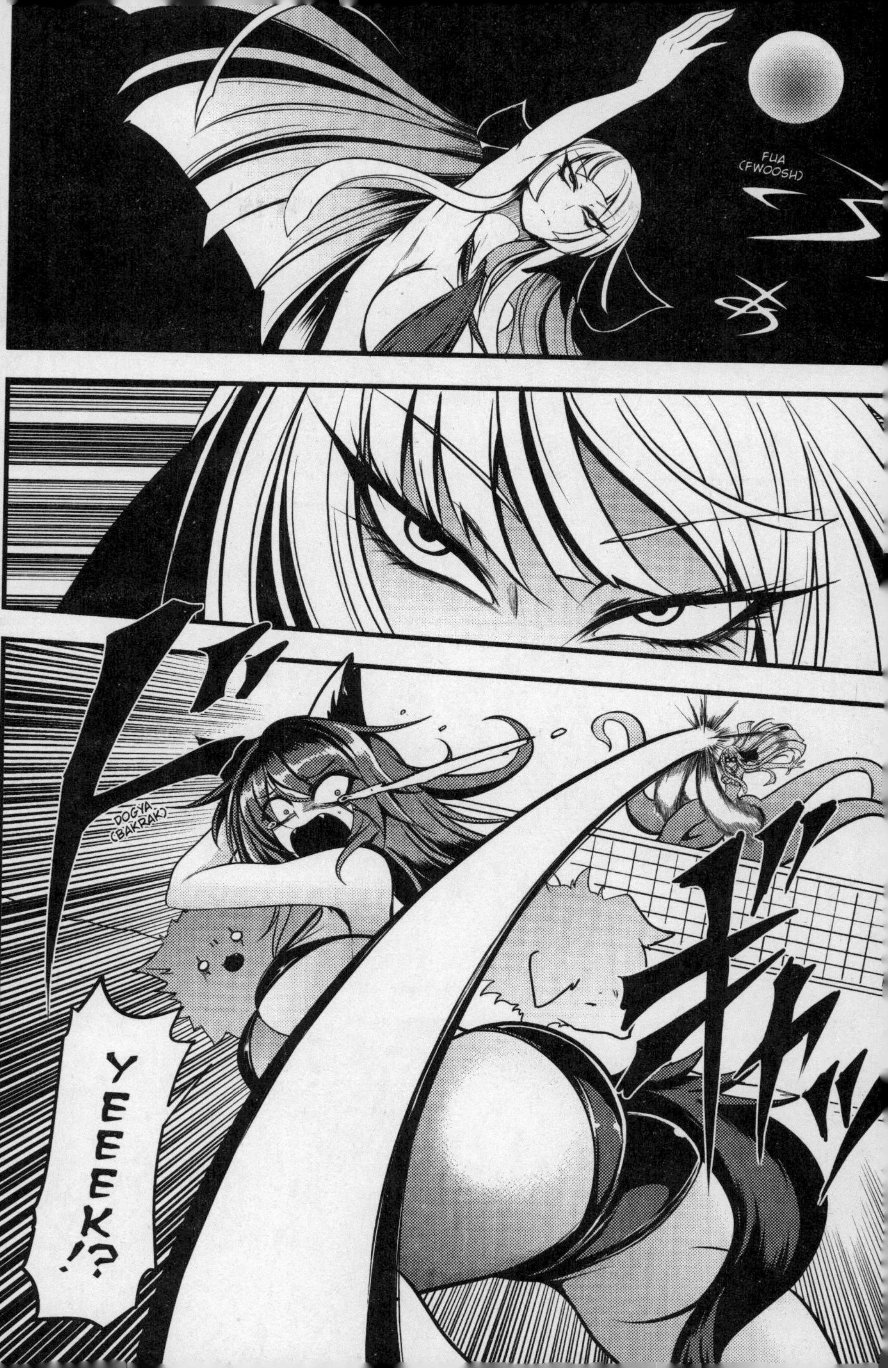
FUA
(FWOOSH)
DOGYA
(BAKRAK)
YEEEEK!?

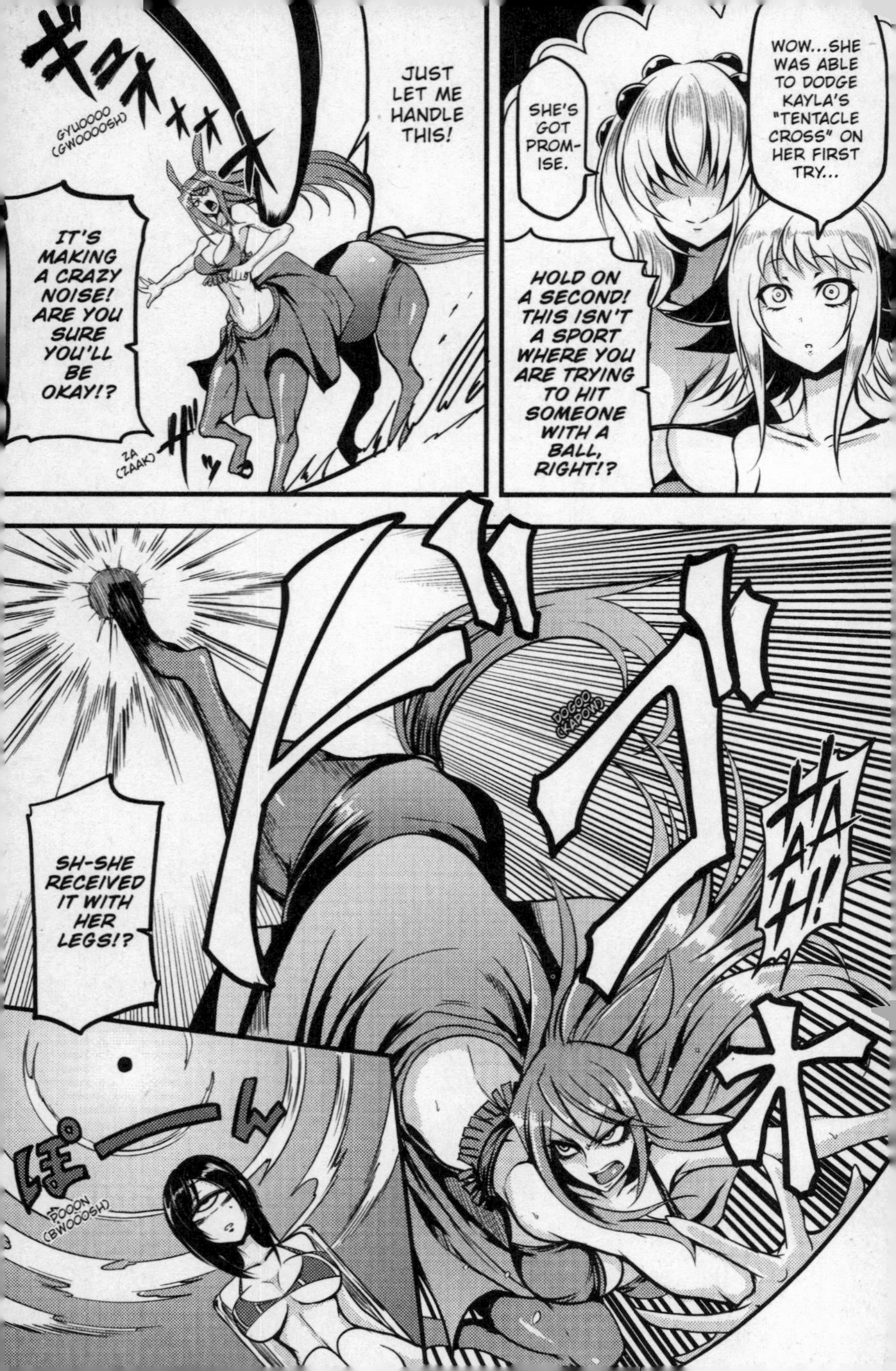

WOW...SHE WAS ABLE TO DODGE KAYLA'S "TENTACLE CROSS" ON HER FIRST TRY...
SHE'S GOT PROMISE.
HOLD ON A SECOND! THIS ISN'T A SPORT WHERE YOU ARE TRYING TO HIT SOMEONE WITH A BALL, RIGHT!?
GYUOOOO (GWOOOOSH)
JUST LET ME HANDLE THIS!
IT'S MAKING A CRAZY NOISE! ARE YOU SURE YOU'LL BE OKAY!?
ZA (ZAAK)
HAAAH!
DOGOO (KAPOW)
SH-SHE RECEIVED IT WITH HER LEGS!?
POOON (BWOOOSH)

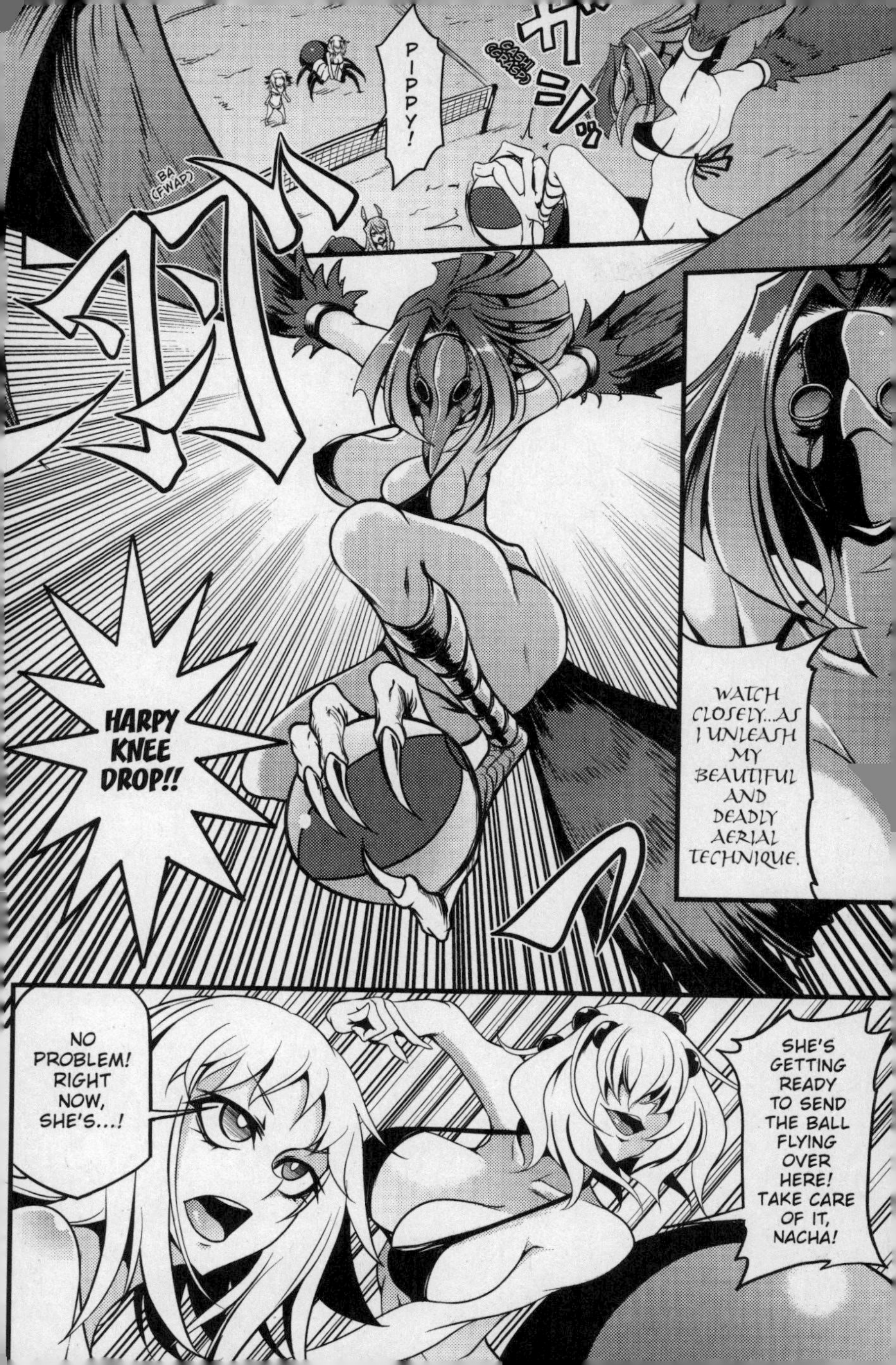

GASHI (GRASP)
PIPPY!
BA (FWAP)
WATCH CLOSELY...AS I UNLEASH MY BEAUTIFUL AND DEADLY AERIAL TECHNIQUE.
HARPY KNEE DROP!!
SHE'S GETTING READY TO SEND THE BALL FLYING OVER HERE! TAKE CARE OF IT, NACHA!
NO PROBLEM! RIGHT NOW, SHE'S...!

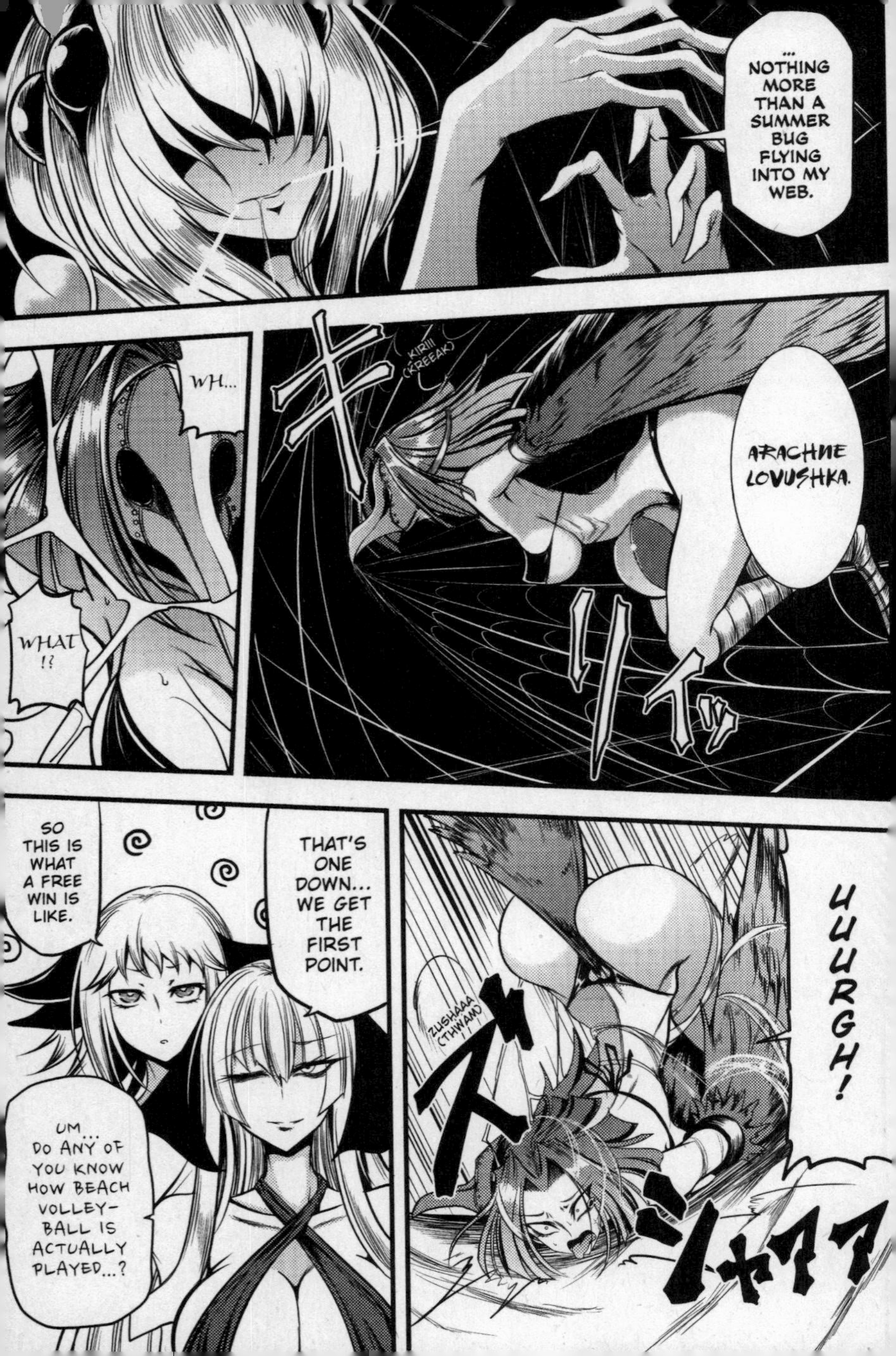

... NOTHING MORE THAN A SUMMER BUG FLYING INTO MY WEB.
KIRIII (KREEAK)
ARACHNE LOVUSHKA.
WH...
WHAT !?
UUURGH!
ZUSHAAA (THWAM)
THAT'S ONE DOWN... WE GET THE FIRST POINT.
SO THIS IS WHAT A FREE WIN IS LIKE.
UM... DO ANY OF YOU KNOW HOW BEACH VOLLEY-BALL IS ACTUALLY PLAYED...?

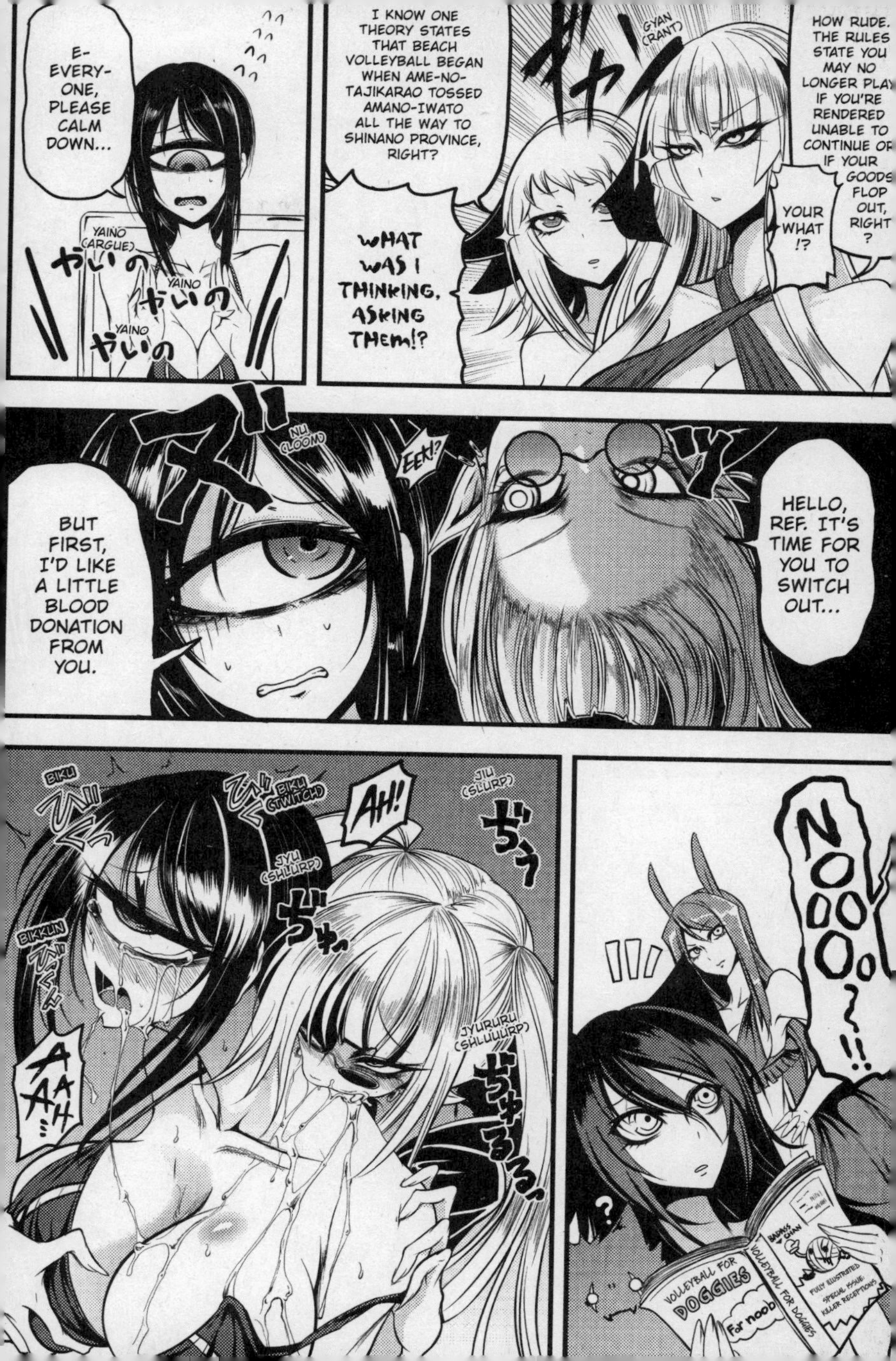
HOW RUDE. THE RULES STATE YOU MAY NO LONGER PLAY IF YOU'RE RENDERED UNABLE TO CONTINUE OR IF YOUR GOODS FLOP OUT, RIGHT?
GYAN (RANT)
I KNOW ONE THEORY STATES THAT BEACH VOLLEYBALL BEGAN WHEN AME-NO-TAJIKARAO TOSSED AMANO-IWATO ALL THE WAY TO SHINANO PROVINCE, RIGHT?
YOUR WHAT!?
WHAT WAS I THINKING, ASKING THEM!?
E-EVERYONE, PLEASE CALM DOWN...
YAINO (ARGUE)
やいの
YAINO
やいの
YAINO
やいの
HELLO, REF. IT'S TIME FOR YOU TO SWITCH OUT...
EEK!?
NU (LOOM)
BUT FIRST, I'D LIKE A LITTLE BLOOD DONATION FROM YOU.
NOOOOoo~!!
!!!
?
VOLLEYBALL FOR DOGGIES
BADASS CHAN
FULLY ILLUSTRATED SPECIAL ISSUE: KILLER RECEPTIONS
VOLLEYBALL FOR DOGGIES
For noob
JIU (SLURP)
AH!
BIKU (TWITCH)
BIKU
JYU (SHLURP)
BIKKUN
JYURURU (SHLUUURP)
AAAH...

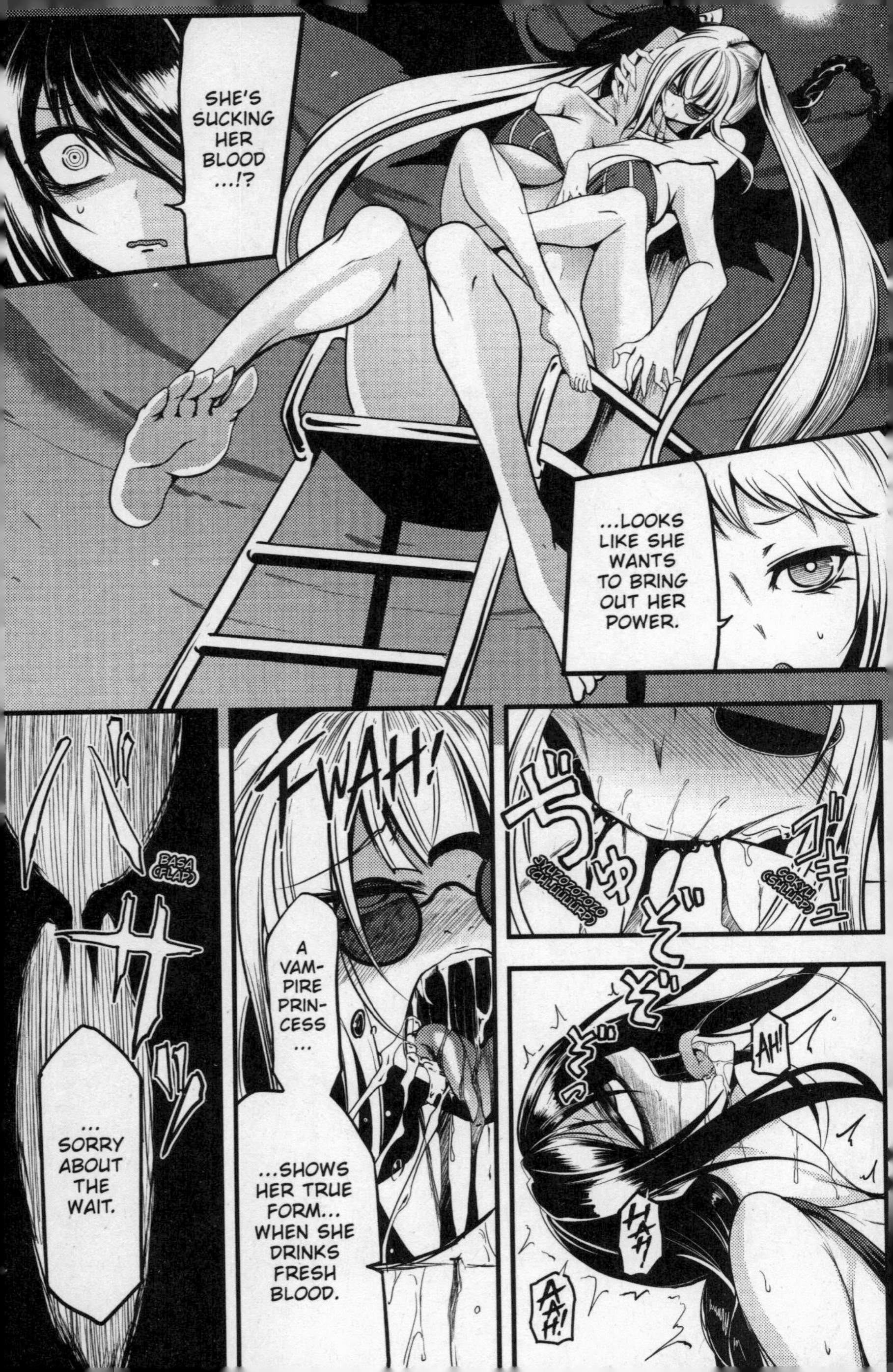
SHE'S SUCKING HER BLOOD ...!?
...LOOKS LIKE SHE WANTS TO BRING OUT HER POWER.
GOKYU (GLUPP)
JYUZOZOZOZO (CHLLLLLURP)
AH!
HAH
AAH!
FWAH!
A VAMPIRE PRINCESS ...
...SHOWS HER TRUE FORM... WHEN SHE DRINKS FRESH BLOOD.
BASA (FLAP)
... SORRY ABOUT THE WAIT.

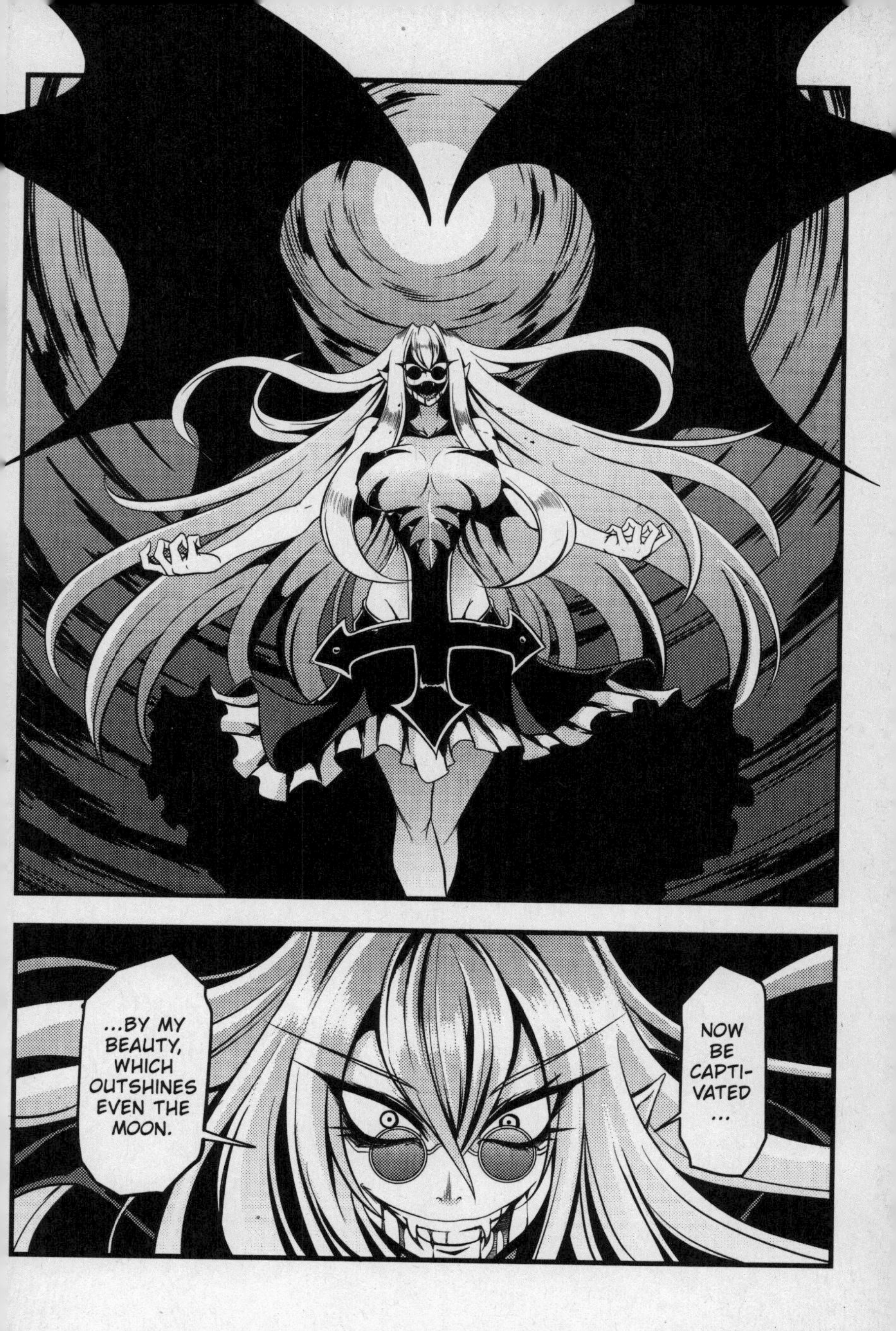
NOW BE CAPTIVATED ...
...BY MY BEAUTY, WHICH OUTSHINES EVEN THE MOON.

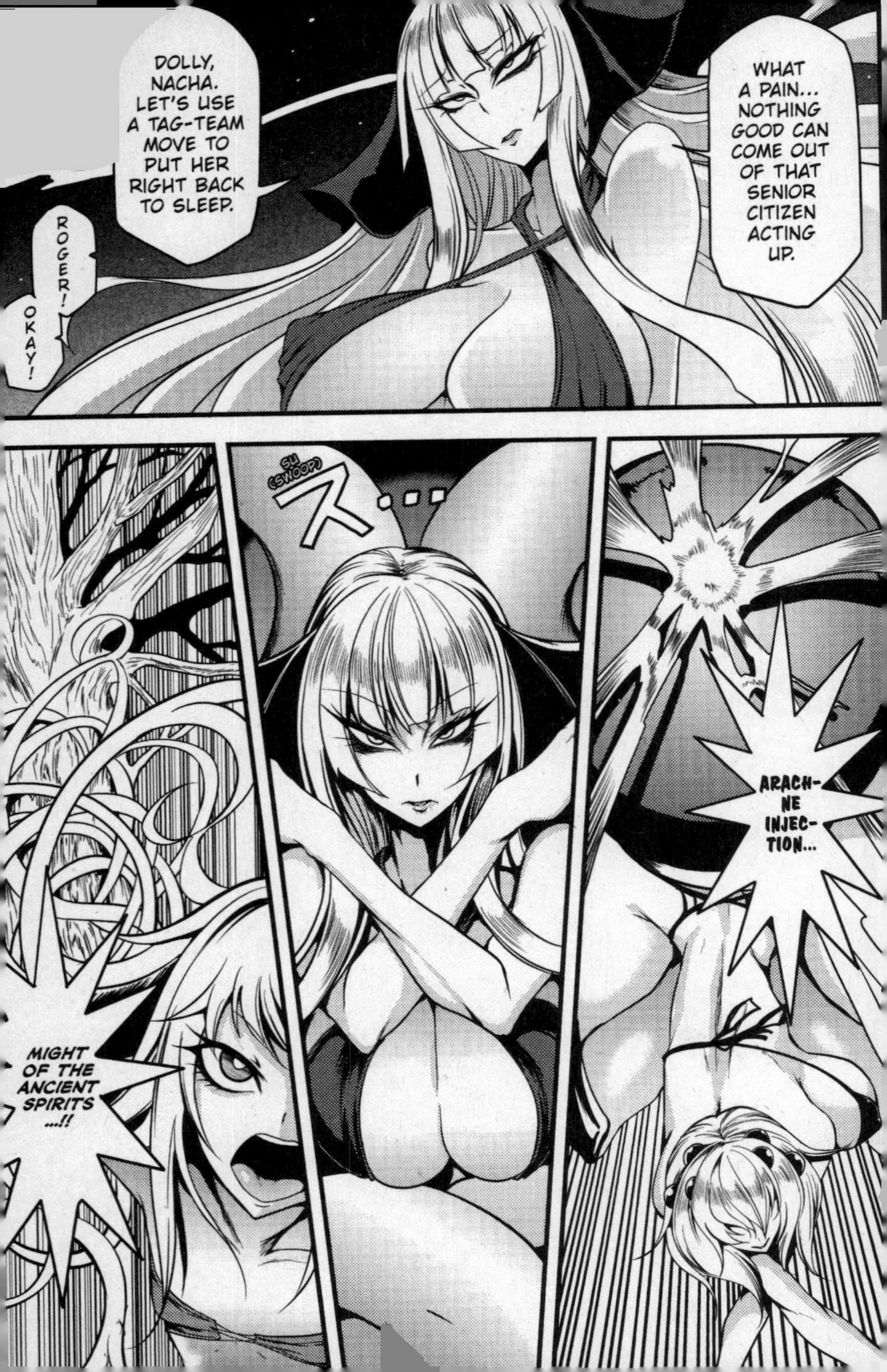
WHAT A PAIN... NOTHING GOOD CAN COME OUT OF THAT SENIOR CITIZEN ACTING UP.
DOLLY, NACHA. LET'S USE A TAG-TEAM MOVE TO PUT HER RIGHT BACK TO SLEEP.
ROGER!
OKAY!
ARACHNE INJECTION...
SU (SWOOP)
ス...
MIGHT OF THE ANCIENT SPIRITS ...!!

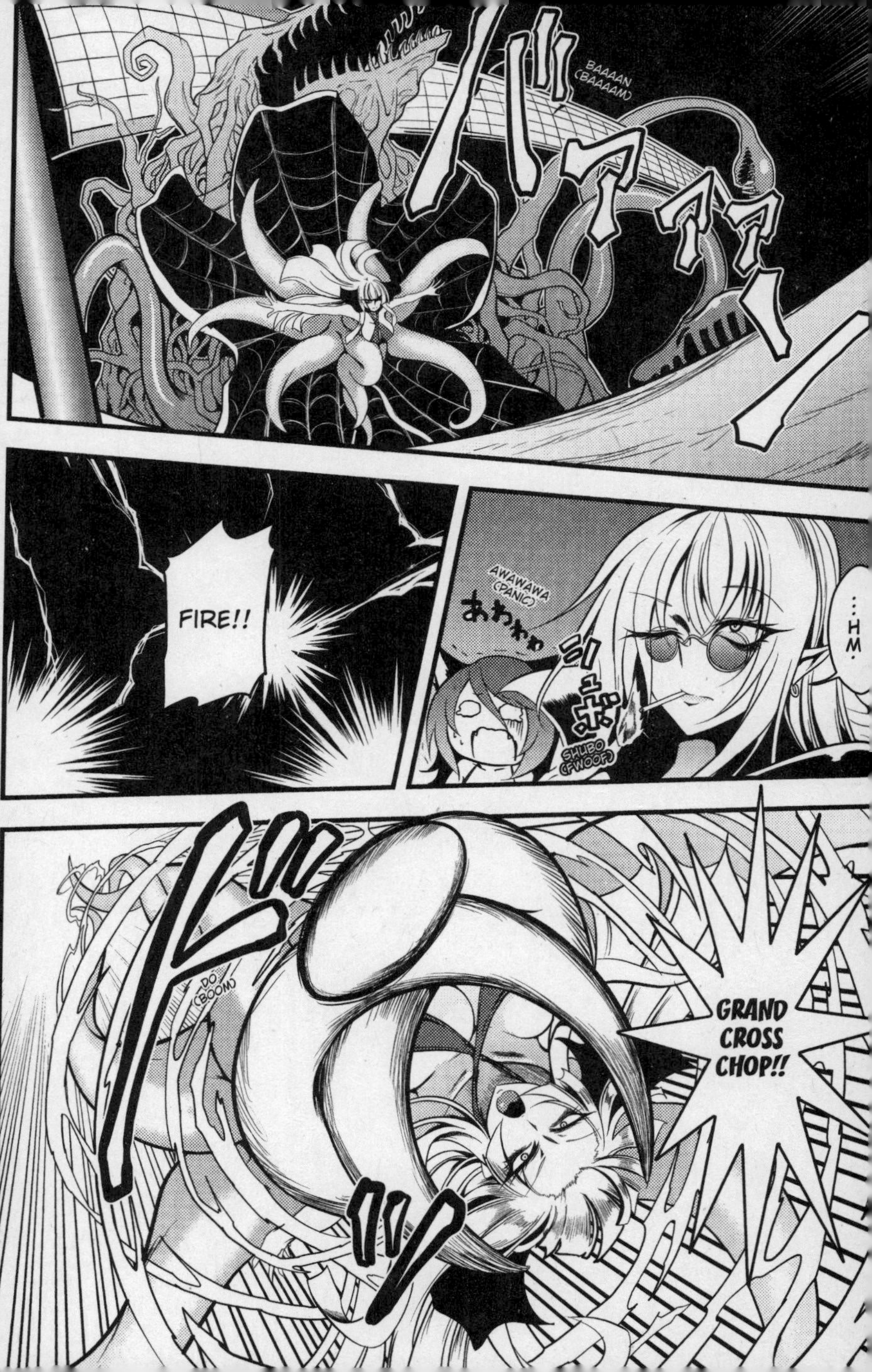
BAAAAN
(BAAAAM)
…HM.
AWAWAWA
(PANIC)
あわわ
シュボ
SHUBO
(FWOOF)
FIRE!!
GRAND CROSS CHOP!!
DO
(BOOM)

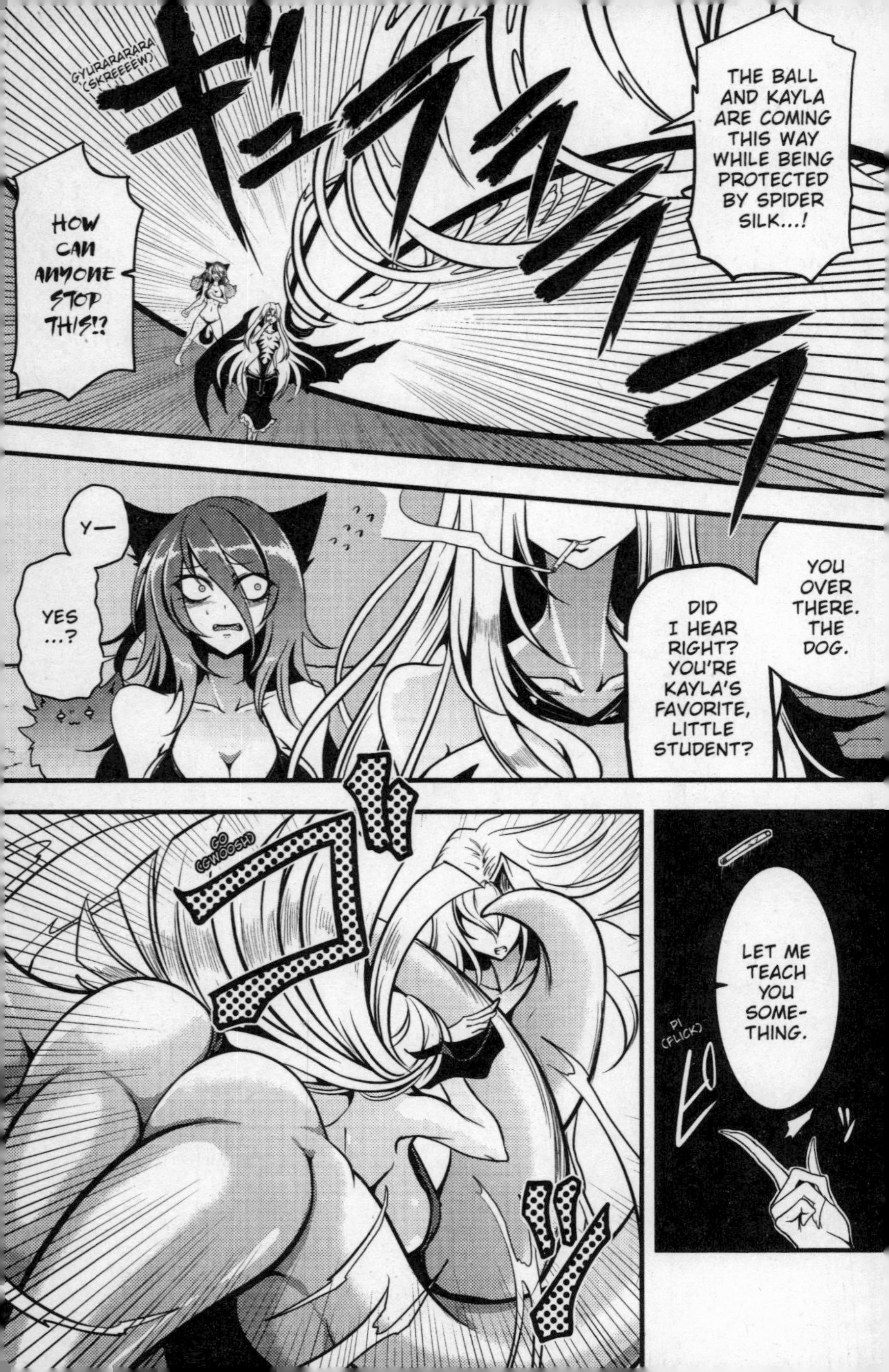
THE BALL AND KAYLA ARE COMING THIS WAY WHILE BEING PROTECTED BY SPIDER SILK...!
GYURARARARA (SKREEEEW)
HOW CAN ANYONE STOP THIS!?
YOU OVER THERE. THE DOG.
DID I HEAR RIGHT? YOU'RE KAYLA'S FAVORITE, LITTLE STUDENT?
Y—
YES ...?
LET ME TEACH YOU SOME-THING.
PI (FLICK)
GO (GWOOSH)

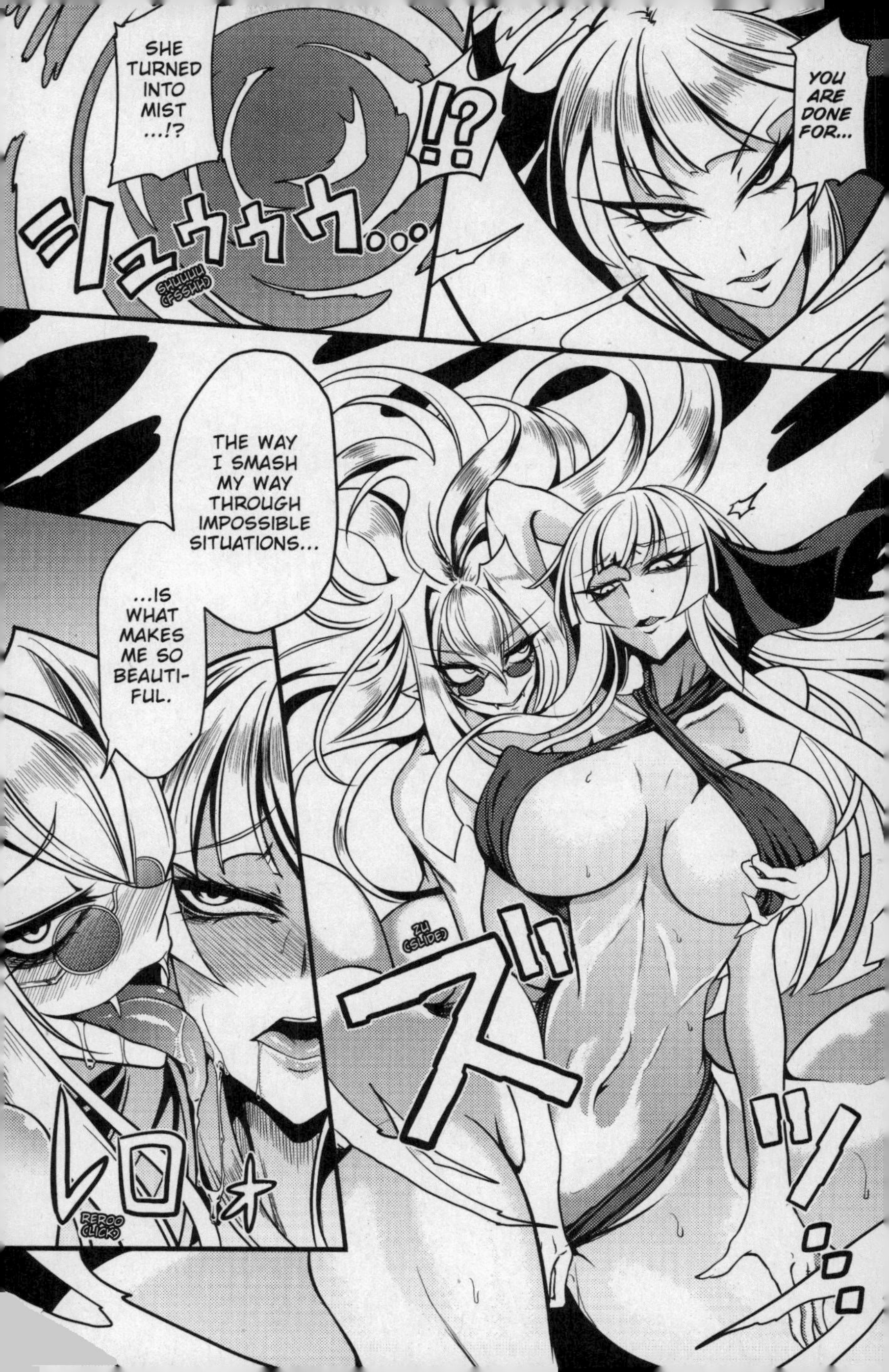
YOU ARE DONE FOR...
SHE TURNED INTO MIST ...!?
!?
SHUUUU (PSSHH)
THE WAY I SMASH MY WAY THROUGH IMPOSSIBLE SITUATIONS...
...IS WHAT MAKES ME SO BEAUTIFUL.
ZU (SLIDE)
REROO (LICK)

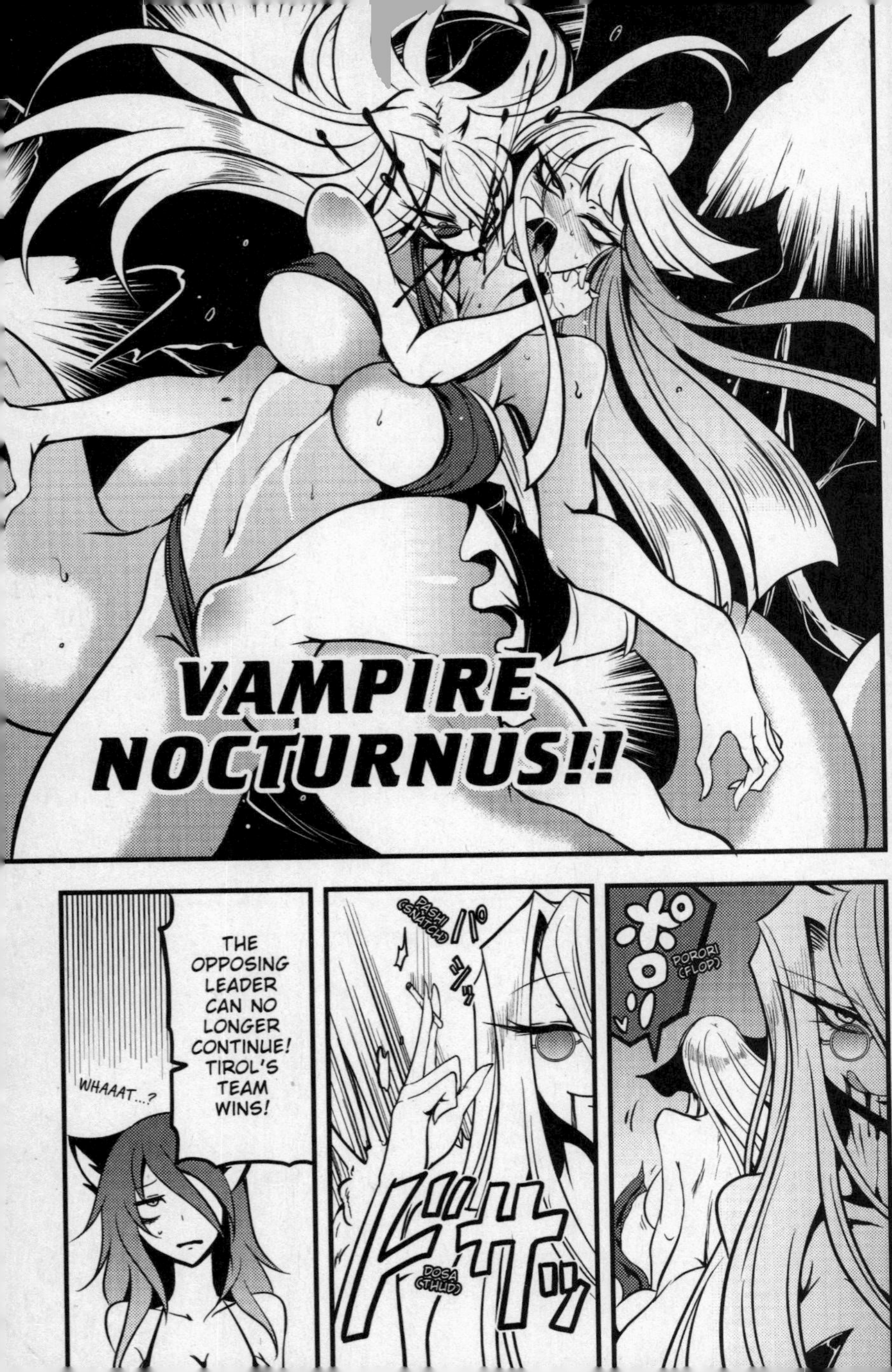
VAMPIRE NOCTURNUS!!
PORORI (FLOP)
PASHI (SNATCH)
DOSA (THUD)
THE OPPOSING LEADER CAN NO LONGER CONTINUE! TIROL'S TEAM WINS!
WHAAAT...?

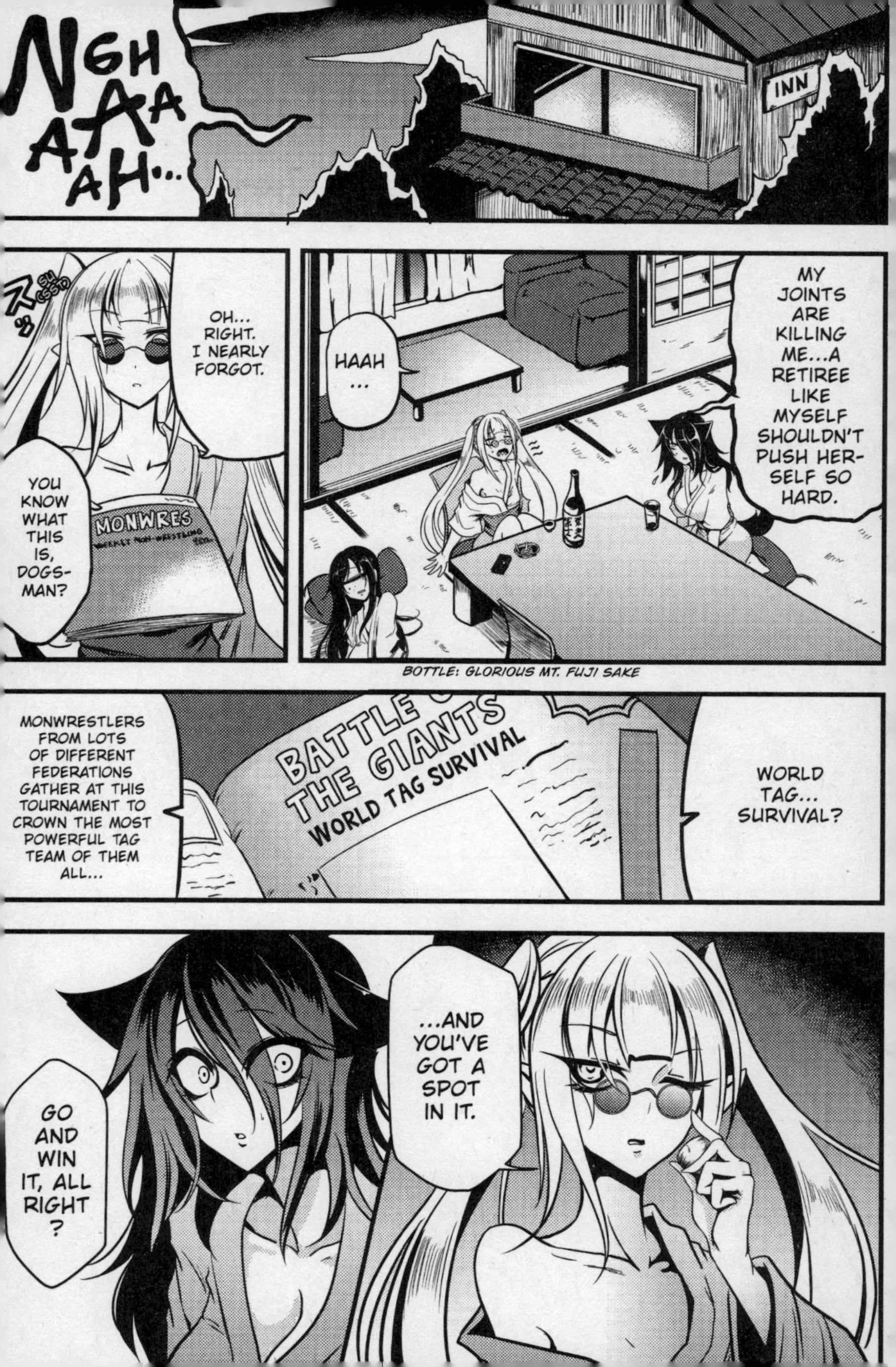
NGH AAAAH...
INN
MY JOINTS ARE KILLING ME...A RETIREE LIKE MYSELF SHOULDN'T PUSH HER-SELF SO HARD.
HAAH...
OH... RIGHT. I NEARLY FORGOT.
YOU KNOW WHAT THIS IS, DOGS-MAN?
MONWRES
BOTTLE: GLORIOUS MT. FUJI SAKE
WORLD TAG... SURVIVAL?
BATTLE
THE GIANTS
WORLD TAG SURVIVAL
MONWRESTLERS FROM LOTS OF DIFFERENT FEDERATIONS GATHER AT THIS TOURNAMENT TO CROWN THE MOST POWERFUL TAG TEAM OF THEM ALL...
...AND YOU'VE GOT A SPOT IN IT.
GO AND WIN IT, ALL RIGHT?

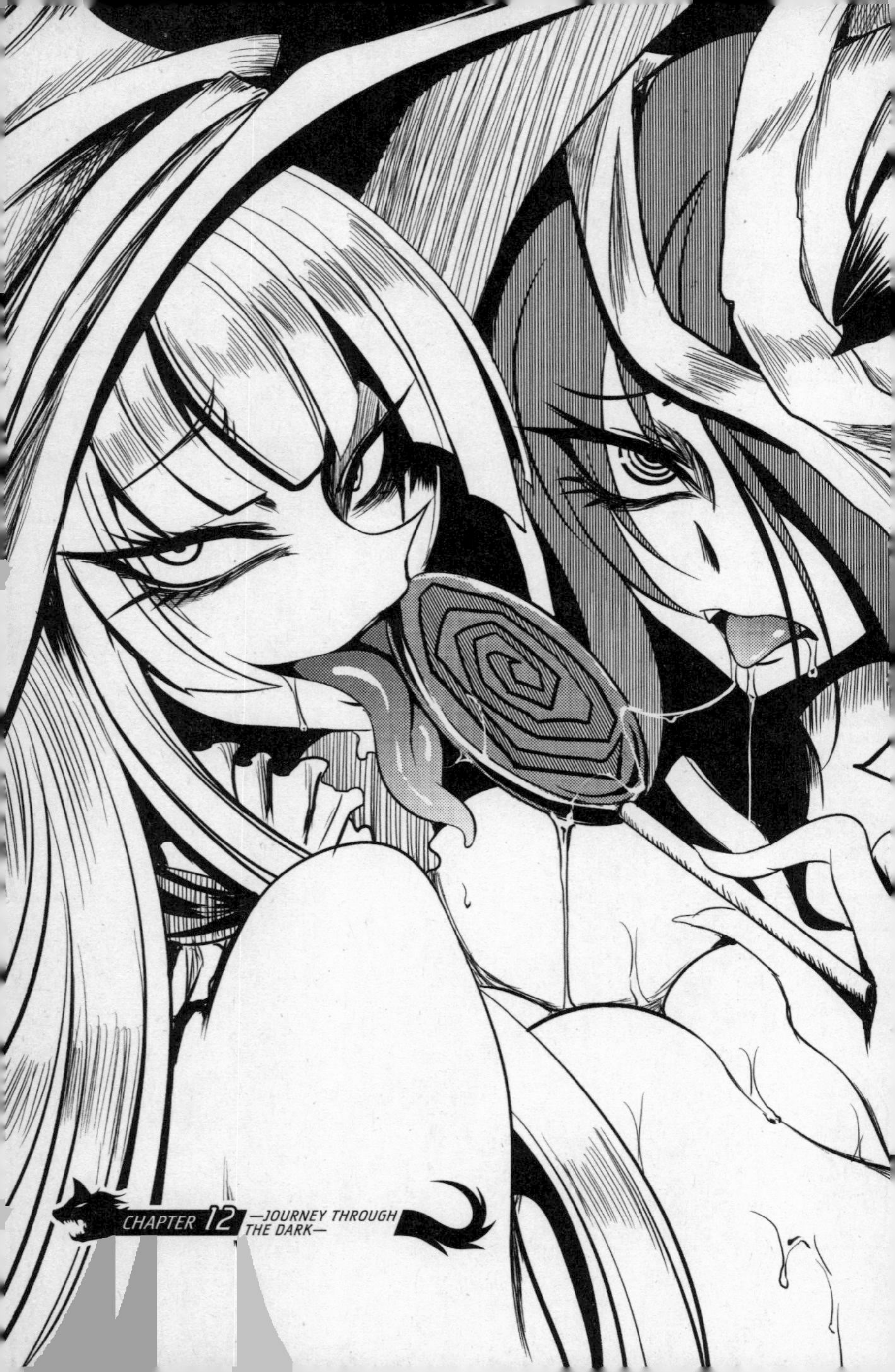
CHAPTER 12
—JOURNEY THROUGH THE DARK—

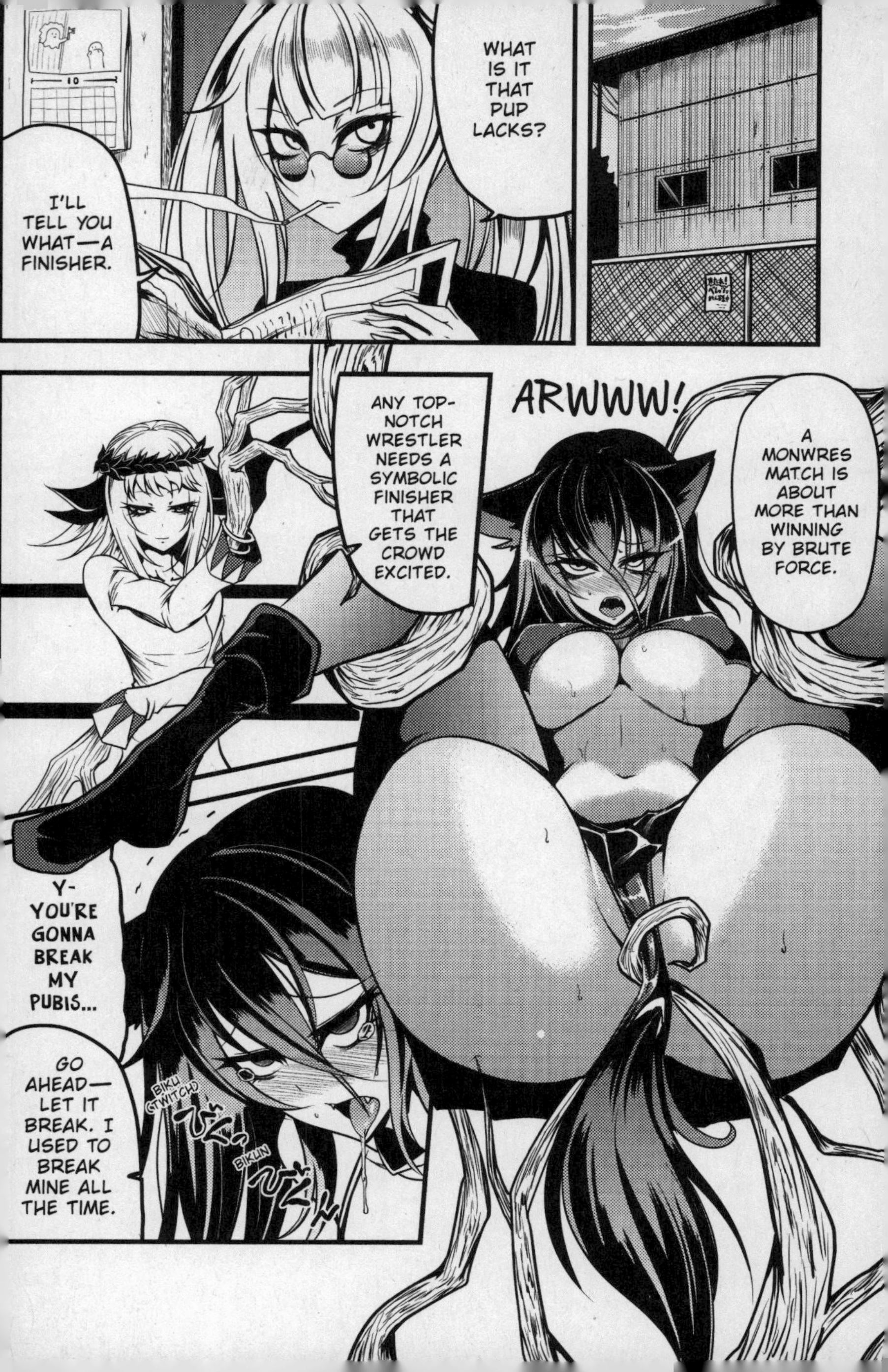
WHAT IS IT THAT PUP LACKS?
I'LL TELL YOU WHAT—A FINISHER.
A MONWRES MATCH IS ABOUT MORE THAN WINNING BY BRUTE FORCE.
ARWWW!
ANY TOP-NOTCH WRESTLER NEEDS A SYMBOLIC FINISHER THAT GETS THE CROWD EXCITED.
Y-YOU'RE GONNA BREAK MY PUBIS...
BIKU (TWITCH)
BIKUN
GO AHEAD—LET IT BREAK. I USED TO BREAK MINE ALL THE TIME.

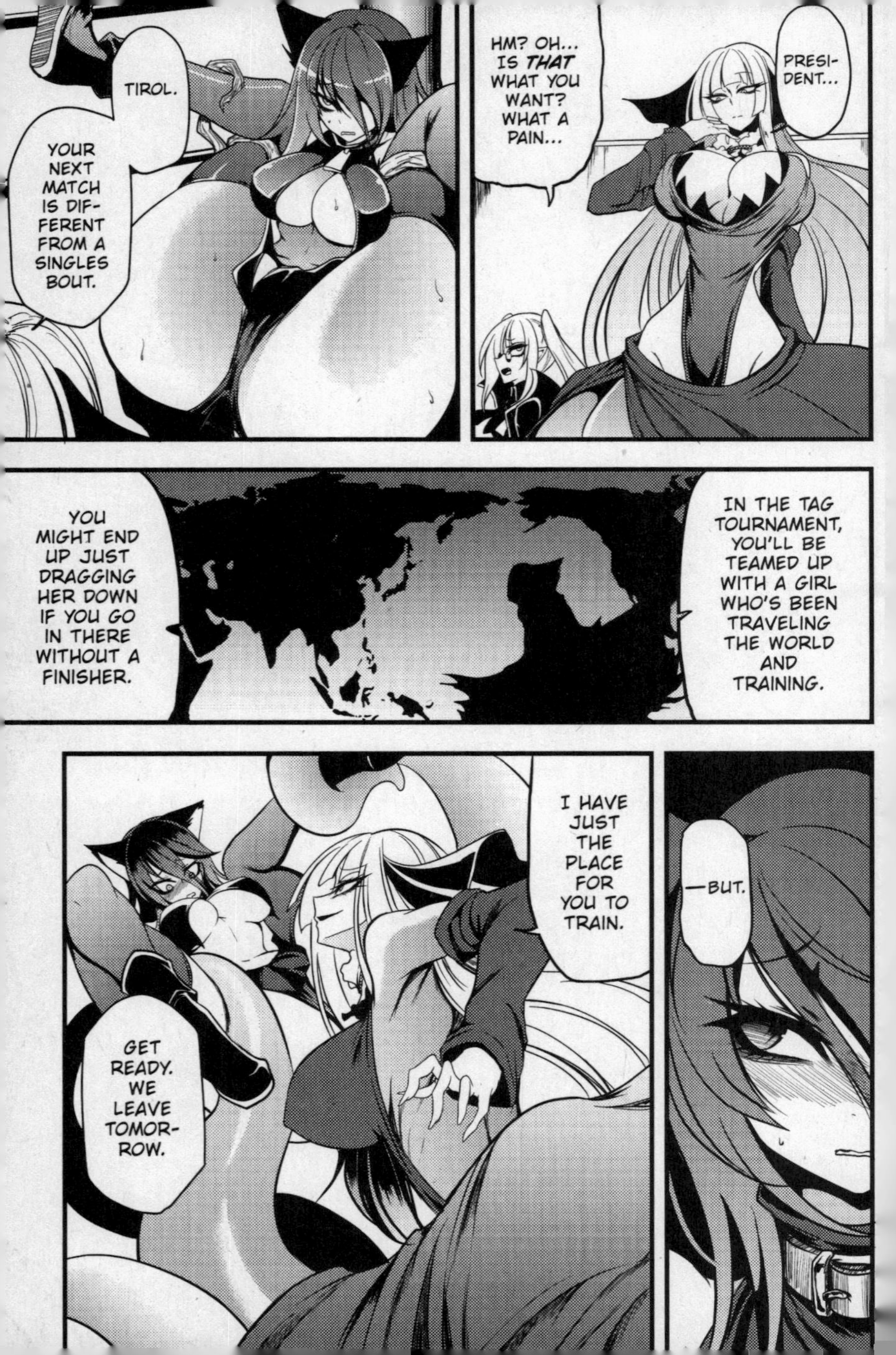
PRESIDENT...
HM? OH... IS *THAT* WHAT YOU WANT? WHAT A PAIN...
TIROL.
YOUR NEXT MATCH IS DIFFERENT FROM A SINGLES BOUT.
IN THE TAG TOURNAMENT, YOU'LL BE TEAMED UP WITH A GIRL WHO'S BEEN TRAVELING THE WORLD AND TRAINING.
YOU MIGHT END UP JUST DRAGGING HER DOWN IF YOU GO IN THERE WITHOUT A FINISHER.
—BUT.
I HAVE JUST THE PLACE FOR YOU TO TRAIN.
GET READY. WE LEAVE TOMORROW.

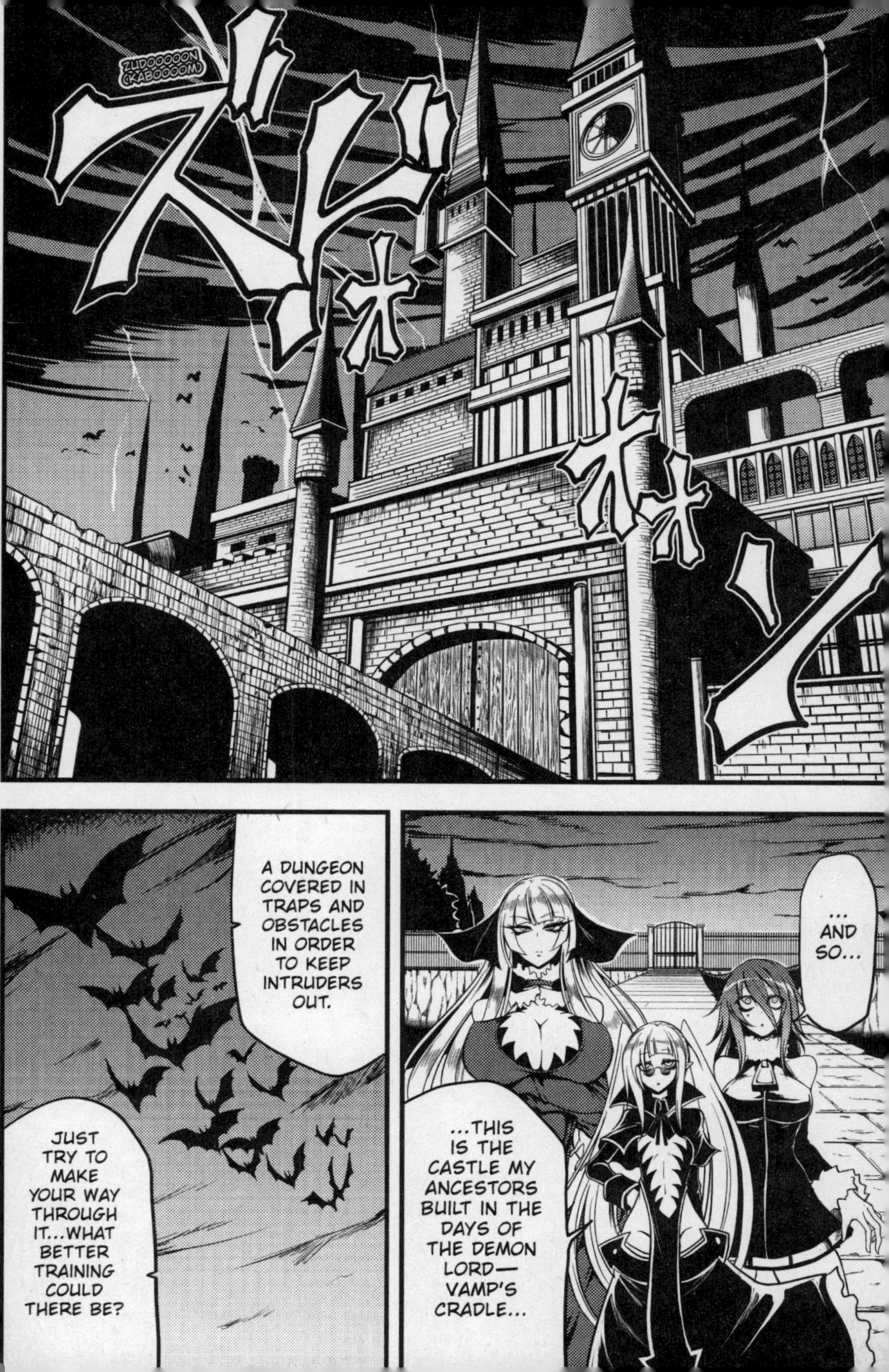
ZUDOOOOON (KABOOOOM)
...AND SO...
...THIS IS THE CASTLE MY ANCESTORS BUILT IN THE DAYS OF THE DEMON LORD—VAMP'S CRADLE...
A DUNGEON COVERED IN TRAPS AND OBSTACLES IN ORDER TO KEEP INTRUDERS OUT.
JUST TRY TO MAKE YOUR WAY THROUGH IT...WHAT BETTER TRAINING COULD THERE BE?

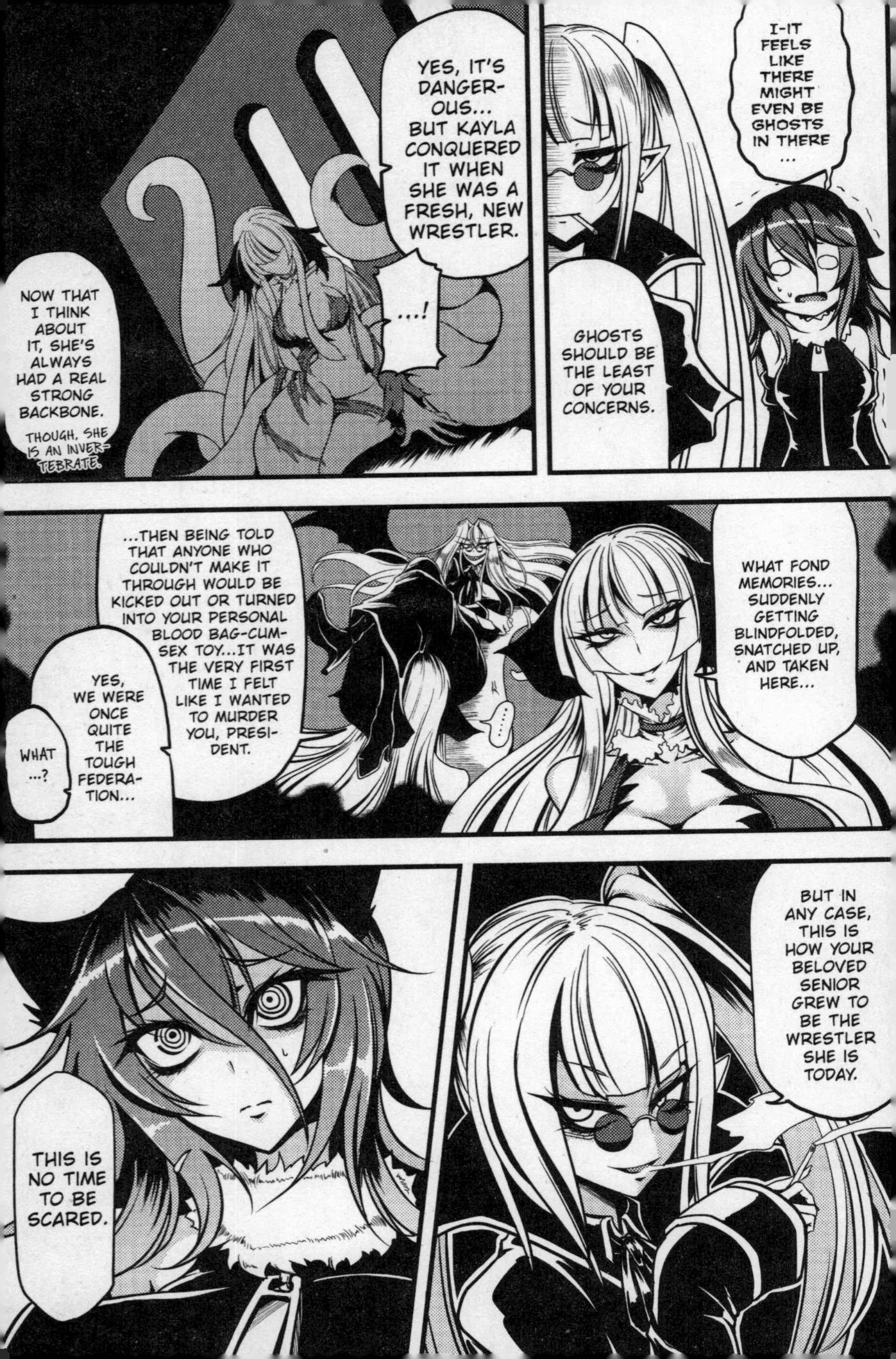
I-IT FEELS LIKE THERE MIGHT EVEN BE GHOSTS IN THERE ...
GHOSTS SHOULD BE THE LEAST OF YOUR CONCERNS.
YES, IT'S DANGER-OUS... BUT KAYLA CONQUERED IT WHEN SHE WAS A FRESH, NEW WRESTLER.
...!
NOW THAT I THINK ABOUT IT, SHE'S ALWAYS HAD A REAL STRONG BACKBONE.
THOUGH, SHE IS AN INVER-TEBRATE.
WHAT FOND MEMORIES... SUDDENLY GETTING BLINDFOLDED, SNATCHED UP, AND TAKEN HERE...
...THEN BEING TOLD THAT ANYONE WHO COULDN'T MAKE IT THROUGH WOULD BE KICKED OUT OR TURNED INTO YOUR PERSONAL BLOOD BAG-CUM-SEX TOY...IT WAS THE VERY FIRST TIME I FELT LIKE I WANTED TO MURDER YOU, PRESI-DENT.
YES, WE WERE ONCE QUITE THE TOUGH FEDERA-TION...
WHAT ...?
BUT IN ANY CASE, THIS IS HOW YOUR BELOVED SENIOR GREW TO BE THE WRESTLER SHE IS TODAY.
THIS IS NO TIME TO BE SCARED.

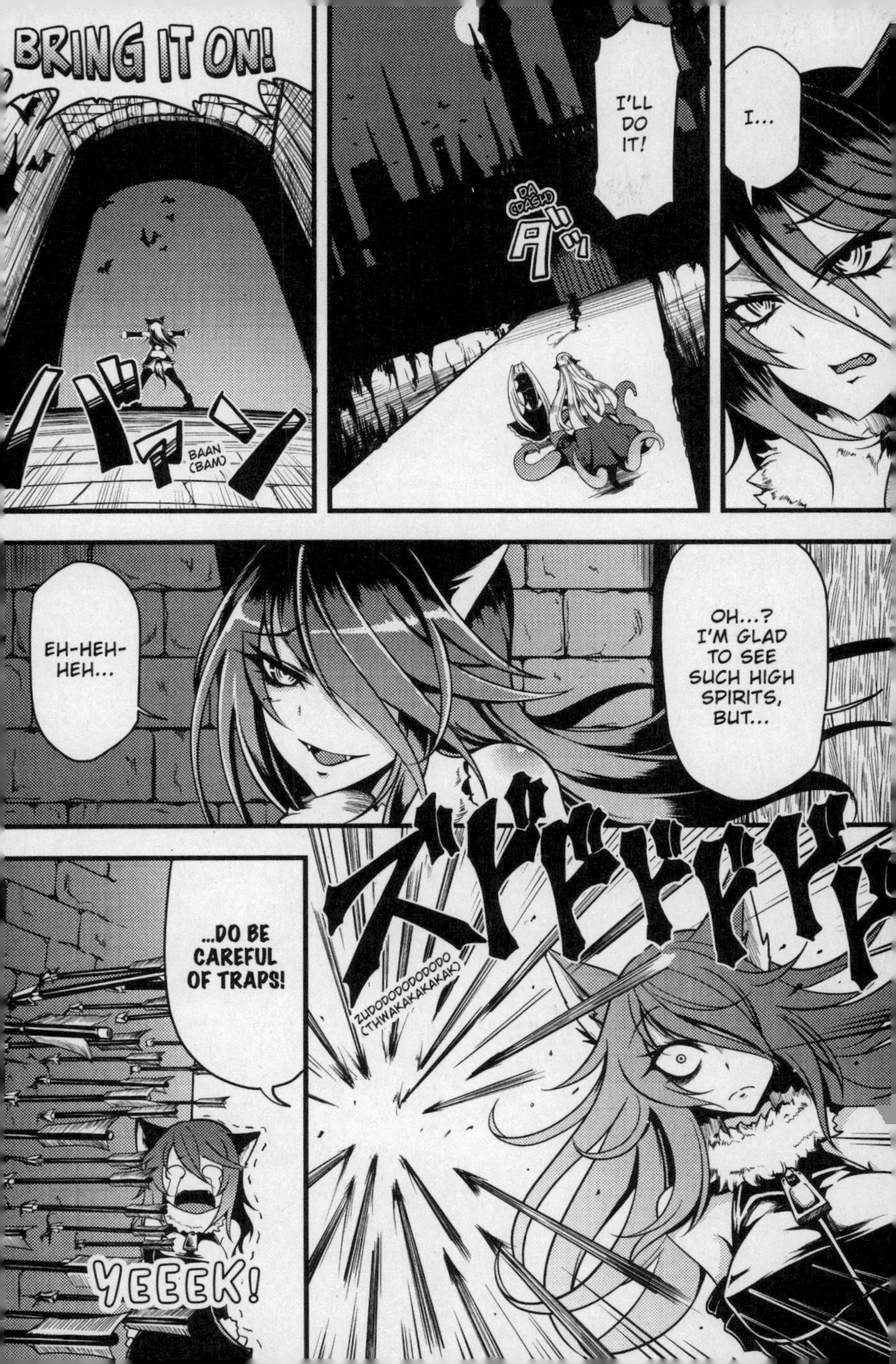
I...
I'LL DO IT!
DA (DASH)
BRING IT ON!
BAAN (BAM)
OH...? I'M GLAD TO SEE SUCH HIGH SPIRITS, BUT...
EH-HEH-HEH...
ZUDODODODODODO (THWAKAKAKAKAK)
...DO BE CAREFUL OF TRAPS!
YEEEK!

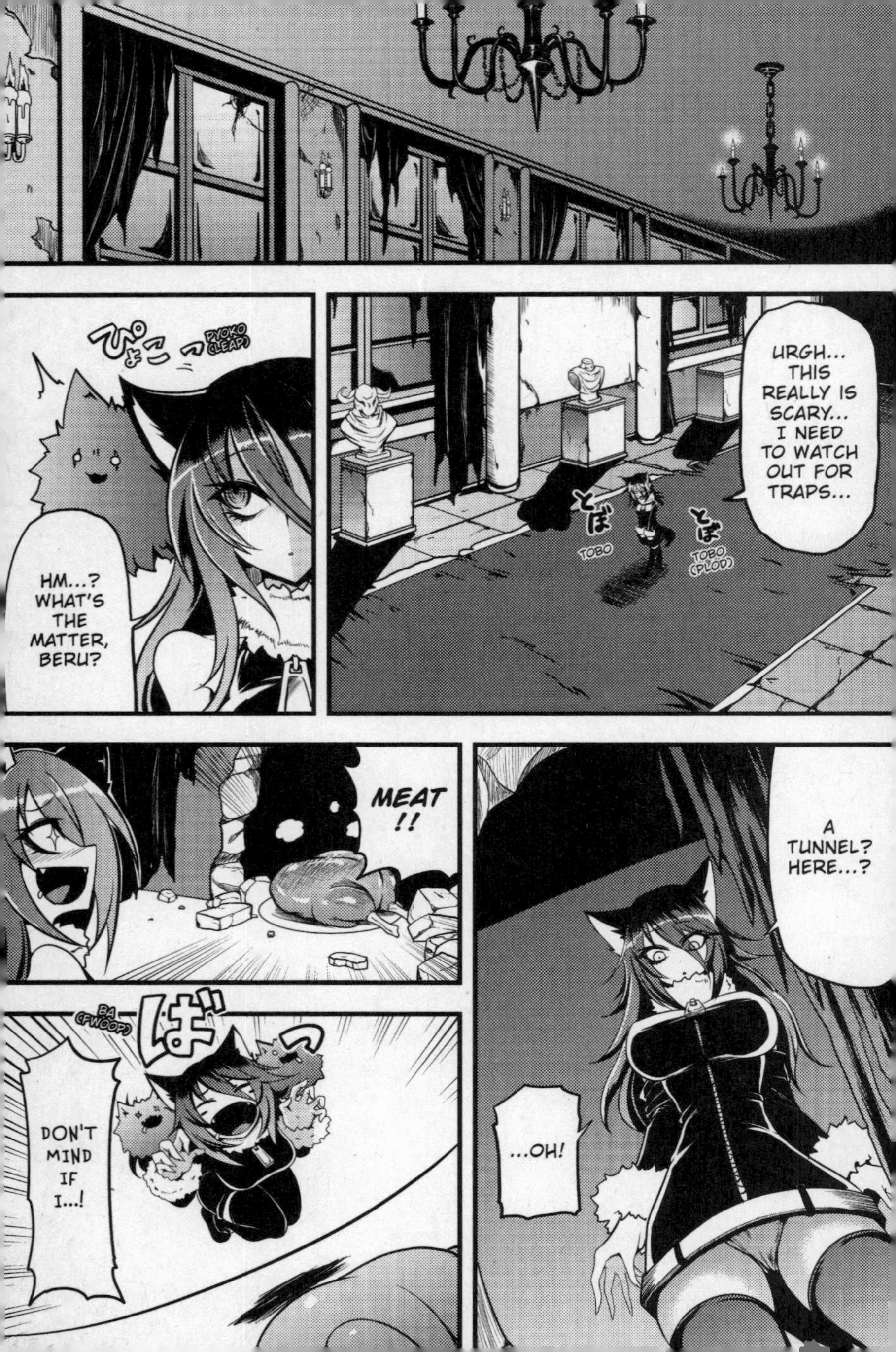
URGH... THIS REALLY IS SCARY... I NEED TO WATCH OUT FOR TRAPS...
とぼ
TOBO
とぼ
TOBO (PLOD)
ぴょこっ
PYOKO (LEAP)
HM...? WHAT'S THE MATTER, BERU?
A TUNNEL? HERE...?
...OH!
MEAT!!
ばっ
BA (FWOOP)
DON'T MIND IF I...!

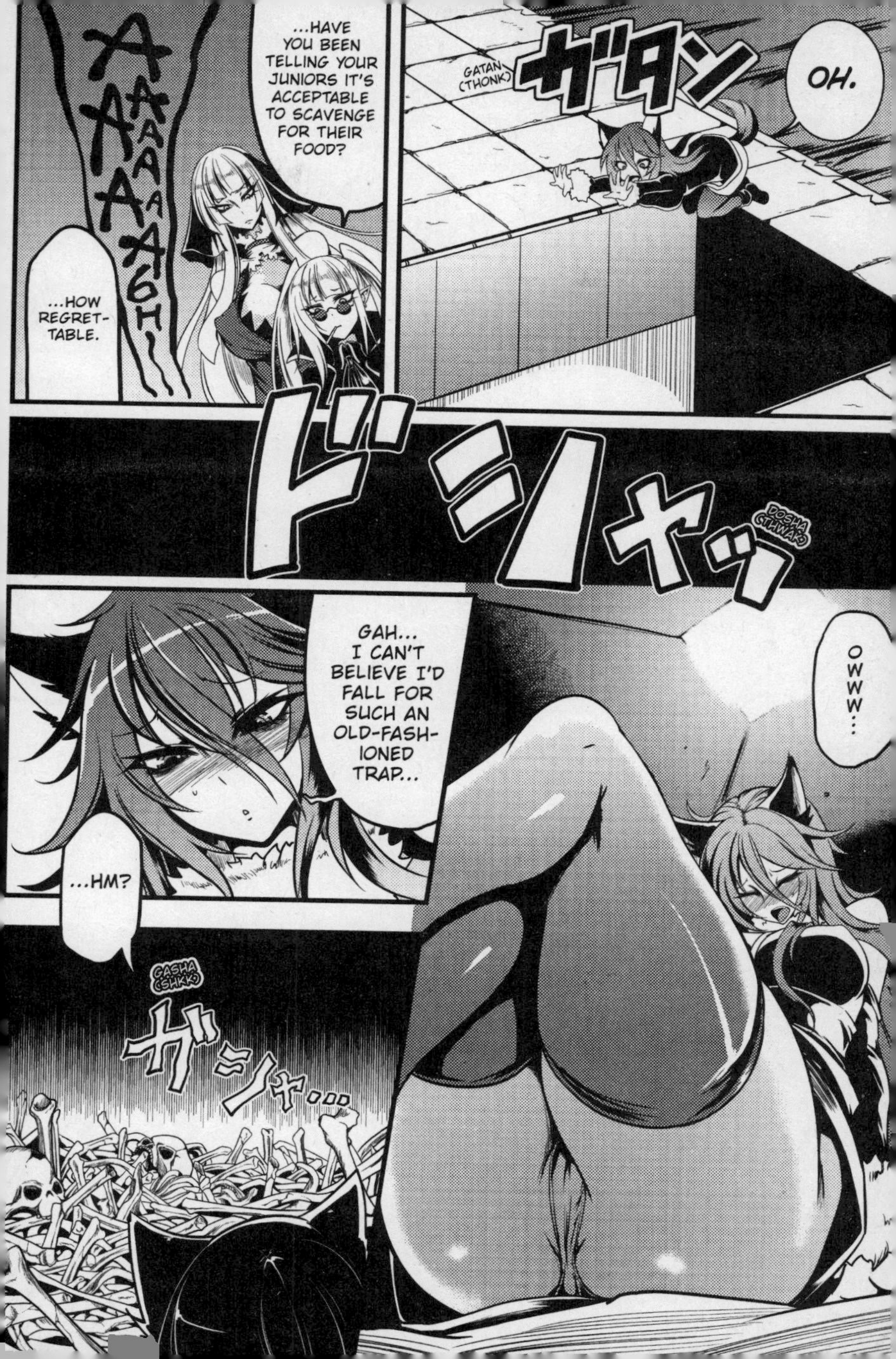
GATAN (THONK)
ガタン
OH.
...HAVE YOU BEEN TELLING YOUR JUNIORS IT'S ACCEPTABLE TO SCAVENGE FOR THEIR FOOD?
AAAAAAAAAGH~
...HOW REGRET-TABLE.
ドシャッ
DOSHA (THWAK)
OWWW...
GAH... I CAN'T BELIEVE I'D FALL FOR SUCH AN OLD-FASHIONED TRAP...
...HM?
GASHA (SHKK)
ガシャ...

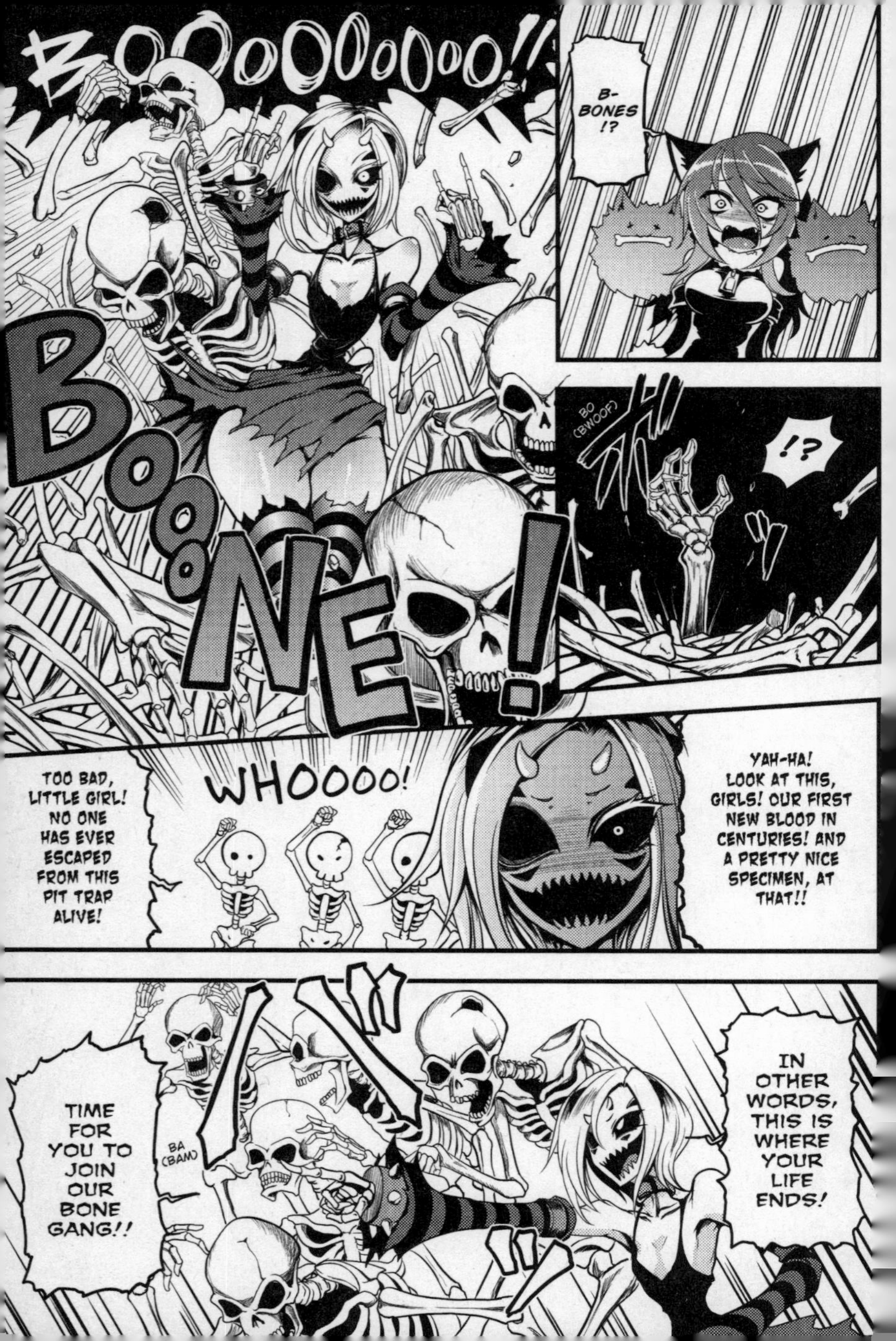

B-BONES!?
BO (BWOOF)
!?
BOOOOOOOOOO!!
BOOONE!
YAH-HA! LOOK AT THIS, GIRLS! OUR FIRST NEW BLOOD IN CENTURIES! AND A PRETTY NICE SPECIMEN, AT THAT!!
WHOOOO!
TOO BAD, LITTLE GIRL! NO ONE HAS EVER ESCAPED FROM THIS PIT TRAP ALIVE!
IN OTHER WORDS, THIS IS WHERE YOUR LIFE ENDS!
BA (BAM)
TIME FOR YOU TO JOIN OUR BONE GANG!!

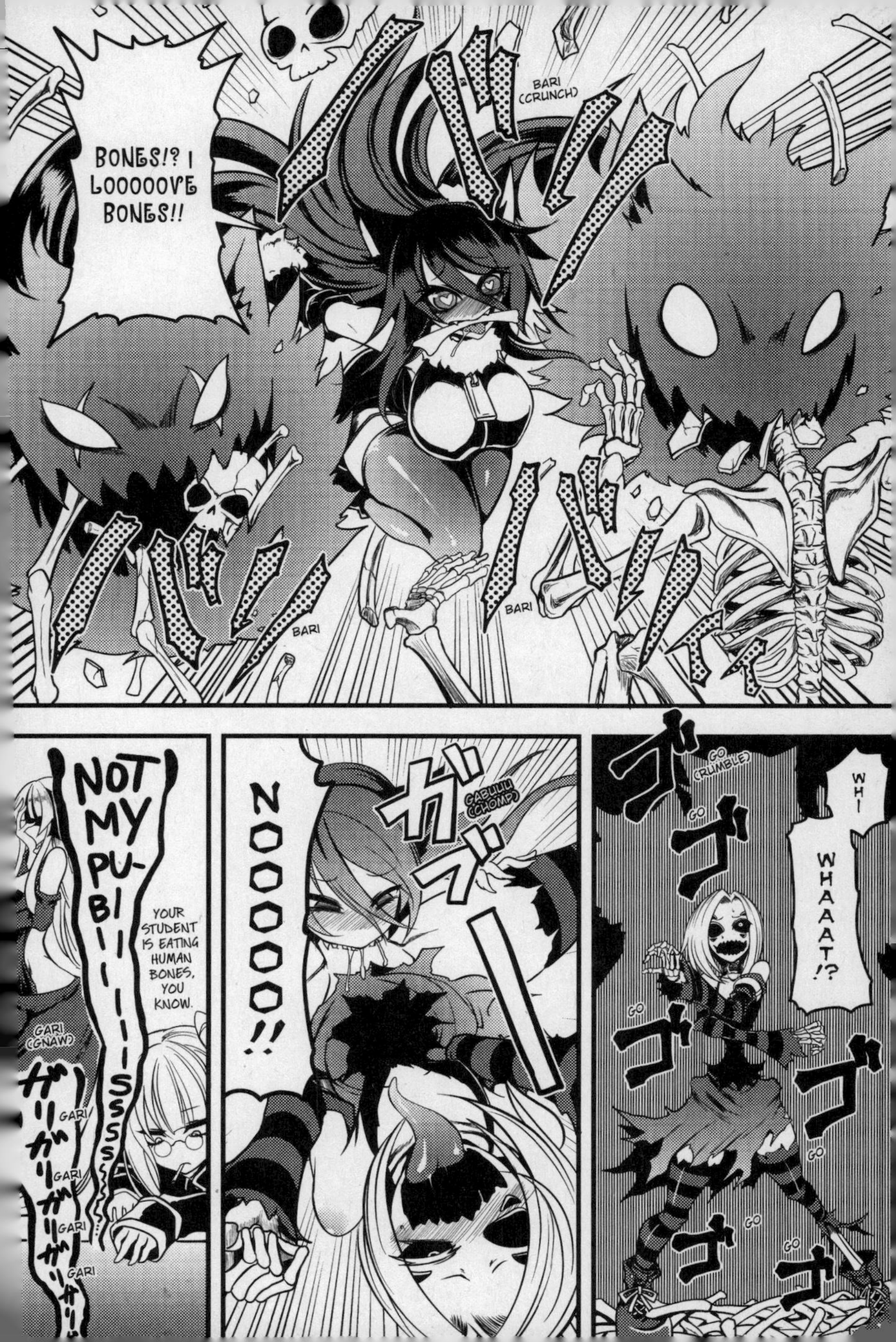
BARI (CRUNCH)
BONES!? I LOOOOOVE BONES!!
BARI
BARI
GO (RUMBLE)
WHI
WHAAAT!?
GO
GO
GO
GO
GO
GABUUU (CHOMP)
NOOOOOO!!
NOT MY PU-PI-I-I-I-I-I-I-ISSSSS
YOUR STUDENT IS EATING HUMAN BONES, YOU KNOW.
GARI (GNAW)
GARI
GARI
GARI
GARI

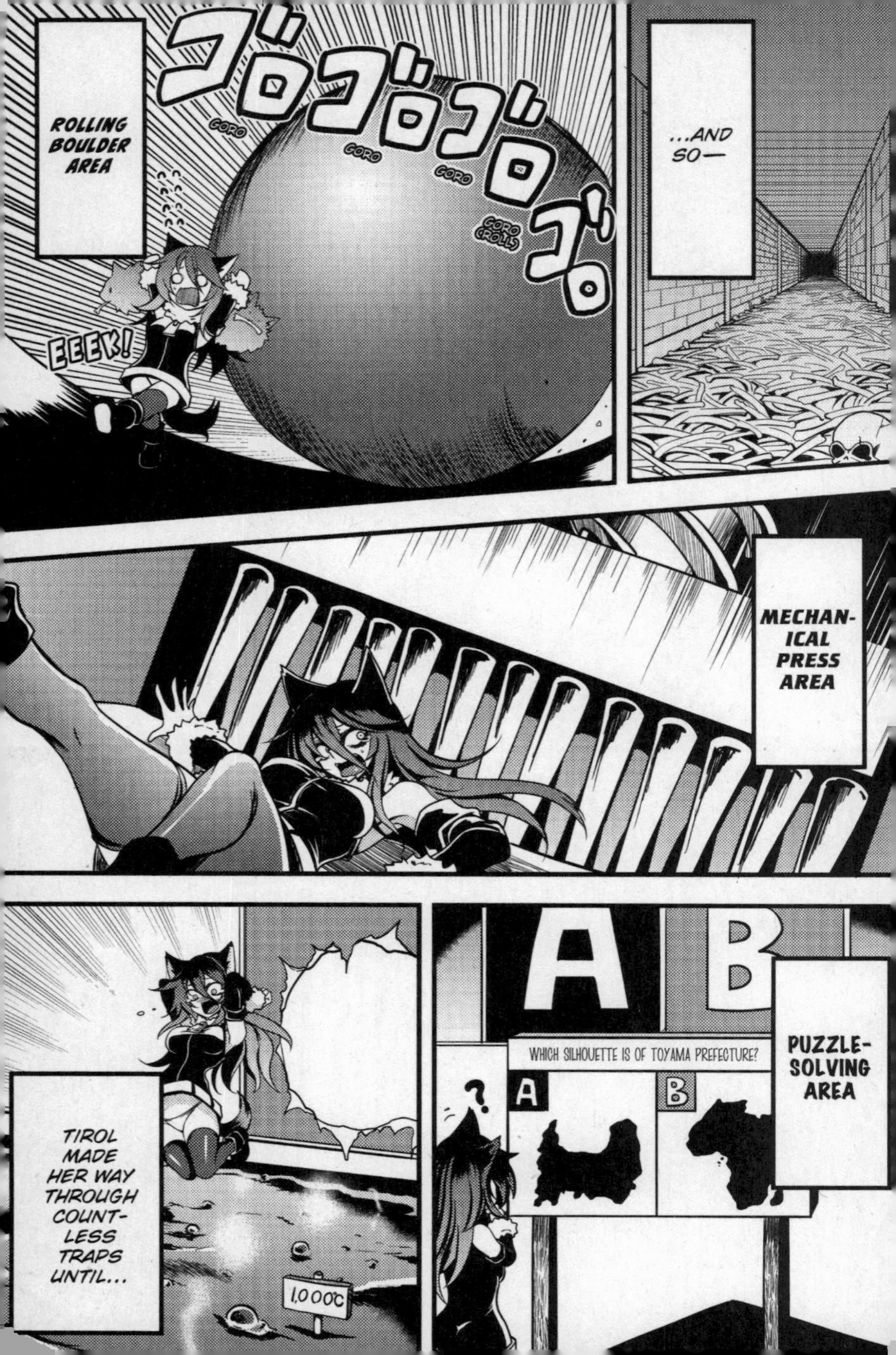
...AND SO—
ROLLING BOULDER AREA
GORO
GORO
GORO
GORO (ROLL)
EEEK!
MECHAN-ICAL PRESS AREA
PUZZLE-SOLVING AREA
A
B
WHICH SILHOUETTE IS OF TOYAMA PREFECTURE?
A
B
TIROL MADE HER WAY THROUGH COUNT-LESS TRAPS UNTIL...
1,000°C

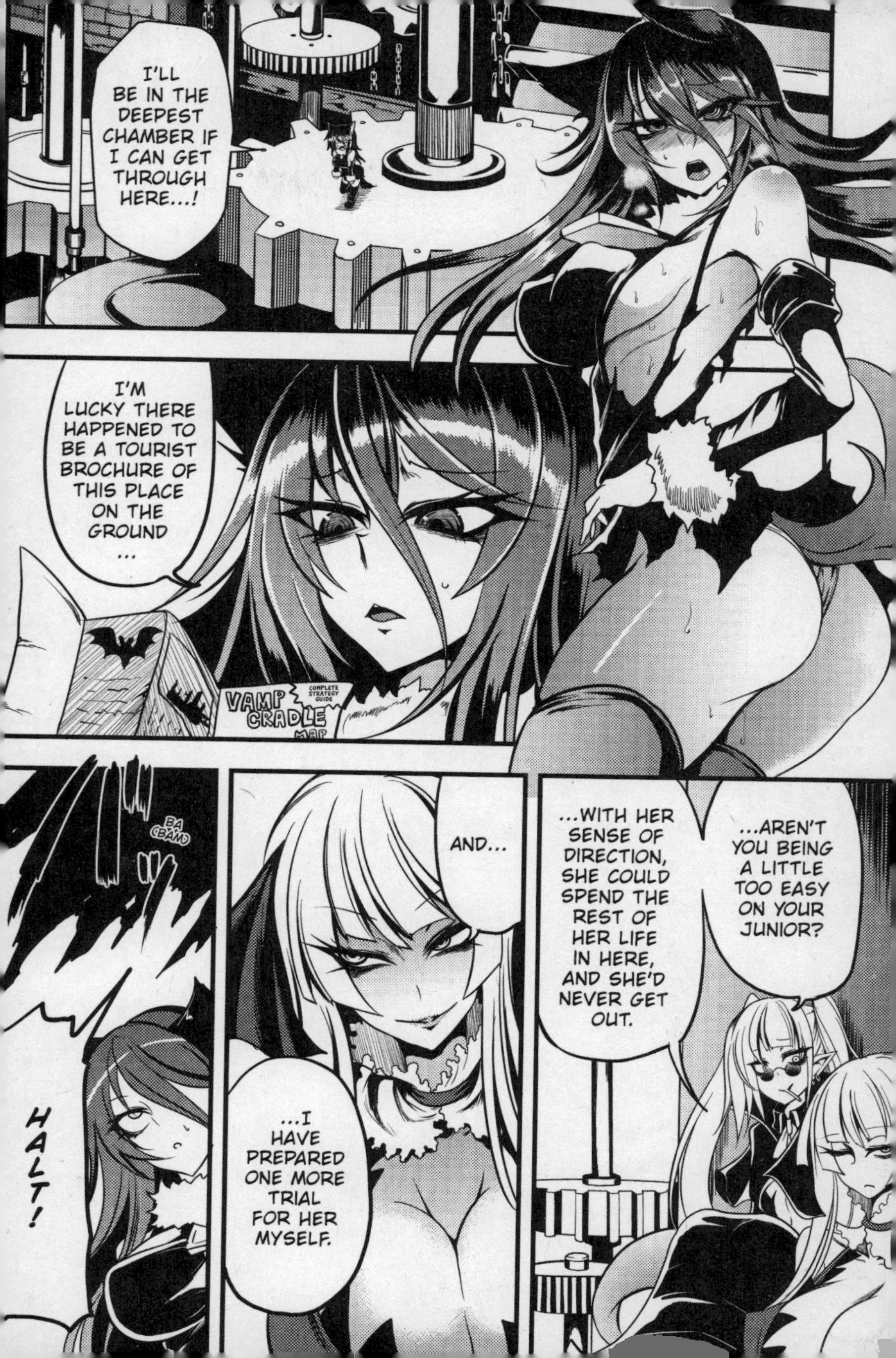
I'LL BE IN THE DEEPEST CHAMBER IF I CAN GET THROUGH HERE...!
I'M LUCKY THERE HAPPENED TO BE A TOURIST BROCHURE OF THIS PLACE ON THE GROUND ...
COMPLETE STRATEGY GUIDE
VAMP CRADLE MAP
...AREN'T YOU BEING A LITTLE TOO EASY ON YOUR JUNIOR?
...WITH HER SENSE OF DIRECTION, SHE COULD SPEND THE REST OF HER LIFE IN HERE, AND SHE'D NEVER GET OUT.
AND...
...I HAVE PREPARED ONE MORE TRIAL FOR HER MYSELF.
BA BAM
HALT!

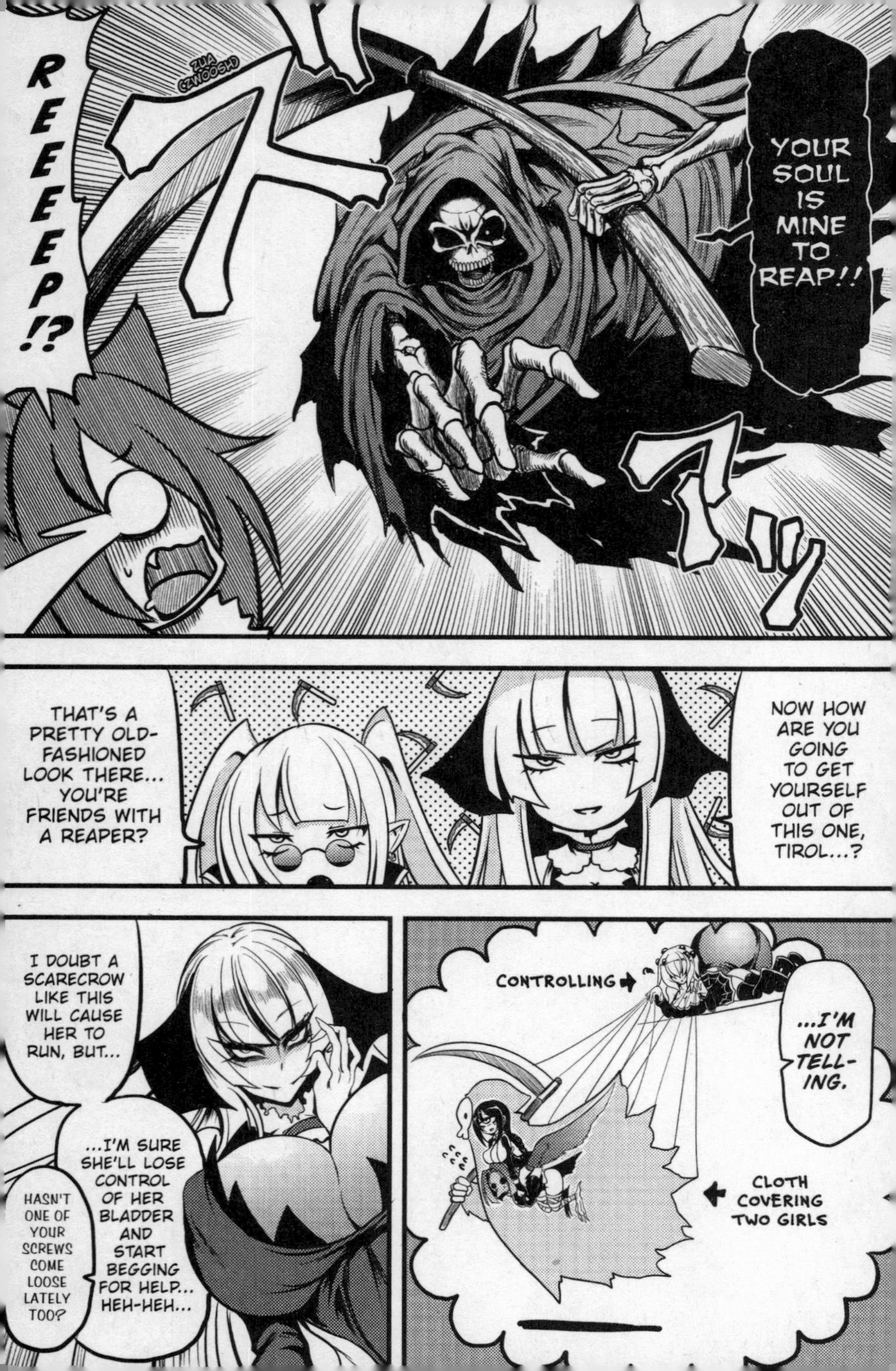
YOUR SOUL IS MINE TO REAP!!
ZUA (ZWOOSH)
REEEEEP!?
NOW HOW ARE YOU GOING TO GET YOURSELF OUT OF THIS ONE, TIROL...?
THAT'S A PRETTY OLD-FASHIONED LOOK THERE... YOU'RE FRIENDS WITH A REAPER?
CONTROLLING
...I'M NOT TELLING.
CLOTH COVERING TWO GIRLS
I DOUBT A SCARECROW LIKE THIS WILL CAUSE HER TO RUN, BUT...
...I'M SURE SHE'LL LOSE CONTROL OF HER BLADDER AND START BEGGING FOR HELP... HEH-HEH...
HASN'T ONE OF YOUR SCREWS COME LOOSE LATELY TOO?

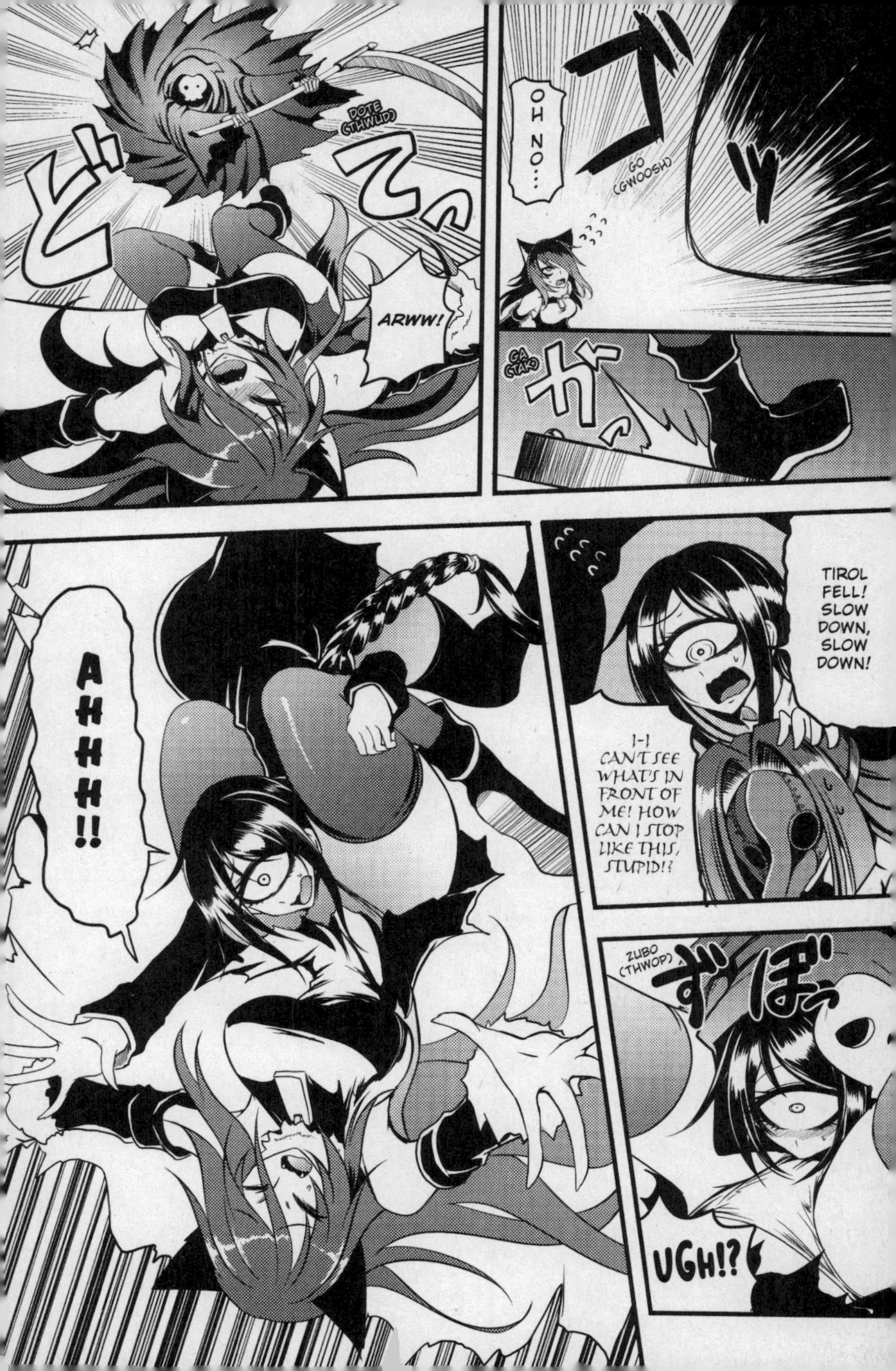

OH NO...
ゴッ
GO (GWOOSH)
がっ
GA (TAK)
どてっ
DOTE (THWUD)
ARWW!
TIROL FELL! SLOW DOWN, SLOW DOWN!
I-I CAN'T SEE WHAT'S IN FRONT OF ME! HOW CAN I STOP LIKE THIS, STUPID!?
ずぼっ
ZUBO (THWOP)
UGH!?
AHHHH!!

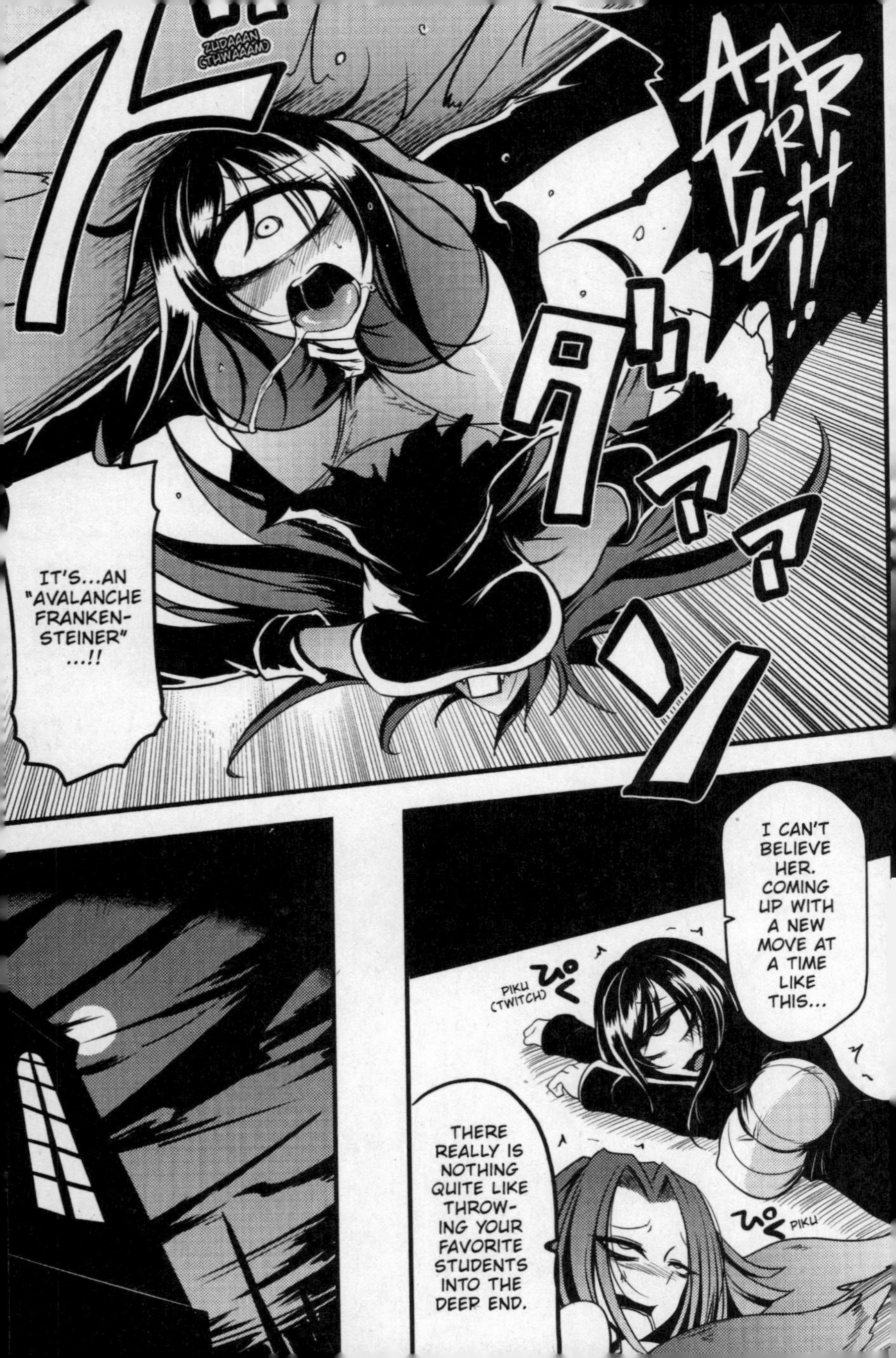
AARRRH!!
ZUDAAAN (THWAAAM)
IT'S...AN "AVALANCHE FRANKEN-STEINER" ...!!
I CAN'T BELIEVE HER. COMING UP WITH A NEW MOVE AT A TIME LIKE THIS...
PIKU (TWITCH)
THERE REALLY IS NOTHING QUITE LIKE THROW-ING YOUR FAVORITE STUDENTS INTO THE DEEP END.
PIKU

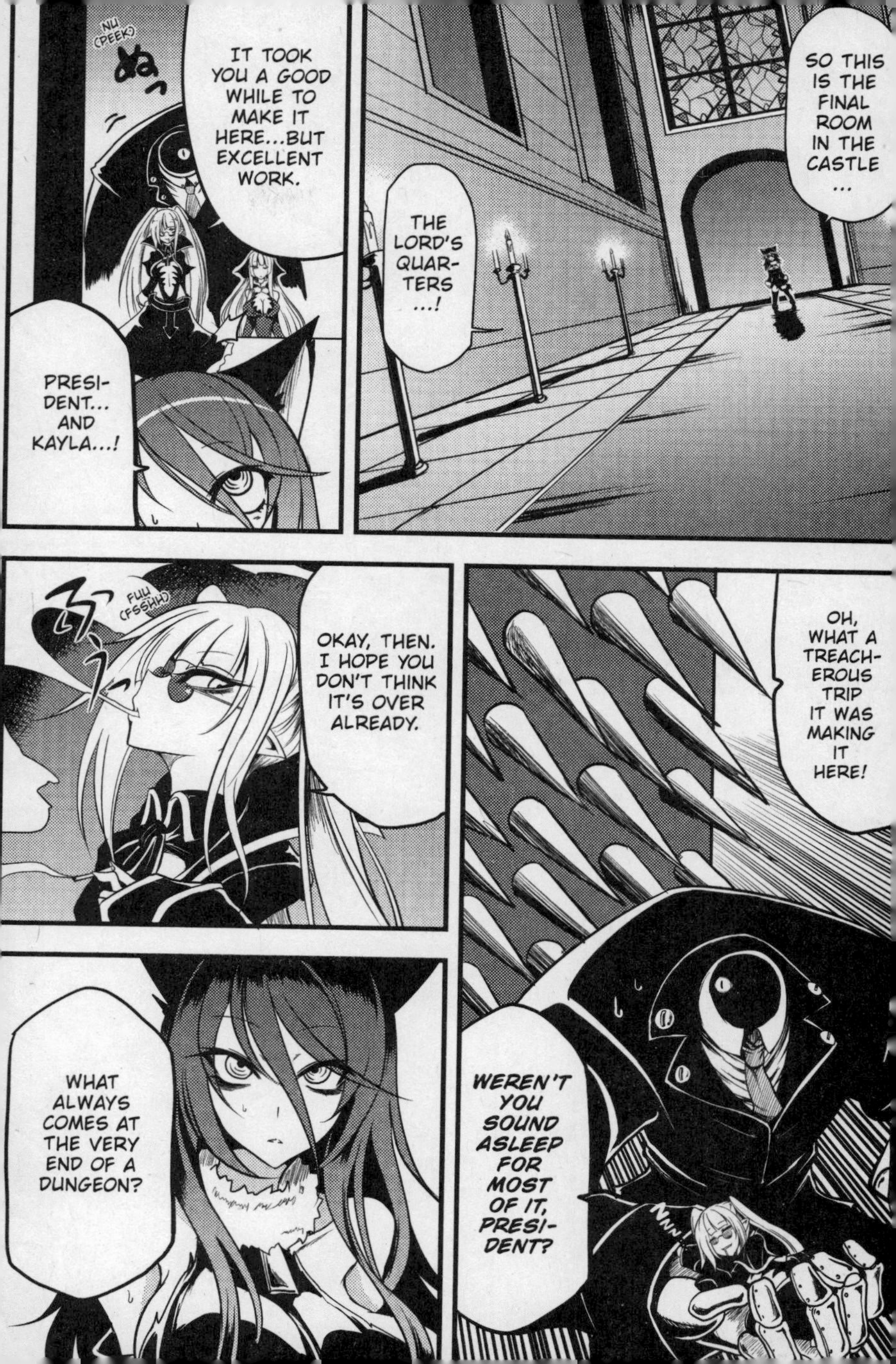
SO THIS IS THE FINAL ROOM IN THE CASTLE...
THE LORD'S QUARTERS...!
NU (PEEK)
ぬっ
IT TOOK YOU A GOOD WHILE TO MAKE IT HERE...BUT EXCELLENT WORK.
PRESIDENT... AND KAYLA...!
OH, WHAT A TREACHEROUS TRIP IT WAS MAKING IT HERE!
WEREN'T YOU SOUND ASLEEP FOR MOST OF IT, PRESIDENT?
FUU (FSSHH)
OKAY, THEN. I HOPE YOU DON'T THINK IT'S OVER ALREADY.
WHAT ALWAYS COMES AT THE VERY END OF A DUNGEON?

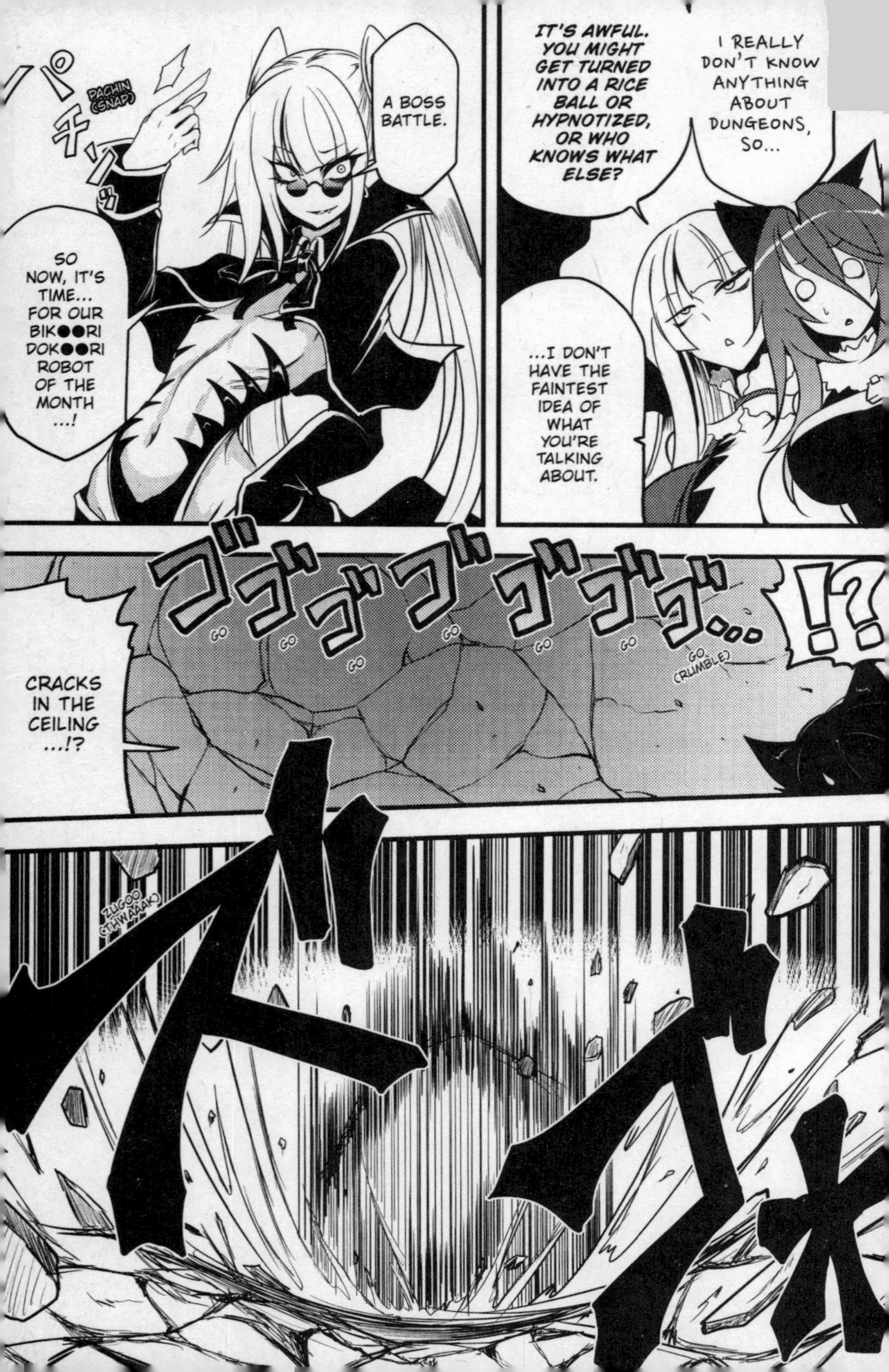
I REALLY DON'T KNOW ANYTHING ABOUT DUNGEONS, SO...
IT'S AWFUL. YOU MIGHT GET TURNED INTO A RICE BALL OR HYPNOTIZED, OR WHO KNOWS WHAT ELSE?
...I DON'T HAVE THE FAINTEST IDEA OF WHAT YOU'RE TALKING ABOUT.
A BOSS BATTLE.
PACHIN (SNAP)
SO NOW, IT'S TIME... FOR OUR BIK●●RI DOK●●RI ROBOT OF THE MONTH ...!
!?
GO GO GO GO GO GO GO (RUMBLE)
CRACKS IN THE CEILING ...!?
ZUGOO (THWAAAK)

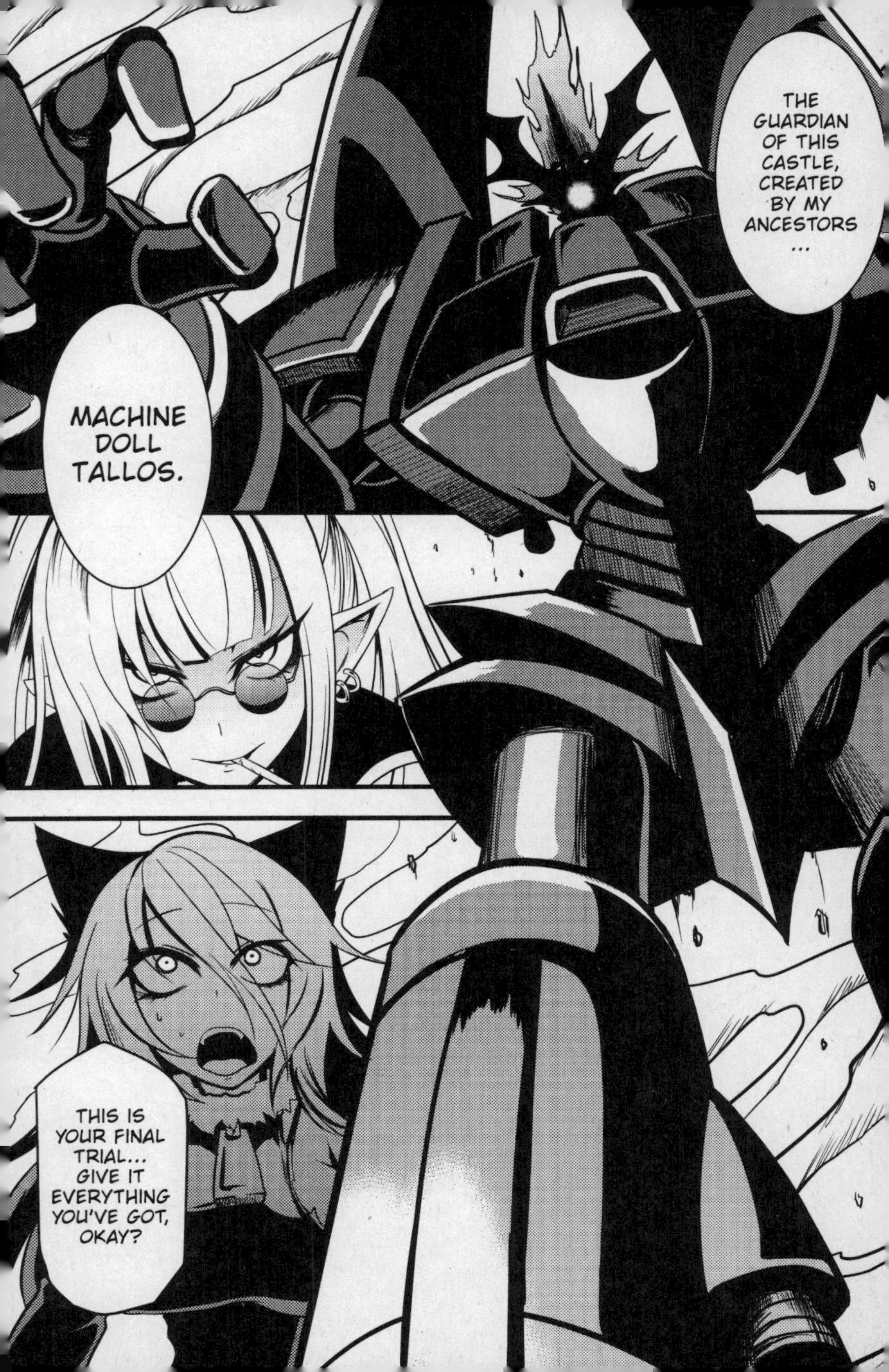
THE GUARDIAN OF THIS CASTLE, CREATED BY MY ANCESTORS ...
MACHINE DOLL TALLOS.
THIS IS YOUR FINAL TRIAL... GIVE IT EVERYTHING YOU'VE GOT, OKAY?

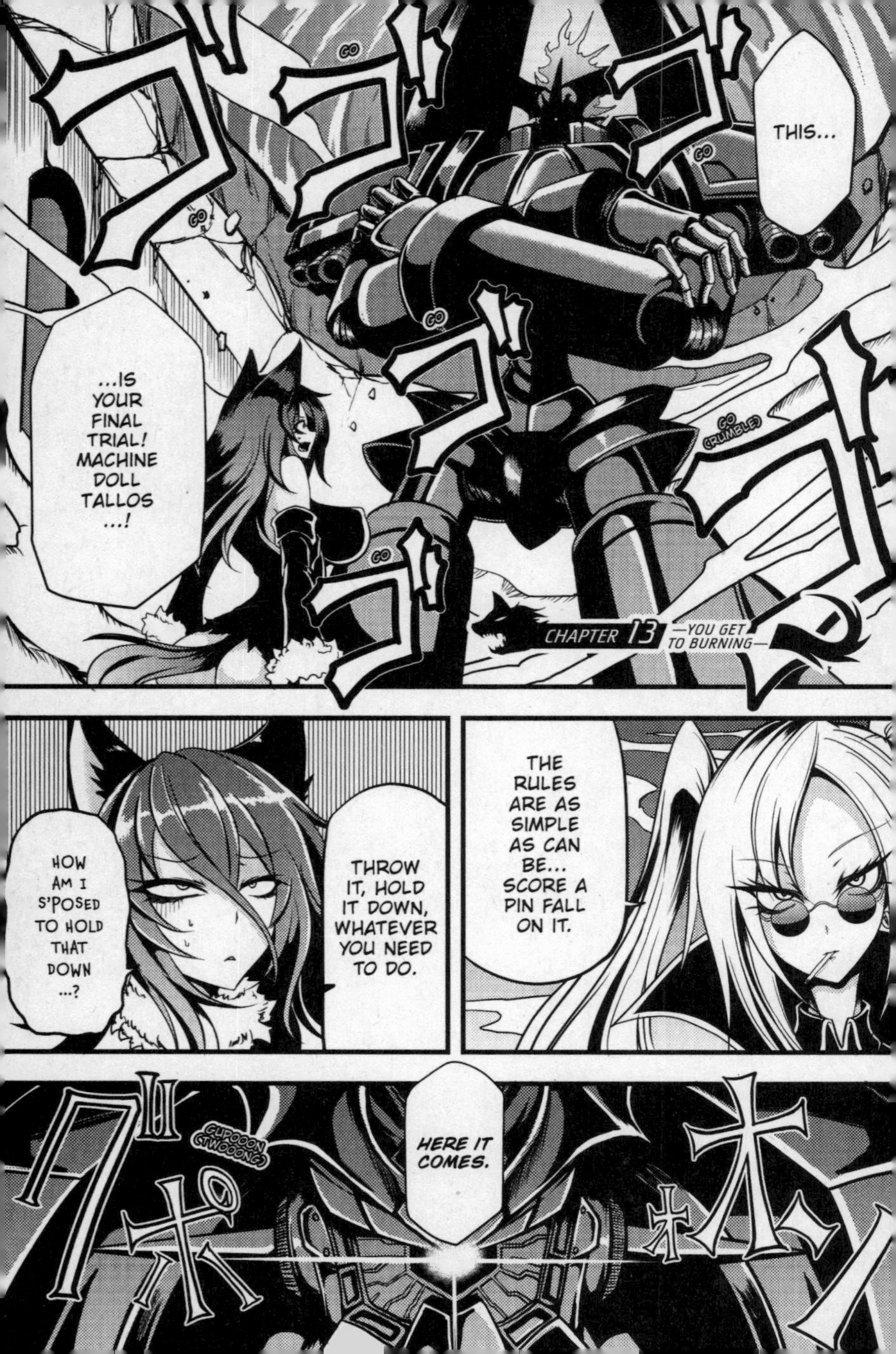
THIS...
GO
GO
GO
GO
...IS YOUR FINAL TRIAL! MACHINE DOLL TALLOS ...!
GO (RUMBLE)
GO
CHAPTER 13 —YOU GET TO BURNING—
THE RULES ARE AS SIMPLE AS CAN BE... SCORE A PIN FALL ON IT.
THROW IT, HOLD IT DOWN, WHATEVER YOU NEED TO DO.
HOW AM I S'POSED TO HOLD THAT DOWN ...?
HERE IT COMES.
GUPOOON (TWOOONG)

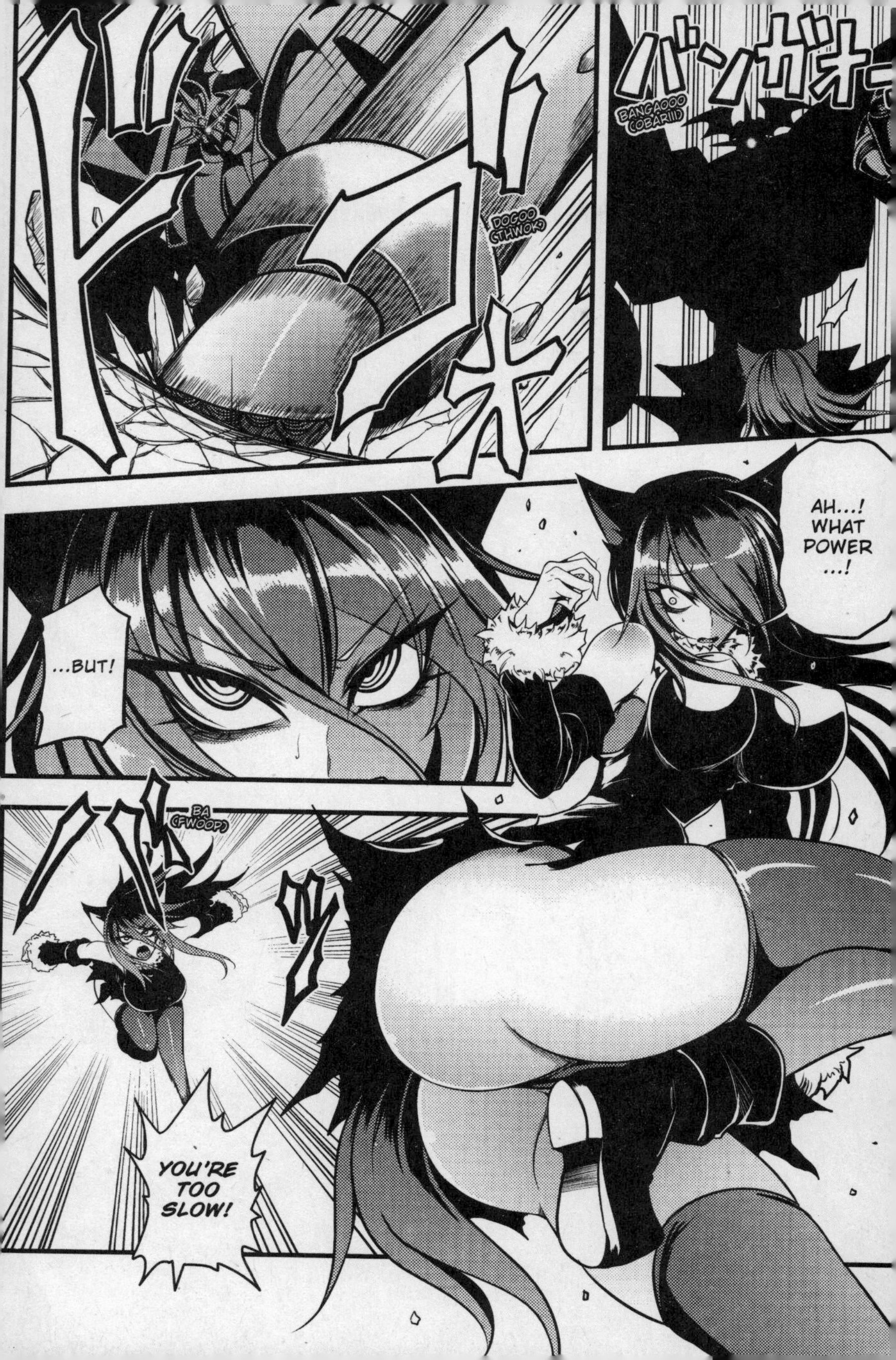
BANGAOOO (OBARIID)
DOGOO (THWOK)
AH...! WHAT POWER ...!
...BUT!
BA (FWOOP)
YOU'RE TOO SLOW!

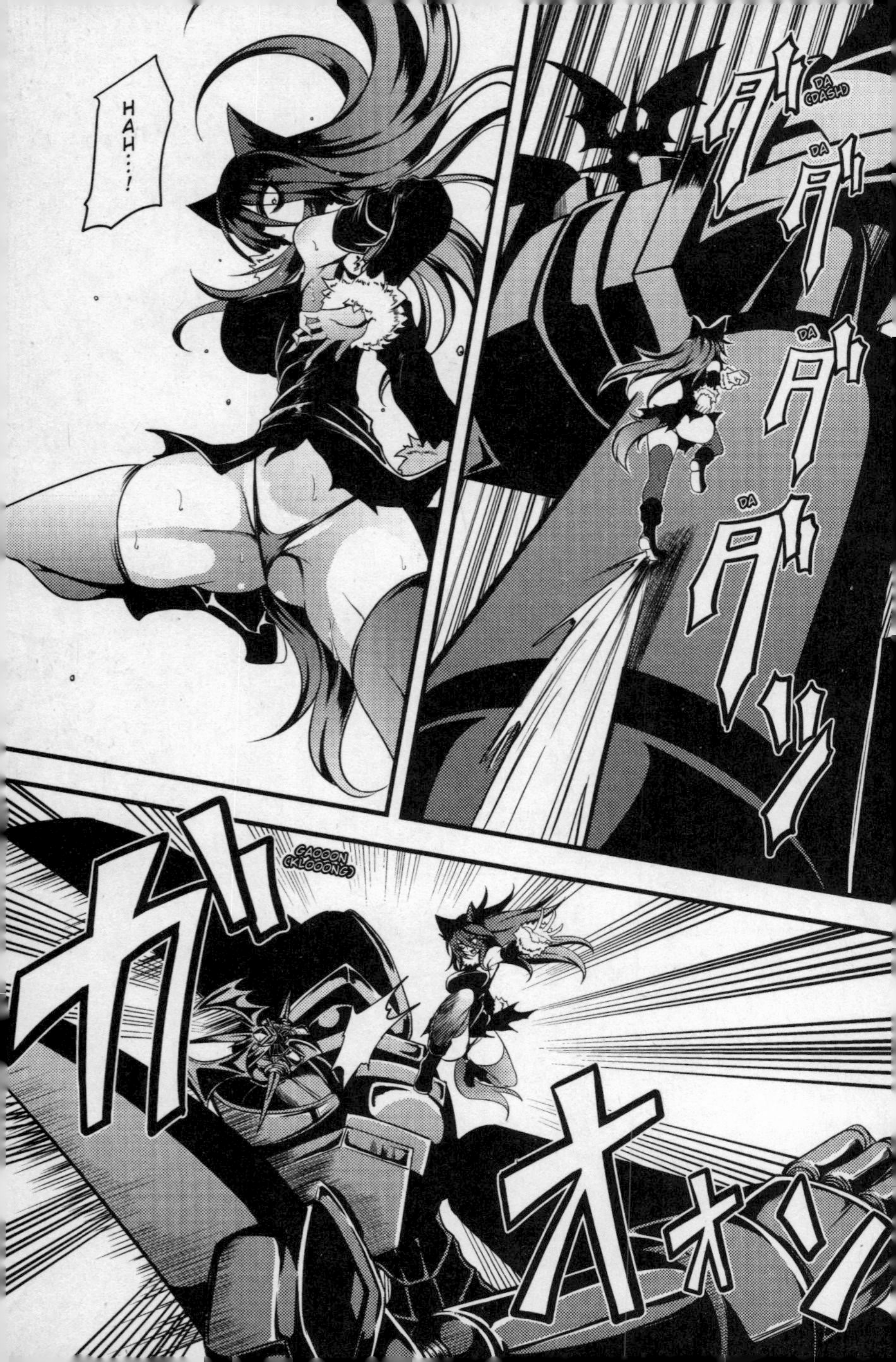
DA (DASH)
DA
DA
DA
HAH...!
GAOOON (KLOOONG)

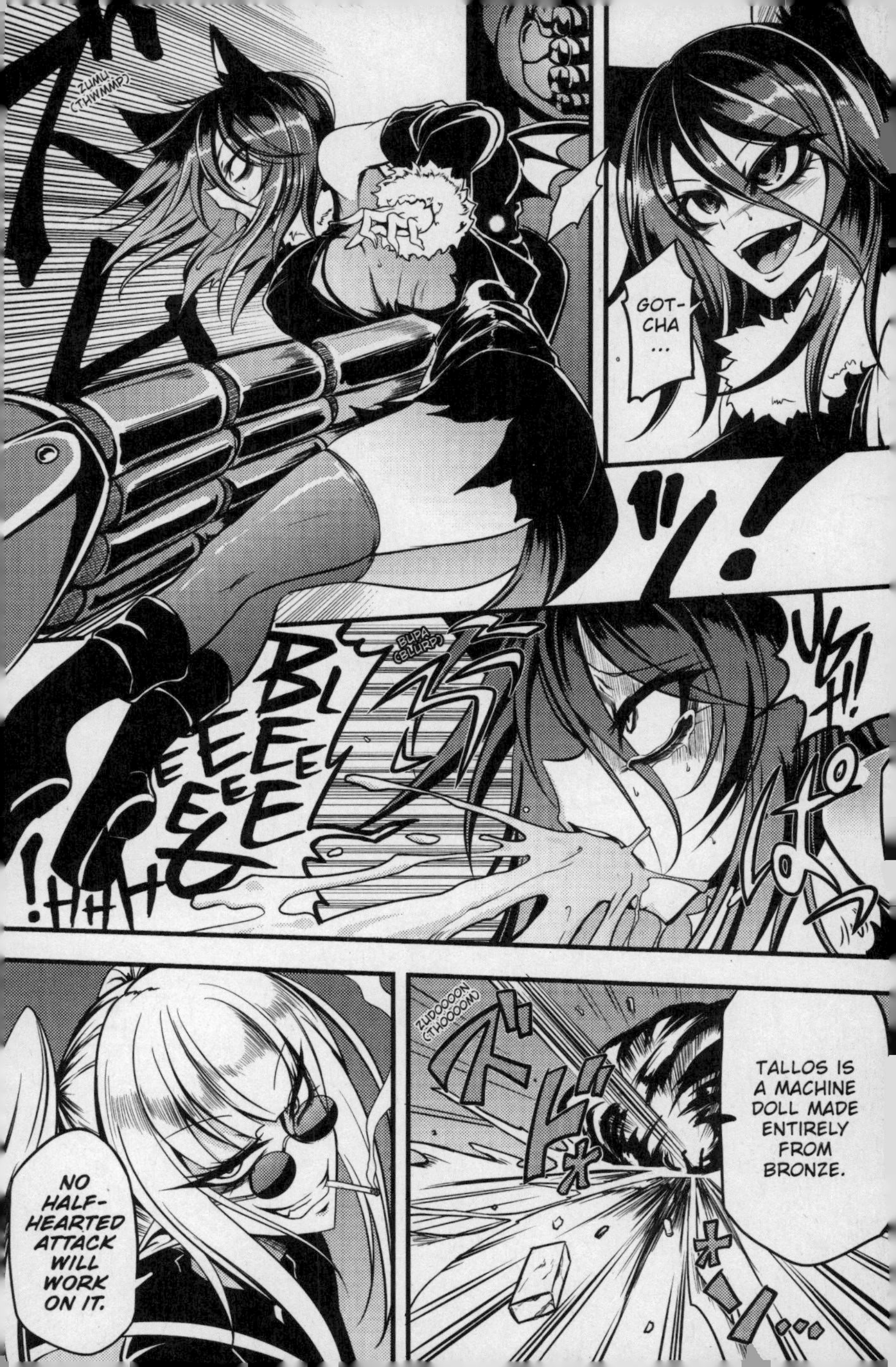
GOT-CHA...
ZUMU (THWMMP)
BUPA (BLURP)
TALLOS IS A MACHINE DOLL MADE ENTIRELY FROM BRONZE.
ZUDOOOON (THOOOOM)
NO HALF-HEARTED ATTACK WILL WORK ON IT.

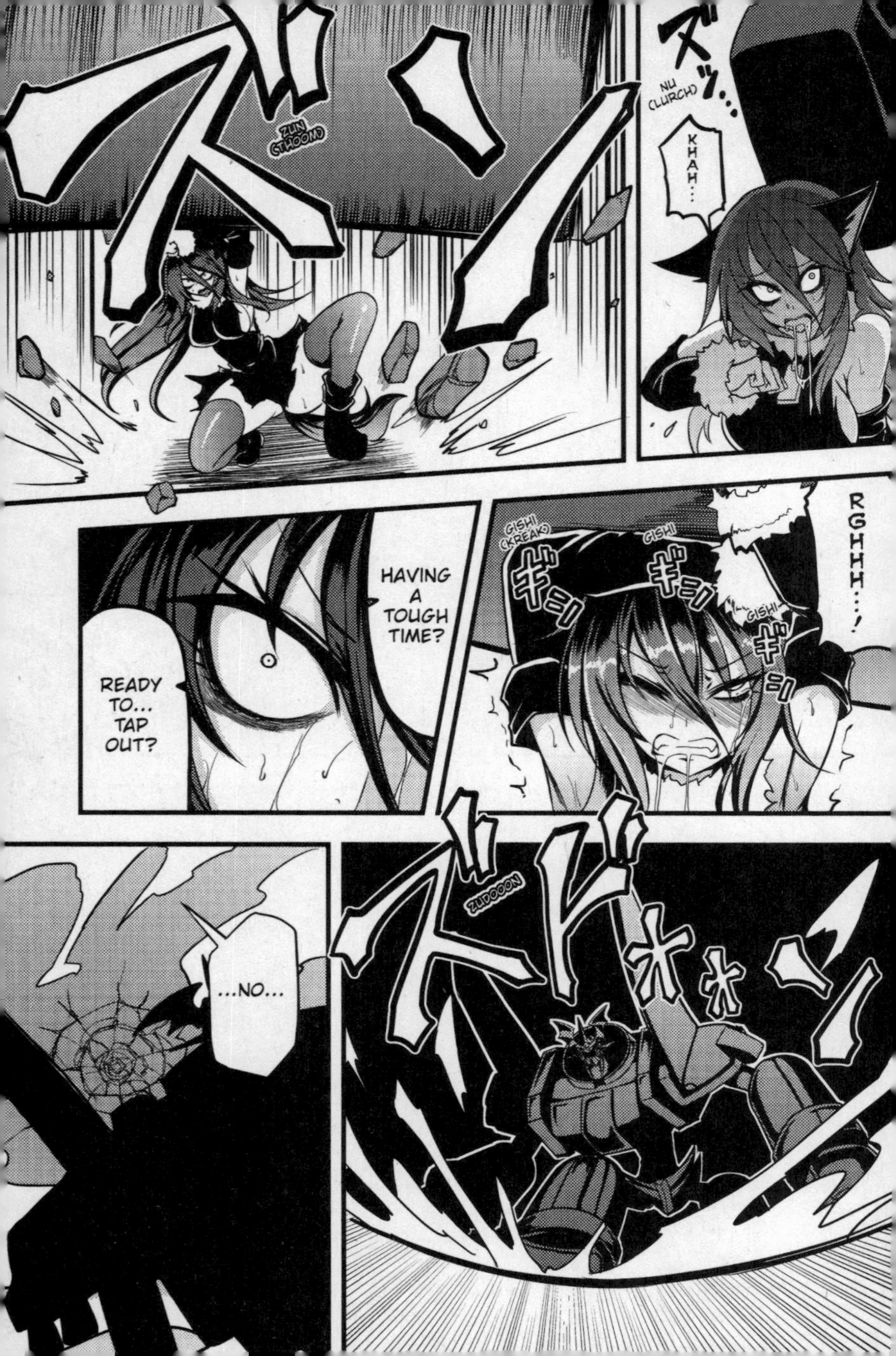
NU (LURCH)
KHAH...
ZUN (THOOM)
RGHHH...!
GISHI
GISHI (KREAK)
GISHI
HAVING A TOUGH TIME?
READY TO... TAP OUT?
ZUDOOON
...NO...

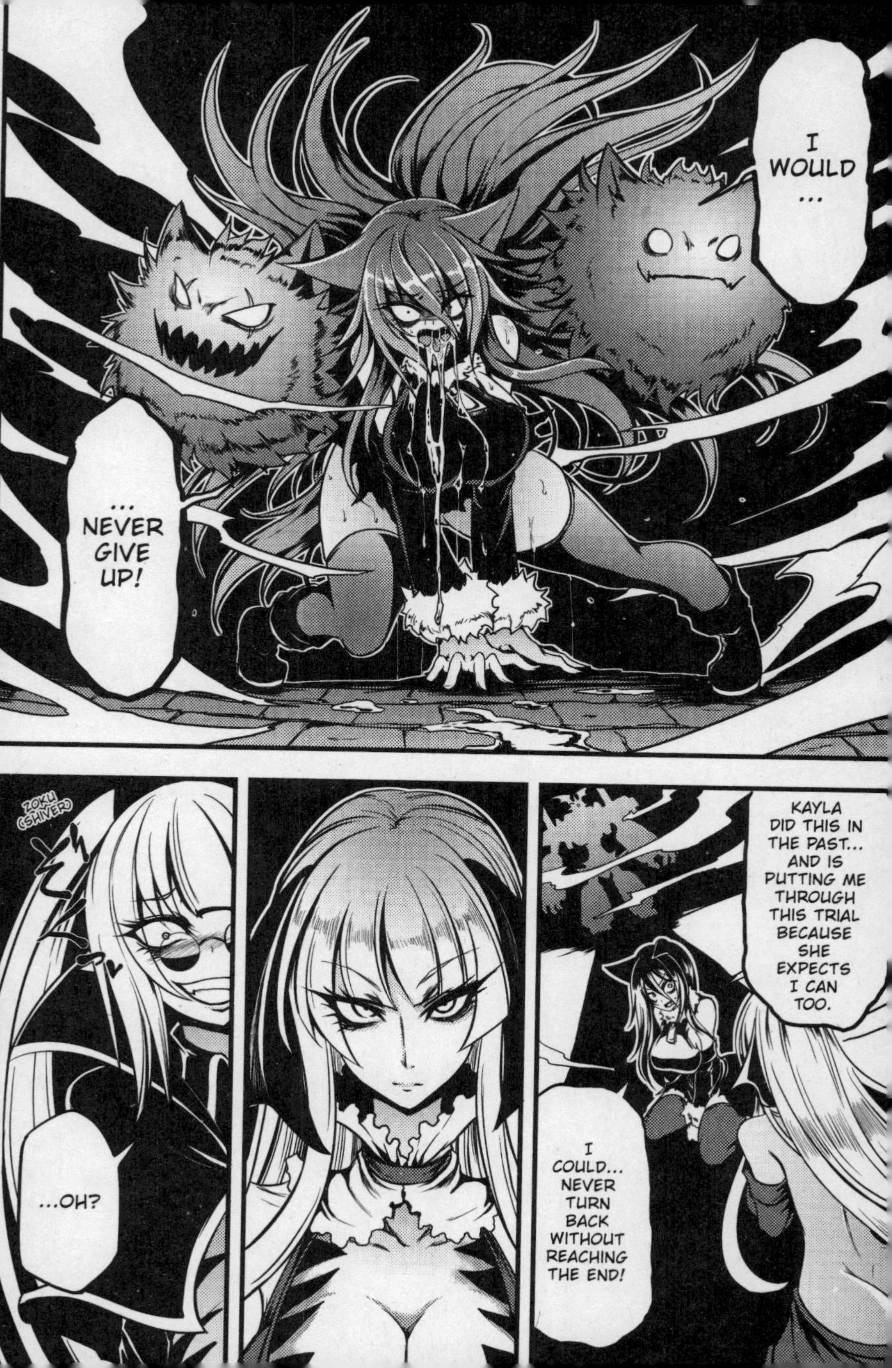
I WOULD...
...NEVER GIVE UP!
KAYLA DID THIS IN THE PAST... AND IS PUTTING ME THROUGH THIS TRIAL BECAUSE SHE EXPECTS I CAN TOO.
I COULD... NEVER TURN BACK WITHOUT REACHING THE END!
ZOKU (SHIVER)
...OH?

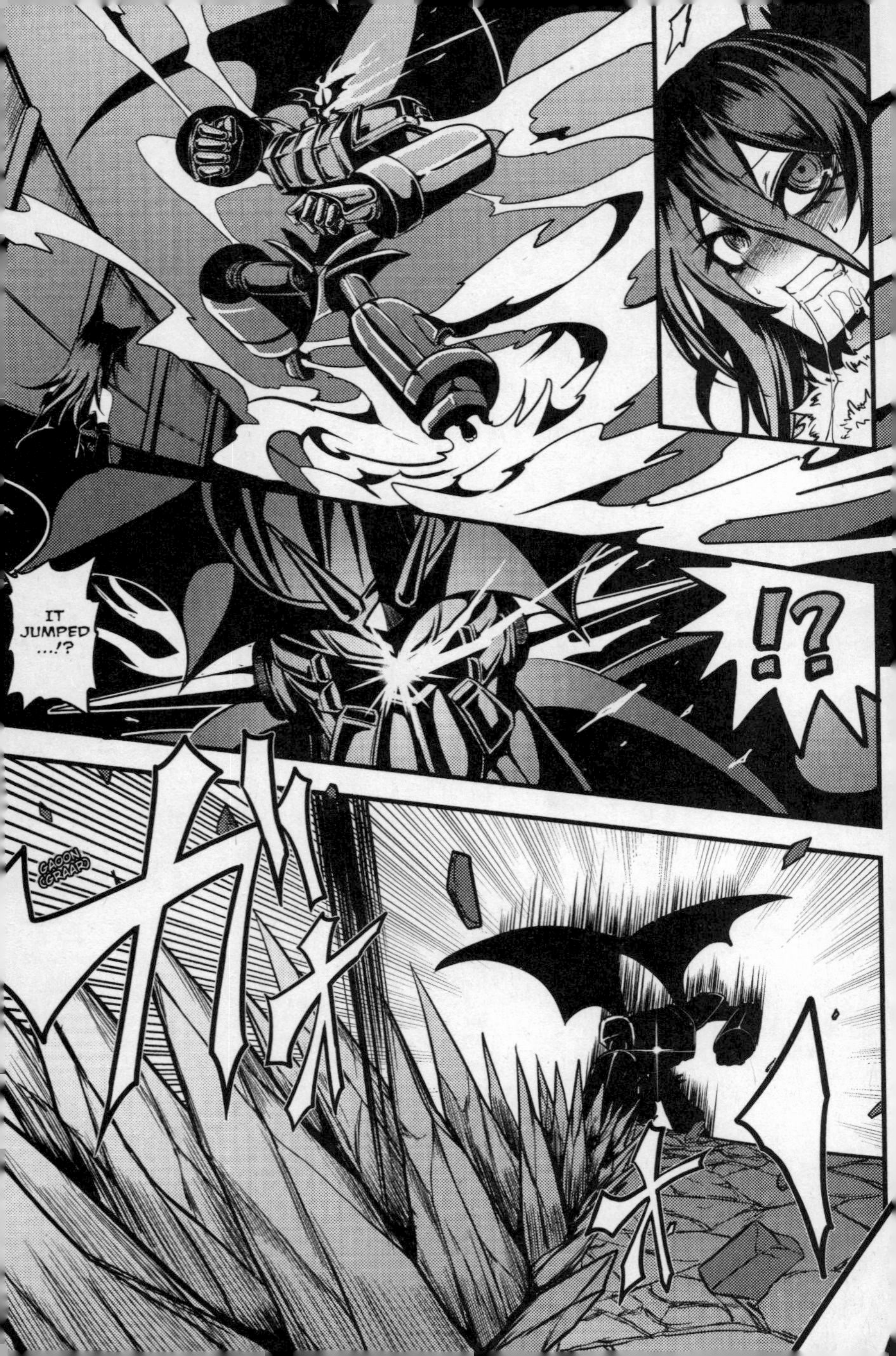
!?
IT JUMPED ...!?
GAOON (GRAAR)

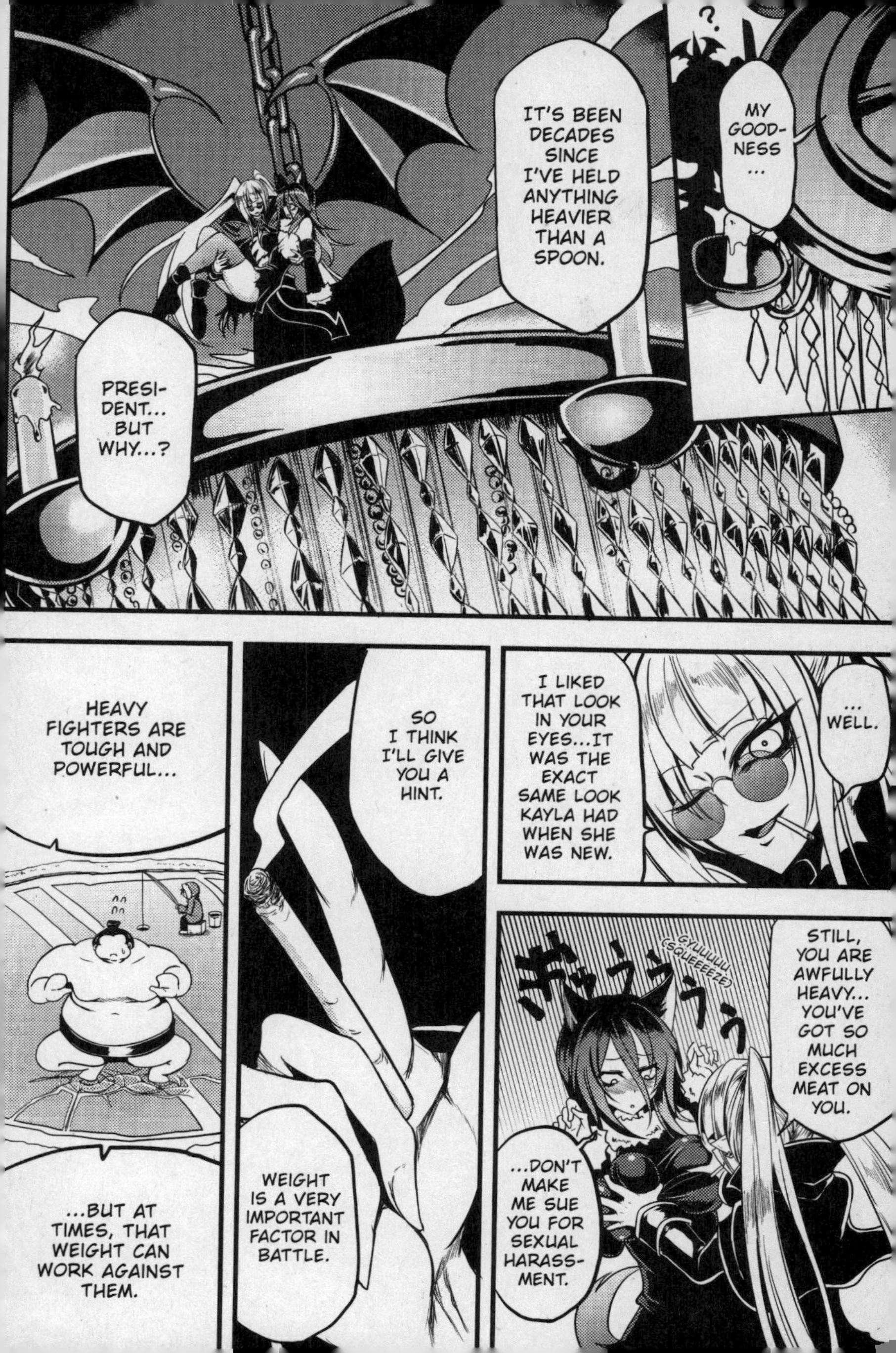
?
MY GOODNESS...
IT'S BEEN DECADES SINCE I'VE HELD ANYTHING HEAVIER THAN A SPOON.
PRESIDENT... BUT WHY...?
...WELL.
I LIKED THAT LOOK IN YOUR EYES...IT WAS THE EXACT SAME LOOK KAYLA HAD WHEN SHE WAS NEW.
GYUUUUU (SQUEEEEZE)
STILL, YOU ARE AWFULLY HEAVY... YOU'VE GOT SO MUCH EXCESS MEAT ON YOU.
...DON'T MAKE ME SUE YOU FOR SEXUAL HARASSMENT.
SO I THINK I'LL GIVE YOU A HINT.
WEIGHT IS A VERY IMPORTANT FACTOR IN BATTLE.
HEAVY FIGHTERS ARE TOUGH AND POWERFUL...
...BUT AT TIMES, THAT WEIGHT CAN WORK AGAINST THEM.

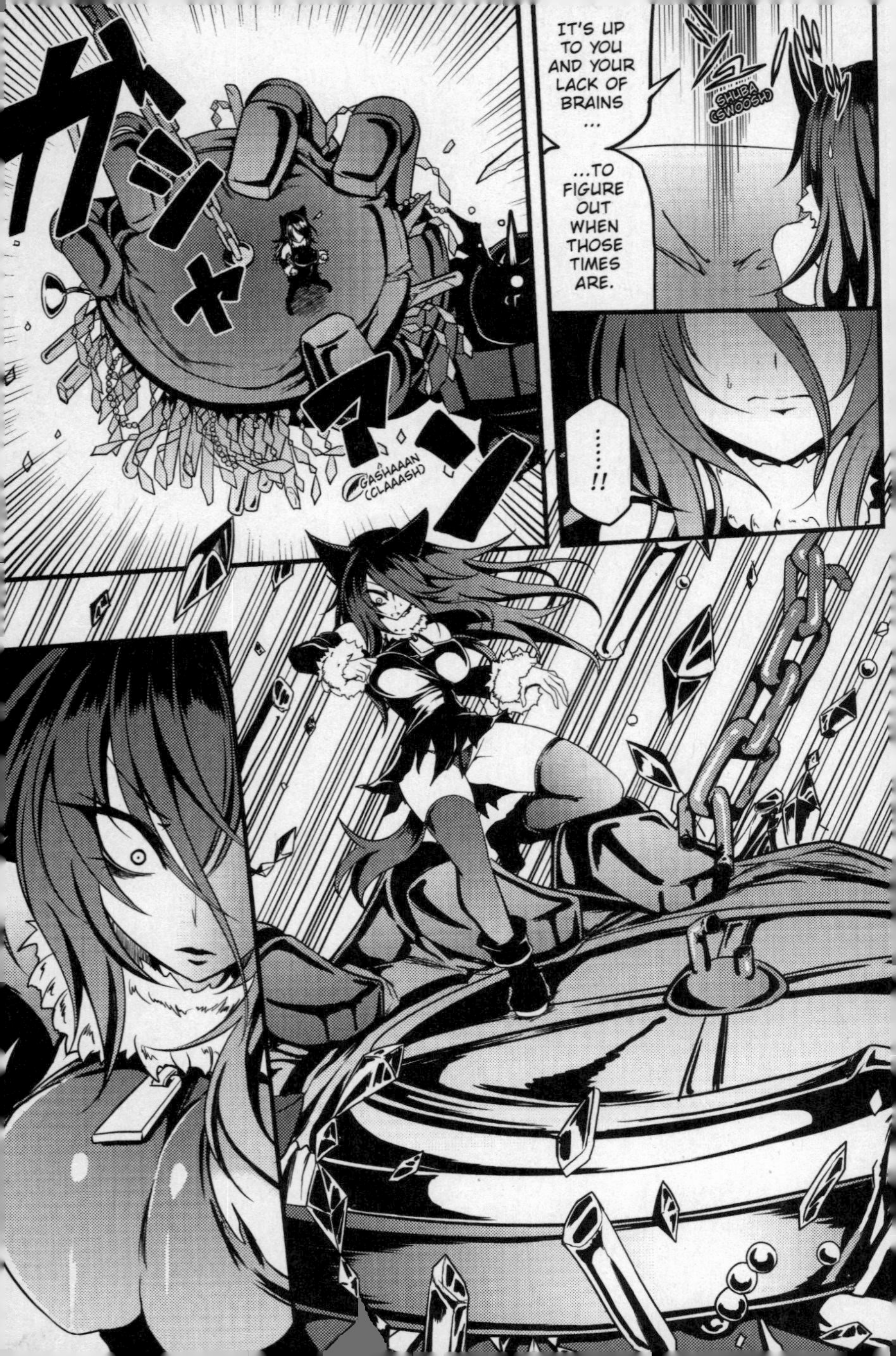
SHUBA (SWOOSH)
IT'S UP TO YOU AND YOUR LACK OF BRAINS ...
...TO FIGURE OUT WHEN THOSE TIMES ARE.
......!!
GASHAAAN (CLAAASH)

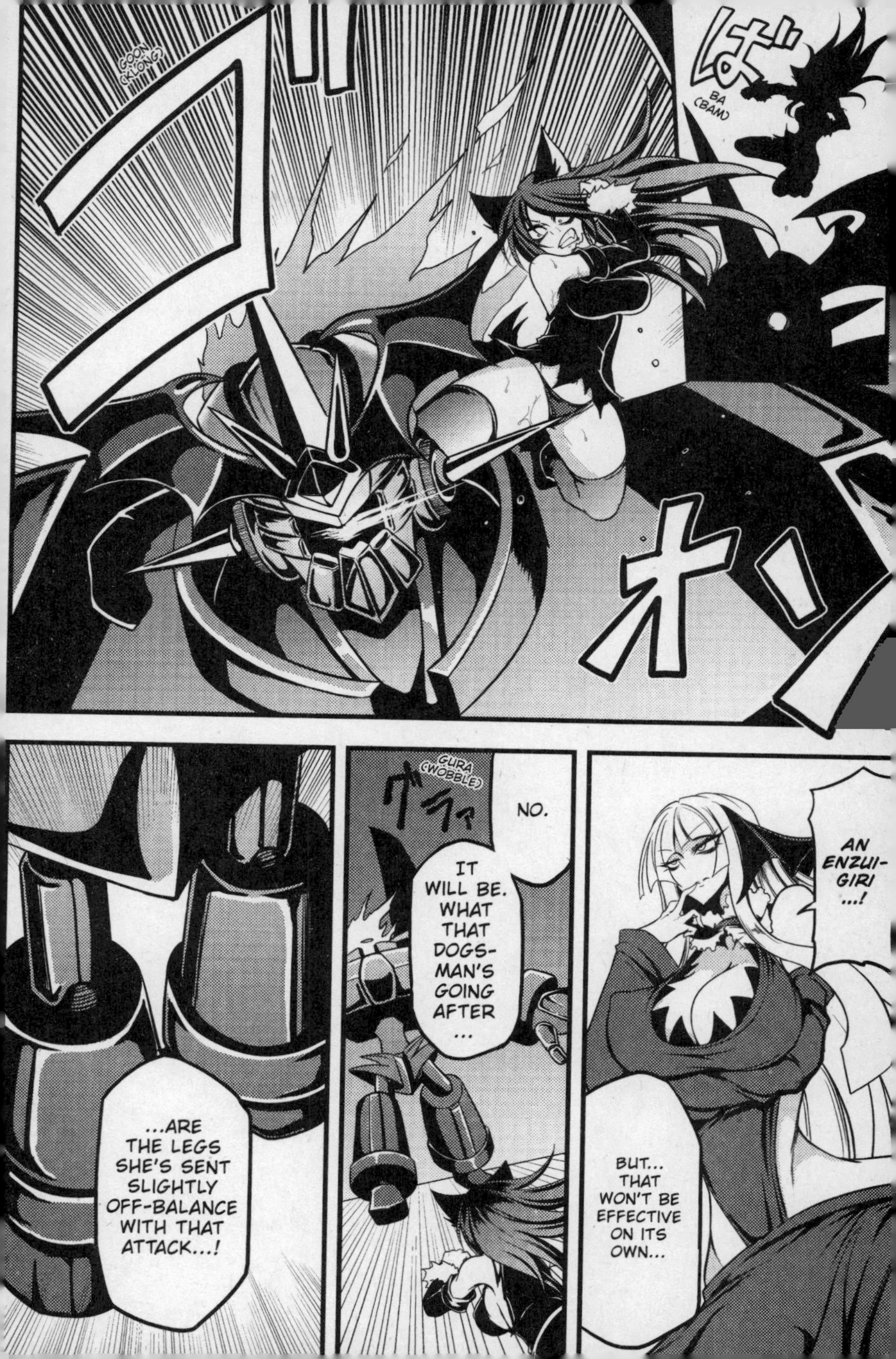
ば
BA (BAM)
GOON (KLONG)
AN ENZUI-GIRI ...!
BUT... THAT WON'T BE EFFECTIVE ON ITS OWN...
GURA (WOBBLE)
NO.
IT WILL BE. WHAT THAT DOGS-MAN'S GOING AFTER ...
...ARE THE LEGS SHE'S SENT SLIGHTLY OFF-BALANCE WITH THAT ATTACK...!

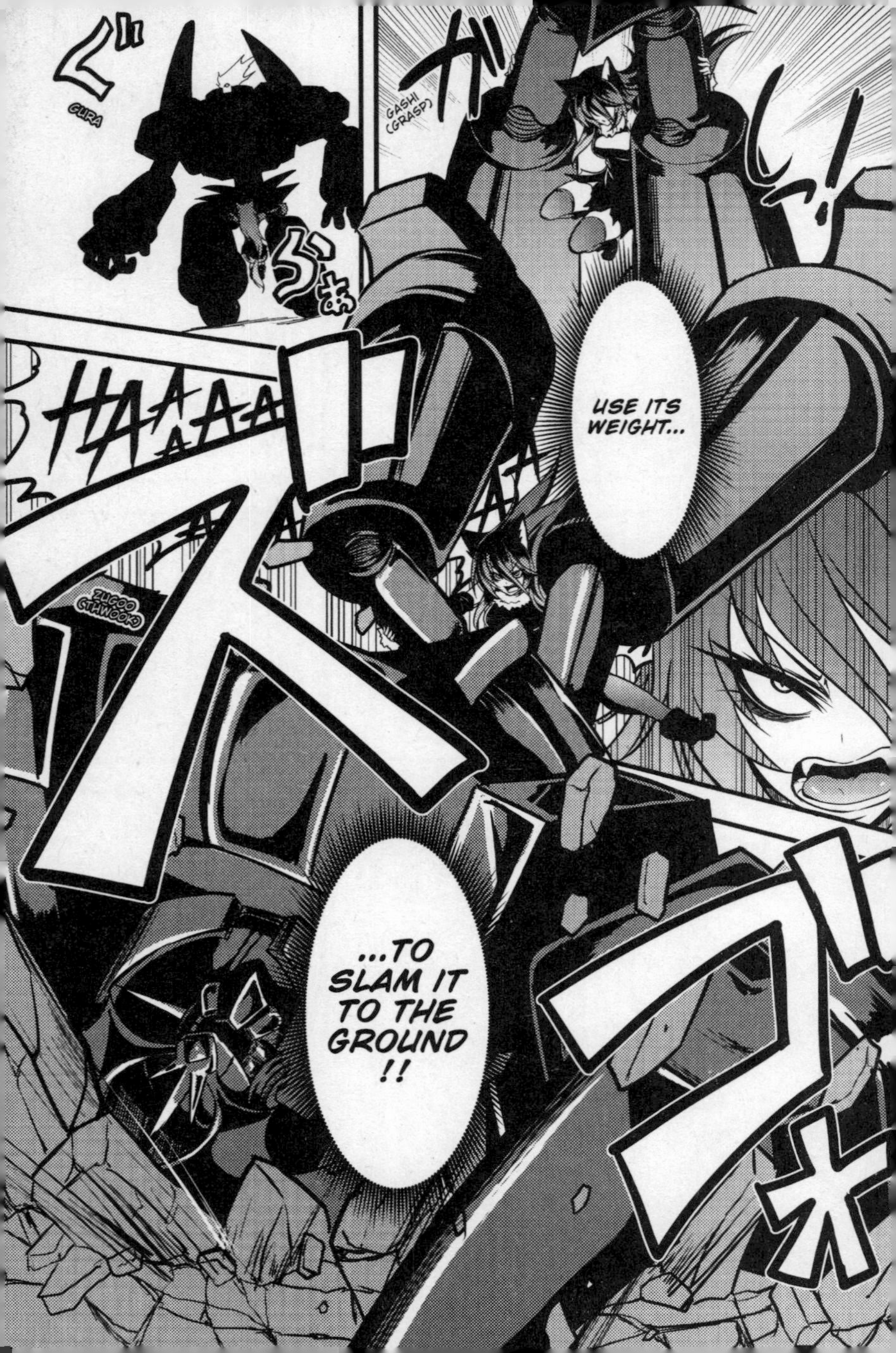
GASHI (GRASP)
GURA
USE ITS WEIGHT...
HAAAAA
ZUGOO (STAWOOK)
...TO SLAM IT TO THE GROUND!!

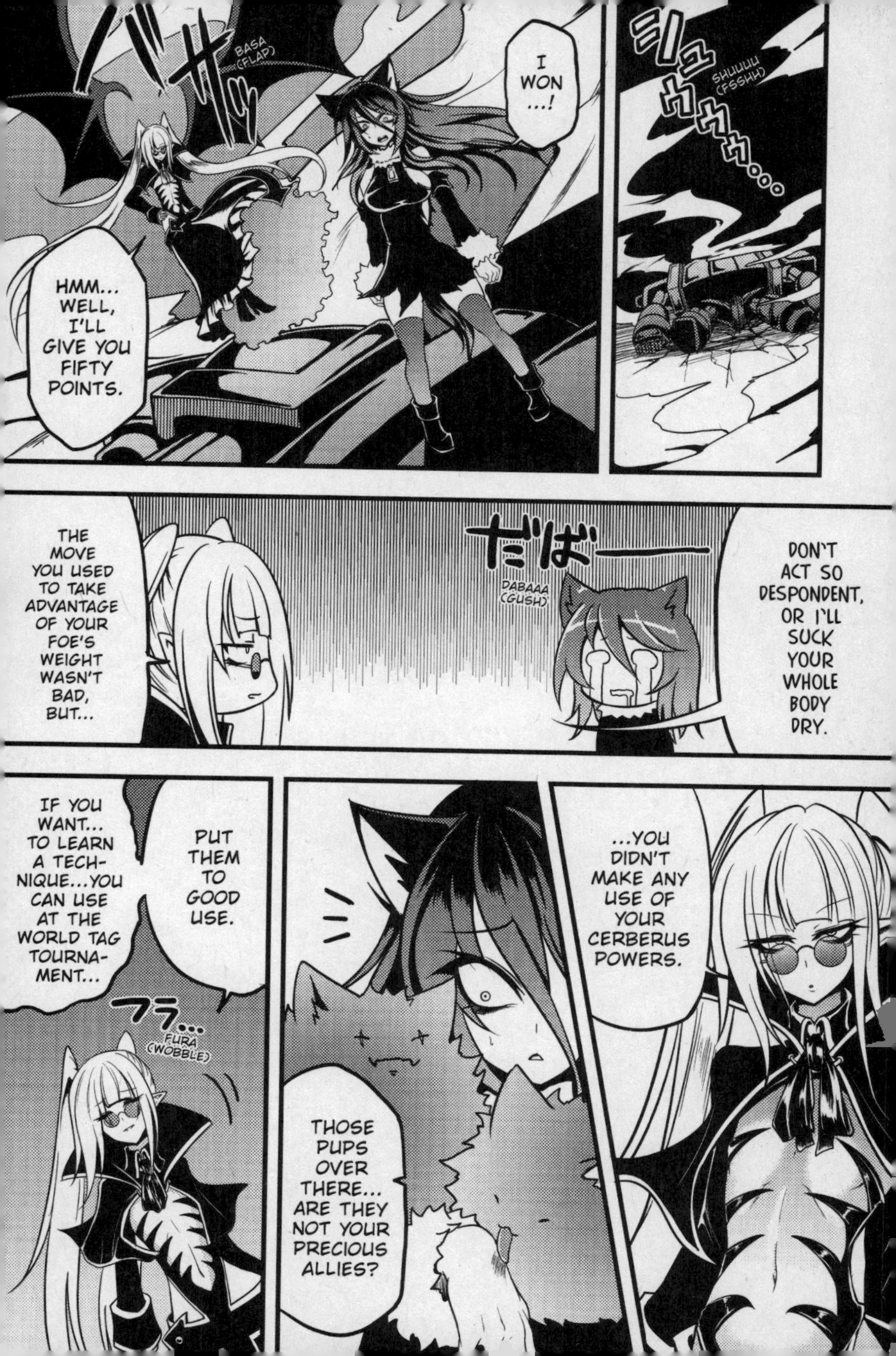

ミュウウウウ...
SHUUUU (FSSHH)
I WON ...!
バサッ
BASA (FLAP)
HMM... WELL, I'LL GIVE YOU FIFTY POINTS.
DON'T ACT SO DESPONDENT, OR I'LL SUCK YOUR WHOLE BODY DRY.
だばーー
DABAAA (GUSH)
THE MOVE YOU USED TO TAKE ADVANTAGE OF YOUR FOE'S WEIGHT WASN'T BAD, BUT...
...YOU DIDN'T MAKE ANY USE OF YOUR CERBERUS POWERS.
THOSE PUPS OVER THERE... ARE THEY NOT YOUR PRECIOUS ALLIES?
PUT THEM TO GOOD USE.
IF YOU WANT... TO LEARN A TECH-NIQUE...YOU CAN USE AT THE WORLD TAG TOURNA-MENT...
フラ...
FURA (WOBBLE)

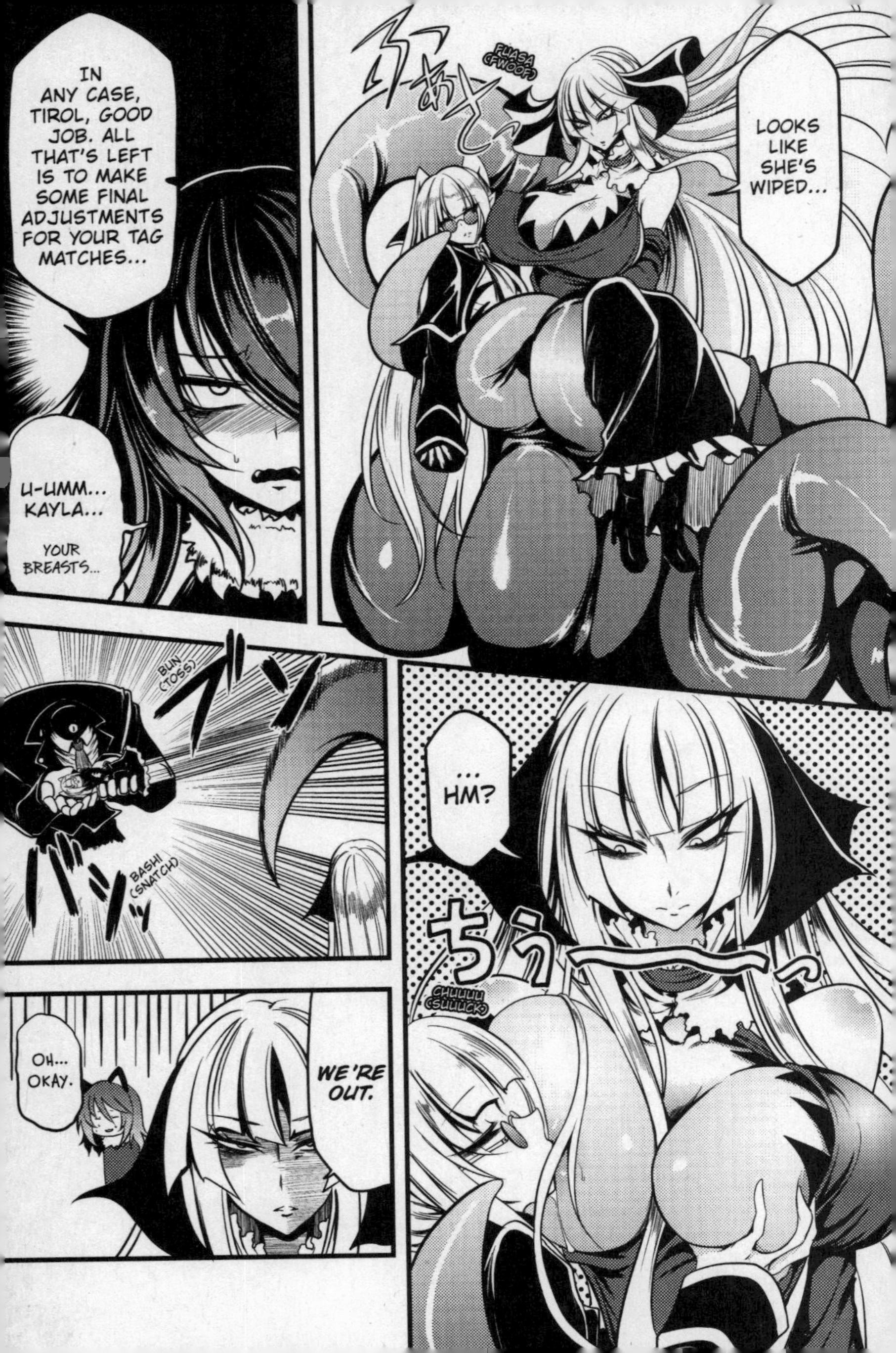
FUASA (FWOOP)
LOOKS LIKE SHE'S WIPED...
IN ANY CASE, TIROL, GOOD JOB. ALL THAT'S LEFT IS TO MAKE SOME FINAL ADJUSTMENTS FOR YOUR TAG MATCHES...
U-UMM... KAYLA...
YOUR BREASTS...
...HM?
CHUUUU (SUUUCK)
BUN (TOSS)
BASHI (SNATCH)
WE'RE OUT.
OH... OKAY.

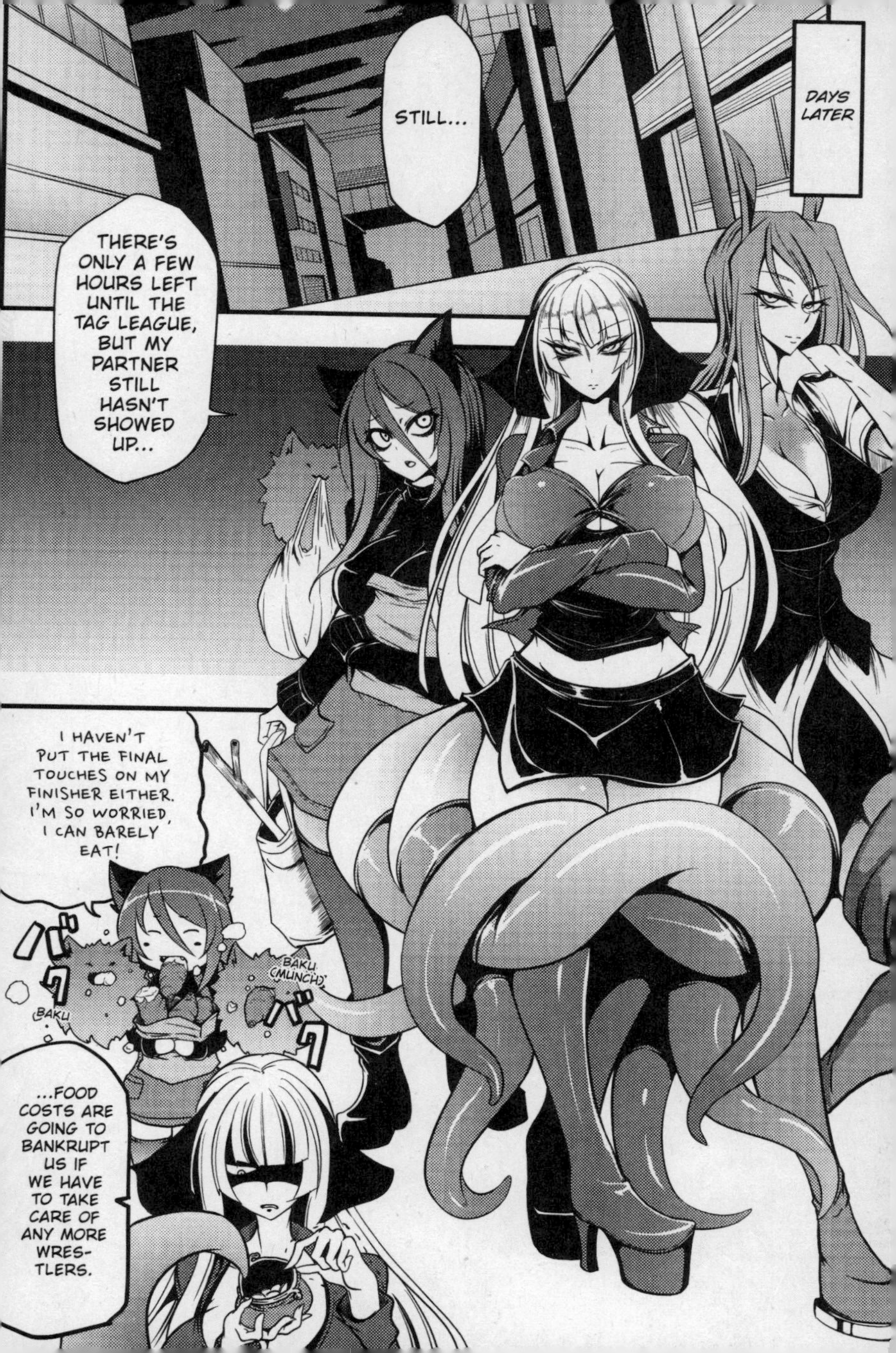

DAYS LATER
STILL...
THERE'S ONLY A FEW HOURS LEFT UNTIL THE TAG LEAGUE, BUT MY PARTNER STILL HASN'T SHOWED UP...
I HAVEN'T PUT THE FINAL TOUCHES ON MY FINISHER EITHER. I'M SO WORRIED, I CAN BARELY EAT!
BAKU (MUNCH)
BAKU
...FOOD COSTS ARE GOING TO BANKRUPT US IF WE HAVE TO TAKE CARE OF ANY MORE WRES-TLERS.

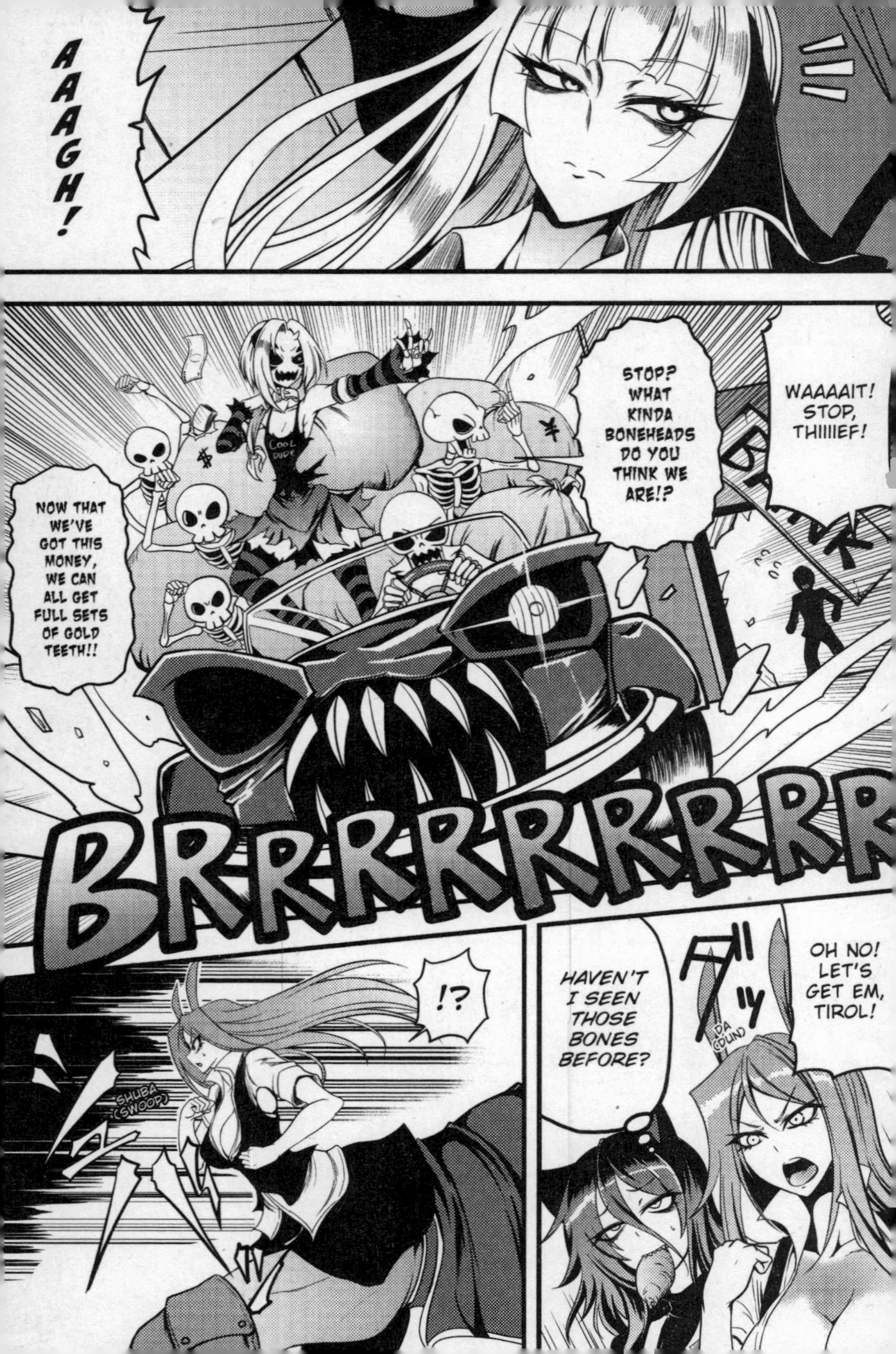

AAAAGH!
WAAAAIT! STOP, THIIIIEF!
STOP? WHAT KINDA BONEHEADS DO YOU THINK WE ARE!?
NOW THAT WE'VE GOT THIS MONEY, WE CAN ALL GET FULL SETS OF GOLD TEETH!!
BRRRRRRRRR
OH NO! LET'S GET EM, TIROL!
DA (DUN)
HAVEN'T I SEEN THOSE BONES BEFORE?
!?
SHUBA (SWOOP)

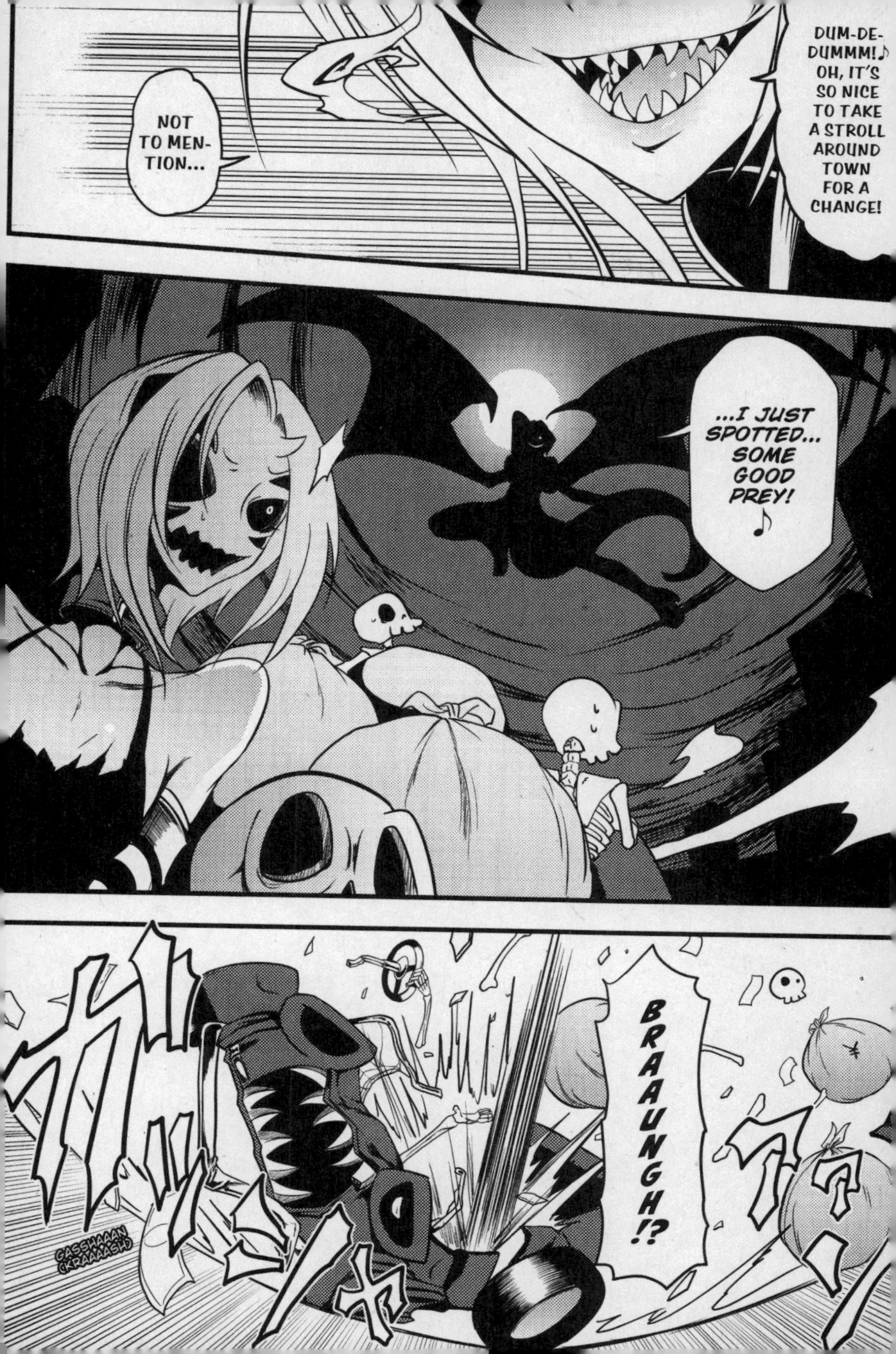
DUM-DE-DUMMM!♪ OH, IT'S SO NICE TO TAKE A STROLL AROUND TOWN FOR A CHANGE!
NOT TO MEN-TION...
...I JUST SPOTTED... SOME GOOD PREY! ♪
BRAAUNGH!?
GASSHAAAN (KRAAAAASH)

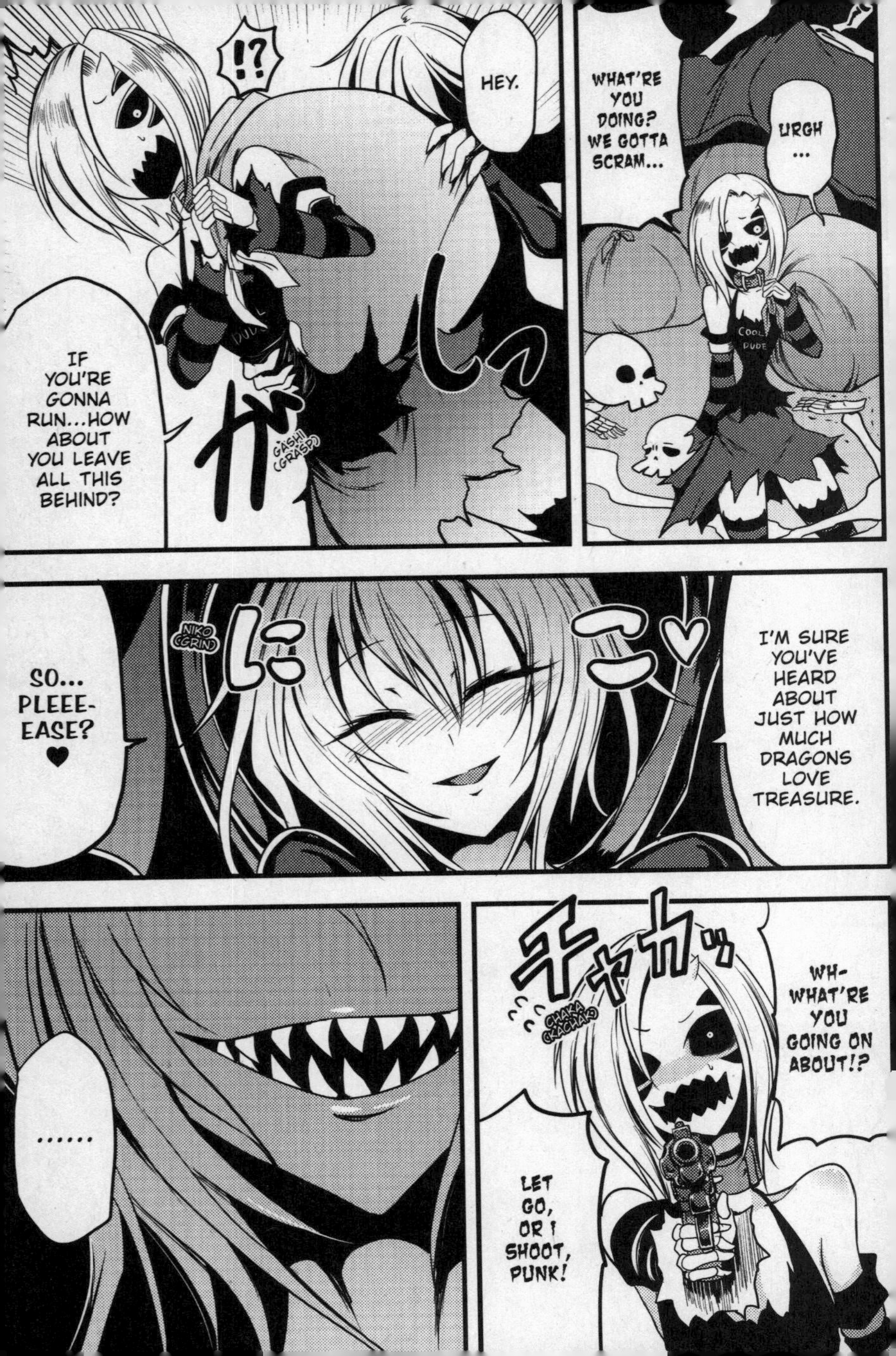
URGH...
WHAT'RE YOU DOING? WE GOTTA SCRAM...
HEY.
!?
GASHI (GRASP)
IF YOU'RE GONNA RUN...HOW ABOUT YOU LEAVE ALL THIS BEHIND?
I'M SURE YOU'VE HEARD ABOUT JUST HOW MUCH DRAGONS LOVE TREASURE.
NIKO (GRIN)
SO... PLEEE-EASE? ♥
CHAKA (KACHAK)
WH-WHAT'RE YOU GOING ON ABOUT!?
LET GO, OR I SHOOT, PUNK!
......

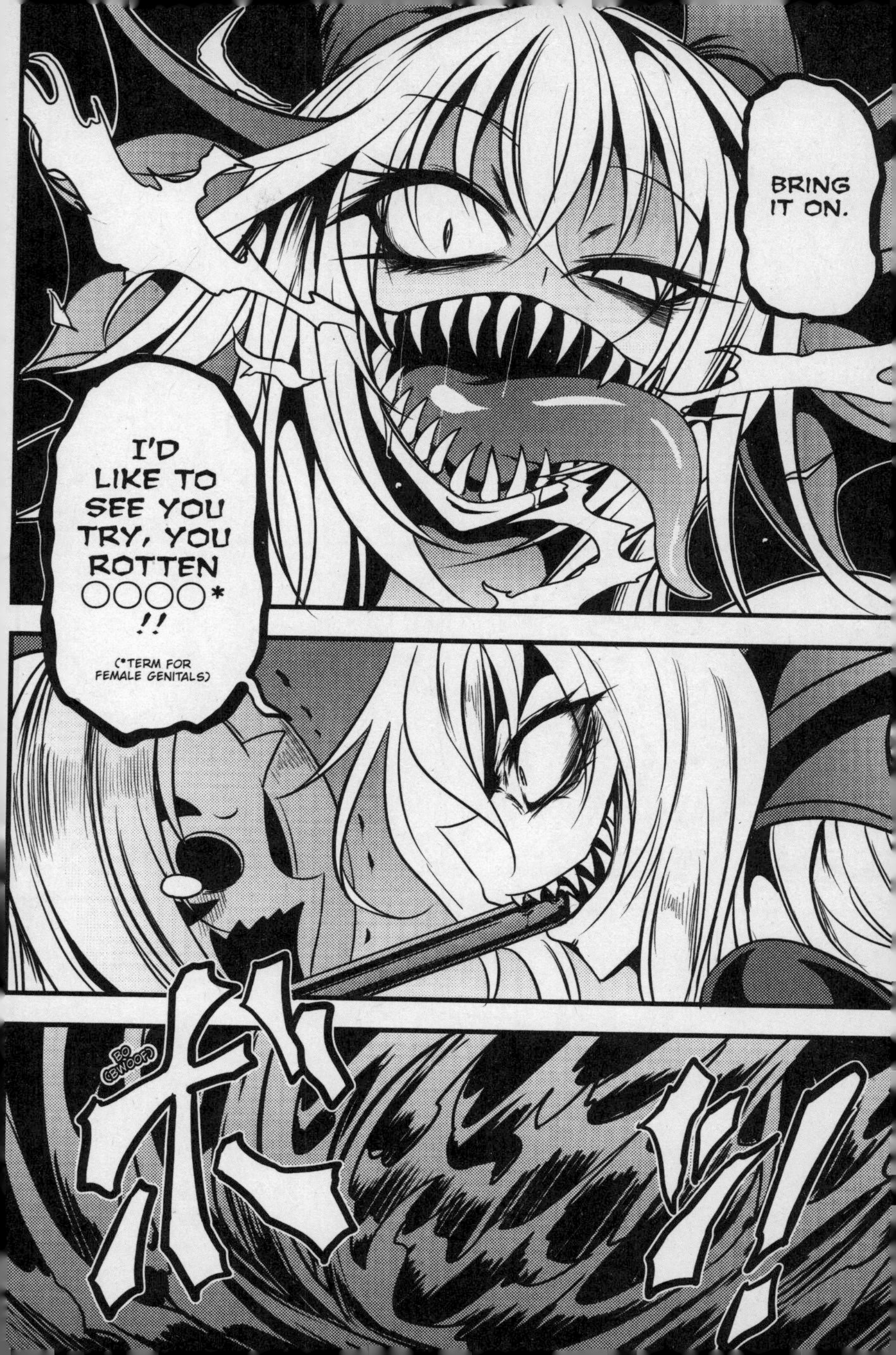

BRING IT ON.
I'D LIKE TO SEE YOU TRY, YOU ROTTEN ○○○○*!!
(*TERM FOR FEMALE GENITALS)
BO (BWOOF)

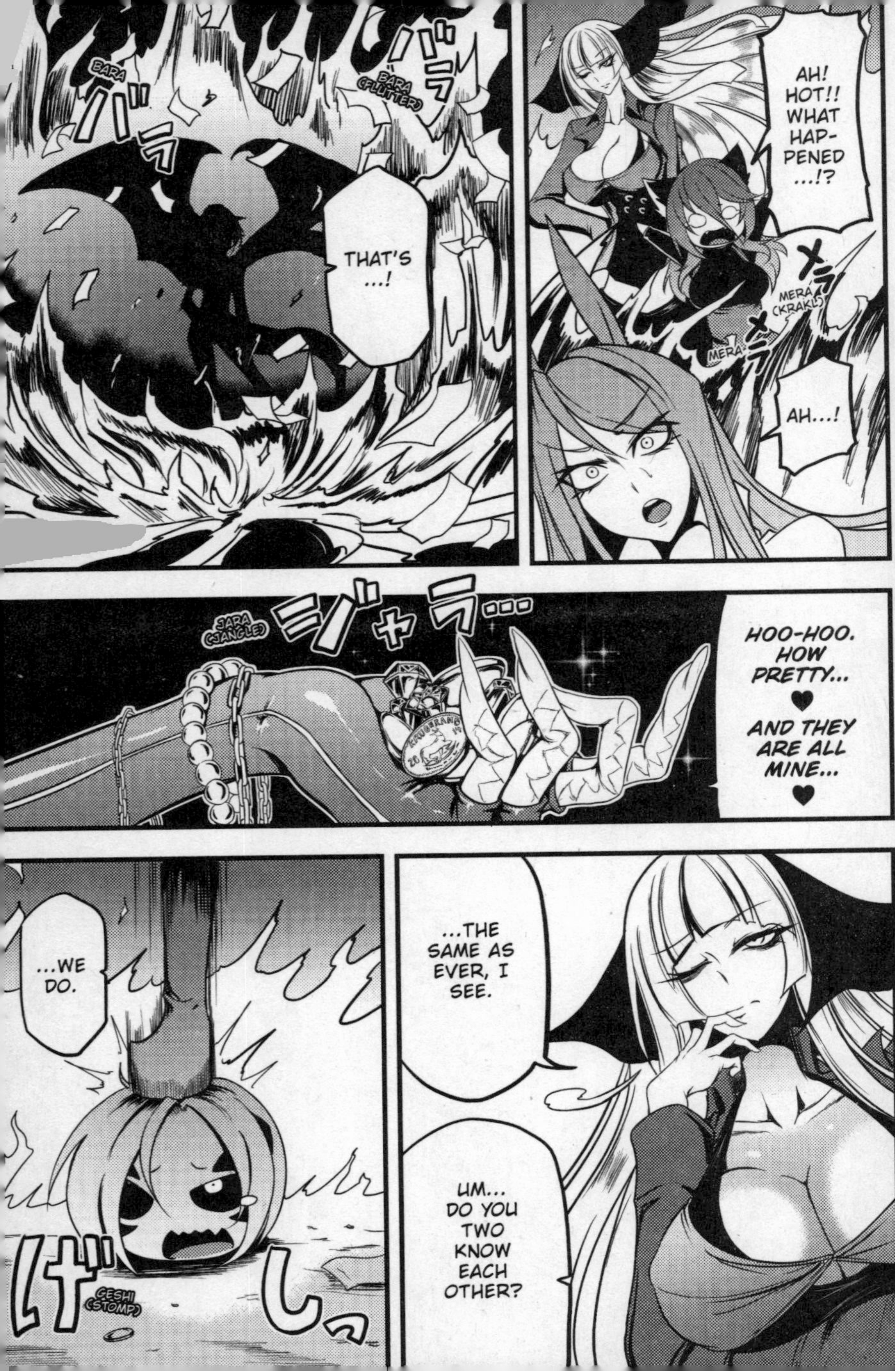
AH! HOT!! WHAT HAP-PENED ...!?
MERA (KRAKL)
MERA
AH...!
BARA (FLUTTER)
BARA
THAT'S ...!
JARA (JANGLE)
HOO-HOO. HOW PRETTY... ♥
AND THEY ARE ALL MINE... ♥
...THE SAME AS EVER, I SEE.
UM... DO YOU TWO KNOW EACH OTHER?
...WE DO.
GESHI (STOMP)

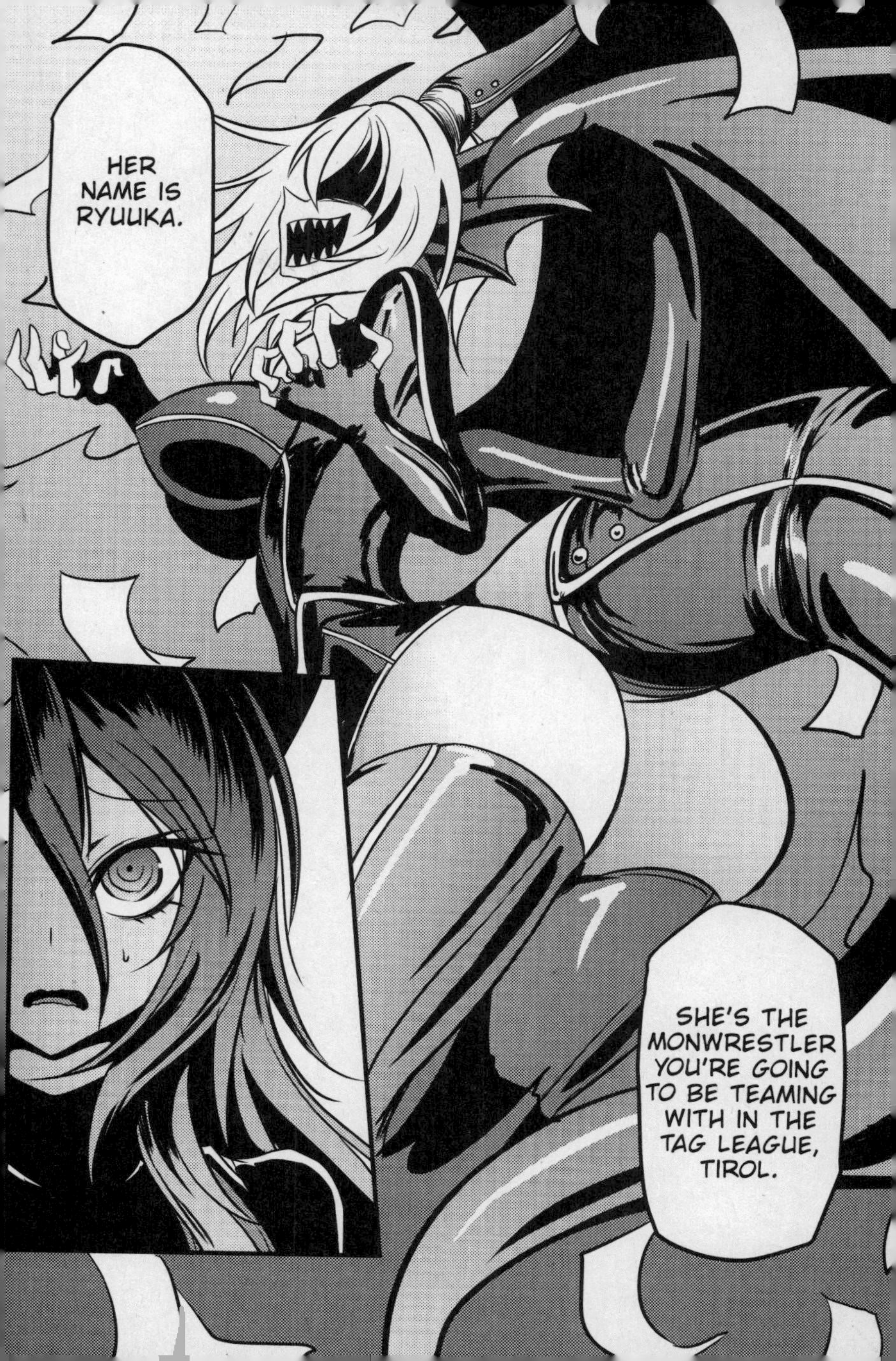
HER NAME IS RYUUKA.
SHE'S THE MONWRESTLER YOU'RE GOING TO BE TEAMING WITH IN THE TAG LEAGUE, TIROL.

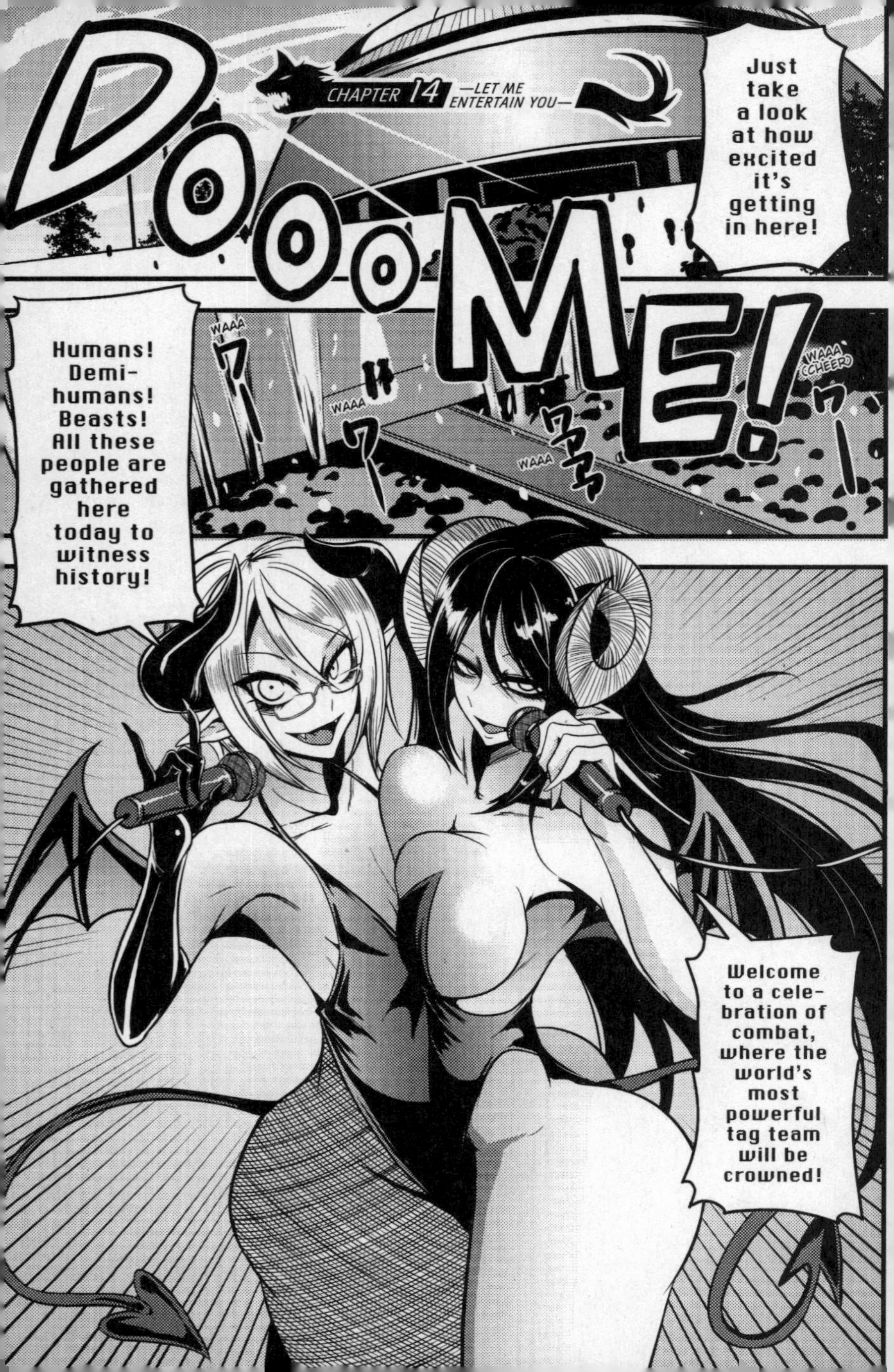
Just take a look at how excited it's getting in here!
CHAPTER 14 —LET ME ENTERTAIN YOU—
DOOOOOME!
WAAA (CHEER)
WAAA
WAAA
WAAA
Humans! Demi-humans! Beasts! All these people are gathered here today to witness history!
Welcome to a cele-bration of combat, where the world's most powerful tag team will be crowned!

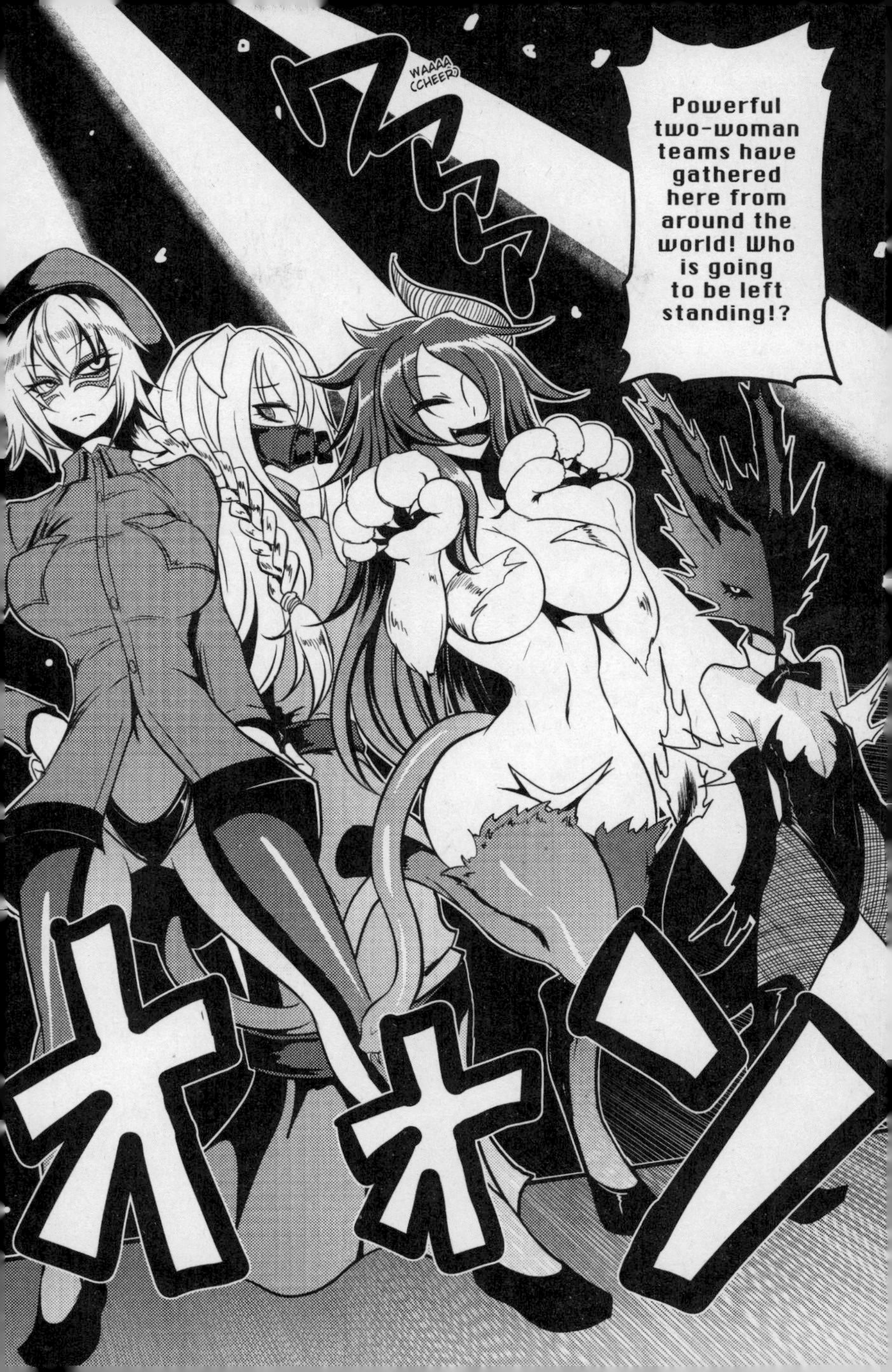

Powerful two-woman teams have gathered here from around the world! Who is going to be left standing!?
WAAAA (CHEER)

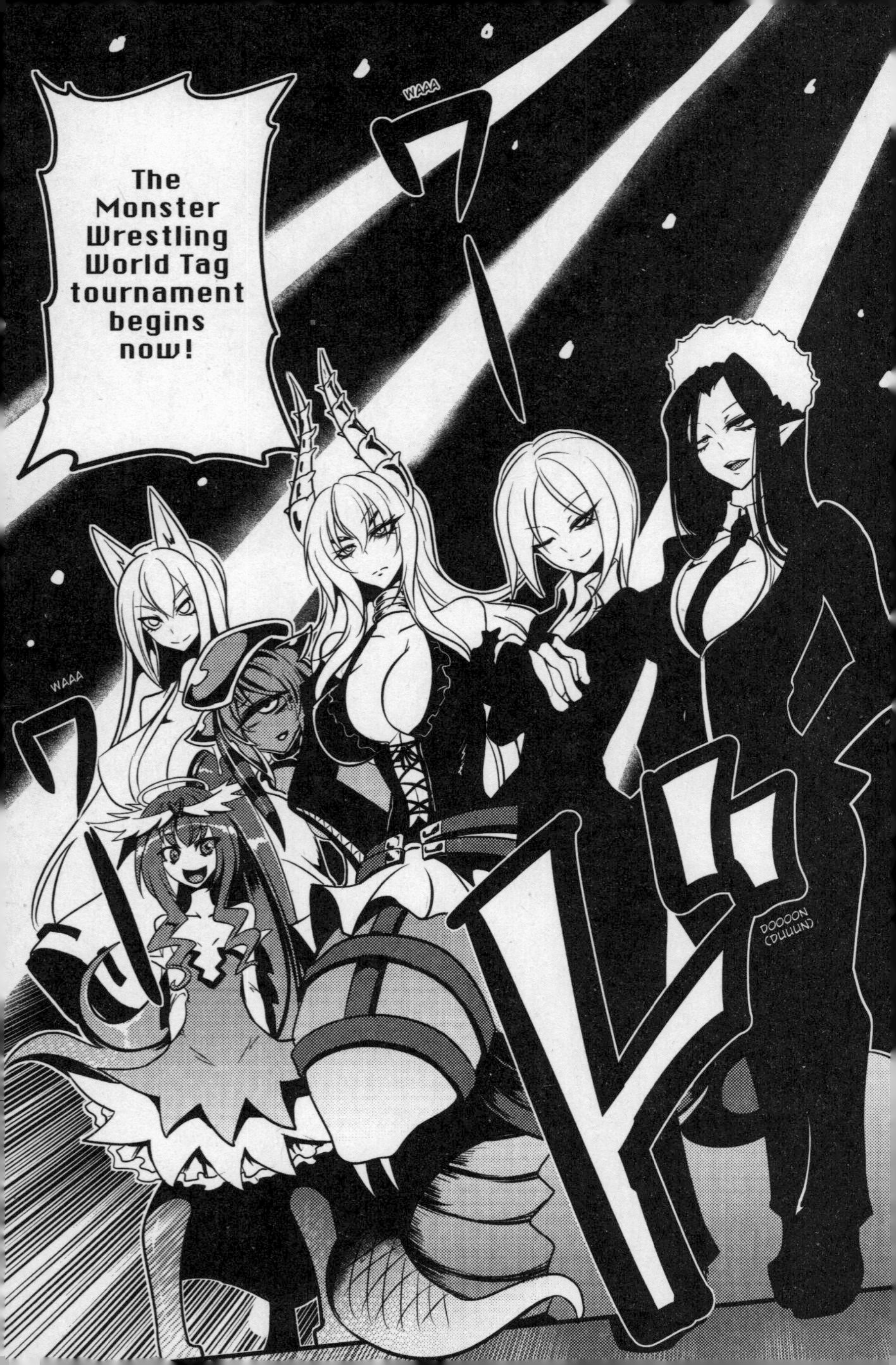

WAAA
The Monster Wrestling World Tag tournament begins now!
WAAA
DOOOON (DUUUN)

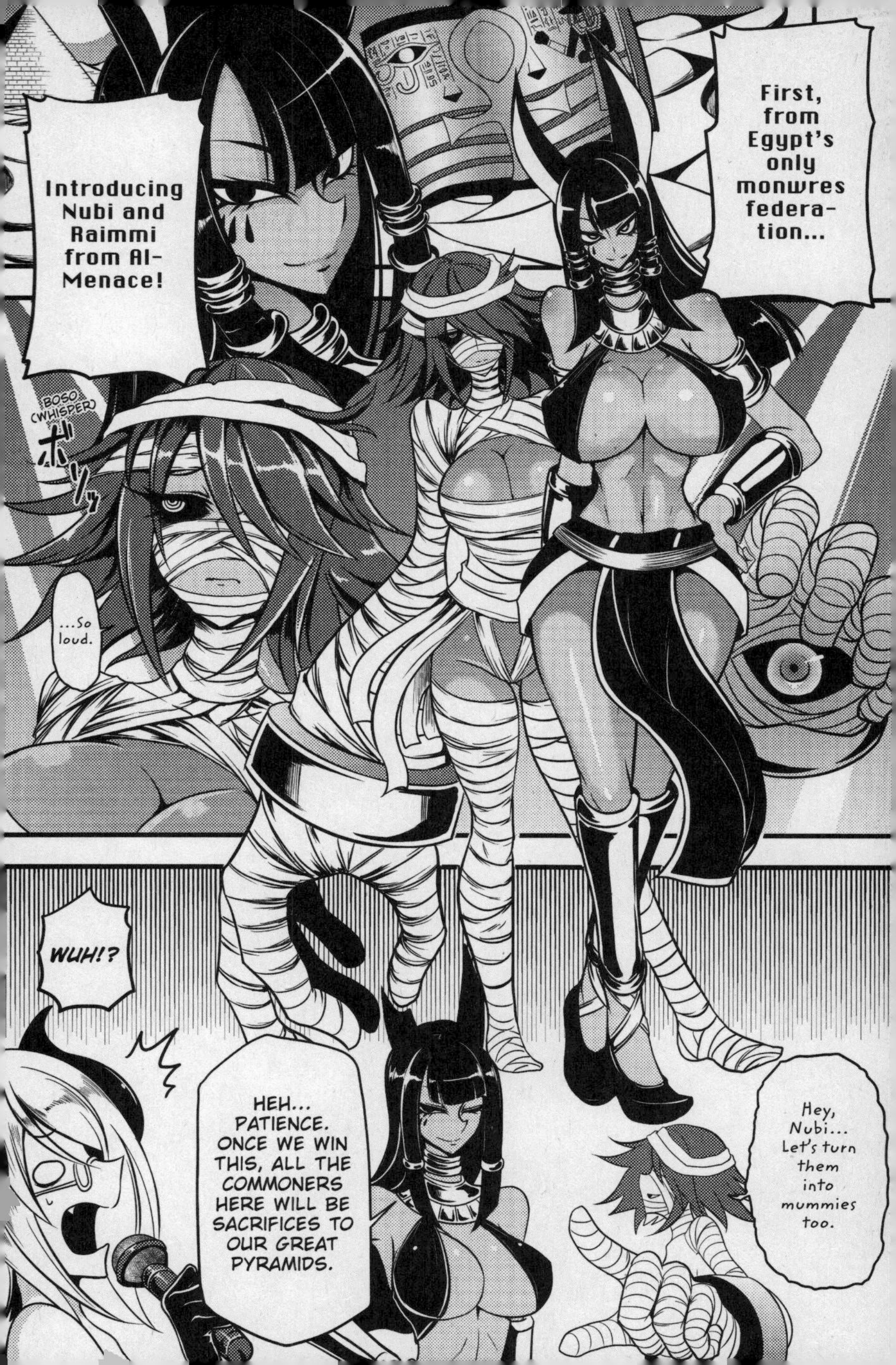

First, from Egypt's only monwres federation...
Introducing Nubi and Raimmi from Al-Menace!
ボソッ
BOSO (WHISPER)
...So loud.
Hey, Nubi... Let's turn them into mummies too.
HEH... PATIENCE. ONCE WE WIN THIS, ALL THE COMMONERS HERE WILL BE SACRIFICES TO OUR GREAT PYRAMIDS.
WUH!?

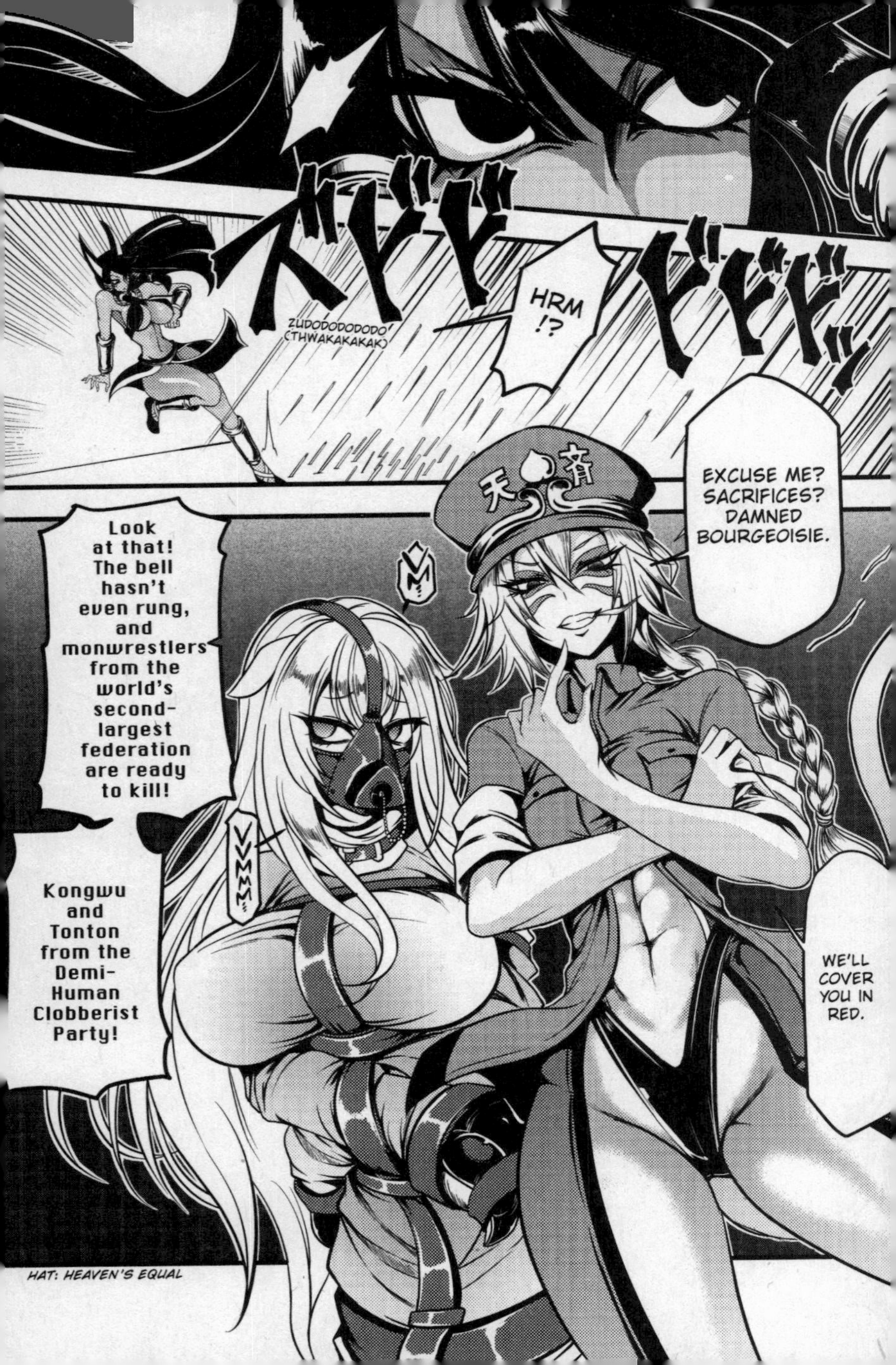
HRM !?
ZUDODODODODO (THWAKAKAKAK)
EXCUSE ME? SACRIFICES? DAMNED BOURGEOISIE.
天 斉
Look at that! The bell hasn't even rung, and monwrestlers from the world's second-largest federation are ready to kill!
VM...
VVMMM...
WE'LL COVER YOU IN RED.
Kongwu and Tonton from the Demi-Human Clobberist Party!
HAT: HEAVEN'S EQUAL

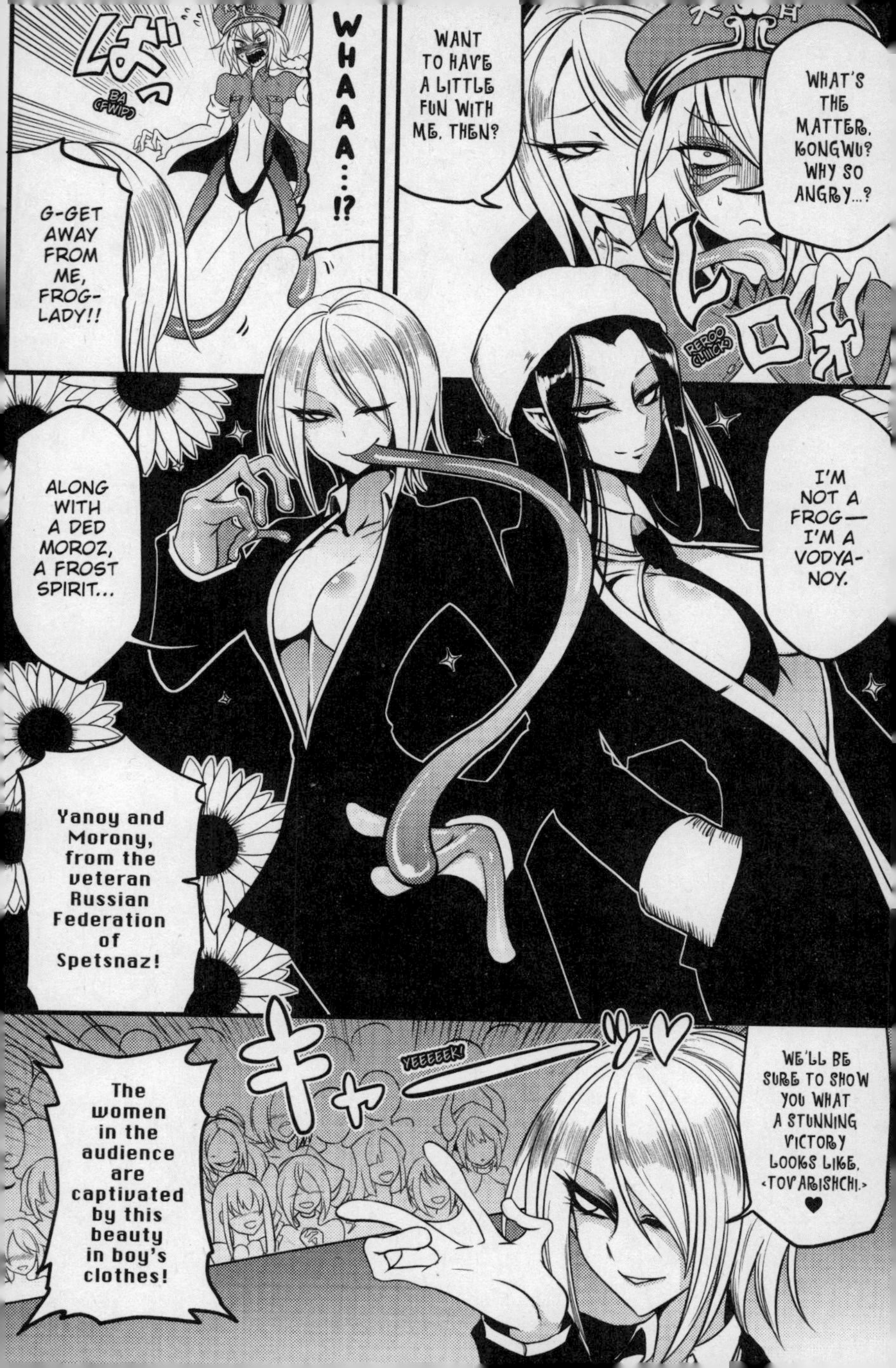
WHAT'S THE MATTER, KONGWU? WHY SO ANGRY...?
レロオ
REROO (LIIICK)
WANT TO HAVE A LITTLE FUN WITH ME, THEN?
WHAAAA...!?
ばっ
BA (FWIP)
G-GET AWAY FROM ME, FROG-LADY!!
I'M NOT A FROG— I'M A VODYANOY.
ALONG WITH A DED MOROZ, A FROST SPIRIT...
Yanoy and Morony, from the veteran Russian Federation of Spetsnaz!
WE'LL BE SURE TO SHOW YOU WHAT A STUNNING VICTORY LOOKS LIKE, <TOVARISHCHI.> ♥
キャ
YEEEEEK!
The women in the audience are captivated by this beauty in boy's clothes!

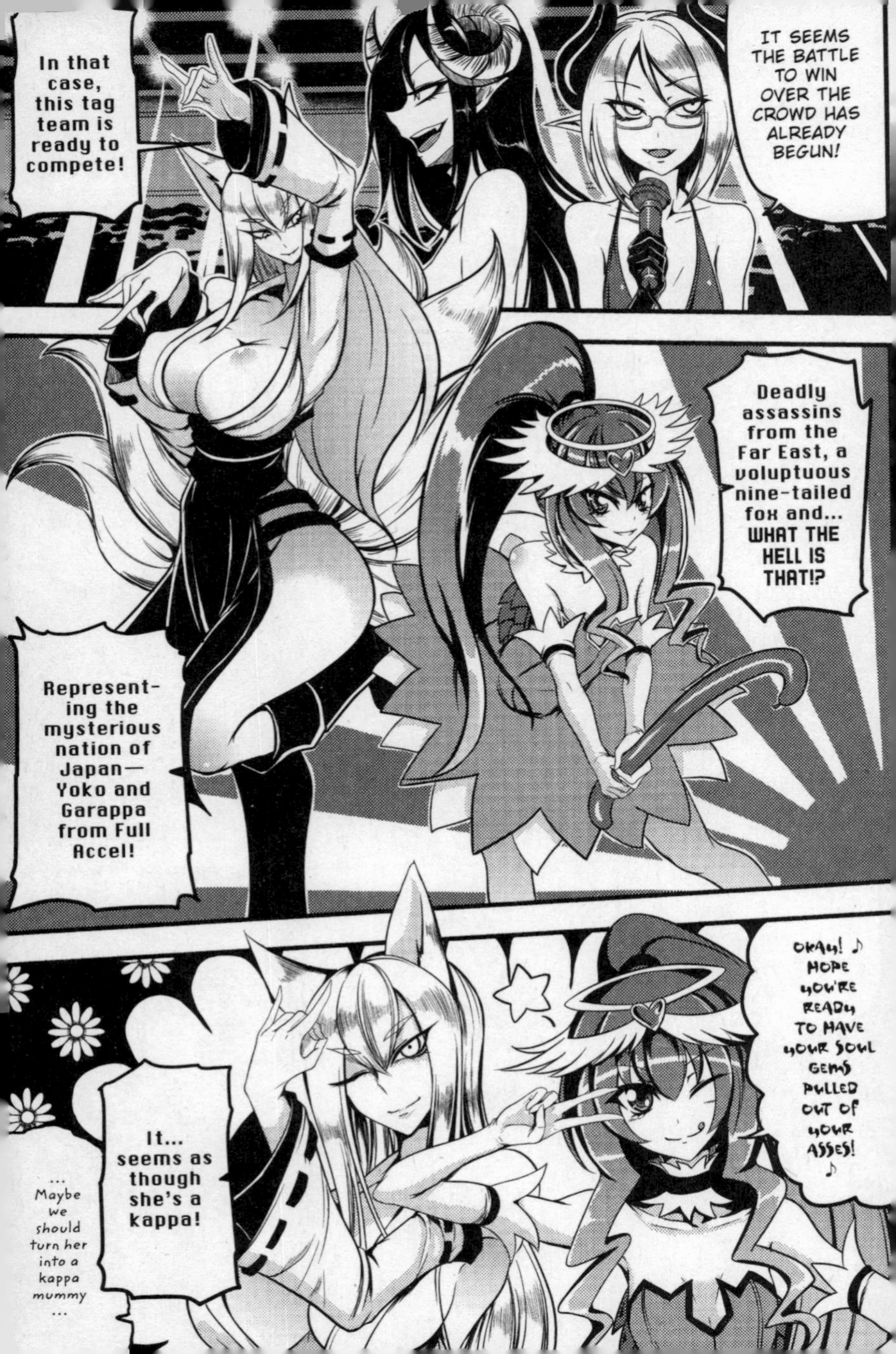
IT SEEMS THE BATTLE TO WIN OVER THE CROWD HAS ALREADY BEGUN!
In that case, this tag team is ready to compete!
Deadly assassins from the Far East, a voluptuous nine-tailed fox and... WHAT THE HELL IS THAT!?
Representing the mysterious nation of Japan—Yoko and Garappa from Full Accel!
OKAY! ♪ HOPE YOU'RE READY TO HAVE YOUR SOUL GEMS PULLED OUT OF YOUR ASSES! ♪
It... seems as though she's a kappa!
...Maybe we should turn her into a kappa mummy...

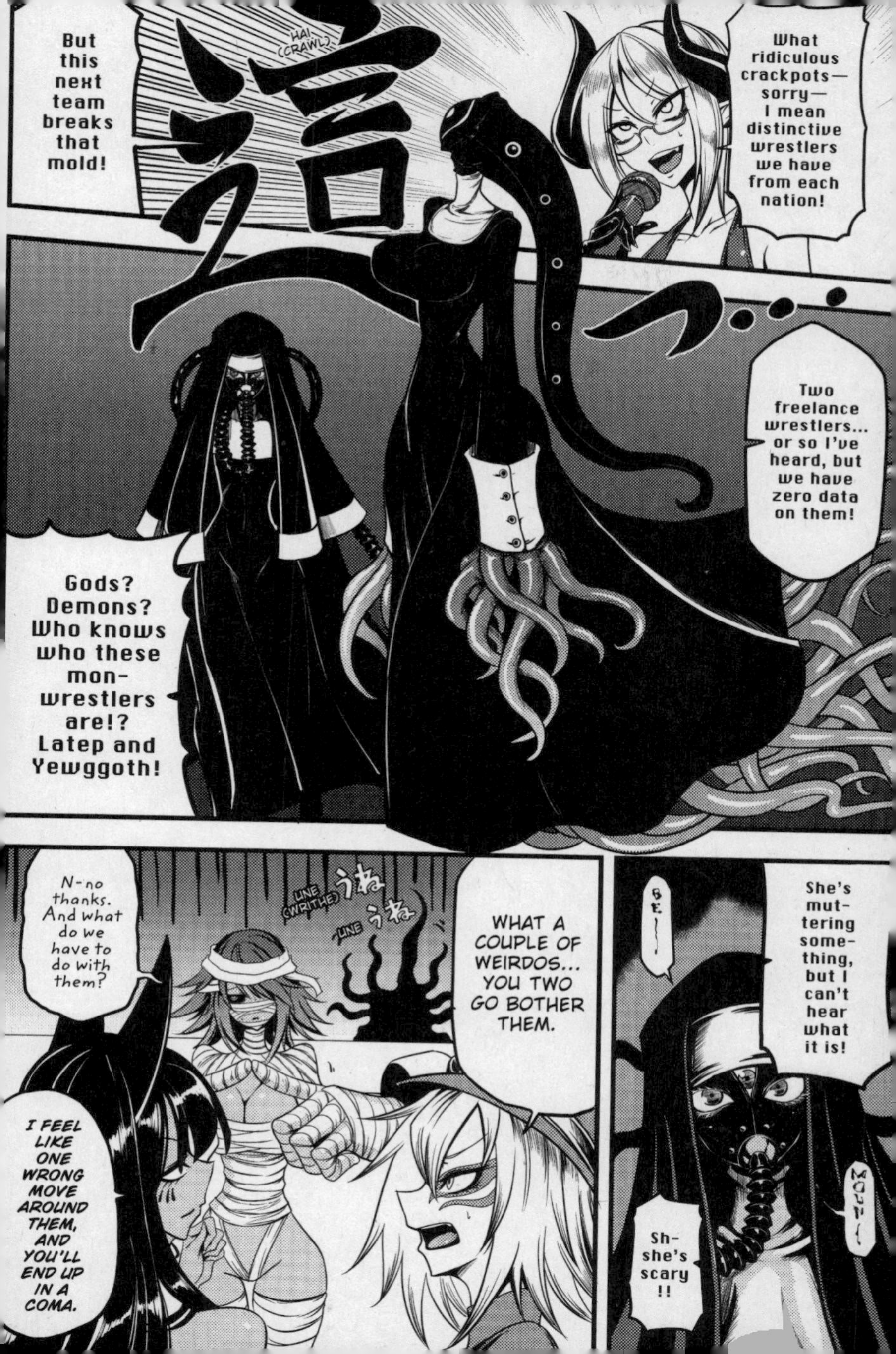
What ridiculous crackpots—sorry—I mean distinctive wrestlers we have from each nation!
HAI (CRAWL)
But this next team breaks that mold!
Two freelance wrestlers... or so I've heard, but we have zero data on them!
Gods? Demons? Who knows who these mon-wrestlers are!? Latep and Yewggoth!
She's mut-tering some-thing, but I can't hear what it is!
Sh-she's scary!!
WHAT A COUPLE OF WEIRDOS... YOU TWO GO BOTHER THEM.
UNE (WRITHE) うね
UNE うね
N-no thanks. And what do we have to do with them?
I FEEL LIKE ONE WRONG MOVE AROUND THEM, AND YOU'LL END UP IN A COMA.

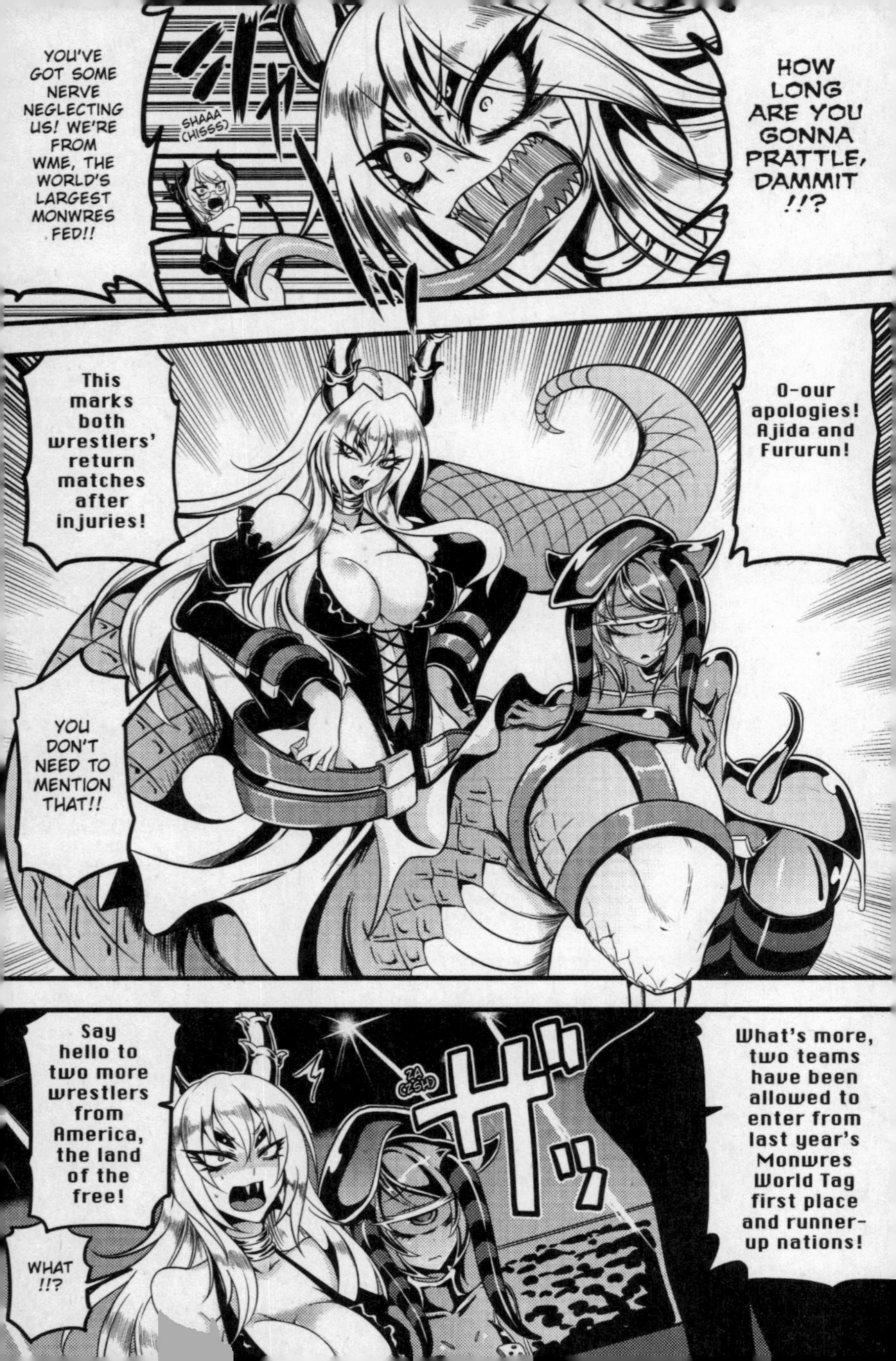
HOW LONG ARE YOU GONNA PRATTLE, DAMMIT!!?
SHAAA (HISSS)
YOU'VE GOT SOME NERVE NEGLECTING US! WE'RE FROM WME, THE WORLD'S LARGEST MONWRES FED!!
O-our apologies! Ajida and Fururun!
This marks both wrestlers' return matches after injuries!
YOU DON'T NEED TO MENTION THAT!!
What's more, two teams have been allowed to enter from last year's Monwres World Tag first place and runner-up nations!
ZA (GZSH)
Say hello to two more wrestlers from America, the land of the free!
WHAT!!?

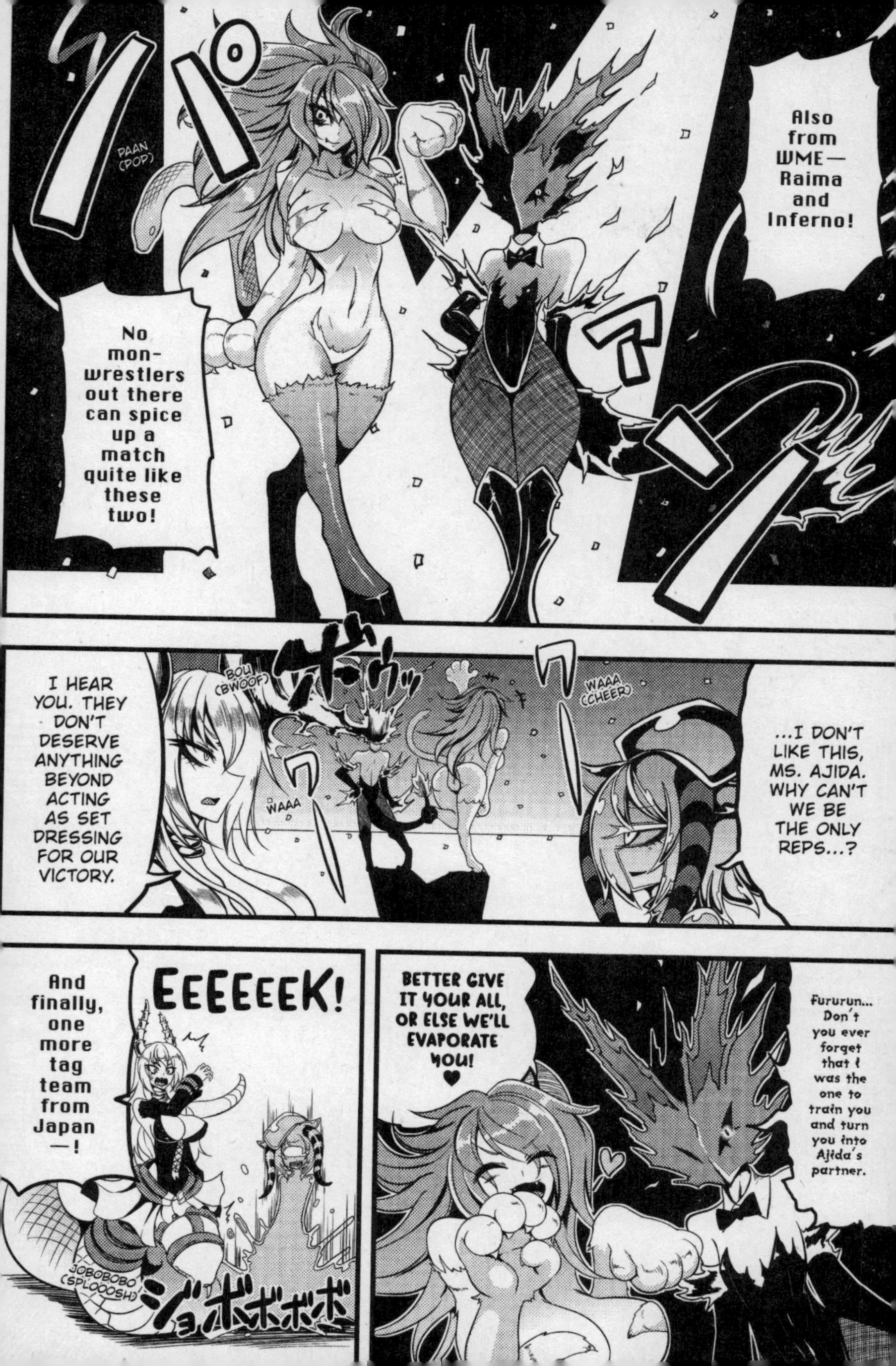
Also from WME—Raima and Inferno!
PAAN (POP)
No mon-wrestlers out there can spice up a match quite like these two!
...I DON'T LIKE THIS, MS. AJIDA. WHY CAN'T WE BE THE ONLY REPS...?
WAAA (CHEER)
BOU (BWOOF)
WAAA
I HEAR YOU. THEY DON'T DESERVE ANYTHING BEYOND ACTING AS SET DRESSING FOR OUR VICTORY.
Fururun... Don't you ever forget that I was the one to train you and turn you into Ajida's partner.
BETTER GIVE IT YOUR ALL, OR ELSE WE'LL EVAPORATE YOU! ♥
EEEEEEK!
And finally, one more tag team from Japan—!
JOBOBOBO (SPLOOOSH)

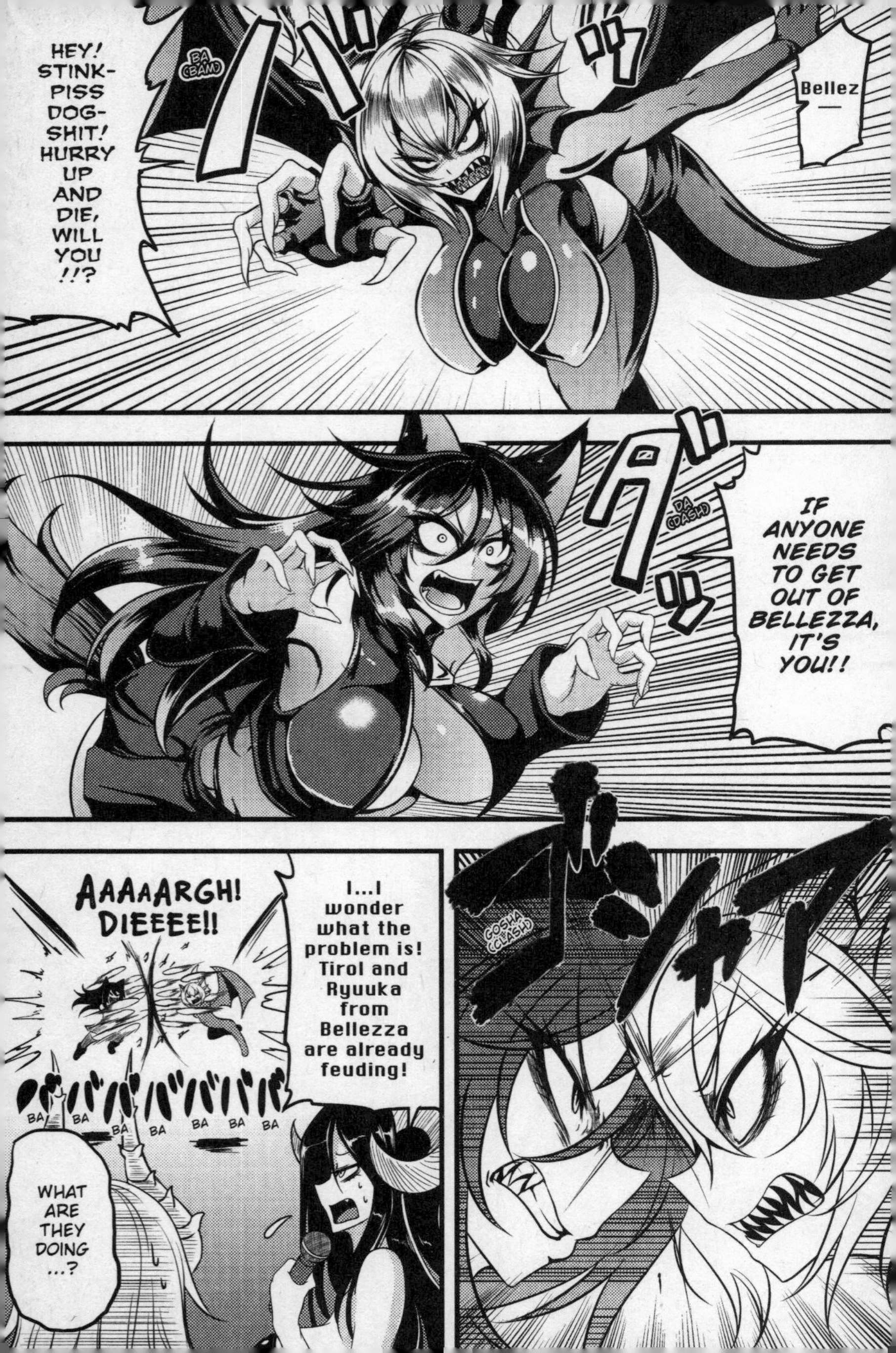
Bellez—
BA (BAM)
HEY! STINK-PISS DOG-SHIT! HURRY UP AND DIE, WILL YOU!!?
DA (DASH)
IF ANYONE NEEDS TO GET OUT OF BELLEZZA, IT'S YOU!!
GOSHA (CLASH)
I...I wonder what the problem is! Tirol and Ryuuka from Bellezza are already feuding!
AAAAARGH! DIEEEE!!
BA BA BA BA BA BA BA
WHAT ARE THEY DOING...?

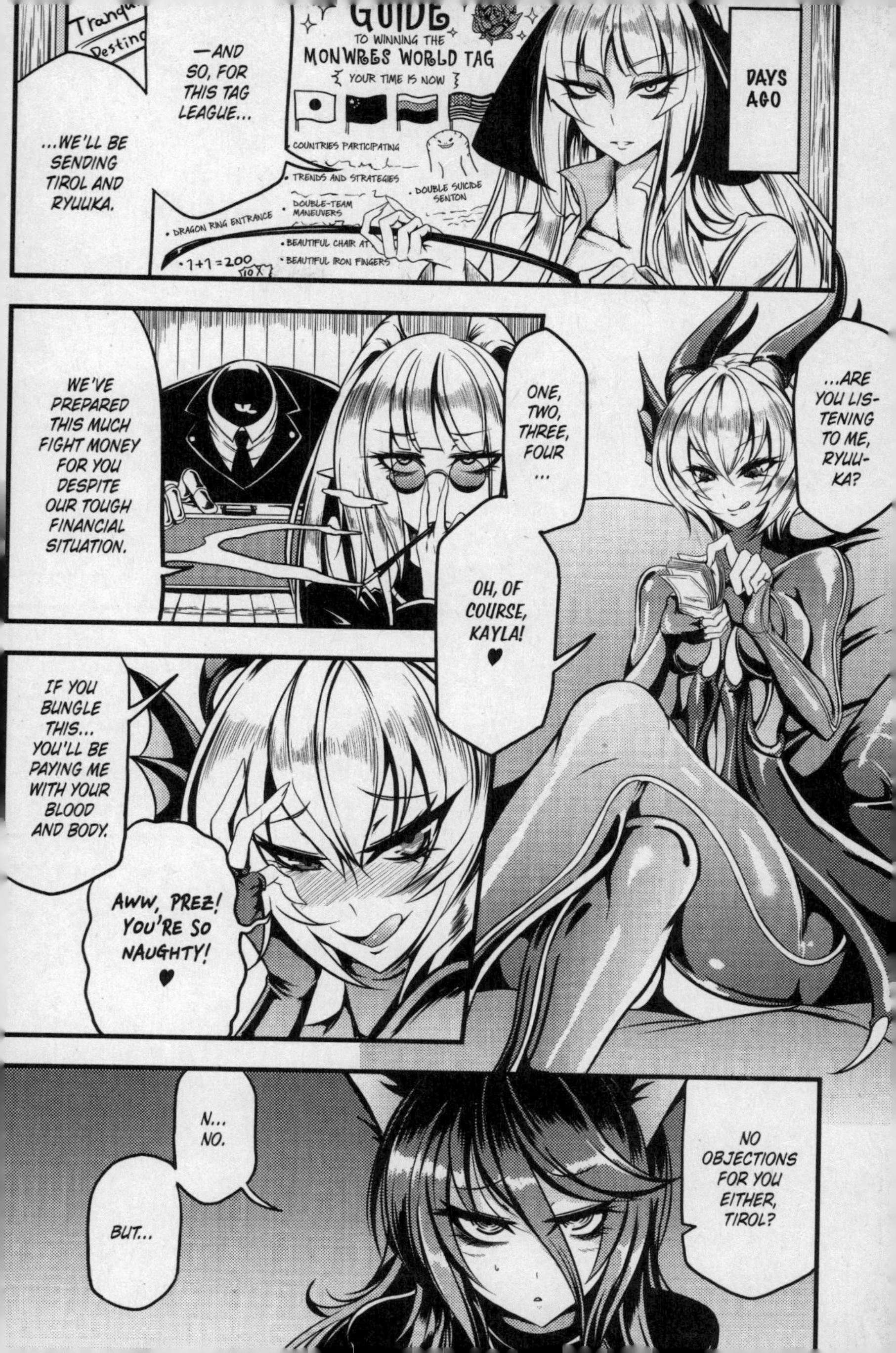
DAYS AGO
GUIDE
TO WINNING THE MONWRES WORLD TAG
YOUR TIME IS NOW
COUNTRIES PARTICIPATING
TRENDS AND STRATEGIES
DOUBLE SUICIDE SENTON
DOUBLE-TEAM MANEUVERS
DRAGON RING ENTRANCE
BEAUTIFUL CHAIR AT
BEAUTIFUL IRON FINGERS
1+1=200
—AND SO, FOR THIS TAG LEAGUE...
...WE'LL BE SENDING TIROL AND RYUUKA.
...ARE YOU LISTENING TO ME, RYUUKA?
ONE, TWO, THREE, FOUR...
OH, OF COURSE, KAYLA! ♥
WE'VE PREPARED THIS MUCH FIGHT MONEY FOR YOU DESPITE OUR TOUGH FINANCIAL SITUATION.
AWW, PREZ! YOU'RE SO NAUGHTY! ♥
IF YOU BUNGLE THIS... YOU'LL BE PAYING ME WITH YOUR BLOOD AND BODY.
NO OBJECTIONS FOR YOU EITHER, TIROL?
N... NO.
BUT...

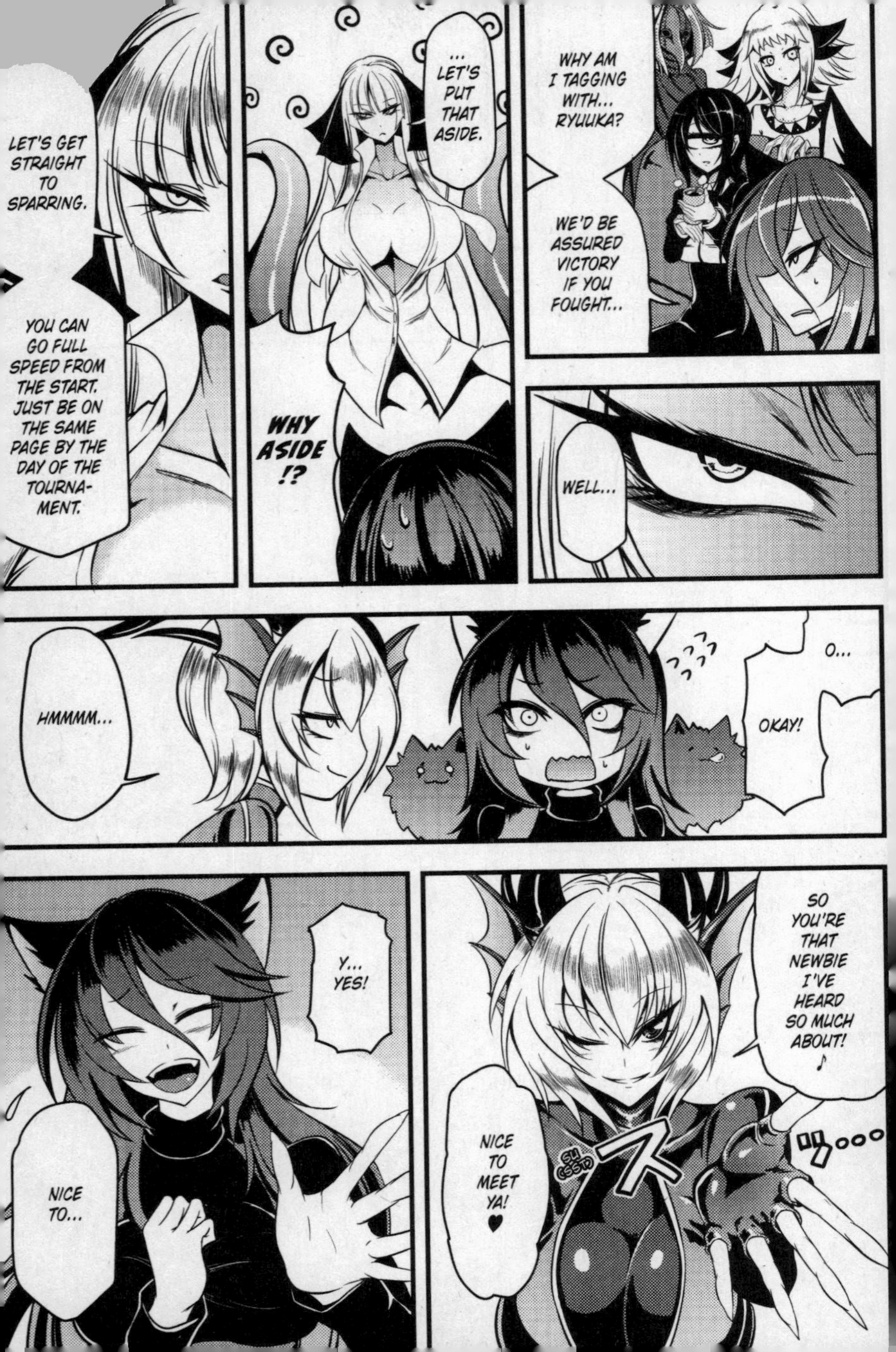
WHY AM I TAGGING WITH... RYUUKA?
WE'D BE ASSURED VICTORY IF YOU FOUGHT...
WELL...
... LET'S PUT THAT ASIDE.
WHY ASIDE !?
LET'S GET STRAIGHT TO SPARRING.
YOU CAN GO FULL SPEED FROM THE START. JUST BE ON THE SAME PAGE BY THE DAY OF THE TOURNA-MENT.
O...
OKAY!
HMMMM...
SO YOU'RE THAT NEWBIE I'VE HEARD SO MUCH ABOUT! ♪
NICE TO MEET YA! ♥
Y... YES!
NICE TO...

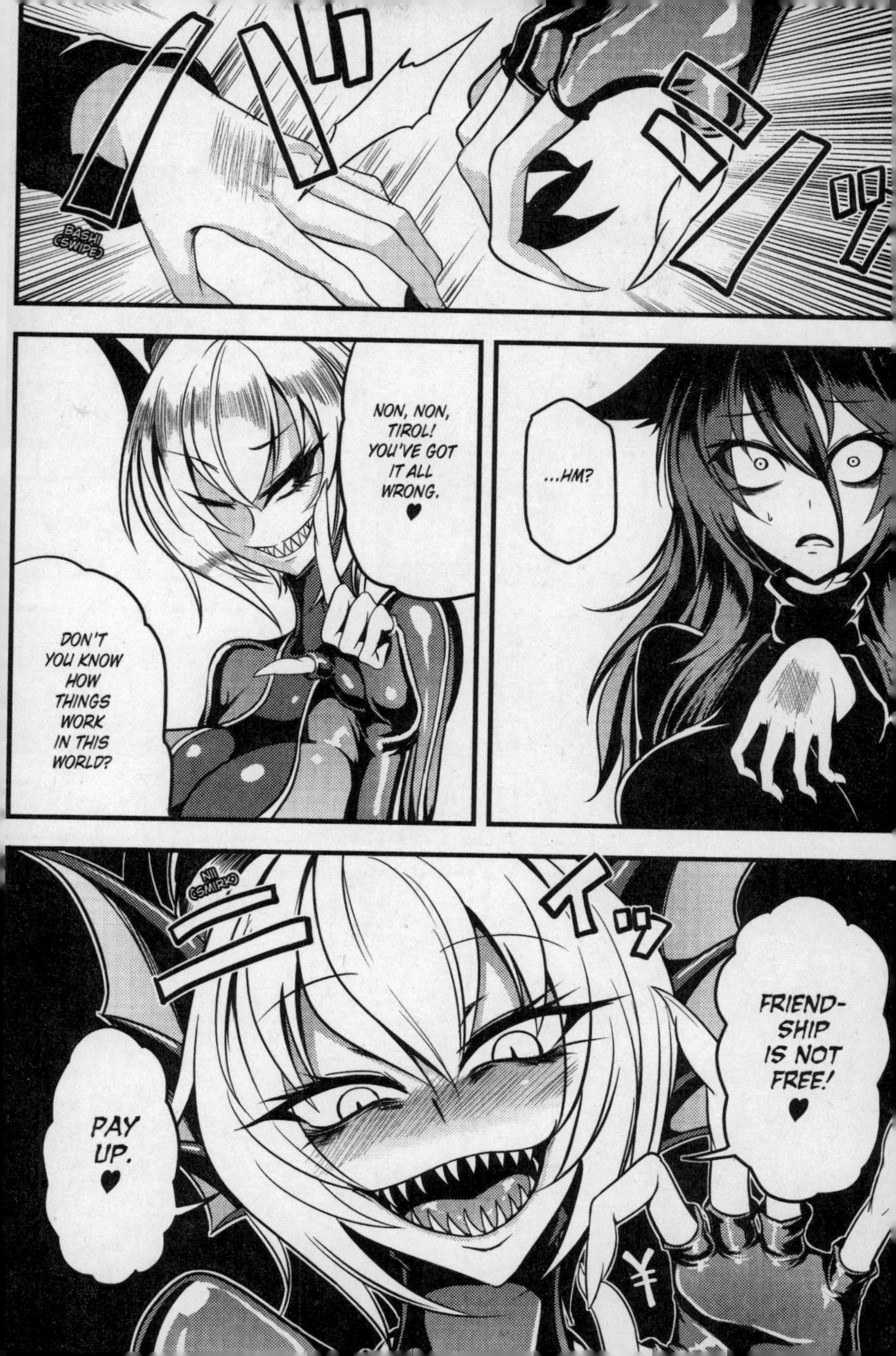
BASHI (SWIPE)
...HM?
NON, NON, TIROL! YOU'VE GOT IT ALL WRONG. ♥
DON'T YOU KNOW HOW THINGS WORK IN THIS WORLD?
NII (SMIRK)
FRIEND-SHIP IS NOT FREE! ♥
PAY UP. ♥
¥

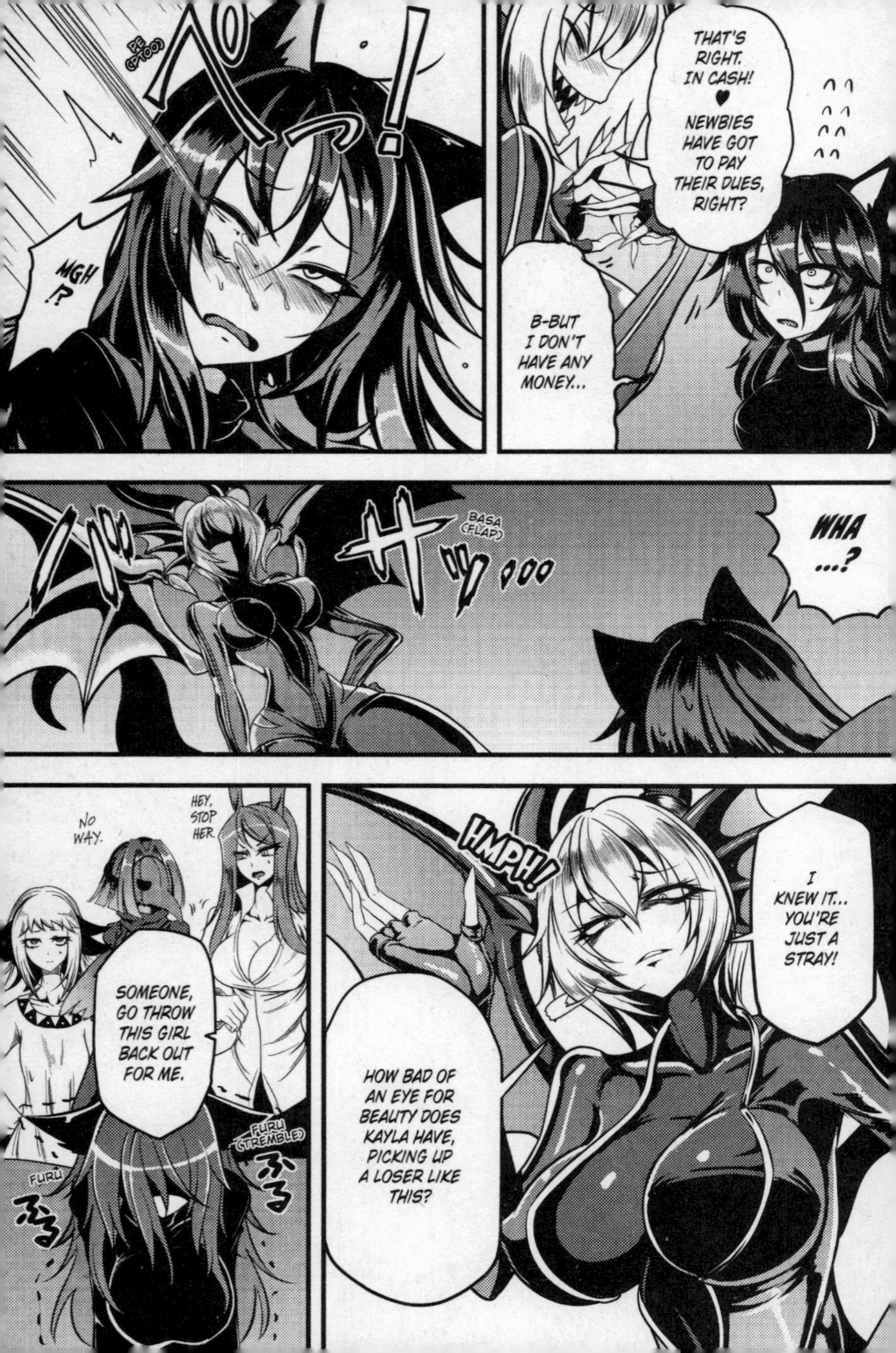
THAT'S RIGHT. IN CASH! ♥
NEWBIES HAVE GOT TO PAY THEIR DUES, RIGHT?
B-BUT I DON'T HAVE ANY MONEY...
PE (P'TOO)
MGH !?
WHA ...?
BASA (FLAP)
HMPH!
I KNEW IT... YOU'RE JUST A STRAY!
HOW BAD OF AN EYE FOR BEAUTY DOES KAYLA HAVE, PICKING UP A LOSER LIKE THIS?
HEY, STOP HER.
NO WAY.
SOMEONE, GO THROW THIS GIRL BACK OUT FOR ME.
FURU (TREMBLE)
FURU

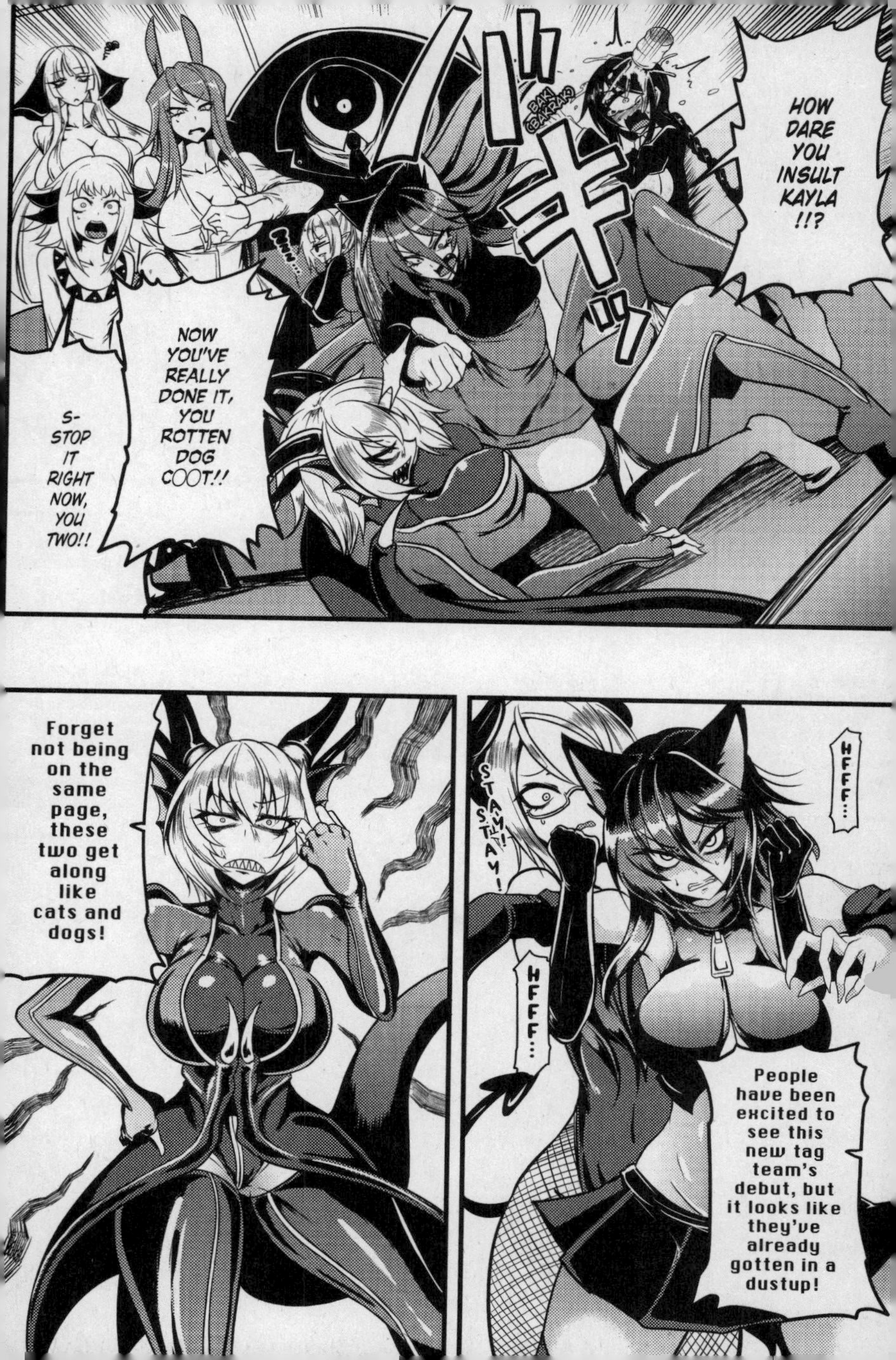
HOW DARE YOU INSULT KAYLA!!?
BAKI (BAKRAK)
NOW YOU'VE REALLY DONE IT, YOU ROTTEN DOG COOT!!
S-STOP IT RIGHT NOW, YOU TWO!!
HFFF...
STAY! STAY!
HFFF...
People have been excited to see this new tag team's debut, but it looks like they've already gotten in a dustup!
Forget not being on the same page, these two get along like cats and dogs!

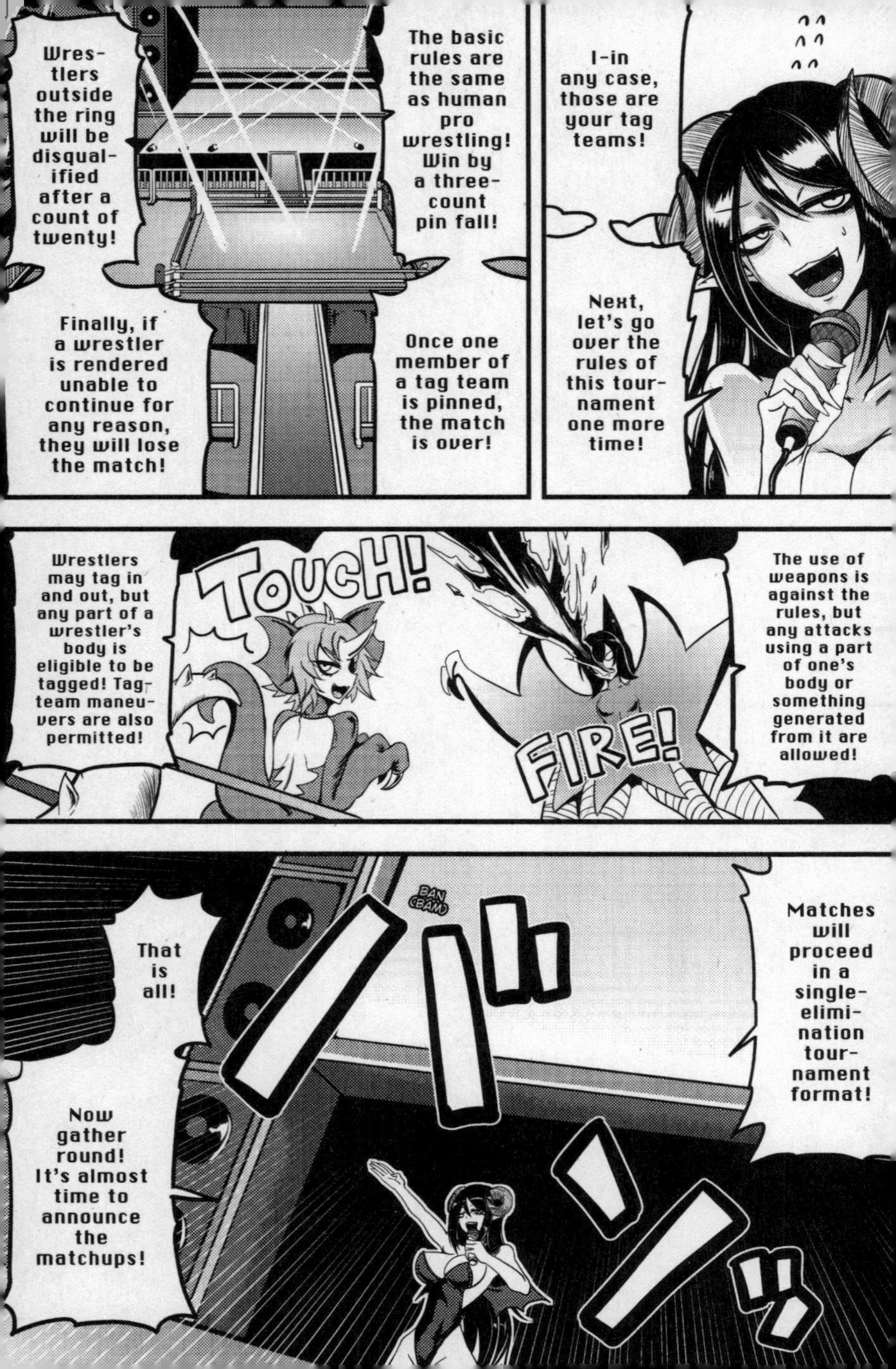

I-in any case, those are your tag teams!
Next, let's go over the rules of this tournament one more time!
The basic rules are the same as human pro wrestling! Win by a three-count pin fall!
Once one member of a tag team is pinned, the match is over!
Wrestlers outside the ring will be disqualified after a count of twenty!
Finally, if a wrestler is rendered unable to continue for any reason, they will lose the match!
The use of weapons is against the rules, but any attacks using a part of one's body or something generated from it are allowed!
FIRE!
TOUCH!
Wrestlers may tag in and out, but any part of a wrestler's body is eligible to be tagged! Tag-team maneuvers are also permitted!
Matches will proceed in a single-elimination tournament format!
BAN (BAM)
That is all!
Now gather round! It's almost time to announce the matchups!

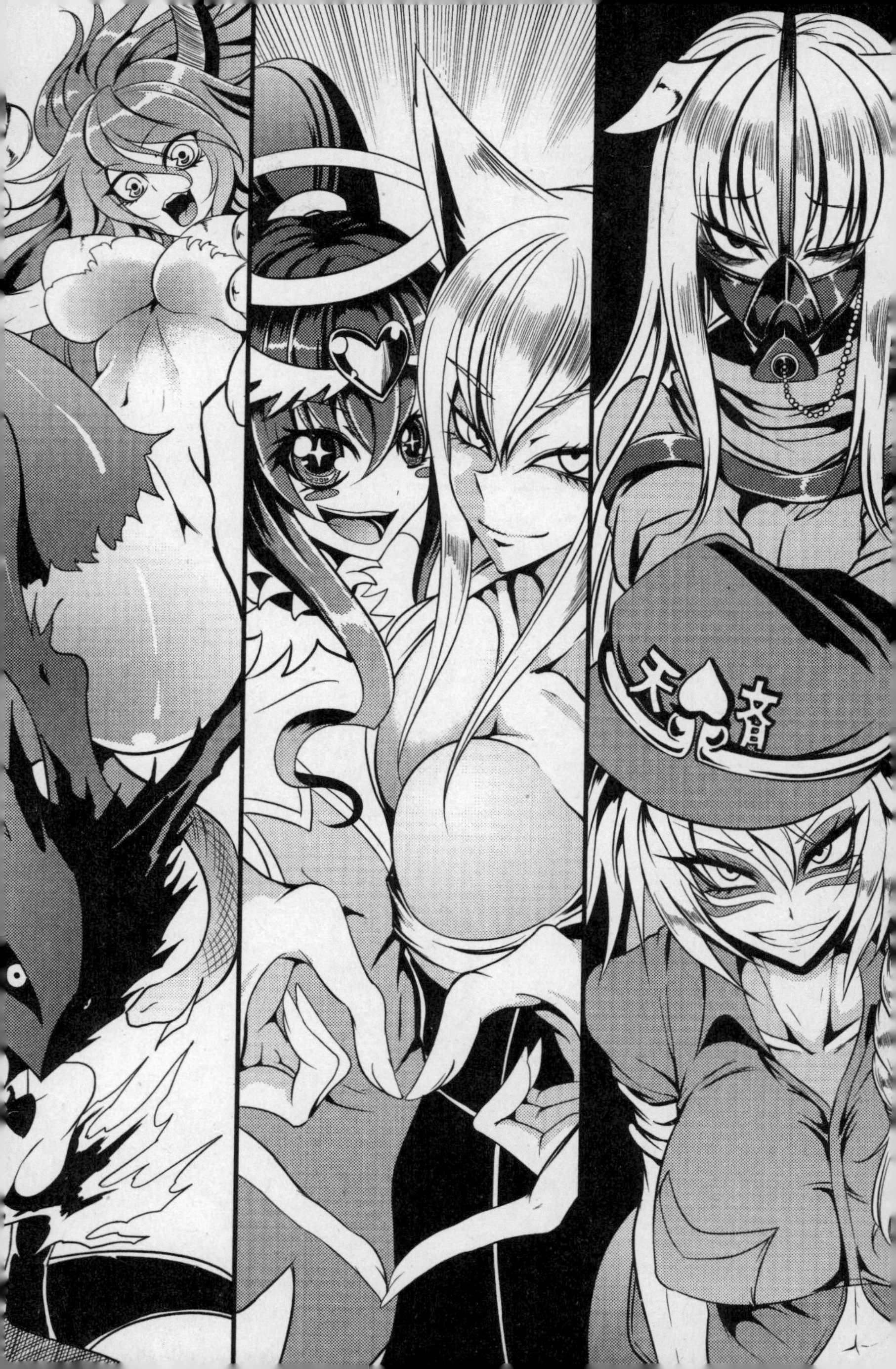
天音

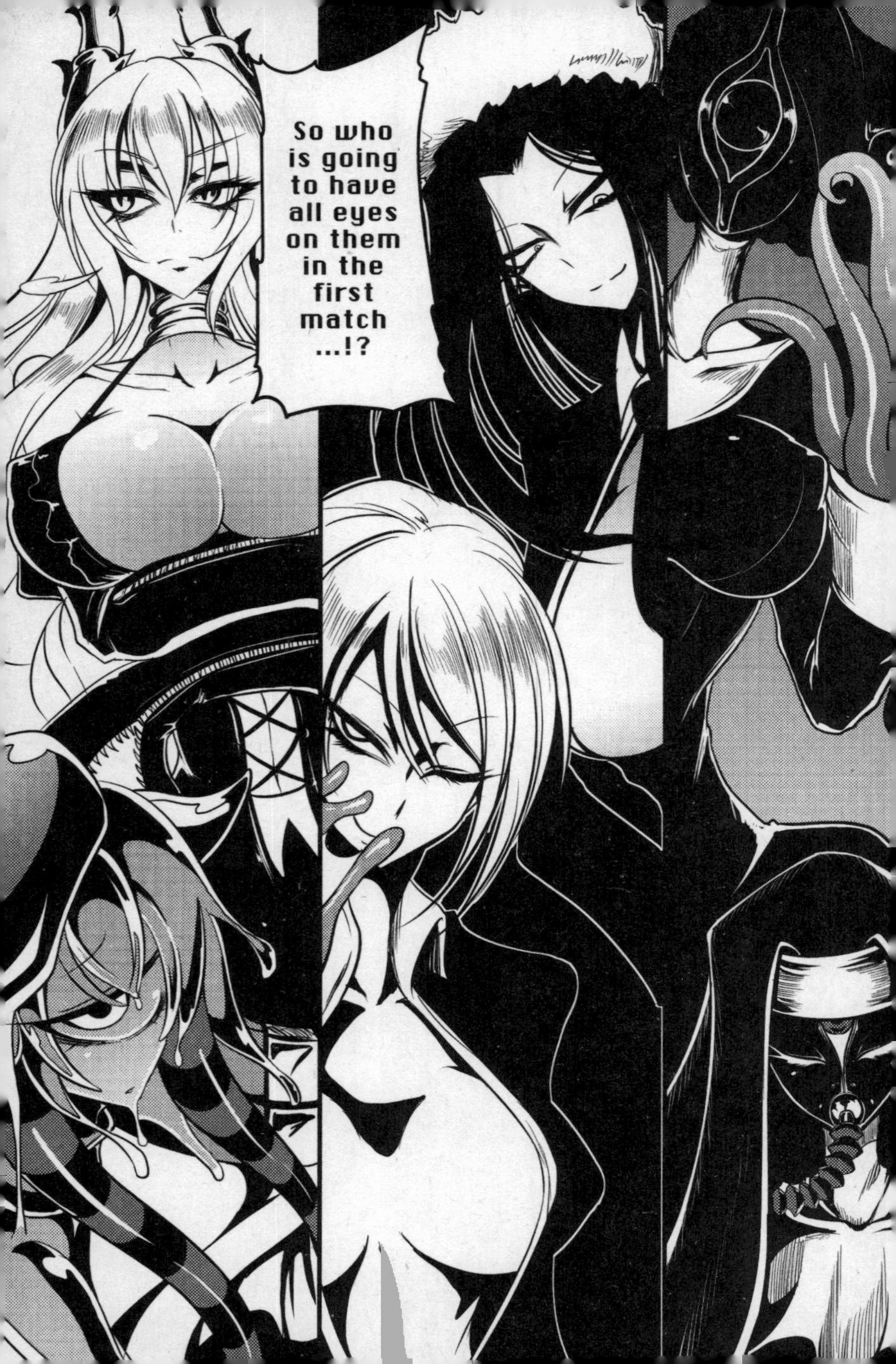
So who is going to have all eyes on them in the first match ...!?

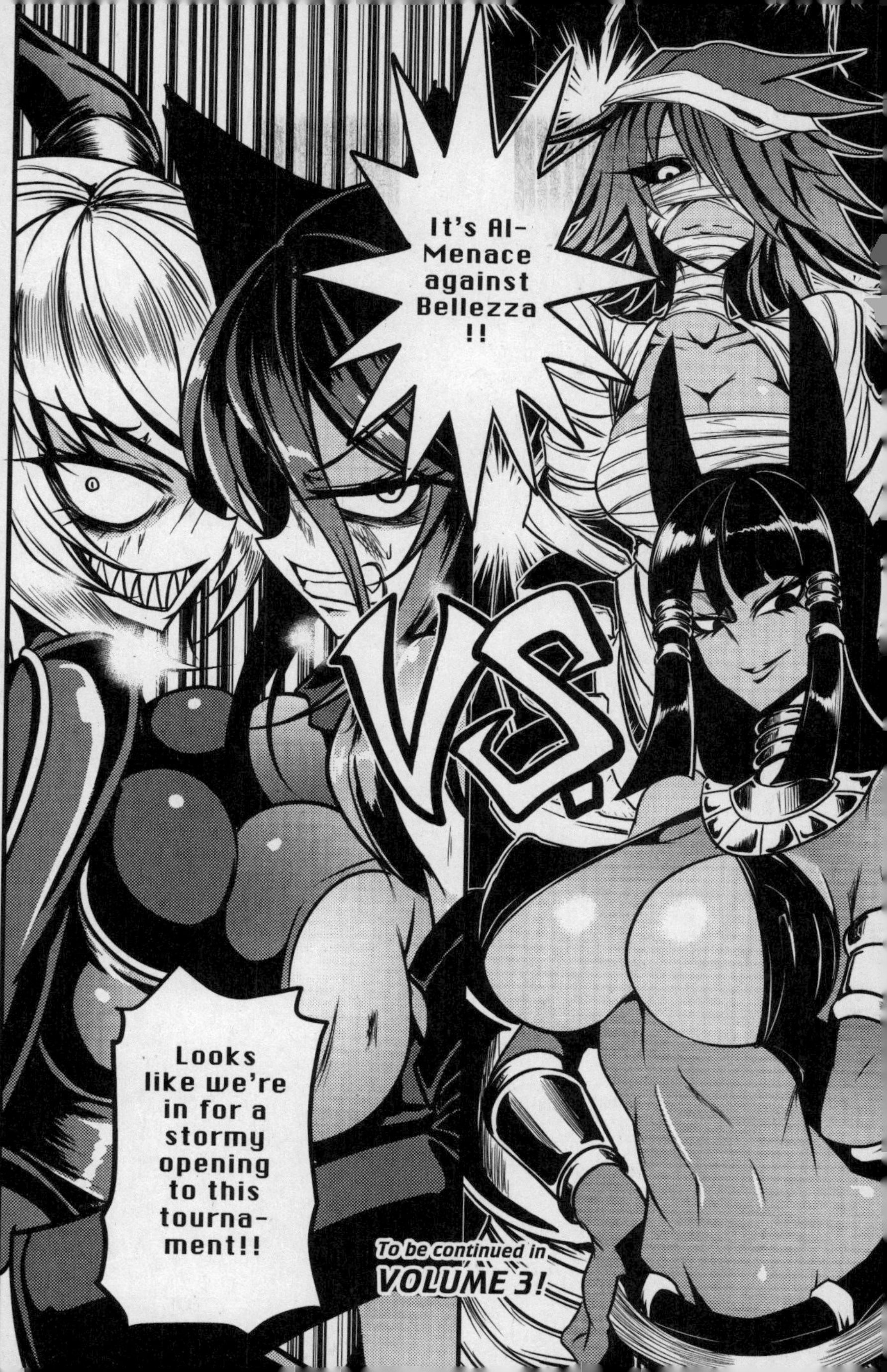
It's Al-Menace against Bellezza !!
VS
Looks like we're in for a stormy opening to this tourna-ment!!
To be continued in VOLUME 3!

DOLLY

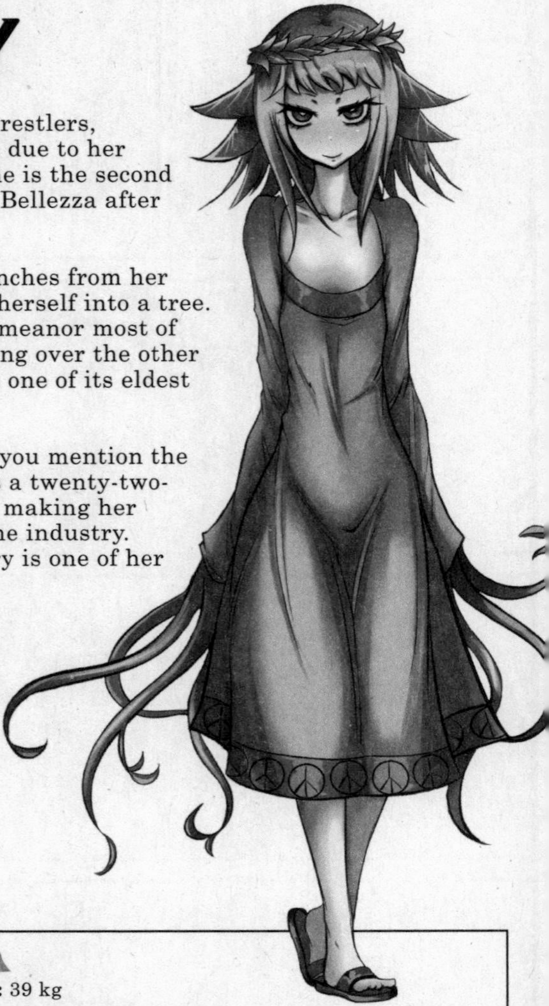

One of Bellezza's monwrestlers, she has a long life span due to her arboreal nature, and she is the second most senior member of Bellezza after Elizabeth.

She is able to grow branches from her body and turn parts of herself into a tree. Dolly has a peaceful demeanor most of the time, kindly watching over the other members of Bellezza as one of its eldest wrestlers.

However, she'll snap if you mention the size of her chest. She is a twenty-two-year monwres veteran, making her knowledgeable about the industry. This is why commentary is one of her strengths.

She and Urus seem to get along very well, and it seems they shared some sort of experience in the past.

Race: Dryad **Age:** 41
Height: 149 cm **Weight:** 39 kg
Likes: Commentary, Urus **Dislikes:** Pests, talking about breast size
Hobbies: Sunbathing (photosynthesis), watching monwres
Her Monwres Principles: To always fight with everything she has and to wrestle as a Bellezza monwrestler would
Special Moves: Dryads Jail
Measurements: B ☠, W54, H71 (cm)

LONELY PARADISE

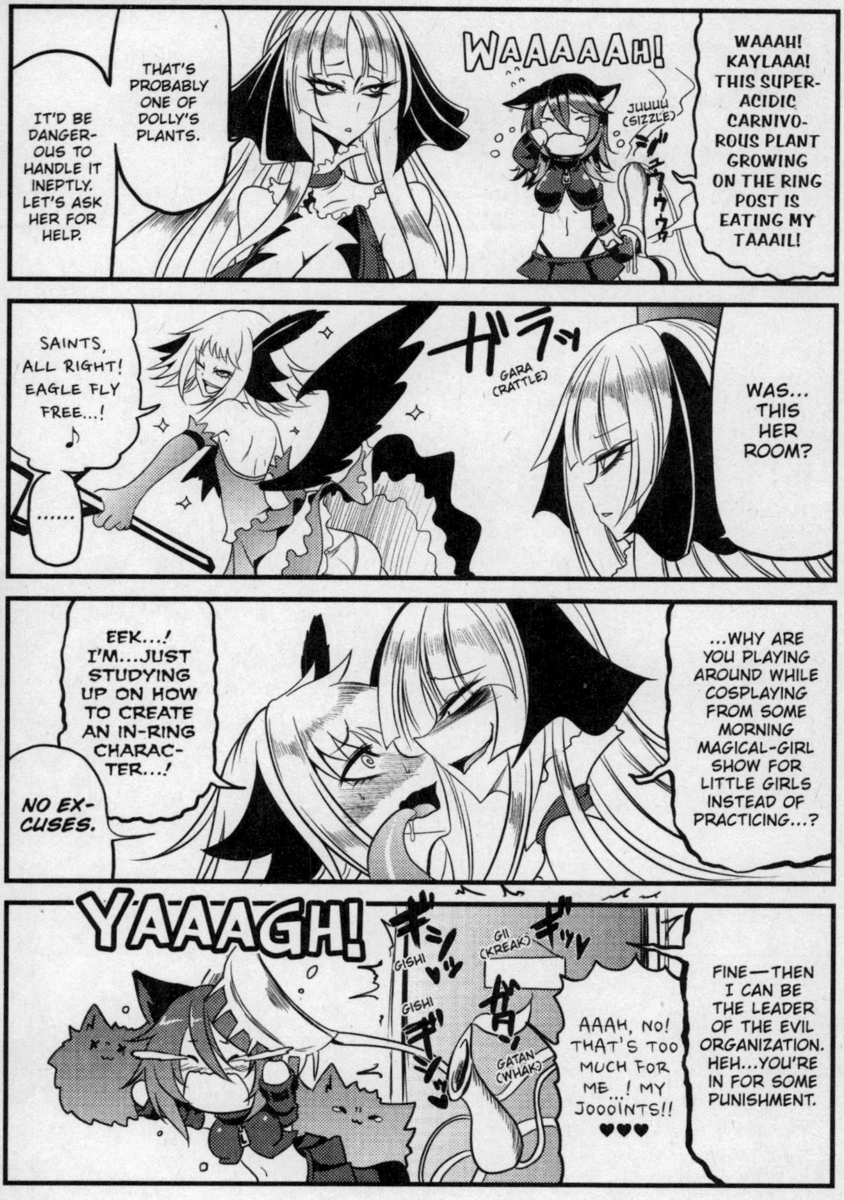
WAAAH! KAYLAAA! THIS SUPER-ACIDIC CARNIVOROUS PLANT GROWING ON THE RING POST IS EATING MY TAAAIL!
WAAAAAAH!
JUUUU (SIZZLE)
THAT'S PROBABLY ONE OF DOLLY'S PLANTS.
IT'D BE DANGEROUS TO HANDLE IT INEPTLY. LET'S ASK HER FOR HELP.
WAS... THIS HER ROOM?
ガラッ
GARA (RATTLE)
SAINTS, ALL RIGHT! EAGLE FLY FREE...! ♪
......
...WHY ARE YOU PLAYING AROUND WHILE COSPLAYING FROM SOME MORNING MAGICAL-GIRL SHOW FOR LITTLE GIRLS INSTEAD OF PRACTICING...?
EEK...! I'M...JUST STUDYING UP ON HOW TO CREATE AN IN-RING CHARACTER...!
NO EXCUSES.
FINE—THEN I CAN BE THE LEADER OF THE EVIL ORGANIZATION. HEH...YOU'RE IN FOR SOME PUNISHMENT.
AAAH, NO! THAT'S TOO MUCH FOR ME...! MY JOOOINTS!! ♥♥♥
GII (KREAK)
GATAN (WHAK)
GISHI
GISHI
YAAAGH!

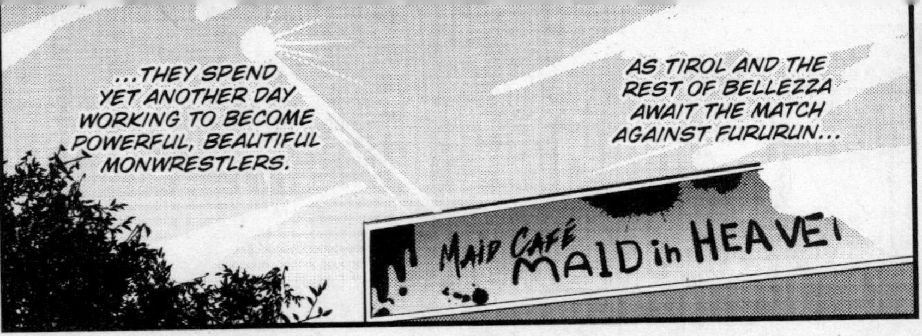
AS TIROL AND THE REST OF BELLEZZA AWAIT THE MATCH AGAINST FURURUN...
...THEY SPEND YET ANOTHER DAY WORKING TO BECOME POWERFUL, BEAUTIFUL MONWRESTLERS.
MAID CAFÉ
MAID in HEAVE

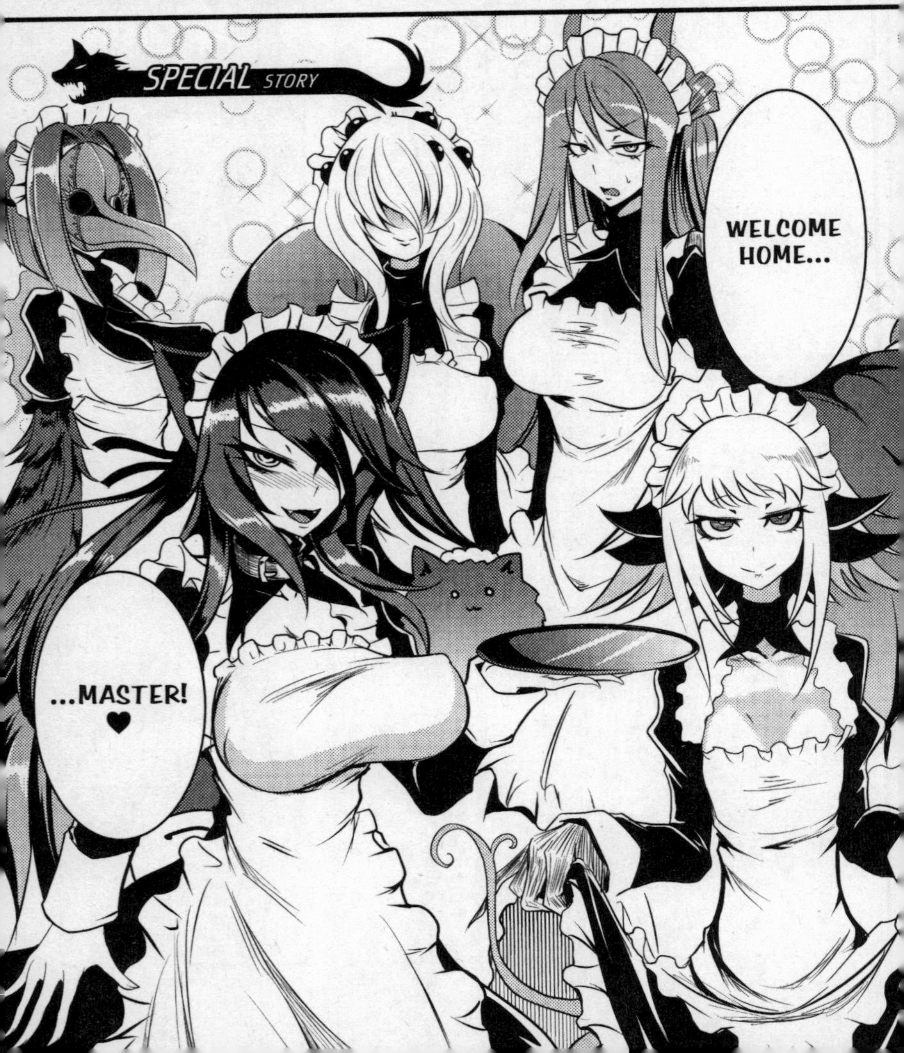
SPECIAL STORY
WELCOME HOME...
...MASTER! ♥

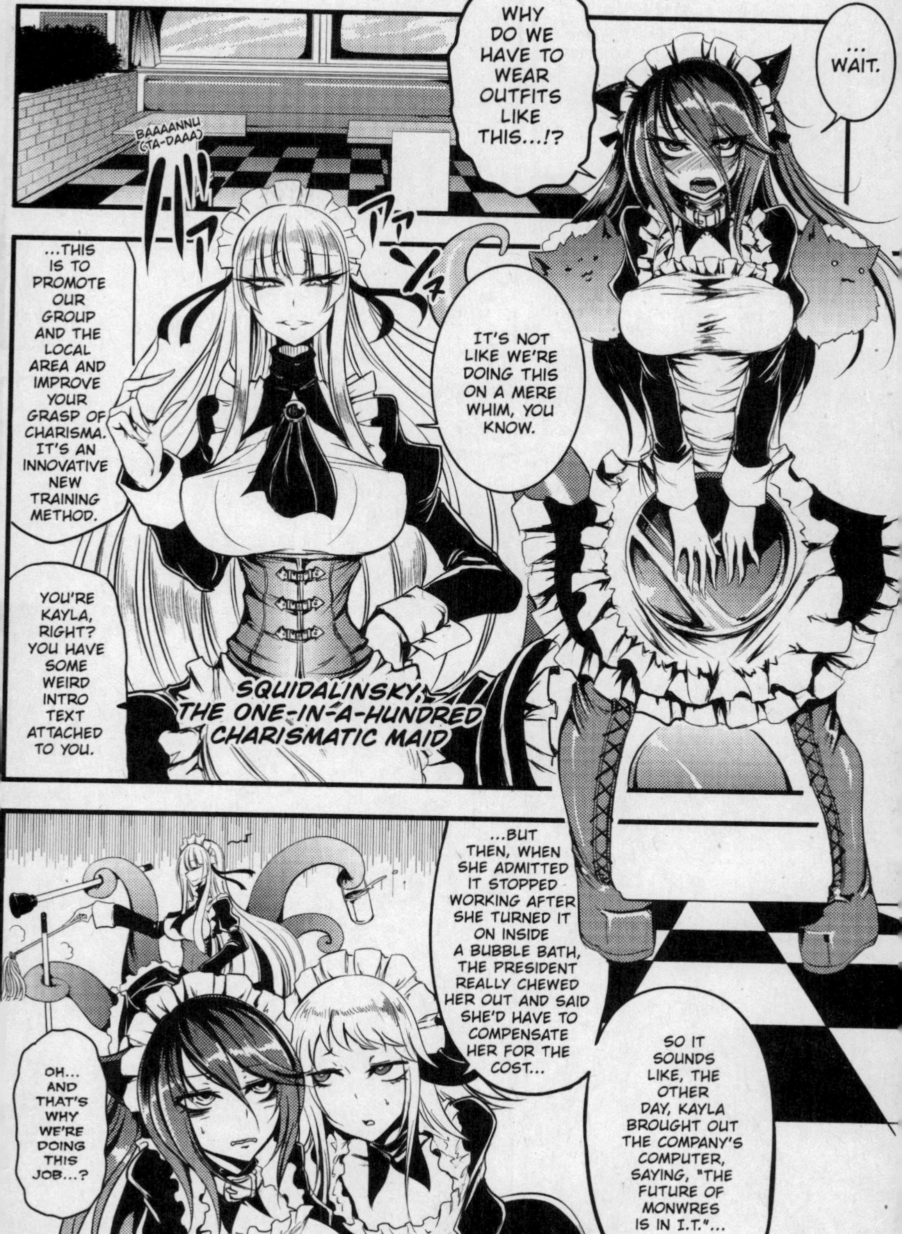

...WAIT.
WHY DO WE HAVE TO WEAR OUTFITS LIKE THIS...!?
BAAAANNU (TA-DAAA)
IT'S NOT LIKE WE'RE DOING THIS ON A MERE WHIM, YOU KNOW.
...THIS IS TO PROMOTE OUR GROUP AND THE LOCAL AREA AND IMPROVE YOUR GRASP OF CHARISMA. IT'S AN INNOVATIVE NEW TRAINING METHOD.
SQUIDALINSKY, THE ONE-IN-A-HUNDRED CHARISMATIC MAID
YOU'RE KAYLA, RIGHT? YOU HAVE SOME WEIRD INTRO TEXT ATTACHED TO YOU.
SO IT SOUNDS LIKE, THE OTHER DAY, KAYLA BROUGHT OUT THE COMPANY'S COMPUTER, SAYING, "THE FUTURE OF MONWRES IS IN I.T."...
...BUT THEN, WHEN SHE ADMITTED IT STOPPED WORKING AFTER SHE TURNED IT ON INSIDE A BUBBLE BATH, THE PRESIDENT REALLY CHEWED HER OUT AND SAID SHE'D HAVE TO COMPENSATE HER FOR THE COST...
OH... AND THAT'S WHY WE'RE DOING THIS JOB...?

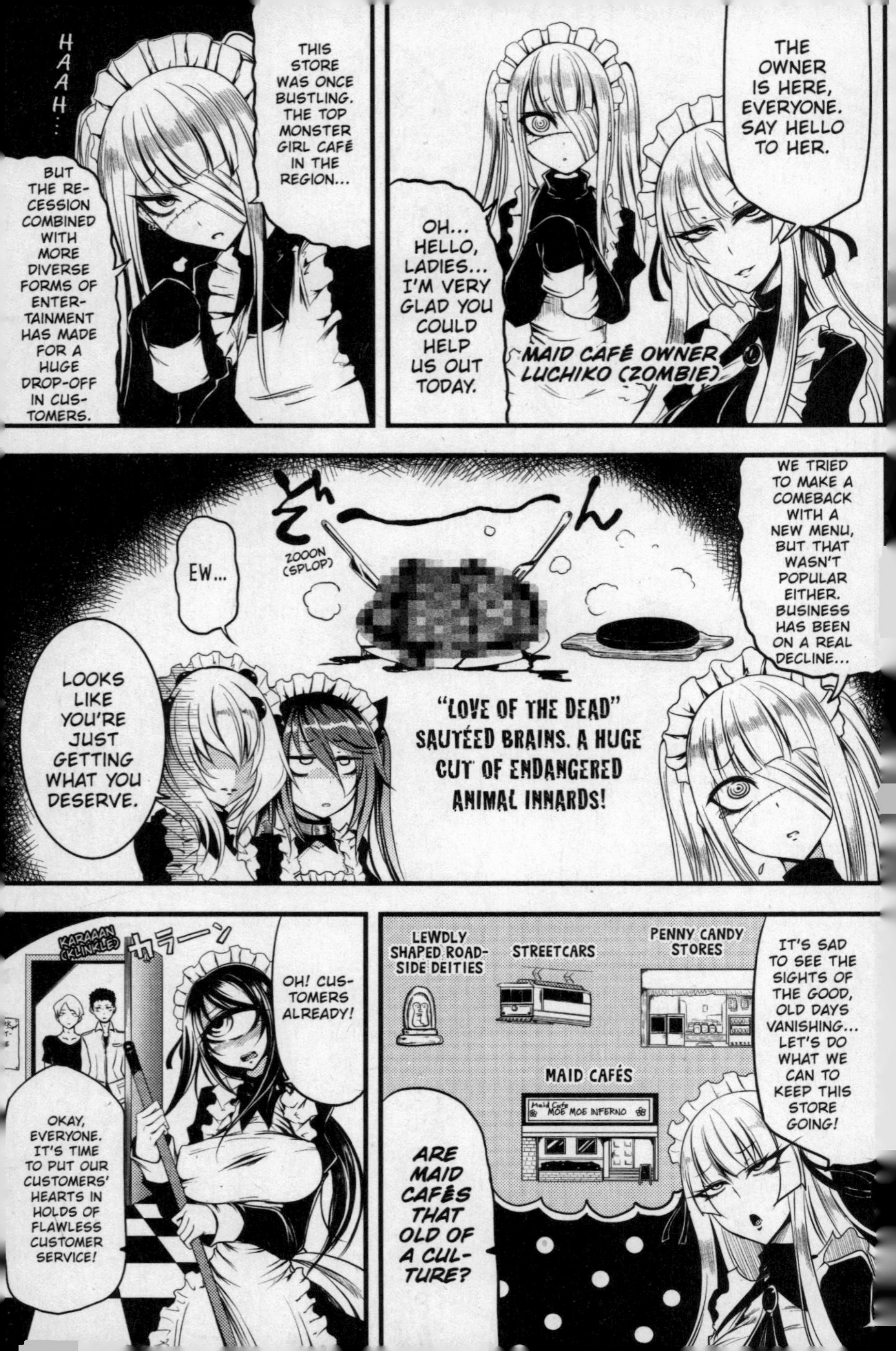
THE OWNER IS HERE, EVERYONE. SAY HELLO TO HER.
OH... HELLO, LADIES... I'M VERY GLAD YOU COULD HELP US OUT TODAY.
MAID CAFÉ OWNER LUCHIKO (ZOMBIE)
THIS STORE WAS ONCE BUSTLING. THE TOP MONSTER GIRL CAFÉ IN THE REGION...
HAAAH...
BUT THE RE-CESSION COMBINED WITH MORE DIVERSE FORMS OF ENTER-TAINMENT HAS MADE FOR A HUGE DROP-OFF IN CUS-TOMERS.
WE TRIED TO MAKE A COMEBACK WITH A NEW MENU, BUT THAT WASN'T POPULAR EITHER. BUSINESS HAS BEEN ON A REAL DECLINE...
ZOOON (SPLOP)
EW...
"LOVE OF THE DEAD" SAUTÉED BRAINS. A HUGE CUT OF ENDANGERED ANIMAL INNARDS!
LOOKS LIKE YOU'RE JUST GETTING WHAT YOU DESERVE.
IT'S SAD TO SEE THE SIGHTS OF THE GOOD, OLD DAYS VANISHING... LET'S DO WHAT WE CAN TO KEEP THIS STORE GOING!
PENNY CANDY STORES
STREETCARS
LEWDLY SHAPED ROAD-SIDE DEITIES
MAID CAFÉS
Maid Cafe MOE MOE INFERNO
ARE MAID CAFÉS THAT OLD OF A CUL-TURE?
KARAAAN (KLINKLE)
OH! CUS-TOMERS ALREADY!
OKAY, EVERYONE. IT'S TIME TO PUT OUR CUSTOMERS' HEARTS IN HOLDS OF FLAWLESS CUSTOMER SERVICE!

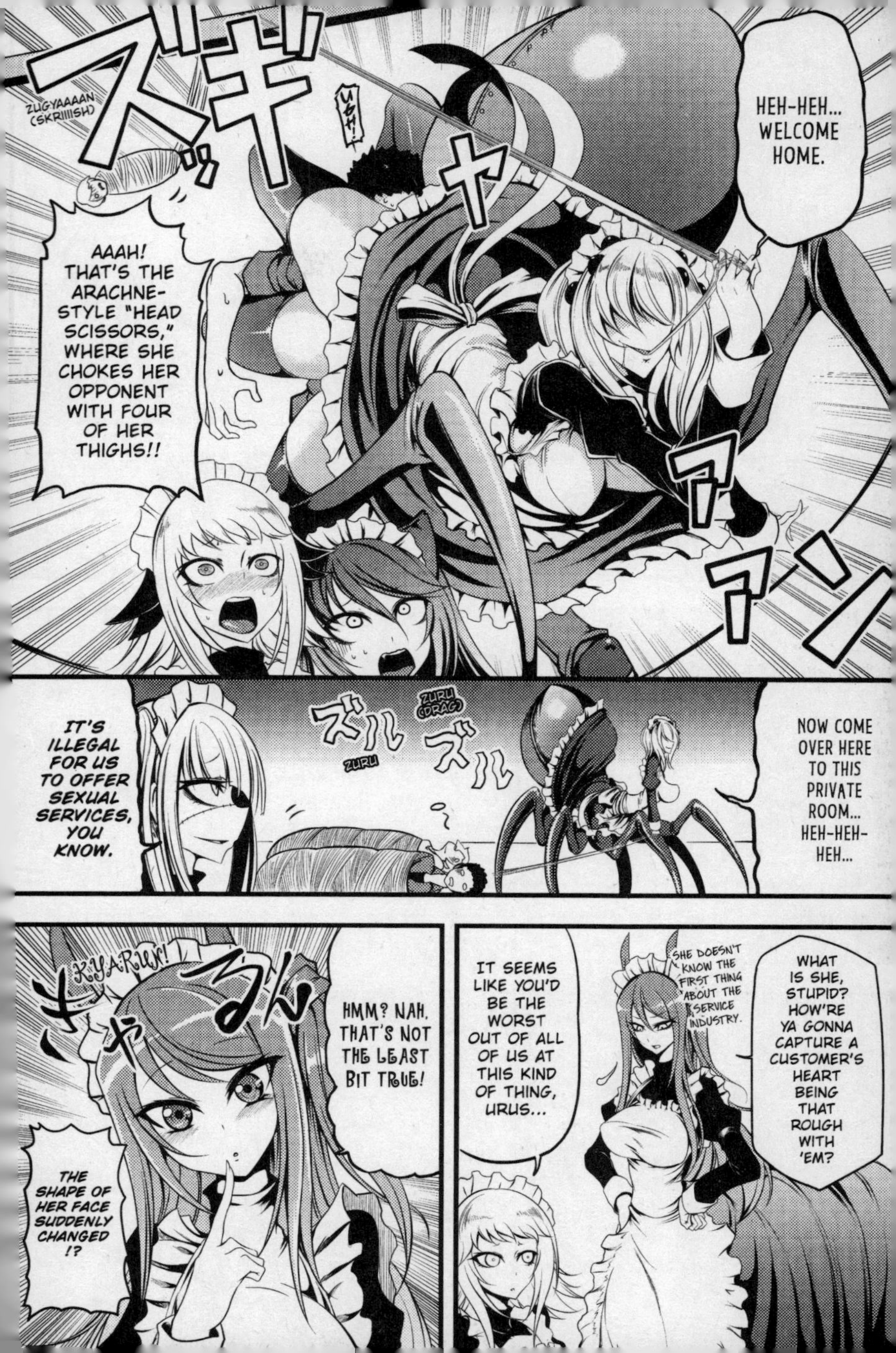
HEH-HEH... WELCOME HOME.
ZUGYAAAAN (SKRIIIISH)
UGH!
AAAH! THAT'S THE ARACHNE-STYLE "HEAD SCISSORS," WHERE SHE CHOKES HER OPPONENT WITH FOUR OF HER THIGHS!!
NOW COME OVER HERE TO THIS PRIVATE ROOM... HEH-HEH-HEH...
ZURU (DRAG)
ZURU
IT'S ILLEGAL FOR US TO OFFER SEXUAL SERVICES, YOU KNOW.
WHAT IS SHE, STUPID? HOW'RE YA GONNA CAPTURE A CUSTOMER'S HEART BEING THAT ROUGH WITH 'EM?
SHE DOESN'T KNOW THE FIRST THING ABOUT THE SERVICE INDUSTRY.
IT SEEMS LIKE YOU'D BE THE WORST OUT OF ALL OF US AT THIS KIND OF THING, URUS...
HMM? NAH. THAT'S NOT THE LEAST BIT TRUE!
KYARUN!
THE SHAPE OF HER FACE SUDDENLY CHANGED!?

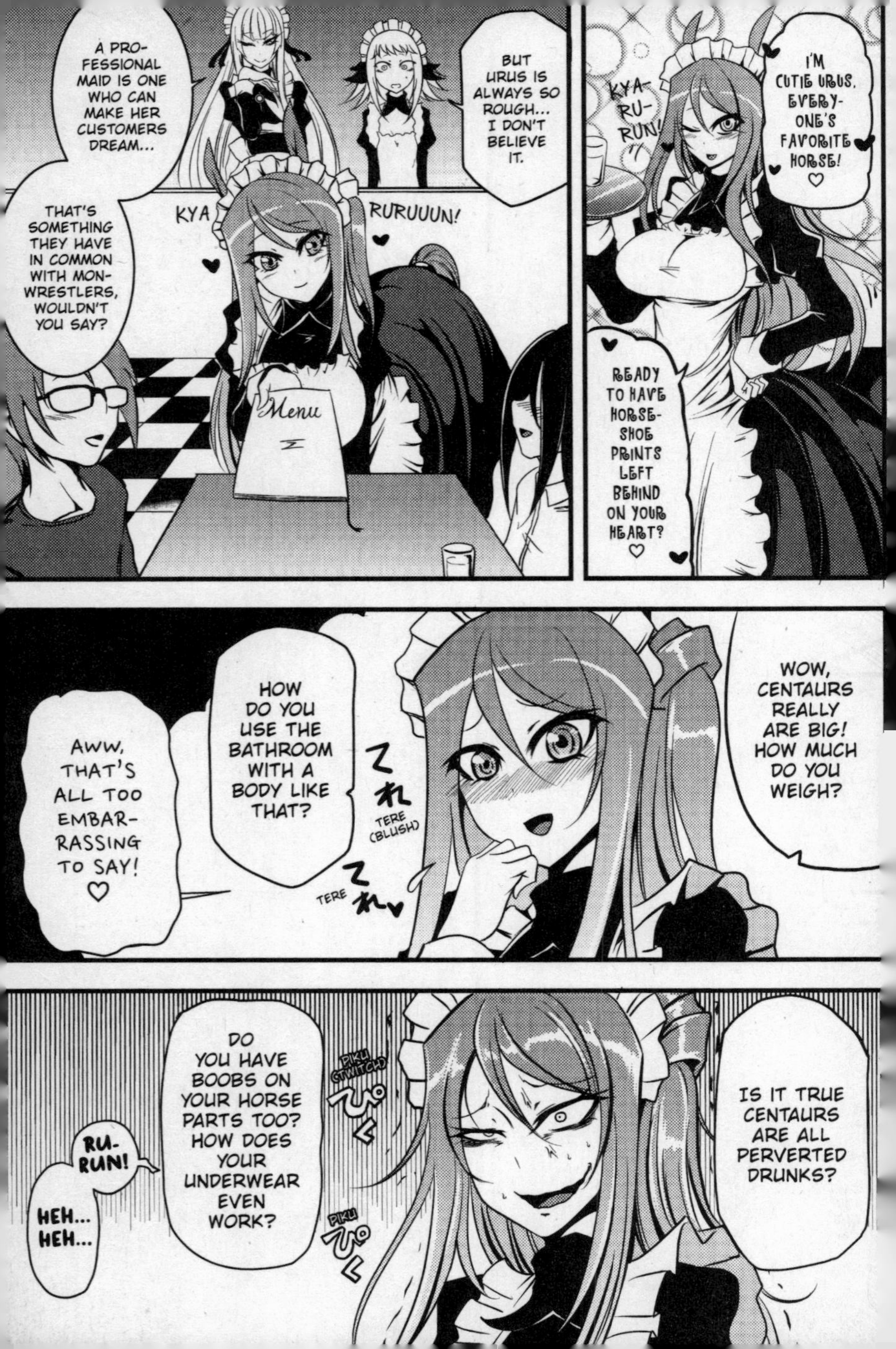
KYA-RU-RUN!
I'M CUTIE URUS, EVERY-ONE'S FAVORITE HORSE! ♡
READY TO HAVE HORSE-SHOE PRINTS LEFT BEHIND ON YOUR HEART? ♡
BUT URUS IS ALWAYS SO ROUGH... I DON'T BELIEVE IT.
A PRO-FESSIONAL MAID IS ONE WHO CAN MAKE HER CUSTOMERS DREAM...
KYA RURUUUN!
THAT'S SOMETHING THEY HAVE IN COMMON WITH MON-WRESTLERS, WOULDN'T YOU SAY?
Menu
WOW, CENTAURS REALLY ARE BIG! HOW MUCH DO YOU WEIGH?
HOW DO YOU USE THE BATHROOM WITH A BODY LIKE THAT?
TERE (BLUSH)
TERE
AWW, THAT'S ALL TOO EMBAR-RASSING TO SAY! ♡
IS IT TRUE CENTAURS ARE ALL PERVERTED DRUNKS?
PIKU (TWITCH)
DO YOU HAVE BOOBS ON YOUR HORSE PARTS TOO? HOW DOES YOUR UNDERWEAR EVEN WORK?
PIKU
RU-RUN!
HEH... HEH...

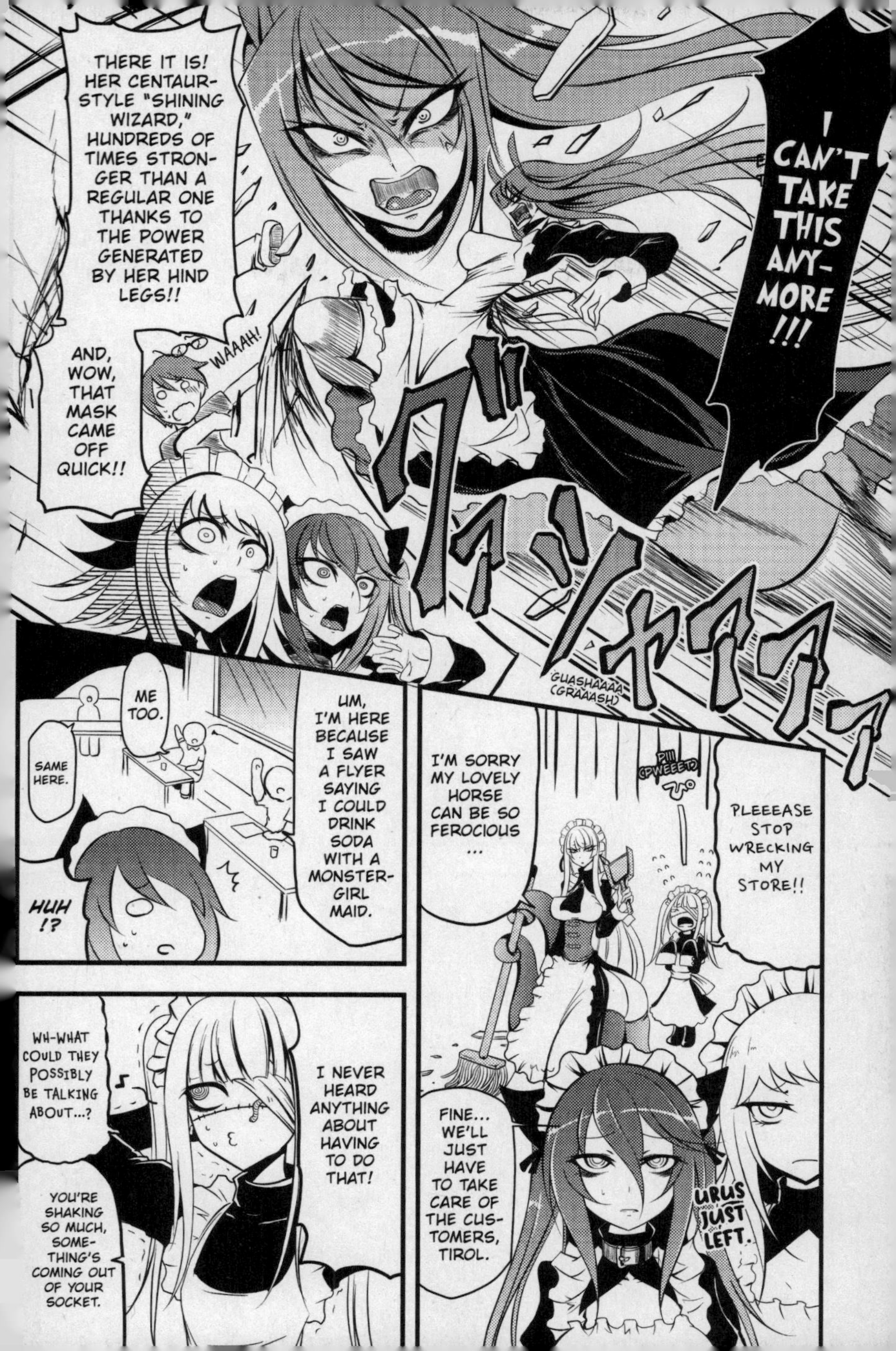
I CAN'T TAKE THIS ANYMORE!!!
THERE IT IS! HER CENTAUR-STYLE "SHINING WIZARD," HUNDREDS OF TIMES STRONGER THAN A REGULAR ONE THANKS TO THE POWER GENERATED BY HER HIND LEGS!!
GUASHAAAA (GRAAASH)
WAAAH!
AND, WOW, THAT MASK CAME OFF QUICK!!
PLEEEASE STOP WRECKING MY STORE!!
PIII (PWEEET)
I'M SORRY MY LOVELY HORSE CAN BE SO FEROCIOUS ...
FINE... WE'LL JUST HAVE TO TAKE CARE OF THE CUSTOMERS, TIROL.
URUS JUST LEFT.
UM, I'M HERE BECAUSE I SAW A FLYER SAYING I COULD DRINK SODA WITH A MONSTER-GIRL MAID.
ME TOO.
SAME HERE.
HUH!?
I NEVER HEARD ANYTHING ABOUT HAVING TO DO THAT!
WH-WHAT COULD THEY POSSIBLY BE TALKING ABOUT...?
YOU'RE SHAKING SO MUCH, SOMETHING'S COMING OUT OF YOUR SOCKET.

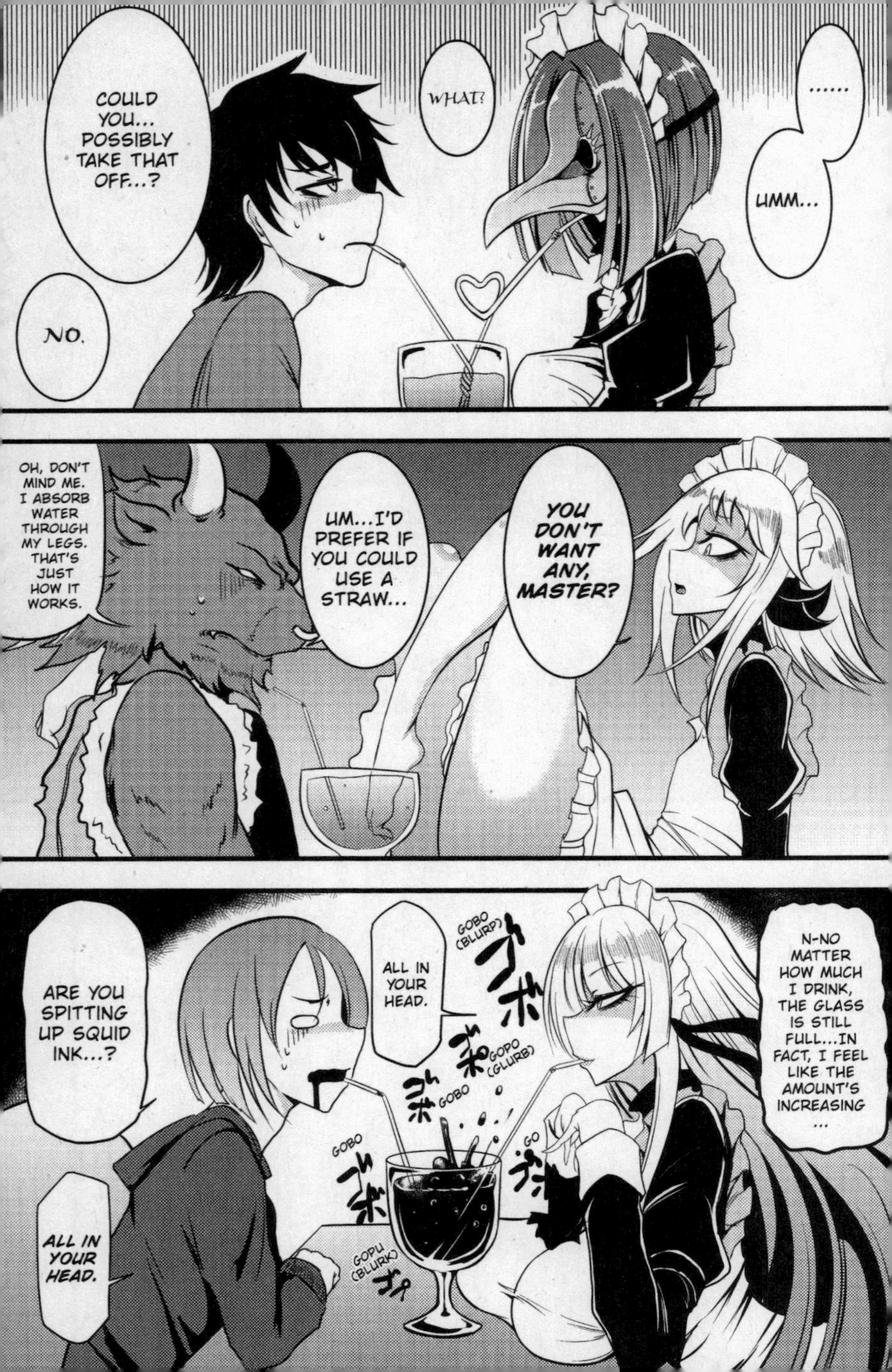
......
UMM...
WHAT?
COULD YOU... POSSIBLY TAKE THAT OFF...?
NO.
YOU DON'T WANT ANY, MASTER?
UM...I'D PREFER IF YOU COULD USE A STRAW...
OH, DON'T MIND ME. I ABSORB WATER THROUGH MY LEGS. THAT'S JUST HOW IT WORKS.
N-NO MATTER HOW MUCH I DRINK, THE GLASS IS STILL FULL...IN FACT, I FEEL LIKE THE AMOUNT'S INCREASING...
GO
GOBO (BLURP)
GOPO (GLURB)
ALL IN YOUR HEAD.
GOBO
GOBO
ARE YOU SPITTING UP SQUID INK...?
GOPU (BLURK)
ALL IN YOUR HEAD.

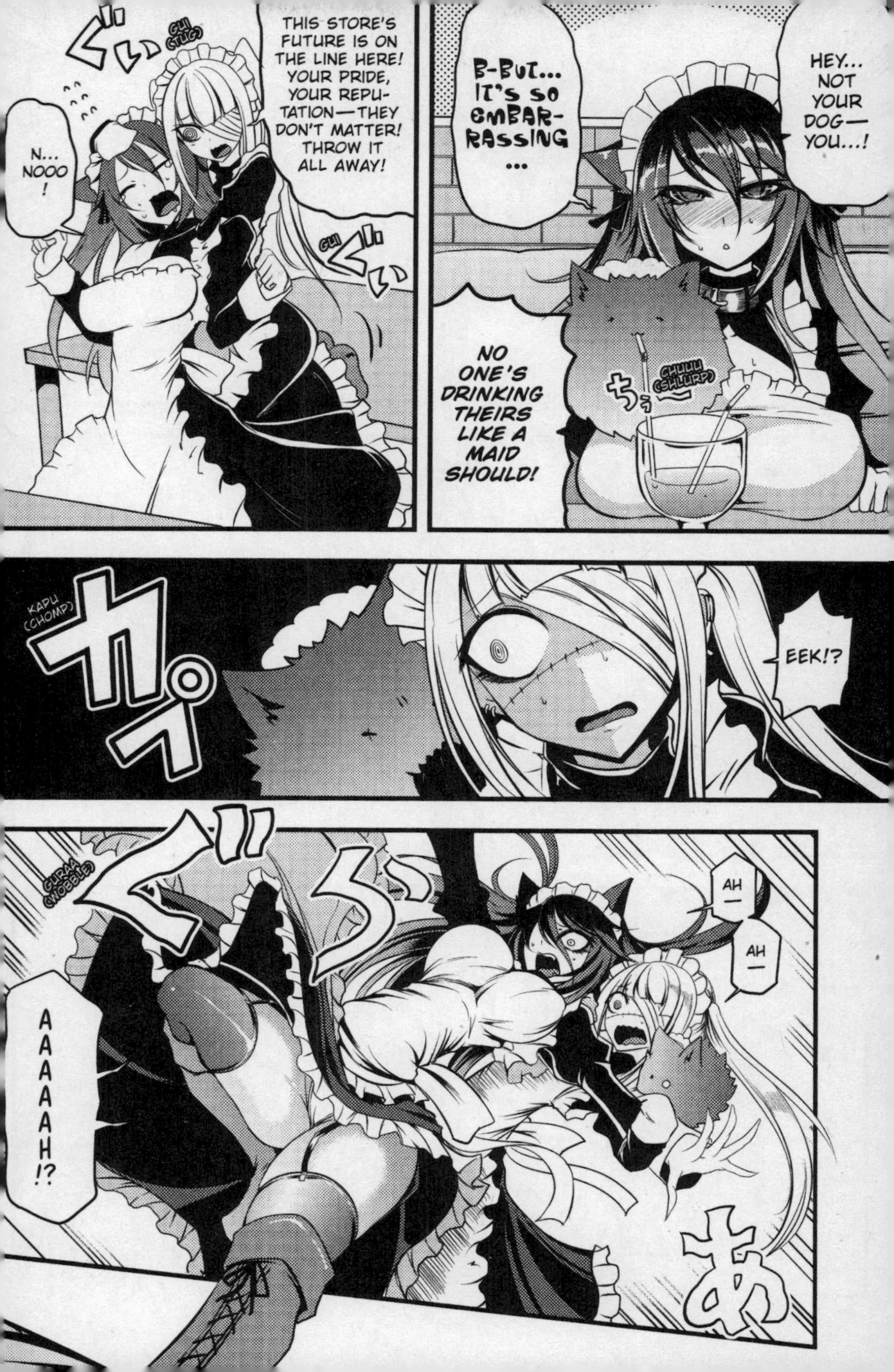
HEY... NOT YOUR DOG— YOU...!
B-BUT... IT'S SO EMBARRASSING...
NO ONE'S DRINKING THEIRS LIKE A MAID SHOULD!
CHUUU (SHLURP)
THIS STORE'S FUTURE IS ON THE LINE HERE! YOUR PRIDE, YOUR REPUTATION—THEY DON'T MATTER! THROW IT ALL AWAY!
GUI (TUG)
GUI
N... NOOO!
EEK!?
KAPU (CHOMP)
AH—
AH—
GURAA (WOBBLE)
AAAAAAH!?

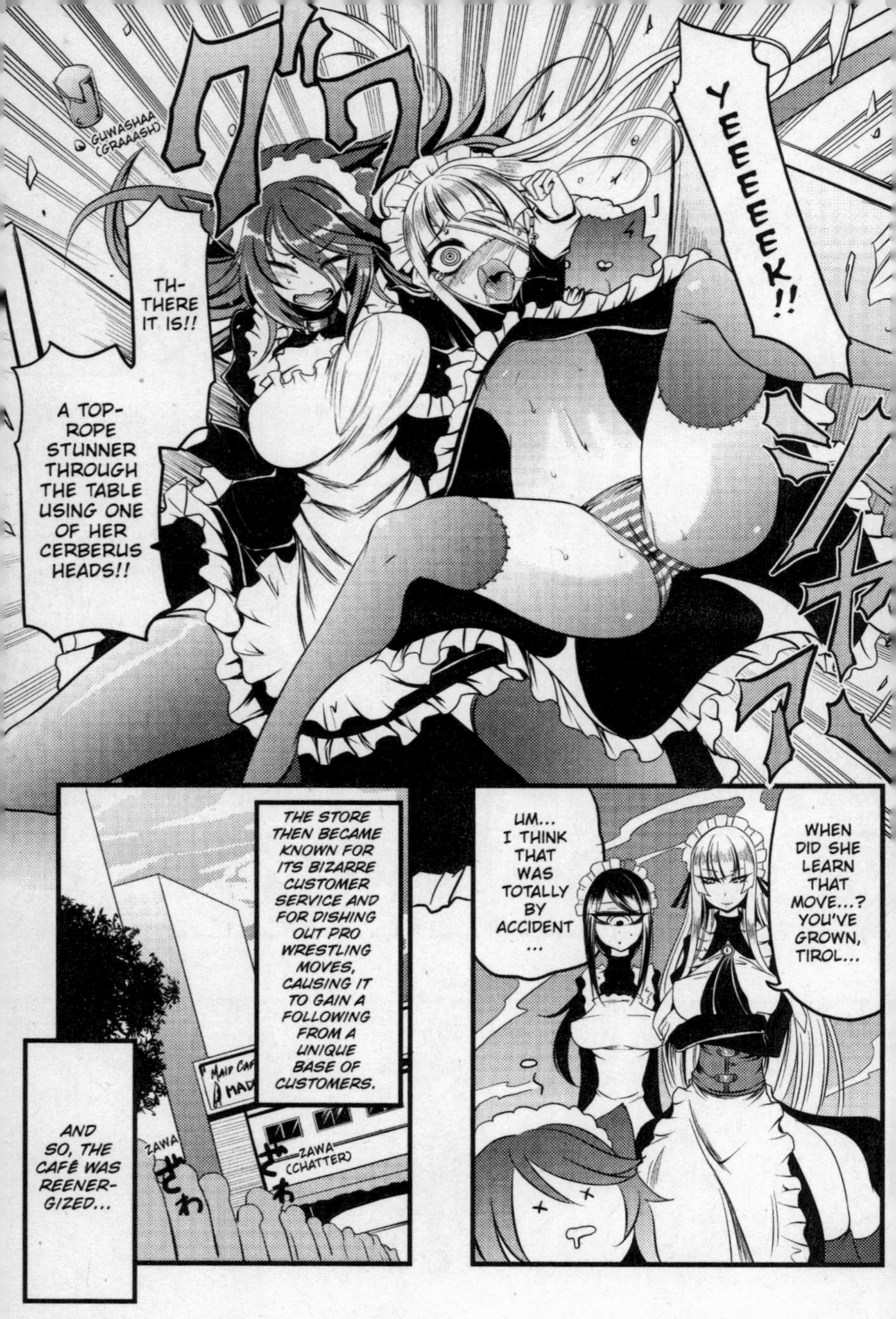
YEEEEEEK!!
GUWASHAA (GRAAASH)
TH-THERE IT IS!!
A TOP-ROPE STUNNER THROUGH THE TABLE USING ONE OF HER CERBERUS HEADS!!
WHEN DID SHE LEARN THAT MOVE...? YOU'VE GROWN, TIROL...
UM... I THINK THAT WAS TOTALLY BY ACCIDENT...
THE STORE THEN BECAME KNOWN FOR ITS BIZARRE CUSTOMER SERVICE AND FOR DISHING OUT PRO WRESTLING MOVES, CAUSING IT TO GAIN A FOLLOWING FROM A UNIQUE BASE OF CUSTOMERS.
ZAWA ZAWA (CHATTER)
AND SO, THE CAFÉ WAS REENERGIZED...

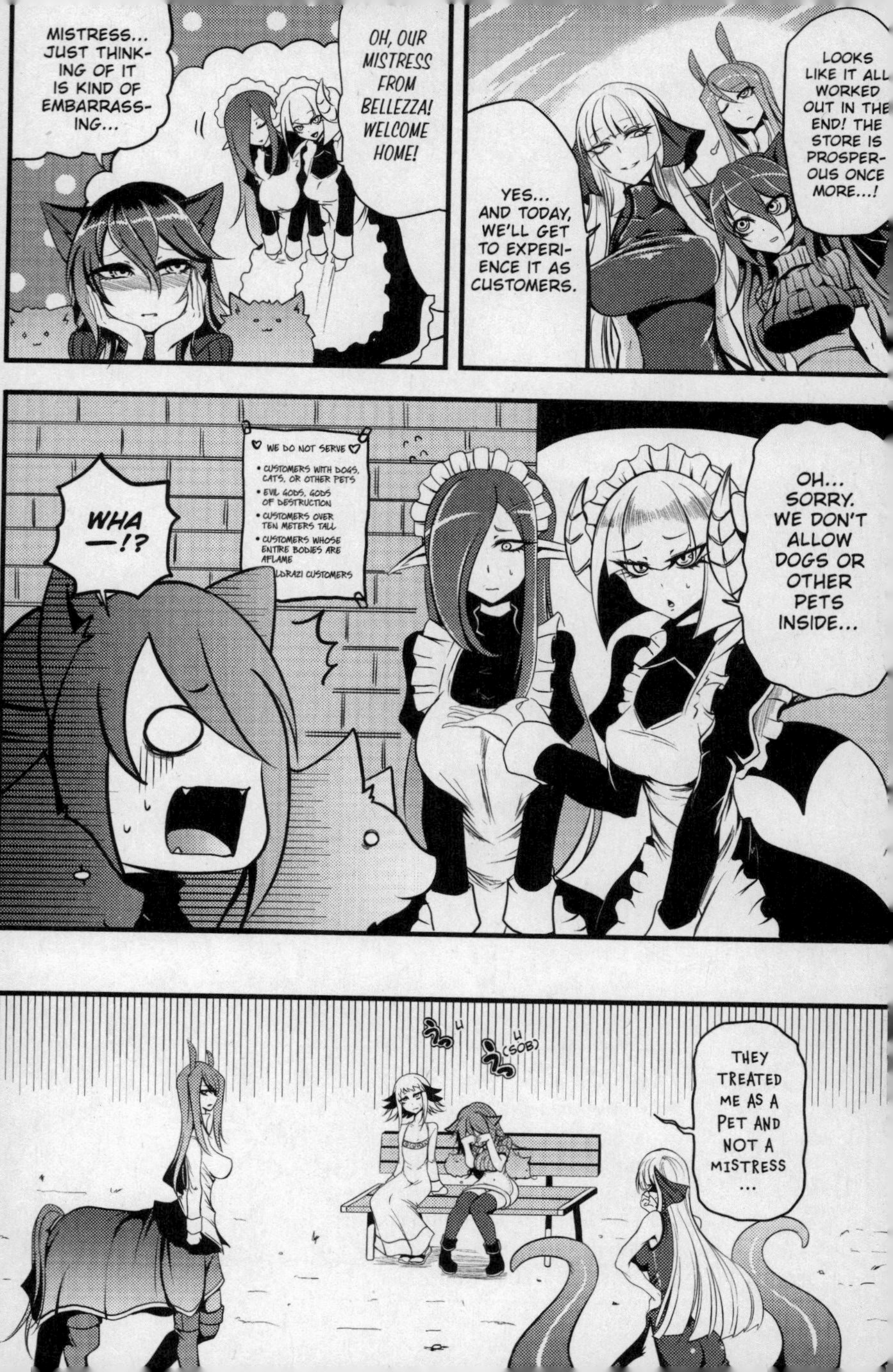
LOOKS LIKE IT ALL WORKED OUT IN THE END! THE STORE IS PROSPEROUS ONCE MORE...!
YES... AND TODAY, WE'LL GET TO EXPERIENCE IT AS CUSTOMERS.
OH, OUR MISTRESS FROM BELLEZZA! WELCOME HOME!
MISTRESS... JUST THINKING OF IT IS KIND OF EMBARRASSING...
OH... SORRY. WE DON'T ALLOW DOGS OR OTHER PETS INSIDE...
WE DO NOT SERVE
• CUSTOMERS WITH DOGS, CATS, OR OTHER PETS
• EVIL GODS, GODS OF DESTRUCTION
• CUSTOMERS OVER TEN METERS TALL
• CUSTOMERS WHOSE ENTIRE BODIES ARE AFLAME
LDRAZI CUSTOMERS
WHA—!?
(SOB)
THEY TREATED ME AS A PET AND NOT A MISTRESS...

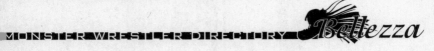

PIPPY

A young, masked Bellezza monwrestler. Powerful aerial attacks using her flight ability are her specialty.

Not only a harpy, she is of a species similar to birds of prey, making her proud and quick to fight.

However, because of her stupidity, she usually finds the tables turned on her, or she's punished by her friends.

She also quickly forgets things and repeats her mistakes because she's birdbrained.

She wears a plague doctor's mask because she likes the design, but she doesn't know what it was originally used for.

Race: Harpy   **Age:** 22
Height: 153 cm   **Weight:** 34 kg
Likes: The sky, meat
Dislikes: Being punished by Kayla and Dolly, having to be patient
Hobbies: Flying as she looks down on other species
Her Monwres Principles: To show her beautiful aerial attacks
Special Moves: Harpy Knee Drop
Measurements: B83, W54, H78 (cm)

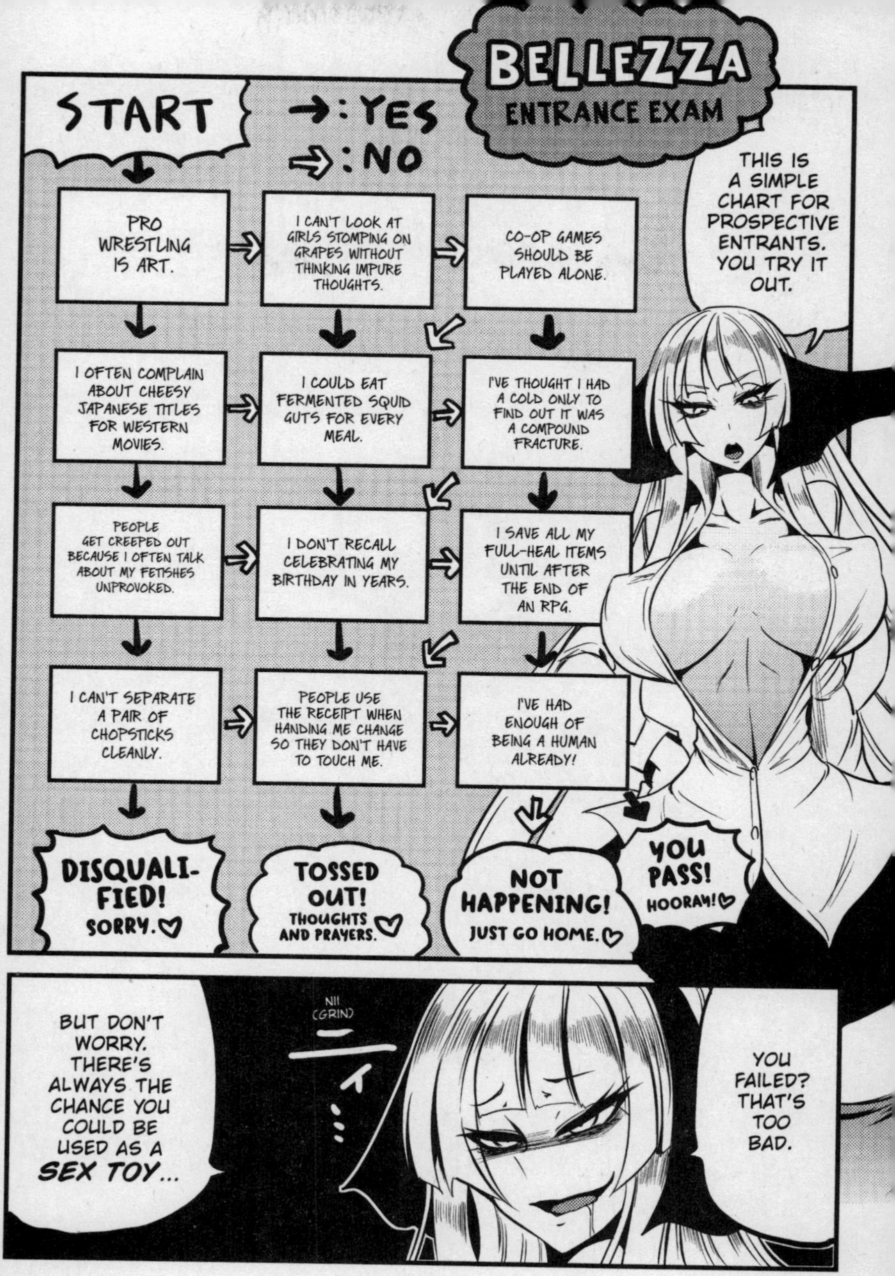
BELLEZZA
ENTRANCE EXAM
THIS IS A SIMPLE CHART FOR PROSPECTIVE ENTRANTS. YOU TRY IT OUT.
START
→: YES
⇨: NO
PRO WRESTLING IS ART.
I CAN'T LOOK AT GIRLS STOMPING ON GRAPES WITHOUT THINKING IMPURE THOUGHTS.
CO-OP GAMES SHOULD BE PLAYED ALONE.
I OFTEN COMPLAIN ABOUT CHEESY JAPANESE TITLES FOR WESTERN MOVIES.
I COULD EAT FERMENTED SQUID GUTS FOR EVERY MEAL.
I'VE THOUGHT I HAD A COLD ONLY TO FIND OUT IT WAS A COMPOUND FRACTURE.
PEOPLE GET CREEPED OUT BECAUSE I OFTEN TALK ABOUT MY FETISHES UNPROVOKED.
I DON'T RECALL CELEBRATING MY BIRTHDAY IN YEARS.
I SAVE ALL MY FULL-HEAL ITEMS UNTIL AFTER THE END OF AN RPG.
I CAN'T SEPARATE A PAIR OF CHOPSTICKS CLEANLY.
PEOPLE USE THE RECEIPT WHEN HANDING ME CHANGE SO THEY DON'T HAVE TO TOUCH ME.
I'VE HAD ENOUGH OF BEING A HUMAN ALREADY!
DISQUALI-FIED! SORRY.♡
TOSSED OUT! THOUGHTS AND PRAYERS.♡
NOT HAPPENING! JUST GO HOME.♡
YOU PASS! HOORAY!♡
YOU FAILED? THAT'S TOO BAD.
NII (GRIN)
BUT DON'T WORRY. THERE'S ALWAYS THE CHANCE YOU COULD BE USED AS A SEX TOY...

ILLUSTRATION FROM OKAYADO

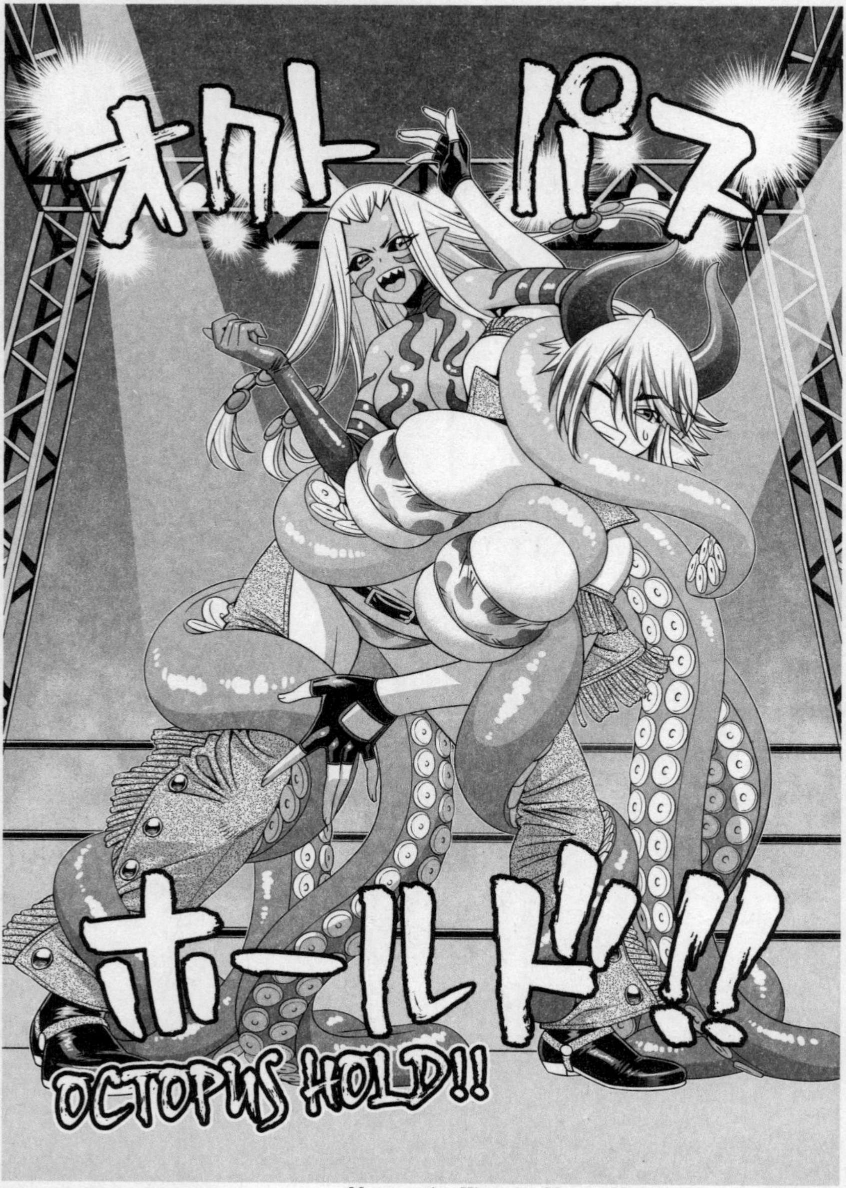
オクトパス
ホールド!!
OCTOPUS HOLD!!

OKAYADO

Manga artist. His series *Monster Musume: Everyday Life with Monster Girls* is fourteen volumes in and serialized in *COMIC Ryu WEB* (published by Tokuma Shoten).

ILLUSTRATION FROM KENKOU CROSS

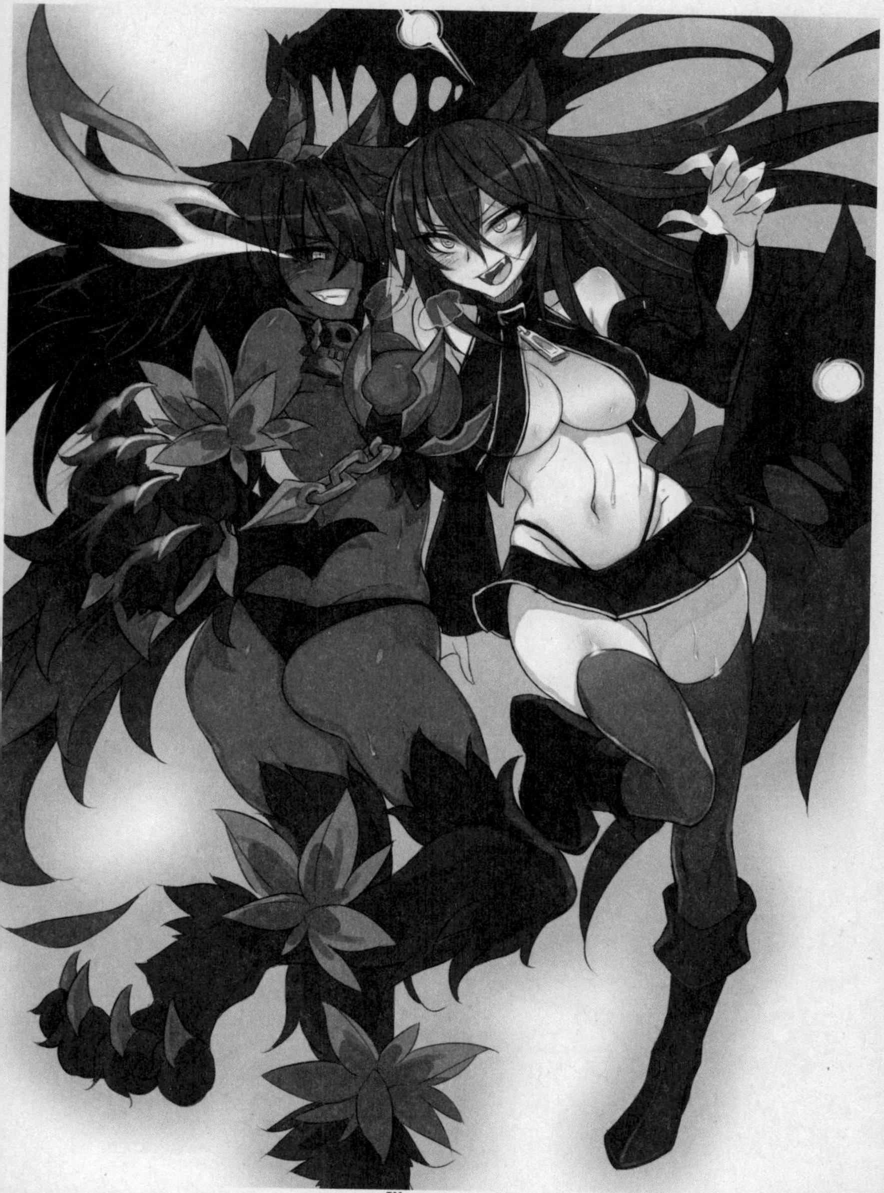

KENKOU CROSS

Illustrator and manga author. Illustrating for books and games, as well as authoring monster girl short story manga, Kenkou Cross is known as a genius wizard in the monster girl community.